Behavioral

Health Services and Delivery

Edited by **Frank Boruch, MD**

American College of Physician Executives
4890 West Kennedy Boulevard, Suite 200
Tampa, Florida 33609
813/287-2000

ISBN: 0-924674-59-8
Library of Congress Card Number: 97-78158

Printed in the United States of America by Hillsboro Printing Company, Tampa, Florida.

Foreword

There is an ebb and flow to the production of a book that surprises and confounds those who work to bring the book about. During the two years that this book has gestated, a few planned chapters disappeared for lack of fit or for lack of author follow-through. Others were added at the suggestion of the editor as the times changed and his vision of the book was altered to reflect a fluid reality. Generally, the book took longer to complete than anticipated, but it is, we think, an accurate snapshot of the state of affairs in the management of behavioral health services.

The first seven chapters are excellent background on the overall environment in which the behavioral health services professional works. In the nineteen remaining chapters, actual and proposed models for service delivery are offered. They show that behavioral health services, as with health care delivery in general, are moving rapidly into a managed care, integrated systems world. The models are particularly important, we think, because they show the degree to which a maximally cognitive, minimally procedural area of health care can adopt current health care management concepts.

This does not mean that the time-based vagaries of behavioral health can be ignored and that compliance with rigid guidelines for professional practice can be demanded. All the inexactness of medical practice are magnified in behavioral health services. What the models show, however, is that the broad strokes of managed care and systems integration are as applicable to behavioral health services as they are elsewhere in health care. The models also show that wise and creative practitioners and managers can adopt emerging management approaches without damage to their profession.

The College owes a special debt of gratitude to Dr. Frank Boruch, the editor of this book. He stayed with our publishing venture through changing times in his professional life and through the agonies of reaching conclusion in the past few months. His stamp is clearly on the book, and we thank him for his unflagging attention to quality and detail.

Wesley Curry
Managing Editor, Book Publishing
American College of Physician Executives
August 1998

Preface

Even in the sophisticated atmospheres of first world countries, there continues to be a stigma attached to and a disregard for the pain engendered by behavioral illness. That stigma exists as an intellectual absurdity when viewed from the perspective of scientific evidence-based knowledge about the molecular biology of behavior. It exists as an embarrassing emotional shortcoming when viewed from the perspective of core values such as honesty and compassion.

This book is designed as a benchmark work to review models, methods, and tools that would help to improve behavioral health care service delivery. It will, ideally, serve as a catalyst for innovations that will prompt a perpetually improving state of behavioral health care that will continuously increase in real worth.

Contributors to this book, however, have elevated it to a higher plane than originally intended by the editor. Readers will experience ideas graciously offered by professionals and experts from disparate fields and organizations that might be better known for their competition than their cooperation. The contributors, though, understand that we in behavioral health care are interdependent. For our collective corpus to be maximally effective in achieving our mission of helping others, we must cooperate.

This book, then, does something that was not purposefully planned. It proclaims that, in our struggle against stigma, bias, and prejudice, and in our efforts toward quality, efficacy, efficiency, and equity, we are all in this together. It opens another window onto a global behavioral health frontier for the elevation of our human condition.

Frank Boruch, MD
Storrs, Connecticut
August 1998

Acknowledgements

Everyone who finds value in this book owes, as I do, gratitude to the legion of individuals it takes to put a book together. Thanks to all those who inspired, all those who expressed interest, all those who supported, all those who contributed labor or ideas or both, and all those who routinely work and sacrifice behind the scenes, those who make things happen.

Special thanks go to the publisher, the American College of Physician Executives, and all the personnel at that outstanding center of learning. Extra special gratitude is extended to Wes Curry at ACPE. He is truly an editor's editor, and a fine human being.

Last, every author who has been included in this text deserves plaudits. Opinions and perspectives are the authors' own. I do not agree with or endorse all that is written, but to grow and learn we must explore the diversity that exists in our field today. I commend and applaud all the authors for their dedication to excellence, their sincerity, their thoughtfulness, and the supreme gift of their individual and collective ideas.

To all the authors, I say "Thank You." — F.B.

To

    Jonathan Sant

        Nicholas Tao

            and Monica Anne,

                with whom I live in love.—*F.B.*

Table of Contents

Section III: Networks

Section IV: Integration

Section V: Location-Based

Section VI: Quality and Outcomes

Section I

An Overview

Chapter 1

A Historial Overview

by Donna Vavala

In early colonial America, citizens with mental disorders were left to roam the countryside or were cared for at home. Over time, workhouses were established for the idle and disorderly, and poorhouses were built to accommodate those who had fallen on hard times. Many of these places eventually became warehouses for the mentally ill.[1]

It was not until 1752 that Pennsylvania Hospital in Philadelphia established the country's first unit for mentally ill patients. (See table on page 2 for chronology of founding of state mental health hospitals.) New York Hospital in New York City followed suit in 1771, and the first free-standing hospital for the mentally ill opened in 1773 as Public Hospital in Williamsburg, Virginia.

However, in the mid-1800s, many mentally ill people were still being dumped in workhouses and poorhouses. Reformer Dorothea Dix, appalled by conditions in these facilities, urged the government to take responsibility. As a result of the national uproar her protests caused, states began building hospitals for the mentally ill.[1] By 1860, 28 of the then 33 states had at least one public mental health hospital.[3] Around the turn of the century, university-affiliated psychiatric hospitals sprang up as institutions of teaching and research, and psychiatric units began to appear in general hospitals.

Most of the country's first mental hospitals were run by lay administrators, with physicians acting in consulting roles. The prevailing theory of the day was that the mentally ill were insensitive to pain, so beatings, temperature extremes, and inhuman living conditions were commonly used in an to attempt to shock patients into sanity. These "treatments" were deemed helpful rather than inhuman.

The era of moral treatment began at the turn of the 19th Century. It focused on humane treatment, kindness, open wards, pleasant surroundings, no or minimal restraints, and structured activity. Cure rates were touted to be 40 percent to 100 percent. However, these claims were found to be grossly exaggerated and hastened the downfall of moral treatment.[3] When moral treatment

A Partial Chronology of the Creation of U.S. Mental Health Facilities[2]

Date	Description of Facility
1650	Puritan leader Roger Williams urged town council of Providence, Rhode Island to provide for the care of a "distracted women," one of the earliest recorded references to public care of the mentally ill in the United States.
1751	The colonial governor of Pennsylvania approved the charter of Pennsylvania Hospital, including treatment of people with mental illness. The hospital opened in Philadelphia in 1752.
1771	Royal charter established New York Hospital in New York City, whose north wing was to be used as "wards or cells for the reception of lunatics." A separate facility, the New York Lunatic Asylum, was built in 1808.
1817	First private mental hospital in the United States, the Asylum for the Relief of Persons Deprived of the Use of Their Reason, opened.
1817	Cornerstone laid for Fayette Hospital in Lexington, Kentucky, but hospital wasn't occupied because of lack of funds. Purchased by the State of Kentucky in 1822 and opened in 1824 as Eastern Lunatic Asylum.
1818	Charlestown branch of Massachusetts General Hospital, later named McLean Asylum for the Insane, admitted first patient.
1824	First mental hospital in Ohio, Commercial Hospital and Lunatic Asylum, opened in Cincinnati.
1824	Connecticut Retreat for the Insane opened in Hartford. Now called Institute of Living.
1828	First state mental hospital opened in Columbia, South Carolina.
1833	State Lunatic Hospital, now Worcester State Hospital, opened in Worcester, Massachusetts.
1836	First patient admitted to Vermont Asylum for the Insane in Brattleboro.
1838	Ohio Lunatic Asylum opened in Columbus.
1840	First Tennessee mental health facility opened near Nashville. Later became Central Hospital for the Insane.
1840	Maine Insane Hospital, now the Augusta Mental Health Institute, opened in Augusta.
1843	New York State Lunatic Asylum opened in Utica.
1847	Butler Hospital for the Insane opened in Providence, Rhode Island.
1848	New Jersey Lunatic Asylum in Trenton admitted first patient.
1848	Louisiana Insane Asylum opened in Jackson.
1848	Indiana Hospital for the Insane, Indianapolis, admitted first patients.
1849	Pennsylvania State Lunatic Hospital opened in Harrisburg.
1851	Illinois State Hospital for the Insane opened in Jacksonville.

A Partial Chronology *(continued)*

1852	First patients admitted to State Hospital No. 1, now Fulton State Hospital, in Fulton, Missouri.
1852	Alabama Insane Hospital opened in Tuscaloosa.
1853	Insane Asylum of California, later called Stockton State Hospital, opened in Stockton.
1859	First mental hospital for criminal patients, New York State Lunatic Asylum for Insane Convicts, opened in Auburn.
1859	First patient admitted to Michigan Asylum for the Insane in Kalamazoo.
1859	Lunatic Asylum West of the Allegheny Mountains opened in Weston, Virginia. (Became first mental health hospital in West Virginia in 1863 during Civil War.)
1860	First state mental hospital in Wisconsin opened in Mendota.
1861	Mount Pleasant State Hospital opened in Mount Pleasant, Iowa.
1861	State Lunatic Asylum opened in Austin, Texas.
1866	First Minnesota mental hospital opened in St. Peter.
1869	Willard Asylum, first state hospital for patients with chronic mental illness opened in Ovid, New York.
1870	Asylum for the Incurable Insane, first public mental health facility in Rhode Island, opened in Howard.
1871	Western State Hospital opened near Tacoma, Washington.
1879	Colorado State Hospital opened in Pueblo.
1879	First public mental hospital in what would become South Dakota opened in Yankton.
1882	First Nevada mental health hospital opened in what is now Sparks.
1883	Arkansas State Lunatic Asylum opened in Little Rock.
1883	Oregon State Hospital opened in Salem.
1885	North Dakota State Hospital opened in Jamestown.
1885	Utah State Hospital opened in Provo.
1887	Arizona State Hospital for the Insane opened in Phoenix.
1889	Wyoming Territorial Insane Asylum opened in Evanston.
1906	First university psychiatric teaching hospital, State Psychopathic Hospital, established at University of Michigan, Ann Arbor.
Note:	A longer chronology of events in the development of psychology in America may be found at http://www.cwu.edu/~warren/addenda.html on the Internet, the full chronology brings the history of psychology to the present.

ended, for most of the remainder of the century, a pessimistic psychiatric ideology prevailed. Patients were held in low esteem in the community and in what would appear today to be contempt by hospitals.[4]

Most mental hospitals were built late in the 19th Century and the early part of the 20th Century. But most provided inferior care, and mental health policy was given low priority as America experienced industrialization and as vast numbers of immigrants flooded the country. The first effort to humanize treatment in the 20th Century was made by Clifford Beers, a former mental patient who exposed the wretched conditions in mental hospitals and worked to change them.[4] A patient at four different institutions over a three-year period, Beers, who had the symptoms of a bipolar disorder, wrote an autobiography, *A Mind That Found Itself,* that inspired the mental hygiene movement of the 1920s and '30s.

Throughout the 19th Century, patient populations comprised predominately acute cases institutionalized for less than a year. Between 1890 and 1940, the proportion of long-term chronic patients increased dramatically. By 1923, more than half of all patients had been hospitalized for five years or longer.[5] In the 20th Century, institutions became places to provide long-term custodial care for the chronically ill population. Given the large numbers of such patients and the disinclination of public sources to recognize funding needs, the institutions became dismal places. The situation was depicted dramatically in the 1948 film "The Snake Pit," for which actress Olivia de Haviland received an Oscar nomination.

Ambulatory care for mentally ill patients burgeoned in the early part of the 20th Century. First, clinics associated with state hospitals were established; then freestanding outpatient clinics were set up. As a result, private psychiatric practices began to flourish.[1] This was the beginning of a strong movement away from institutionalization of all but the most seriously ill patients and probably presaged the later deinstitutionalization phenomenon. Of course, the deinstitutionalization movement was fueled by a wide array of other factors, most notably public and political dismay with the quality of facilities and services.

During the 1930s, the New Deal legitimized the concept of the welfare state, enlarged the scope of federal activities, and emphasized the importance of scientists and intellectuals in the formulation and implementation of policy. In 1936, the Mental Hospital Survey Committee was created through the collaborative efforts of a number of major medical associations. Within a few years, the committee had produced several studies of mental hospitals and, by 1943, it began awarding grants to investigate a variety of diseases.[5]

The most substantial changes in mental health services and facilities followed World War II. By 1940, state mental hospital census had reached 410,000. Another 59,000 patients were in veterans', county, and city institutions. In that year, a total of 105,000 people were admitted to state institutions (82,000 for the first time); 59,000 were discharged (70 percent of whom had either recovered or improved); and 32,000 died. Public hospitals cared for nearly 98 percent of all institutionalized patients and, in 1940, their aggregate budget reached $144 million.[5] In today's dollars, that budget would be more than $1.6 billion, using Consumer Price Index adjustments.

4

In 1940, psychiatry was still considered an institutional specialty; more than two-thirds of the members of the American Psychiatric Association (APA) practiced in public institutions. Public hospitals were still considered the most appropriate setting for treating the mentally ill. In the early 1940s, shock therapies were commonly used in all mental hospitals. An estimated 75,000 patients received some form of shock therapy between 1935 and 1941.[5]

Psychosurgery was popular in the 1940s and into the late 1950s (the lobotomy was introduced in 1936). By 1951, 18,608 psychosurgeries had been performed.[5] The methods, particularly lobotomies, fell into increasing disfavor because of adverse publicity and because of increasing opposition to them in the psychiatric profession, and have largely disappeared from practice. By the time Ken Kesey's *One Flew over the Cuckoo's Nest* appeared in 1962, the practices he harpooned were on a downward track. Their demise may also have been hastened by the advent of pharmacology as a primary treatment methodology for mental illnesses. A search of various databases failed to disclose more up-to-date statistics on psychosurgery, but the lack of information itself suggests that the methodologies, at least in their previous forms, are rare if not extinct. According to Weiner, "Although psychosurgery for violent behavior is accepted clinical practice in Sweden, Japan, India, and Australia, since the 1970s it has been used in the United States only rarely."[6]

Psychiatrists discovered during World War II that neuropsychiatric disorders were more serious than previously recognized, that environmental stress associated with war contributed to mental problems, and that early treatment in noninstitutional settings produced favorable outcomes. These findings were the basis for claims in 1945 that early identification of symptoms and treatment in community settings could reduce future hospitalization and possibly prevent serious illness.[5] As mentioned earlier, these findings and subsequent advances in psychopharmacology likely fueled the deinstitutionalization movement.

The post-war era also produced a new breed of young physicians whose thinking was shaped by these astonishing findings. They were attracted by psychodynamic and psychoanalytic concepts and, after 1945, many of them assumed leadership positions within the specialty and attempted to pioneer new community-oriented policies.

In 1946, Congress enacted the Hill-Burton Act, which provided generous federal subsidies for hospital construction, particularly in rural and generally underserved areas of the country. Thousands of new beds, many of them for psychiatric care, were added in a short period. In the same year, the National Institute of Mental Health (NIMH) was established within the National Institutes of Health as a comprehensive research program on mental illness and health.

Another prominent piece of legislation, the National Mental Health Act, also passed during 1946 at the prompting of Robert H. Felix, MD, an early proponent of community psychiatry. The act ended the tradition of federal inactivity and incorporated three goals: to train mental health personnel by providing fellowships and institutional grants; to support research relating to the cause, diagnosis, and treatment of psychiatric disorders; and to award grants to states to assist in establishing clinics and treatment centers and to fund demonstration studies dealing with prevention, diagnosis, and treatment of patients at public hospitals.

The National Mental Health Act led to formation of the National Mental Health Advisory Council to achieve these goals, most notably the charge to encourage development of clinics and treatment centers in all the states. Before 1948, half of all states had no mental health clinics. By 1949, all but five had at least one. Six years later, there were 1,234 outpatient psychiatric clinics, of which two-thirds were state-subsidized.[5]

When World War II ended, the nation's public health hospitals, a significant public source of mental health services, had seriously deteriorated, yet their census continued to rise steadily. By 1945, it stood at 462,000. In 1946, the U.S. Public Health Service's Committee on Psychiatric Standards and Policies established the Central Inspection Board and concluded an agreement with the American College of Surgeons to assume responsibility for inspecting public health hospitals by 1951. Throughout its existence, the board was never able to successfully develop rating techniques and approved less than half of the public health hospitals it inspected. In 1953, of 45 hospitals it inspected, only two were approved. The American College of Surgeons disagreed with the board's ratings and passed 25 of those hospitals. The board was terminated in 1960.[5]

By the late 1940s, the Governors' Council directed its Council of State Governments to conduct a comprehensive analysis of care and treatment of the mentally ill to provide state governments with data. A year later, it issued "The Mental Health Programs of the Forty-Eight States," a report that anticipated the activism of states in the mental health field during the 1950s. A study of training and research followed and was completed in 1953. In 1954, the governors convened a conference devoted to mental health and adopted a 10-point program embodying the basic themes from the two studies. This historic meeting set the stage for expansion in preventive and community-based care.[5]

During the 1950s, mental health hospitals returned to public favor. Psychotropic drugs created hope for many mentally ill patients. By 1956, antidepressants first appeared. During this era, there was a greater sensitivity toward the methodological problems of identifying and explaining diagnoses. In 1952, the American Psychiatric Association published the first edition of *Diagnostic and Statistical Manual: Mental Disorders (DSM-1)*. The manual revealed the intellectual, cultural, and social forces that transformed psychiatry after World War II. It divided mental disorders into two categories: those that are a result of brain function (infection, trauma, disease) and those that hinder social adjustment and in which brain function is secondary to the illness (psychotic, manic depressive, paranoid, phobic).[5]

The Joint Commission on Mental Illness and Health was formed in 1955 and existed for six years, during which time a number of scholarly studies were conducted. The commission's work led to passage of federal legislation that undermined the traditional emphasis on institutional care for the severely mentally ill. Its final report in 1961, "Action for Mental Health," portrayed the shortcomings of the mental health service system and recommended increasing manpower and services to maximize existing services. But the recommendations were hazy and hard to implement.[5]

However, the Health Amendments Act of 1956 did force an increase in the supply of nurses and other public health workers. Title V of the Act authorized a new program of federal grants to state and local governments. It modified the National Mental Health Act of 1946 to increase funds for mental health and greatly increased the importance of NIMH's role in mental health policy. Amendments in 1956 to the Social Security Act of 1935 provided benefits for people age 50 and older who were unable to work because of a physical or mental condition. The age limitation was deleted four years later.[5]

During the 1950s and 1960s, interprofessional tensions among the various professions in the mental heath care arena altered jurisdictional boundaries and roles. Federal policy encouraged training of nonmedical professionals, and there was great debate about their ability to offer psychotherapy without medical supervision. In the 1960s, psychiatric activists and their supporters promoted community-based outpatient treatment and insisted it was possible to identify those at high risk and intervene to avoid hospitalization. The federal Short-Doyle Act shifted the focus of state policy away from a reliance on institutional care and treatment, and counties and cities began to establish more facilities. This marked the end of the traditional mental hospital after nearly 150 years.[5]

Financing of the mental health system underwent dramatic changes during the 1960s. In the private sector, third-party health insurance coverage expanded rapidly after World War II. By 1970, about 80 percent of the population was covered, but the coverage was spotty. By 1971, all Blue Cross plans in the United States offered some psychiatric benefits.

In 1960, the old age assistance and medical assistance for the aged program was legislatively amended to permit payment for short-term treatment in public mental hospitals for up to 42 days. Two years later, the Department of Health, Education, and Welfare (now the Department of Health and Human Services) revised the regulations to allow welfare payments to conditionally discharged patients, a move to return people to the community sooner.[5]

The mental health community had high hopes of new funding and big changes in mental health when President John F. Kennedy took office. His personal interest in the field was well known. In 1963, Kennedy signed the Community Mental Health Centers Act, which provided $150 million in grants for construction over three years. The goal was to reduce reliance on mental hospitals. Resident populations at mental health hospitals fell dramatically during this period.

A law was passed in 1965, during Lyndon Baines Johnson's tenure in the White House, that focused on building a national system of community mental health centers. But the timing was bad. The Vietnam War was raging, and the goal of building and staffing 2,000 centers by 1980 was not to be. Additionally, the relationship between the specialty of psychiatry and the centers faltered. The number of psychiatrists associated with centers plummeted. Instead they were staffed by clinical psychologists, social workers, and nonprofessionals.[5]

Medicare and Medicaid, established in Social Security Act Amendments passed in 1965 and designed to provide medical care for the poor and elderly, included psychiatric benefits. There was a lifetime limit of 190 days for inpatient services in psychiatric hospitals; there were no limitations at general hospital psychiatric units. Possibly as a result, the 1960s marked a shift in the location of services and an increase in the volume of cases. For instance, in 1955, 77.4 percent of episodes occurred in mental hospitals and 22.6 percent in outpatient facilities. Thirteen years later, the respective figures were 47.3 and 52.7. Outpatient centers were being used by people who had never had access to mental health services. Although outpatient treatment increased dramatically, inpatient treatment was unaffected. The median stay for patients in long-term mental care was 8.4 years in 1962.[5]

In 1969, elderly people with mental disorders were being sent to nursing homes instead of to state hospitals because of the passage of Medicare and Medicaid. The nursing home population rocketed from 470,000 to 928,000 as a result.[3] By limiting Medicaid and Medicare funds for elderly patients in mental hospitals, the legislation encouraged states to refer them to nursing homes, where federal payments were more generous. By 1977, 14 percent of Medicaid funds were spent on patients in state hospitals versus 53 percent spent on patients in nursing homes. Meanwhile, public hospitals were admitting more young people, but they were releasing them sooner.[5]

By 1970, the thinking among psychodynamic and biological psychiatrists merged, and the treatment of choice of both sides was a combination of individual, group, and milieu therapies, in conjunction with drug therapy. As the psychoanalytic psychiatrists retired from the profession, they were replaced by those more committed to biological explanations of mental disorders. The new thinkers stressed the importance of integrating psychiatry and medicine and of exploiting new medical technologies to explain the biology of mental disorders. The emphasis shifted from psychosocial rehabilitation to examination of pathology and diagnosis.[5]

In the 1970s and 1980s, the welfare system came under fire from a political constituency determined to curtail government responsibilities and activities. As a result, many chronically and severely mentally ill people were often left without access to support services or even to the basic necessities of life. By the 1980s, the plight of the homeless mentally ill had become a problem of staggering dimensions.[5]

During his presidency, Jimmy Carter trotted out the President's Commission on Mental Health. Although it only existed during 1977, the commission did confirm the fact that people with chronic mental disabilities were being released into the community without basic skils and resources for coping with their new lives and that half were being readmitted within a year of discharge, a finding that was seconded in a General Accounting Office (GAO) report that same year.[7] The process of deinstitutionalization began in the 1950s, but the backlash wasn't felt until the 1970s.

Deinstitutionalization prompted two major developments in the delivery of mental health care. First, patients with acute mental illness episodes had traditionally been seen at local hospitals, while chronic patients tended to be treated at mental hospitals. After deinstitutionalization, the treatment profiles of these two types of patients began to approximate each other. Deinstitutionalization, therefore, ended the two-class system of mental health care.

The second impact of deinstitutionalization was in readmissions. While chronic populations at state hospitals decreased, total admissions continued to rise until 1972, mostly because of read-missions. Patients spent less time in the hospital, but they entered the hospital many more times. In 1969, readmissions accounted for 47 percent of all admissions. In 1972, that figure rose to 54 percent. There was no shift in funding to allow services to follow patients.[3]

Expansion of federal entitlement programs hastened the discharge of many patients during and after the 1970s. Between 1970 and 1986, the number of inpatient beds in state and county insti-tutions dropped from 413,000 to 119,000. Length of stay fell to 28 days. By 1983, general hospi-tals accounted for almost two-thirds of the nearly three million inpatient psychiatric episodes and were the most popular hospitalization site for mental illness.[7]

The National Alliance for the Mentally Ill was founded in 1972 to unite families of the mentally ill in an advocacy organization that played an increasingly important role in the politics of men-tal health during and after the 1980s. The organization strives to eliminate discrimination and restrictions on access to essential treatments and life supports such as employment, housing, health insurance, and social contact for the mentally ill.

In 1980 Congress passed the Mental Health Systems Act. It assumed federal leadership in improving community services and recommended planning, accountability, performance con-tracts between providers of mental health care and general medical care, and protection of patient rights. However, the election of Ronald Reagan as President led to a 25 percent cut in fed-eral funding and conversion of federal mental health programs into a single block grant to the states. In 1981, the Omnibus Budget Reconciliation Act provided a block grant to states for men-tal health services and substance abuse and repealed most of the provisions of the Mental Health Systems Act. This reversed more than three decades of federal involvement and leader-ship in mental health services. During the following decade, the states and local communities took up the mantle.[7]

Also in 1980, the Disability Amendments legislation mandated that the Social Security Administration review the eligibility of all Supplemental Security Income (SSI) and Supplemental Security Disability Income (SSDI) recipients every three years. It was thought this move would save $218 million over the next five years. When President Reagan took office, there were about 550,000 disabled people receiving assistance, including the mentally ill. The admin-istration wielded the clause like an ax to deny benefits to thousands of new applicants and to chip out others. The mentally disabled, who accounted for 11 percent of SSDI recipients but rep-resented 30 percent of those cut from the program, were hit hard The Social Security Administration projected it would save $3.5 billion by 1985 simply by defining disability more narrowly and weeding out those who did not fit the parameters. A public outcry ensued, and, by mid-1983, the administration caved in under strong public pressure and reversed its policy.[7]

The '90s have wrought many more changes. When Congress failed to pass a health care reform plan early in President Clinton's first term, the states generated initiatives to move the process along. Medicaid now comprises 20 percent of the states' budgets, so states are turning to the solution the private sector has been using around the country: managed care. Medicaid managed care doubled in enrollment between 1987 and 1992 and again between 1992 and 1994, with eight million beneficiaries now enrolled. State Medicaid agencies have been experimenting with managed care since about 1985, but the experiment has become a full-fledged movement.

As of May 1995, 28 state mental health systems were affected by Medicaid reforms, and many have moved to a variety of managed care models. Arizona has the oldest Medicaid managed care program. It added a behavioral health carve-out in 1990.[5] Most of the state initiatives have relied on primary care management or limited, prepaid plans for certain subgroups of people, such as Aid to Families with Dependent Children (AFDC).

More states have since developed statewide reform proposals and have applied to the Health Care Financing Administration (HCFA) for research and demonstration waivers through which they can be relieved of Medicaid regulations. With these waivers, states can transfer financial risk to fully capitated managed care organizations and streamline Medicaid enrollment procedures by narrowing eligibility. The impact on public mental health systems is that states are receiving waivers from the prohibitions concerning services in mental health facilities and are covering acute inpatient mental health services provided by state-run facilities. In this way, states can offer a more comprehensive mental health benefit because of federal financial participation.[7] In many states, Medicaid supports about one-third of community health programs, has been the only source of new revenue for the past five years, and is often the only funding source for community support and rehabilitation services. While state mental health authorities run state psychiatric hospitals, Medicaid controls spending for inpatient psychiatric treatment.[7]

With disability defined more narrowly, many people do not fit the parameters of access to managed care. Public mental health systems have traditionally specialized in uncompensated care and have defined populations, not individuals. And, because of limited resources, they have been unsuccessful in meeting the needs of the population. Under managed care, the payer must specify the exact group of consumers to be enrolled, which is bound to affect access. Utilization management also affects access, because state mental health authorities are now trying to decide how to manage patients in the public mental health system. This raises the questions of whether these authorities should retain responsibility for eligibility determination and enrollment and of how much administrative and bureaucratic costs will be. Gatekeeping decisions by managed care organizations, when the public mental health system is involved, will have to be based on the authorities' assignment of financial and clinical risk and on the incentives this assignment creates for the various placement and treatment options.[7]

As part of a proposed health care reform initiative, the American Managed Behavioral Healthcare Association and the National Association of State Mental Health Program Directors produced the "Managed Behavioral Healthcare Cost Report for the Commercial Insured and Uninsured Populations" in May 1994. The analysis was designed to determine the costs of providing comprehensive, affordable health and substance abuse benefits to the American public. Under the Health Security Act, the Clinton Administration estimated such benefits would cost $241 per person per year. However, the study revealed that national averages do not reflect state differences in health care reform and that the data in estimated Medicaid behavioral health care costs are somewhat uncertain. The report showed that the benefits could be provided for $202 to $228 per person per year. Cost savings come from a move to managed care strategies, such as case management and contracting with effective partners. The report found that the estimated 1994 aggregate costs showed dramatic savings in a fully managed program, as compared to a less managed fee-for-service system. However, it must be noted that the conclusions of the report have been widely challenged.

Members of the American Managed Behavioral Healthcare Association were polled for the report. They constitute 17 of the country's largest and best-known managed behavioral health care companies, providing or managing care for more than 65 million Americans. The National Association of State Mental Health Program Directors represents 55 state and territorial mental health authorities, who are collectively the largest purchasers/providers of mental health care in the United States.

Of all these organizations, 53 percent have at least some of their care delivered through staff-model clinics. About 88 percent conduct reviews of medical records, access standards, cancel/fail rates, complaint and appeal review, and resolution. Nearly two-thirds use multidisciplinary reviews. Compliance is measured by 93 percent of members.

All members conduct patient satisfaction surveys. A total of 91 percent graded providers as satisfactory or excellent, 82 percent were satisfied with access, and 89 percent were satisfied overall.[8] This is a far cry from the workhouse incarceration, inhuman conditions, and experimental shock therapies of previous years.

Still, according to NIMH, mental disorders today affect five million adults and cost the United States more than $150 billion each year for treatment, for social service and disability payments, for lost productivity, and for premature mortality. One in 10 Americans experiences some disability from a diagnosable mental illness in the course of any given year, NIMH says.

The U.S. investment in mental health research, which is less than one percent of the yearly costs of mental illnesses, shows that our system requires policies that acknowledge that mental illnesses can be diagnosed precisely and treated effectively, according to the NIMH. And an analysis conducted in 1995 for the Senate Appropriations Committee projected that appropriate and timely treatment of severe mental disorders would produce a 10 percent decrease in the use and cost of medical services by people with these illnesses, yielding savings greater than the cost of providing the treatment services.

In recent years, the study of the brain, behavior, and mental illnesses has been heightened greatly by incredible advances in molecular biology, biomedical imaging, structural chemistry, immunology, psychology, and computer science. New knowledge of the neurochemistry of the brain has led to a new generation of psychotherapeutic drugs not available as recently as a decade ago. These medications are revolutionizing treatment of severe mental illnesses, according to NIMH, and the future holds much more potential.

References

1. Talbott, J. *Unified Mental Health Systems: Utopia Unrealized.* San Francisco, Calif.: Jossey-Bass, Inc., Publishers, 1983.

2. A longer chronology of events in the development of psychology in America may be found at http://www.cwu.edu/~warren/addenda.html on the Internet.

3. Talbott, J. *The Death of the Asylum.* New York, N.Y.: Grune and Stratton, 1978.

4. Mechanic, D. *Mental Health & Social Policy.* Englewood Cliffs, N.J.: Prentice-Hall, Inc., 1969.

5. Grob, G. *From Asylum to Community: Mental Health Policy in Modem America.* Princeton, N.J.: Princeton University Press, 1991.

6. *Psychiatric News,* June 6, 1996, p. 16.

7. Grob, G. *The Mad Among Us: A History of the Care of America's Mentally Ill.* New York, N.Y.: The Free Press, 1994.

8. Melek, S. American Managed Behavioral Healthcare Association and National Association of State Mental Health Program Directors Managed Behavioral Healthcare Cost Report for the Commercial Insured and Uninsured Populations, in conjunction with Foster Higgin and Milliman & Robertson, May 13, 1994.

Donna Vavala is a freelance writer and editor in Brooksville, Florida.

Chapter 2

The Once Current State of Affairs in Behavioral Health Care Service Delivery

by Frank Boruch, MD

The Big Picture

There is no truly "current" landscape of behavioral health care service delivery, because the scenery is always changing. We are in a state of flux, where the only constant is a continued succession of varying models, methods, and tools for providing care.

Service Structures

Managed care, for example, has evolved to a position of preeminence among models of behavioral health care service delivery in the United States. It is credited, at least in part, with a decrease in the rate of increase of behavioral health care costs; shifts in service delivery sites, such as decreased utilization of psychiatric and chemical dependency treatment hospital beds; and rigorous resource management molded by an economic philosophy of cost control. Seventy-five percent of all employees with health plans are now enrolled in some form of managed care. This represents a dramatic shift from just a decade ago, and even within this evolution there is further dramatic and ongoing evolution. For instance, when we had reason to reflect on managed care organizations a few short years ago, we found ourselves thinking almost exclusively about health maintenance organizations (HMOs). Today, our thinking includes other dominant variants of managed care participants, such as preferred provider organizations (PPOs) and independent practice associations (IPAs). IPAs, on behalf of circumscribed groups of independent clinicians, contract with payers to service the health care needs of a number of health plan enrollees. IPAs can be, and some are, clinician-owned and clinician-directed behavioral health specialty operations. A relatively new variant is the professional affiliation group (PAG), whose nature is virtual rather than corporate, but it can negotiate for contractual provision of behavioral health care service delivery.

When we think about types of health care delivery models that have been successful at increasing market share for their plans, we turn to point-of-service (POS) options. In this model, enrollees can, at some added out-of-pocket cost, exercise an option to receive care from clinicians of their choice even when the clinicians are not identified as belonging to a formally identified and endorsed network or group. Point-of-enrollment (POE) options provide health care services as outlined in formal benefit schedules and through a defined network of clinicians. Except in emergencies, POE members who receive care outside of the network pay the full cost of these services themselves.

When we talk about HMO equivalents that also contract directly with payers, combine health care coverage with health care service, presubscribe members for prepaid revenues, bear financial risk, build limited clinician networks, and use the tools of managed care to control costs, we now mention provider-sponsored networks (PSNs). One target for providers in a PSN is to design an organizational structure in which they, rather than a health plan administration, retain organizational control.

As we watch Congress, we see the Balanced Budget Act of 1997, which allows provider-sponsored organizations (PSOs) to serve the Medicare population through the establishment of Medicare risk contracts. PSO legislation is notable for several reasons. Federal spending on Medicare benefits approximates $200 billion/year. PSOs will be able to compete for the managed care risk contract monies in the Medicare+Choice market. This could represent a significant economic boost for initiatives to promote provider-driven management of health care services. PSOs will now have a direct connection to the Health Care Financing Administration (HCFA), our nation's largest purchaser of health care services, and HCFA views PSOs as entities put together and operated by providers who share financial risk and hold majority financial interest in the PSO and who are actually delivering health care to patients.

Four common types of organizations that could meet HCFA's criteria for PSOs are group practices, the already mentioned IPAs and PSNs, and physician/hospital organizations (PHOs). PHOs are joint clinician and hospital ventures created so that the resulting combined body can establish a single contracting, marketing, and service entity.

Last, we must now also recognize organizations that exist primarily to manage and/or provide practice management, administrative, and other support services to and/or "own" clinical practices. Examples of these entities are management services organizations (MSOs), and physician practice management companies (PPMCs). University Behavioral Associates (UBA), a behavioral health MSO based in New York, is described as "a not-for-profit company that provides the standard services of a behavioral management services organization addressing issues of access, utilization and case management, information management, credentialing, claims processing, quality assurance and member services, financial reporting, and contract consultation."[1]

Consumers

Engines driving behavioral health care change are themselves changing. Traditional patients, for example, had little if any influence over their employers' health insurance selection decisions, and, even if they had, they seldom had enough quality or cost knowledge to make informed decisions about value. Now, however, those who were once patients have matured into stakeholder consumers of health care products and services. Their demands are maturing, too. Collectively, they know as much or more about issues such as quality, availability (access, cost, choice), and health plan variations as do employers or other agents who make volume purchasing decisions.

These stakeholder consumers are demanding demonstrable health care value, and, increasingly, they are seeing value in the promotion of well-being as much as they see it in efficient and efficacious treatment of pathology.

This means that behavioral health care service organizations, in formulating competitive strategies, must attend to the expectations of healthy consumers as much as they attend to the concerns of ill patients or large payers.

Stakeholder health care consumers are also asking for guarantees , by law, of basic health care provisions. Patients' bill of rights legislation involves an initiative that would legally mandate health plans to provide subscribers with some basic benefits and protections. Some analysts advise that laws creating health care "rights" could raise health care costs to the extent that the number of uninsured would increase. Consumer advocates, however, are working with lawmakers on bill of rights legislation precisely because they believe that legal guarantees of some basics, such as choice of doctors, would better balance the health care power scale between consumer stakeholders and health plans. The hope is that a legislated bill of rights would pave the way for more consumer-friendly, affordable health care, with more health care security for more people than now have it.

Congress is also considering a proposed Patient Access to Responsible Care Act (PARCA) introduced by Representative Charles Norwood (R-Ga.). This act aims to increase protection for the patient by abrogating the preemption of state malpractice laws currently provided for in the Employee Retirement Income Security Act (ERISA). Injured parties would then be able to sue managed care health plans within state malpractice law. Other PARCA provisions would include a mandated point-of-service alternative choice for managed care patients and a legal mandate that health care professionals be involved when utilization standards are developed.

Consumer stakeholders are no longer content to rely on market forces to give them what they want. They are now pursuing an alliance with legislators to mold laws that will give them what they believe health care consumers are entitled to expect.

The Market

Although its position is challenged regularly now, health care in America, including behavioral health care, holds the status of a commodity. As such, it is subject to the motley and evanescent forces of that change master we identify as "the market." To survive as a provider of behavioral health care, the small provider now has to grow or be aligned with a larger, growing organization. Stasis can equal demise. To succeed now as anything more than a very local and very restricted or niche market provider of behavioral health care, the provider or provider system needs its own capital for growth, or access through its greater whole, to channels of growth capital. The mergers and buyouts we read about so frequently in behavioral health care are not accidents. The market demands competition, and competition demands rapid change with ever-improving products, service, and pricing. As positive revenue margins have become slimmer to bolster value, behavioral health care organizations have become larger and larger to benefit from economies of scale and skill never before seen in the history of mental health.

The June 1997 edition of *Managed Healthcare News* reviewed two such growth phenomena.[2] Advocate Health Care is joining with Behavioral Health Systems to form Advocate Behavioral Health Partners. Behavioral Health Systems alone serviced more than 100,000 lives prior to the partnering. But that example, even with its rather large denominator of covered lives, represents a relatively modest operation compared to some other mergers or mergers in progress. Green Spring Health Services, Inc., and Ceres Behavioral Healthcare System "have established a limited liability company that has acquired all of the assets of Ceres Behavioral Health Systems." Moreover, in spring 1997, Green Spring announced plans to acquire Mainstay, Inc., as a wholly owned subsidiary. That maneuver would add yet another 600,000 behavioral health members to Green Spring's fold of covered lives.[3] At the time of this writing, the Green Spring marketing department estimated that the company served the behavioral health care needs of 16 million people.

Also in 1997, Value Health, Inc. and Columbia/HCA HealthCare Organization agreed to merge. Columbia already had (besides more than 300 hospitals, more than 100 outpatient surgery centers, and many home health care centers) a behavioral health service organization with almost 150 locations. Subsequent to the merger, it was announced that the Value Behavioral Health component of Value Health, Inc., will be sold to FHC Health Systems, owners of Options Health Care, Inc. At last count, Value Behavioral Health as a stand-alone organization is thought to be serving in the neighborhood of 16 million lives, while FHC through its Options subsidiary, serves yet another 6 million lives for behavioral health care.[4] Magellan Health Services, which owns majority interest in Green Spring Health Services, has also been pursuing a vigorous growth strategy. It recently acquired both Merit Behavioral Health Care Corp. and Human Affairs International, Inc. (HAI), whose prior affiliation was with Aetna U.S. Healthcare.[4] Magellan might, with something like 60 million covered lives, be considered the largest behavioral health care manager in America.

Grand proportions offer organizations the hope of grand efficiencies of size and skill. Grand proportions, combined with market dominance in any area, could also afford a behavioral health care organization increased control over premiums charged, payments made to practitioners, and benefits offered to enrollees.

This trend is inversely correlated with the number of self-employed physicians and with the monetary value of solo practices. The May 1997 edition of *Physician Practice Options* reports that, in 1983, only 25 percent of physicians were "employed," whereas, in 1995, 45 percent of doctors chose to become employees. Furthermore, within the past four years, the monetary worth of solo practices has dipped by approximately 20 percent.[5] Solo and small group behavioral health care practices have little or no leverage in negotiating payments for services with large health care organizations. This zero-leverage position can be expected to contribute to further erosion of the revenue base and relative monetary value of solo and small group behavioral health care practices.

Even if they opt to become part of larger behavioral health care service delivery organizations, some practitioners are enhancing their individual marketability by diversifying and augmenting their clinical skills. Psychiatrists, for example, are combining their specialty with advanced formal training in primary care medicine. About 25 percent of our nation's medical schools now offer dual residency training in primary care and psychiatry. Other clinicians are pursuing graduate business degrees to bolster their financial security while they seek opportunities to participate more meaningfully in the decision-making processes that govern the directions of behavioral health care change. Still others are engaged in acquiring expertise that would allow them to successfully engage in relative niche market activities. One example here might involve implementation and provision of managed behavioral health care services within the criminal justice system.

Some doctors are attempting to add weight to their influence in the health care arena by grafting themselves onto unions. It may once have been almost unheard of in nonpublic quarters, and even now may seem unusual, but physicians and labor unions are seeing mutual potential benefits in an alliance.

Others are forming new corporate structure alliances among themselves. Behavioral health care clinicians see the same strengths that health plans see in grand proportions. So, clinicians are joining together under their own corporate canopies to give themselves negotiating leverage with health plans and insurers. By forming such alliances, clinicians also hope to maintain, or take back, control over clinical decisions. The more numerous the corporate affiliates, the better positioned would the group be to pay for state-of-the-art information and administrative systems management services.

Eventually, because the new corporate entities need to compete in a price-sensitive environment, their utilization management behaviors may come to resemble those of existing, mature health plans. Still, if behavioral health care clinical decisions are clearly and exclusively made by behavioral health care clinicians, such structures would be attractive to prospective enrollees. And if the structures are large enough to wield clout in negotiating contracts, health plan and insurer profit margins could be threatened.

Health care may be a trillion-dollar-a-year industry, but even a trillion is a finite number. If one player gets more money from the pool, another player has to get less; likewise for control. If consolidation among clinicians offers them more control over their clinical practices, health plans and insurers will have less control.

Uncertainty about just who will call the money shots, just who will control clinical decision making, and just what role any current participant will have in the future will add fuel to the fire of flux in behavioral health care.

It might also be noted that, paralleling a recent decline in applications for medical schools, some behavioral health care clinicians, including psychiatrists, are looking outside the health care arena for income diversity and a renewed sense of professional well-being. The current economy is strong. Full-time and part-time opportunities in a wide range of fields are attractive to clinicians who prefer to work on a change in their professional life-styles rather than work on trying to influence change in a health care environment over which they feel they have little control. This group sees greater potential for personal enrichment and economic reward outside rather than inside the present world of behavioral health care.

Financing

Because the market is money sensitive, financing of behavioral health care service delivery has come under close scrutiny. Health plan member and payer premiums or dues, patient copayments, and fee-for-service payments represent the lion's share of steady cash flow for health insurance and health service organizations. Just as managed care is the prevailing preferred model of service delivery, so too is capitation the prevailing preferred method of payment for service delivery. Major payers negotiate to remunerate health plans on a capitated basis. Health plans, in turn, negotiate to remunerate providers on a capitated basis. Many billions of dollars are invested in the capitation system for managed care financing. Capitation appears to have helped control costs better than the traditional fee-for-service model. But, today, our emphasis on the importance of the pricing of health care (and, therefore, on capitation's contribution to the system of pricing) is being challenged. Dr. Paul M. Ellwood Jr., the man who gave HMOs their name, was reported by the *New York Times* as saying that he set out to create a system of competition between health care providers based on price and quality, but what has evolved instead is a system of competition based almost completely on price.[6] Fee for service may have provided an incentive in the direction of doing too much. The potential jeopardy of capitation, especially if pricing assumes a position superordinate to quality, is to provide an incentive in the direction of doing too little. In a study jointly conducted by the Washington Business Group on Health and Watson Wyatt Worldwide (Second Annual Study on Value in Health Care), close to half of companies with up to 1,000 employees are reported as saying that quality is suffering because of the emphasis on health care pricing.[7] There was even sponsorship of an unsuccessful but noteworthy legislative initiative in Oregon in 1996 to make capitation illegal.

There are other challenges to capitation. It has been said, for example, that "capitation, far from being a market-oriented solution, actually prevents the formation of a dynamic price system necessary to optimize marketplace trades of medical goods and services."[8] Capitation can be viewed as an economic incentive vehicle to promote prevention and education programs in health care, even as it rewards efforts to foster efficiency and efficacy in health care service delivery. Capitation, along with managed care, helped to decrease the rate of increase in health care costs so that, in the past few years, total spending on health care has been steady at 13.6 percent of our total gross domestic product. But profit margins have narrowed dramatically for health plans and insurers. Capitation financing is no longer able to help contain what looks like upcoming widespread and significant increases in health plan dues and insurance premiums. Stringent capitation, which never did capture popular appeal among clinicians or patients, is now viewed as just one possible choice among a growing variety of ways to pay for behavioral health care. Capitation is undergoing some de-capitation changes.

The health care voucher is one alternative to rigid capitated financing in the expanding pool of ways by which consumers might finance payments to providers so that providers, in turn, can finance their health care service operations. In this finance system, a payer allocates some specific dollar amount to the consumer, and the consumer retains the right to choose various benefit packages from different health plans. The consumer would pay more for augmented benefit menus and might pay nothing for basic benefit programs. Unused cash might be tapped for monetary or benefit credits in case of major medical catastrophe. The federal government's

Federal Employee Health Benefit Plan (FEHBP) offers employees specific cash credit amounts and covers almost 9 million lives. This gives the payer control over its health care costs while allowing consumers to choose health plans, benefits, and particular clinicians that they feel are optimal and would provide the best care for them, at an appropriate cost.

Another option, allowed now by most states, is the Medical Savings Account (MSA). These accounts were established by Congress in 1996 for the self-employed and for small businesses with up to 50 employees. In 1999, Medicare will implement a pilot project wherein Medicare beneficiaries will also participate in MSA accounts. MSAs, which might be considered second cousins to Independent Retirement Accounts (IRAs), but for medical rather than retirement purposes, represent an experimental system under evaluation. In this finance system, an employer elects a deduction on federal income taxes for real money contributions to each employee's medical savings account. The employer then buys a health insurance policy with a very high deductible ($1,500-4,500) for employees and their families, who might be asked to contribute a portion of insurance premiums. Employees use the money in their medical savings accounts to pay medical bills, including those for behavioral health services. When bills exceed both the medical savings account balance and the insurance deductible, the insurance policy comes into effect. Employees could spend money from their medical savings accounts for other than medical purposes, but they would incur both a percentage penalty and a tax liability for those monies. Employers can contribute an equivalent of 65-75 percent of the insurance deductible amount to medical savings accounts for, respectively, individuals or families. At year's end, any balance that might remain in a tax-exempt medical savings account could be invested and earn money for the account holder.

MSAs clearly give control over health care dollar allocation decisions to the consumer. With an MSA, the person who makes the discretionary financial decision is the same person who makes the clinical decision about what health care, when, where , and with whom, is best for them. Furthermore, there are no restrictions on mental health benefits with MSAs.

Flat-fee case rates are yet another alternative to global capitation for population bases. In a capitated system, monies are paid to providers for a patient group, even when some patients in the pool do not access service. With case rates, predetermined dollar amounts are paid to behavioral health care providers only when patients with specific diagnoses present for services. Both Green Spring Mental Health Services and Merit Behavioral Care Corporation, for example, "have started paying these 'case rates' to some mental health provider groups for patients who are not severely ill."[9]

Behavioral healthcare compensation structures of the future seem destined to be built around what are being called pay-for-performance systems. These systems, even when they involve some characteristics of capitated compensation, could have as much or more in common with traditional fee-for-service payment as they do with capitation methods. However, a critical feature of pay-for-performance systems is, and will be, a contractual agreement for a significant portion of potential payments for service to be tied to documented value parameters such as positive patient treatment outcomes data. In this system, the flow of dollars to health plans and/or providers is less when service value indicators are static or fall, and the flow of dollars increases when measurable improvements in value and outcomes are demonstrated. Such structures help to answer the challenge for pricing systems to be more dynamic, and for payment systems to be more market-performance oriented.

Other sources of capital available to behavioral health care providers, for more rapid infusion of money to support progress and growth, are the same as those available to other business enterprises. When we review common types, we are impressed again with the need for exalted size, because market history teaches that organizations with the clout of majestic scale have more access opportunities for large capital transactions than do small operations. Some of the more common sources of capital for behavioral health care organization expenditures and expansion include venture capital; strategic partner equity or debt; subordinated debt placed privately; sale and lease-back arrangements with real estate; notes; initial public offerings (IPOs); equity pooling; and, of course, traditional bank loans.

Parity

The availability of growth capital for behavioral health care service delivery systems would be academic if behavioral health care were not included with other health care coverage in health plan and insurance benefit menus. Even now, there may be more than 60 million men, women, and children in the United States who have no plan or insurance coverage for behavioral health ailments. Initiatives for parity are intrinsic to today's state of behavioral health care affairs.

Equivalence in benefits between behavioral health care and general medical health care is referred to as "parity." The National Mental Health Association (NMHA) commissioned a parity survey conducted by Caravan Research Opinion Corporation International in spring 1997. The survey revealed that 93 percent of us believe that behavioral health issues should be treated the same as other illnesses by health plans and insurance companies. However, 96 percent of all health plans placed special limits on behavioral health benefits.[10]

Helen Thomson, a representative in California's State Assembly, has sponsored a bill that would mandate health plans to "provide coverage for the diagnosis and medically necessary treatment of mental illness under the same terms and conditions applied to other medical conditions."[11] If the California Assembly passes Representative Thomson's bill, California would join a growing collection of states that have mandated some form of parity. Colorado, one of the most recent states to do so, mandates that insurers (although not self-insured companies) cover schizophrenia; major depression; and bipolar, schizoaffective, obsessive-compulsive, and panic disorders in the same way they cover illnesses identified traditionally as organic in nature. In Vermont, parity bill H-57 became law on June 10, 1997. That measure prohibits health plans from placing arbitrary limits, caps, or fees on mental health and addiction treatment services. Other states that have legislated some variation of parity include Arkansas, Connecticut, Indiana, Maine, Maryland, Minnesota, Missouri, New Hampshire, North Carolina, Oklahoma, Rhode Island, South Carolina, and Texas. The National Alliance for the Mentally Ill believes that as many as 30 other states are now giving consideration to behavioral health parity legislation. History will credit Maryland as being the first state, in 1993, to enact parity legislation for chemical dependency and mental illness.

On the federal level, in September 1996, the President signed into law a bill that included a behavioral health parity amendment mandating that annual or lifetime dollar limits that insurers impose on treatment costs must be the same for mental and physical disorders if those insurers offer mental health benefits at all. The Mental Health Parity Act went into effect on January 1, 1998. The amendment, which was sponsored by Senators Paul Wellstone (D-Minnesota) and Pete Dominici (R-New Mexico), was an attenuated version of their initially sponsored legislation for full parity. It does not, for example, require insurers to offer behavioral health benefits as the senators would have liked. Advocates are, however, expected to take advantage of parity's recent momentum by encouraging legislation that would require insurers to offer truly equivalent coverage for all physical and behavioral illness. For example, in 1997, the Substance Abuse Treatment Parity Act bill was introduced into Congress and now seems to be acquiring increasing support. Furthermore, a bipartisan coalition of representatives recently introduced federal legislation that would fortify and augment mental health parity gains that are already mandated by federal law.

In June 1997, the U.S. Senate approved a children's parity amendment (as part of the budget reconciliation bill) that would require nondiscriminatory mental health benefits in health plans enrolling children with federal funds.[12] President Clinton signed that $24 billion Children's Health Insurance Program (CHIP) amendment into law (Public Law 105-33) in August 1997. The $24 billion will be provided to states between now and the year 2002 so that health care services can be purchased for low-income, uninsured children. There is a mental health benefit for children in the law, but state plans reflect significant variability in mental health benefits, and CHIP falls short of offering eligible children true parity. Still, it represents a dramatic, positive step forward in the effort to eliminate inadequacies in current behavioral health care coverage for children.

The potential impact of universal parity on total health care costs is, as might be expected, being vigorously analyzed in many quarters. Parity received a kind of economic endorsement through an interim report prepared for Congress by the National Advisory Mental Health Council (NAMHC). Senator Dominici has said that the interim report, titled "Parity in Coverage of Mental Health Services In an Era of Managed Care," suggests that parity, "in combination with managed care, results in lower costs and lower premiums within the first year of implementation."[13] A RAND study designed to "simulate the consequences of removing coverage limits for mental health care as required by the Mental Health Parity Act" concluded that "the cost consequences of improved coverage under managed care, which by now accounts for most private insurance, are relatively minor."[14] The study indicates that eliminating current restrictions on mental health benefits would add just $1-7 per enrollee per year to the cost of a managed care plan. The federal Substance Abuse and Mental Health Services Administration (SAMHSA) commissioned a study of the economic impact of parity. Results of that work indicate that "private insurance premiums would increase about 3.6 percent for full parity based on an aggregate of health plans including HMOs, fee-for-service, and preferred provider organizations."[15]

The Equal Opportunity Employment Commission has also reinforced the legal foundation for parity at the job site. On April 29, 1997, the Commission declared that the Americans with

Disabilities Act (ADA) disallows employers from questioning prospective employees about any mental illness history and mandates that employers make "reasonable accommodations" to provide mentally ill people with the capacity to do their jobs.[16]

Parity has also assumed the status of a single-focus topic worthy of national conference attention. For example, the Employer Behavioral Healthcare Partnership and CentraLink, in cooperation with the Midwest Business Group on Health, sponsored an event titled "Pragmatic Parity" as part of the Executive Healthcare Leadership Series.

Quality

Parity would be irrelevant, however, if there were no surety about the quality of clinical interventions in behavioral health care. Dr. Paul Elwood, mentioned earlier in this chapter as a person who believes that quality has not yet assumed its proper weight or place in the health care equation, has been instrumental in the past in helping to transform the American health care service delivery structures into what they are today, so his ideas about today's areas for improvements are worth noting. He believes that current quality measures look primarily at processes, at things that are done. He now champions the measurement of treatment outcomes as the gold standard, ideally, to be contractual requirements for health care service delivery systems. In outcomes measurement, an attempt is made to assess changes in a patient's or a group's health status, quantify those changes, and identify attribution for those changes in health to treatment experienced by the patient or group.

Dr. Elwood is not alone. He, along with groups such as the American Association for Retired Persons, unions such as the AFL-CIO, employers such as General Motors, and agencies such as the Health Care Financing Administration all endorse the Foundation for Accountability (FACCT).[6] FACCT intends to offer outcomes measurement recommendations based on criteria for evaluating care itself, rather than for evaluating the processes of delivering care. Of significance for those of us in behavioral health, FACCT has seen fit to address depression among three disease states for which it issued its first recommended criteria for evaluating care.

The Joint Commission on Accreditation of Health Care Organizations (JCAHO) recently published its Comprehensive Accreditation Manual for Managed Behavioral Health Care delivery systems and plans to link accreditation with the outcomes of patient care.[17] Meanwhile, the Council on Accreditation of Services for Families and Children (COA) and the Commission for the Accreditation of Rehabilitative Facilities (CARF) are both working with JCAHO to promote cooperation and shared recognition of accepted standards.

In March 1997, President Clinton appointed two psychiatrists to the Advisory Commission on Consumer Protection and Quality in the Health Care Industry. The appointed psychiatrists are Herbert Pardes, MD, Dean of Columbia University's College of Physicians and Surgeons, New York, New York, and Steven Sharfstein, MD, President and Medical Director of Sheppard Pratt Health Care System, Baltimore, Maryland. The appointees are reported to have observed that "the appointment of the commission reflects a widening belief that the focus in managed care has been for too long on cutting costs and not enough on quality of care."[18] President Clinton has since directed federal health plans to comply with a Consumer Bill of Rights endorsed by the President's Quality Commission.

Many others are involved in advocacy, development, and implementation of tools designed to provide assessments and improve the quality of behavioral health care. Some are specifically involved in the creation of what we have recently come to identify as report cards for behavioral health care service providers. These report cards afford structure for ongoing data collection and analyses in order to assess, continuously, the performance of behavioral health care service delivery systems.

When I asked my computer, in June 1997, to search for information on "mental health quality report cards," it found 1.46 million related listings. Hewitt Associates, Rowayton, Connecticut, surveyed 200 corporate health plan managers and found that 56.6 percent expect to rely on more detailed quality of care assessments in selecting health plan options.[19] Report cards are here to stay, and they are still so young in their developmental age that we can expect to see lots of changes in their substance and utilization in the immediate future.

Several organizations are deploying versions of behavioral health care report cards. The Center for Mental Health Services (CMHS), a unit of the Substance Abuse and Mental Health Services Administration (SAMHSA) within the U.S. Department of Health and Human Services (DHHS), sponsors the Mental Health Statistics Improvement Program (MHSIP), which is described as a consumer-oriented mental health report card. The American Managed Behavioral Healthcare Association (AMBHA) sponsors Performance Measures for Managed Behavioral Healthcare Programs (PERMS). The National Committee for Quality Assurance (NCQA), which was established in 1979 to survey HMOs and other managed care organizations, has also released a report card of standards specifically for its Managed Behavioral Health Accreditation Program.

NCQA is the organization that sponsors the Health Plan Employer Data and Information Set (HEDIS). Introduced in 1991, HEDIS is at its 3.0 permutation as of this writing. Besides being used to review managed commercial health care systems, HEDIS 3.0 is now used by public offi-cials to evaluate managed Medicaid health plans (HEDIS 3.0 incorporates and updates a coex-isting version of Medicaid HEDIS). Furthermore, the Health Care Financing Administration (HCFA) is expected to mandate use of portions of HEDIS 3.0, including all the behavioral health care reporting measures, by Medicare HMOs. NCQA is now publishing HEDIS data from health plans on the Internet at http://www.ncqa.org. Any consumer can also get NCQA health plan review results by calling NCQA's automated accreditation status line at 888/275-7585. HEDIS could be construed as the modern-day equivalent of an indigenous managed care health plan evaluation tool.

Even HEDIS is in an almost constant state of change. For one thing, as noted by Paul Elstein, Director of the Quality and Performance Standards Team, Office of Managed Care, HCFA, "There is no question that HEDIS 3.0 is still primarily a set of process measures."[20] For another, NCQA expects HEDIS itself to continually improve. The next version of HEDIS is already being con-structed and should be ready soon. NCQA's future iterations of HEDIS will probably place more weight on valid, reliable, and reproducible clinical behavioral health care outcomes study data. In a March 31, 1998, press release, NCQA President, Margaret E. O'Kane, addressed new initiatives, saying that "with Accreditation '99, results count." Accreditation '99 is described by NCQA as an effort incorporating selected performance measures from HEDIS and the "nation's first, true performance-based accreditation program for managed care plans." Summary reports will aggregate performance data and reflect a health plan's strengths and weaknesses in five categories: access and service, qualified providers, staying healthy, getting better, and living with illness. NCQA adopted the new reporting structure on the basis of the Consumer Information Framework created by FACCT.

Scientific, evidence-based behavioral health care outcomes studies are becoming the vital ingredient in measuring quality. An entire recent issue of *Psychiatric Annals* was devoted to "Treatment Outcomes in Clinical Practice." In one article in the issue, Sperry identified clinical psychiatric practice as being involved in an "outcomes revolution" wherein, "with the assistance of outcomes data, all can strive to be the best they can with particular patients with particular presentations."[21] Fink wrote that "fortunately, the field of outcomes research in the areas of mental illness and substance abuse is robust and evolving."[22] Outcomes measurement is so robust that Merck-Medco Managed Care, L.L.C. has established a new business unit called the Center for Outcomes Measurement and Performance Assessment.[23] The unit was created to help managed care organizations garner NCQA accreditation and to develop and execute outcomes studies for interested clients.

Medco Containment was a profitable mail order prescription management company when, in 1992, it bought American Biodyne, Inc., which was successful itself as a managed behavioral health care company. The acquisition created Medco Behavioral Care. In 1993, Merck Pharmaceuticals purchased Medco. Merck-Medco is a powerhouse with a strategic plan. It sees its Center for Outcomes Measurement and Performance Assessment as part of a successful future.

Another industry giant, Aetna, through the Aetna Foundation and Aetna U.S. Healthcare, set aside a $15 million Quality Care Research Fund that is designed to bolster research targeting improvements in health care outcomes. Grants valued at $6 million have been awarded to researchers looking at ways to improve depression treatment outcomes in managed care environments.

We are witnessing the evolution of behavioral health care outcomes measurement/management into an enterprise considered important, attractive, and profitable enough to warrant the development of discrete public and private entities specifically established to improve care for consumers and to access expanding market opportunities in the behavioral health quality arena.

"Re-Somethings"

The evolution of outcomes management has added urgency to initiatives for change in the processes of delivering behavioral health care to the consumer. Industrialized countries around the globe are exploring fundamental alterations in their models and methods of providing behavioral health care services. Goals for change supersede single line item entries such as cost control. The "prize" that attracts the effort encompasses nothing short of a perpetually improving, scientific evidence-based behavioral health care that continuously increases in real value. In fact, the more forward-looking organizations in the more forward-looking cultures of the world are simultaneously competing and cooperating with one another to achieve this goal, so that they can secure their share of compelling opportunities in the globalization of behavioral health care.

Major emphasis in this effort is being placed on improvements in resource management. The human resources involved in health care service delivery are at the core of this focus. A host of action oriented "re-" words are being used to describe this phenomenon: reforming, revitalizing, reshaping, remolding, reframing, reinventing, rethinking, restructuring, redesigning, and reengineering. In the world of behavioral health care, these "re-ings" are being sculpted by simple constructs that exude genius when threaded together.

We know that one-half of all behavioral health services provided in America through the formal medical care sector are provided by primary care clinicians.[24,25] We are able to demonstrate that behavioral health is a critical factor in the interactive balance among the immune, endocrine, and central nervous systems. Behavioral states and physical health are interrelated.[26] We know, too, that educational, behavioral, and psychosocial interventions in medical settings can reduce the costs of medical care and improve health outcomes.[27]

When these constructs are threaded together, we see an explanation for why so much of the current strategy for behavioral health care service delivery reformation also involves primary health care service delivery reformation and a meaningful, consistent integration of the two.[28] Smooth cooperation, collaboration, and coordination among conventional allopathic and alternative health care personnel, patient educators, family, community, support systems, and the identified patient offers potential for a greater health yield than proprietary compartments of clinical attention proffered by fragmented sources of care and support. When applied to a union of behavioral health care with primary and specialty medical care, such a meld is being identified as "integration." The third national Primary Care Behavioral Healthcare Summit, in 1997, presented by the Institute for Behavioral Healthcare, in joint sponsorship with the Primary Care/Behavioral Healthcare Partnership and CentraLink, was subtitled "The Leadership Forum on Integrating Behavioral Healthcare and the General Medical Sector."

There are many examples of initiatives to improve on our efforts to integrate behavioral and traditional medical care. Several years ago, Group Health Cooperative of Puget Sound (GHC) made a commitment to develop service delivery units of behavioral health and primary health care professionals who share authorities and responsibilities in coherent clinical management of shared cases. GHC is now studying the impact of its efforts. It believes it has "boosted compliance with antidepressant therapy and achieved better outcomes by forging a closer alliance among primary care physicians, psychiatrists, and other mental health providers."[29]

Mike Quirk, PhD, Director of Behavioral Health at GHC, adds that technically, in primary care, the primary care provider is ultimately the clinician responsible for a patient's care, while behavioral health consultants attached to primary care teams work with team members in a 50-50 partnership. Symptomatic patients are seen by behavioral health consultants in a brief educational, consultative primary care general consultation (PCGC) visit. The majority of these patients are said to have their needs met through the PCGC. When more intense intervention is appropriate, patients are referred to behavioral health specialists.[30]

Part of the GHC strategy involves use of the mental health consultant's expertise to assist primary care clinicians in the development of cognitive-behavioral skills so that primary care physicians can help patients immediately and directly by, for example, coaching patients in methods to cope more successfully with stressors. Even when GHC behavioral health clinicians are no longer actively involved with recovering depressed patients, GHC's primary care clinicians oversee these patients' progress by monitoring their status and maintaining successful treatment strategies.

Such intense, blended integration of behavioral health and primary care professional services in patient treatment and case management reflects a fundamental change in the traditional character of behavioral health care service delivery. Some advise that even more fundamental change is necessary. Michael Hammer, whose reengineering ideas arguably promoted the largest business restructuring effort of this decade, believes that "managed care organizations are at ground zero, and survival and success will require radical, revolutionary thinking."[31] Hammer and Noetzel define reengineering as "the fundamental rethinking and radical redesign of business processes to bring about dramatic improvement." They believe that reengineering principles can and should be applied to patient care. Apparently, as echoed in various health care organizations' initiatives to fundamentally integrate behavioral health care with primary health care and alter the very culture of behavioral health services delivery, there are many within health care who would agree with Hammer and Noetzel.

The Institute for Behavioral Healthcare sponsors an annual Behavioral Healthcare Tomorrow Conference. The 1997 executive luncheon keynote address was titled "Thriving in Market Chaos by Reinventing Behavioral Healthcare." The "re-something" phenomenon in behavioral health care is a powerful initiative that commands attention...and action.

Tools of Progress

Fundamental and radical changes are also metamorphosing the tools we use to effect positive outcomes in behavioral health care. In fact, this category includes so many exciting developments and dramatic advancements that to mention them all would require a separate text. Pharmaceuticals, neurobiology, systems and business theories, chronobiology, psychotherapies, complexity science, somatic therapies, psychoneuroendocrinology, virtual therapies, brain/neuro-imaging techniques, chaos theories, research, computers, the Internet, and information management systems would be included in such a tome. Others, such as quality improvement techniques, innovative service delivery methods, assertive community treatment initiatives, cooperation between private and public entities for a common good, program modeling, management strategies, clinical guidelines, and a home-based orientation for behavioral health care delivery, are afforded space in this volume. Still others, such as the connectedness between mind, body, and spirit, have become popular tools used by many thousands of people to leverage improvements in their states of well-being. This chapter concludes with brief mention of just two of the many tools of progress that could well change the landscape of behavioral health care dramatically, and soon.

Healing at a Distance

From Greek, we get "tele," which means far off or at a distance. From Latin, we get "medicina," which means the healing art. Put the two together, exercise some literary license, add a touch of the method involved, and we get an acceptable definition of telemedicine—health care that occurs when providers and receivers are separated in space, time, or both, yet are united virtually, or as far as effect is concerned, through modern communications technology. Telemedicine, by this definition, might actually have had its birth (though not its name, which was conceived by Thomas Birch, MD, in the 1970s) in the late 18th and early 19th centuries with the advent of the electromagnetic telegraph.

Or, if one prefers to date modern telemedicine's beginning with the invention of our most ubiquitous piece of telemedicine equipment, the telephone, 1849 might be the year, and Antonio Meucci, who was living in Cuba, would be the person who really got telemedicine started.[32] Mr. Meucci's wife was an invalid, confined to the third floor of their home in Havana. He constructed a gadget capable of transmitting some caliber of speech through electrical impulses to enable him to talk with (and provide psychosocial therapeutic support for) his wife while he was in the basement of their home. If this is an accurate reflection of history, Mr. Meucci may also have been the first person to develop a system of behavioral health service delivery through the use of modern communications technology. He may have been the originator of telepsychiatry, or behavioral telehealth care a quarter of a century before Alexander Graham Bell invented the first telephone capable of sustained articulated speech, and a few years prior to the development of facsimile wire transmissions.

The next big foundation block for behavioral telehealth care came with the development of the first electronic television system by Philo T. Farnsworth in 1927. The BBC inaugurated its black-and-white television service in 1936, and CBS, in 1951, began transmitting regular commercial color programming. Motion image behavioral telehealth care was formally introduced soon thereafter. It was initially implemented in the 1950s and 1960s in Omaha at the University of Nebraska Medical Center's Nebraska Psychiatric Institute. Through a closed-circuit television system, specialists from the Institute were able to provide clinical consultations to Norfolk State Hospital, which was 112 miles away, and to enrich the clinical research and training capacities of both institutions.

Then events really began to boil. Fiberoptic cables replaced copper wiring. Satellites were launched and programmed for communication. Computer chips and processors became so small, so powerful, and so economical that computers entered the commercial market and the citizenry was in a position to access the internet. Now, millions of people around the world, through the World Wide Web, transmit and receive text, still images, sound, and motion images with their personal computers. Cellular phones spread across the globe, and, in 1995, the Personal Communication Service (PCS) was introduced commercially. The PCS is a mobile communication system based on digital signals. It offers specialized phone service and has capacities, at a minimum, for pager, answering machine, voice mail, and fax service. The first Internet phones also hit the market in 1995. Several software makers support innovative video telephony applications allowing people half a world away from each other to make voice and video contact with their multimedia computers over the Internet. No computer? No problem. Systems are available that will adapt to your television and phone line, resulting in a fully functional video phone right in your living room or office. And various new Internet Protocol (IP) phone services permit, again without need for a personal computer, use of the Web for dialing around the country or the globe.

Every behavioral health professional in America can now access the technology to engage in behavioral telehealth care. Interested clinicians can maneuver within a wide price range and invest just a few hundred dollars for basic analog systems, or spend thousands of dollars for state-of-the-art systems. There are hundreds of telemedicine vendors for everything from video conferencing platforms that meet international standards, to home-based hardware, software, and peripheral telemedicine equipment. Interesting and informative telemedicine Internet sites include the Federal Telemedicine Gateway at http://www.tmgateway.org and the Telemedicine and Telehealth Networks news magazine at http://www.telemedmag.com. There are at least two telemedicine industry trade groups—the American Telemedicine Association (ATA), and the Association of Telemedicine Service Providers (ATSP). There are many established behavioral telehealth care programs that have paved the way, and growth in the industry proves that it is here to stay. There are dozens of behavioral health programs around the country using telemedicine technology to augment their services. The Southwest Montana Telepsychiatry Network, for example, provides psychiatric care, video peer visits, specialty consultations, public service, and educational programs across a 12-county area encompassing almost 30,000 square miles.[33]

Through the network developed by the Southwestern Virginia Telepsychiatry Project, three rural communities are linked for services with the state hospital. In this way, behavioral health care is provided to residents across eight counties. The telemedicine project at Kansas University Medical Center (KUMC) provides, among other things, behavioral health care assessments, crisis interventions, family counseling, and individual and group psychotherapy through interactive, real-time, audiovisual telecommunications to more than a dozen distant locations.[34]

In an October 1996 National Institutes of Health (NIH) press release, Secretary of Health and Human Service (HHS), Donna E. Shalala, said that "telemedicine offers us some of our best and most cost-effective opportunities for improving quality and access to health care." The release went on to report that the National Library of Medicine (NLM) is budgeting $42 million to fund 19 telemedicine projects. These projects were announced in combination with a Health Care Financing Administration (HCFA) demonstration project that enables Medicare to pay for health services delivered via telemedicine.

Drag anchors are slowing the expansion of behavioral telehealth care. Challenges slowing its growth exist in areas of design, implementation, scientific proofs of value, financing, licensing, assignment of risk liability, data security, regulatory requirements, and ethics. Advantages, however, continue to drive growth and progress. Health care benefits include reduction of clinician and patient isolation, correction of unequal distribution of services, improved access, new market opportunities, enhanced resource utilization, more rapid clinical assessments and interventions, and decreased costs. Because of such benefits, leaders in telemedicine believe it holds out the realistic possibility, for the first time in history, of rapid and equal access to health care.[35]

Nearly one-third of all rural hospitals now have telemedicine programs,[36] and, within 4 or 5 years, industry analysts predict, "20 percent of all home health care visits will be delivered via telemedicine."[37] There is, today, no insurmountable obstacle for behavioral health care centers in Manhattan to provide service for villagers on a hillside in Nepal. One small, 25-pound mobile unit has already demonstrated that it can successfully execute sophisticated studies for, and relay data and images back to, experts located millions of miles away. That mobile unit, which landed on Mars on July 4, 1997, is called Sojourner. Its name suggests something temporary. What is permanent is the impact that telecommunication technology will have on behavioral health care and the force with which behavioral telehealth care will alter our concept of care itself.

Biotechnology

Burrus and Gittines predict that medicine and agriculture will change the most because of biotechnology.[38] They point out our existing technical abilities to map and refigure the genetic code. This is identified as recombinant DNA technology, with potential to eradicate or, conversely, augment any specific trait. Some compounds have the capacity to prevent the otherwise predetermined expression of particular genes. Those powerful blocking compounds are known as Antisense RNA, and they hold the potential to block and prevent the development of genetically determined disease states.

Agriculture has already changed dramatically as a result of bioengineering. For example, in 1996, 75 percent of all the cotton grown in Alabama was genetically engineered. Our soybean crop includes 8 million acres of genetically engineered produce. Even more eye opening, however, is the fact that 1996 saw the release in Florida of our first genetically engineered insect! The bioengineered predator mite is programmed to kill bugs that harm consumer crops such as strawberries.[39] Genetically modified organisms (GMOs) are (literally) part of the American landscape.

Any reader who doubts that behavioral health care could be changed as dramatically as agriculture has been changed by biotechnology should consider the following reports. Researchers have found evidence that they believe "supports the existence of a vulnerability locus for schizophrenia on chromosome 8p."[40] Other investigators report that the human leukocyte antigen (HLA) DRB1 gene locus on chromosome 6p "may partially account for the genetic predisposition to schizophrenia."[41] Still other genetic researchers studying early-onset bipolar disorder suggest that a "gene deleted at the 22q11 chromosomal locus may be involved in its pathogenesis."[42] Several studies by a number of international researchers investigating schizophrenia and bipolar disorders have pinpointed the area known as 22q as one that harbors genes that, if malfunctioning, could increase the risk of mental illness.

The May 1997 edition of *Clinical Psychiatry News* recounts a report by Dr. John J. Ratey indicating that a specific anomaly in the DRD2 gene found on chromosome 10 "can be found in nearly half of all children with attention deficit hyperactivity disorder." Rao[43] writes that "the most commonly employed method for studying linkage and identifying the genomic location of disease genes has been the lod score, or maximum likelihood, method." He adds that, "when the lod score method has succeeded in more genetically complex disorders, the success came with the disorders in which more Mendelian-appearing subtypes (that is, subtypes where mode of inheritance could be identified) exist—e.g., early-onset Alzheimer's disease." Alzheimer's disease loci have been attributed to chromosomes 1, 14, and 21. Disturbances in affect are among the most common of psychiatric manifestations that trouble patients with neurodegenerative Huntington's Disease. In 1993, IT15 was identified as the unstable gene responsible for causing Huntington's Disease.[44] Novelty-seeking behavior is linked to a gene on chromosome 11, and anxiety levels may be modulated by a gene on chromosome 17.[45]

The federal government is engaged in a $3 billion effort to find and decode the more than 60,000 human genes. Target date for this project's finalization is just seven years away. One privately funded effort aims "to unravel the entire human genetic code by 2001."[46] An international effort, called the Human Genome Project, is also dedicated to identifying every gene in the human body within the next few years. Once the genes are identified, the next task will be to delineate the function of each of them.

Furthermore, the age of genetic testing has arrived. Such tests, if not already considered to be a routine segment of diagnostic medicine, will soon become so. We already have genetic testing available for disease states (Down's Syndrome, Huntington's Disease) we think of as being associated with behavioral illness.

The University of Pennsylvania Health System maintains a Web site about its Institute for Human Gene Therapy (IHGT) at http://www.med.upenn.edu/ihgt/. The IHGT is within the university's Division of Medical Genetics under the Department of Molecular and Cellular Engineering. Here, gene therapy is defined as an "approach to treating diseases based on modifying the expression of a person's gene toward a therapeutic goal." Although in its formative stages, it also "has a good potential for disease prevention."

There are two general strategies involved in gene therapy. *Ex vivo* methods modify the DNA structure of harvested host cells cultured outside the body prior to implanting them into a patient. *In vivo* methods implant "vectors" such as alternative cell types (modified viruses or synthetic particle complexes), which deliver therapeutic genes to cells.

If the correction of a genetic defect is limited to the patient, this is termed somatic cell gene therapy. In germ cell gene therapy, manipulation of gene expression is passed on to post-treatment offspring.

Genetic manipulations of the future will not be limited to the treatment of disease states. One step past gene transfer designed to address a life-saving need to eliminate pathology is gene transfer designed to address a life-enhancing desire to effect perceived improvement in some common trait variable, such as temperament. "Enhancement" is the term currently used to describe the latter mode of molecular and cellular engineering utilization.

There is a Web site, called "Genebrowser," dedicated to biotechnology and gene therapy, and there is a weekly magazine, called "Gene Therapy," that reviews the field. There is also, now, an American Society of Gene Therapy that can be reached by e-mail at asgt@u.washington.edu.

The National Institutes of Health (NIH) held its Gene Therapy Policy Conference on March 9, 1998, in Bethesda, Maryland. The conference topic was "Lentiviral Vectors for Gene Delivery." Presentations were made by experts representing both public and private arenas from as near as the New England Regional Primate Research Center and from as far away as the University of Geneva.

If you wonder where you've been while all this was going on, you haven't been anywhere. It's all new. The first human trials of gene therapy only took place in 1990. The Institute for Human Gene Therapy was only formed in 1993, with only single-digit numbers of gene therapy clinical trials in its first four years. The previously mentioned Lentiviral Vector for Gene Delivery conference was only the second scheduled NIH policy conference on gene therapy. The American Society for Gene Therapy scheduled its inaugural meeting in Seattle, Washington, for May 28-31, 1998.

It's all new, but the pace of progress in gene therapy is furious. There are enormous potential clinical gains to be made through genomics. Although technical challenges involved in gene therapy are staggering, there are also giant economic gains to be made by some. More than one biotechnology company is repositioning itself to be primarily a genomic enterprise. The business of winning patents on genetic discoveries could determine who will be the sellers of a potentially lucrative biological medical resource and who might control the money magnet commercialization of a new biological industry in human physical and behavioral enhancement.

Biotechnology is gaining strength in its abilities to gather pertinent data and to analyze those data with the help of ever more powerful computer hardware and software. It already has the theoretical capacity to help us understand, prevent, diagnose, and treat a variety of genetically determined behavioral health disorders. Its next natural step would be to put the new knowledge, as it is acquired, to practical use and thereby change the face of behavioral health care. Biotechnology opens windows for health maintenance, disease avoidance, assessment, treatment types, and cosmetic interventions that were not even dreamed of a few short years ago. Experts are already engaged in serious debate about the ethical and legal challenges arising from current capabilities and future prospects of applied biotechnology.

We already provide the public with genetic testing and counseling. We know that the state of our behavioral health has genetic components. We know that our long-term antidepressant treatments lead to the regulation of specific target genes.[47] We are engaged, at the moment, in clinical trails of gene therapy to treat illness. A complete map of our genetic code is in the offing.

Will we see, in our professional lifetimes, standard gene analysis and modification for population bases with inherited disease states, or for anyone and everyone who can afford the cost of gene transfer enhancement? Will prospective parents contract with new age, high-technology vendors to bioengineer, perhaps from their molecularly altered gene pool, what they would view as a "perfect" baby, free from physical and behavioral disease determining chromosome anomalies, and genetically predisposed to optimal physical attributes, personality characteristics, and joyous emotional vitality? It could happen.

Scottish researchers have been successful in cloning a sheep, known rather fondly as "Dolly," from a six-year-old adult sheep's udder cell. On April 13, 1998, Dolly, who was impregnated by a male of her species, gave birth to a healthy baby lamb. Dolly's artificial cloning did not interfere with natural breeding and reproduction processes—good news for cloning enthusiasts. Since Dolly, both sheep and cattle have been cloned with the incorporation of human genes. Hope exists that whole herds of cloned animals with some human genes will one day provide valuable human proteins (such as blood clotting factor for hemophiliacs) in their milk. Pharmaceuticals on the cloned hoof could be right around the next pasture. A newspaper article, referring to two rhesus monkeys born in August 1996 and cloned from embryo cells, reported that experts said this cloning success "adds to a growing body of evidence that there are no insurmountable biological barriers to creating multiple copies of a human being."[48]

Whether or not the U.S. Congress institutes legislative bans on human cloning, there are entrepreneurs and cloning volunteers prepared to work, somewhere in the world without legal obstacles, to clone human beings. Molecular and cellular engineers might add that traits, such as vibrant behavioral health and happiness, might be among the various selections from which people might choose to alter their clonegy.

Brave Old World
This chapter concludes with a futuristic flavor while being printed on inert paper in a finite book that has obvious physical limitations and the handicap of stasis in the information it conveys. Changes in behavioral health care today are occurring so fast that the second edition of this volume may only be appropriate in digital cybertext format, so that updates can be more easily incorporated as soon as events unfold.

This leaves us where we started at the chapter's beginning. Change is the only reliable constant in behavioral health care service delivery, and today's once current state of affairs is already part of a brave old world.

References

1. "MSOs: A Model for Regaining Control—An Interview with Bruce J. Schwartz, MD." *Psychiatric Practice and Managed Care* 3(4):3,4,9, July-Aug. 1997.

2. "Partnership Creates Behavioral Organization." *Managed Healthcare News* 13(6):38-9, June 1997.

3. "Mainstay Joins Green Spring Network." *Behavioral Healthcare Tomorrow* 6(4):22, Aug. 1997.

4. Curley, R. "Industry Roundup." *Behavioral Healthcare Tomorrow* 7(2):15-6, April 1998.

5. "News and Commentary." *Physician Practice Options*, May 1997.

6. Belkin, L. "But What About Quality?" *New York Times Magazine*, Dec. 8, 1996, pp. 68-71,101,106.

7. "Employers Look at Quality." *Physician Executive* 23(5):5, May-June 1997.

8. Emery, D., and others. "The Political Economy of Capitated Managed Care." *American Journal of Managed Care* 3(3):397-416, March 1997.

9. Kilgore, C. "Insurers Experiment with Flat-Fee Case Rates." *Clinical Psychiatry News* 25(6):1, June 1997.

10. News release from National Mental Health Association, Washington, D.C., June 4, 1997.

11. "California Legislator Backs Parity." Psychiatric News 32(8):45, April 18, 1997.

12. "Senate Votes Parity for Children under Block Grants." *Psychiatric News* 32(15):1, Aug. 1, 1997.

13. "Report to Congress Confirms Parity Cuts Health Care Costs". *Psychiatric News* 32(10):1, May 16, 1997.

14. Sturm, R. "How Expensive Is Unlimited Mental Health Care Coverage under Managed Care?" *JAMA* 278(18)1533-7, Nov. 12, 1997.

15. "Federal Study Demonstrates Affordability of Parity." *Psychiatric News* 33(8):23, April 17, 1998.

16. "New Guidelines Help Employers Accommodate Mentally Ill." *Psychiatric News* 32(11):1, June 6, 1997.

17. Oss, M. "Accreditation: Adapting to Change." *Behavioral Health Management* 17(3):4, May-June 1997.

18. "Sharfstein, Pardes Appointed to Presidential Commission." *Psychiatric News* 32(8):1,38,39, April 18, 1997.

19. Beauregard, T., and Winston, K. "Employers Shift to Quality to Evaluate and Manage Their Health Plans." *Managed Care Quarterly* 5(1):51-6, Winter 1997.

20. "HEDIS: Cutting through the Confusion." *Behavioral Health Management* 17(2):24-5, March-April 1997.

21. Sperry, L. "Treatment Outcomes: An Overview." *Psychiatric Annals* 27(2):85-9, Feb. 1997.

22. Fink, P. "Treatment Outcomes, a Postscript." *Psychiatric Annals* 27(2):133-4, Feb. 1997.

23. "Merck-Medco Establishes Outcomes Measurement Center." *Managed Healthcare News* 13(6):3, June 1997.

24. Reiger, D., and others. "The De Facto U.S. Mental and Addiction Disorders Service System." *Archives of General Psychiatry* 50(2):85-94, Feb. 1993.

25. Narrow, W., and others. "Use of Services by Persons with Mental and Addictive Disorders: Findings from the National Institute of Mental Health Epidemiologic Catchment Area Program." *Archives of General Psychiatry* 50(2):95-107, Feb. 1993.

26. National Institute of Mental Health. *Neuro-Immunology and Mental Health*. Rockville, Md.: U.S. Department of Health and Human Services, Public Health Service, National Institute of Health, National Institute of Mental Health, Sept. 1994, pp. IV-V.

27. Sobel, D. "Rethinking Medicine: Improving Health Outcomes with Cost-Effective Psychological Interventions." *Psychosomatic Medicine* 57(3):234-244, May-June 1995.

28. Strosahl, K. "New Dimensions in Behavioral Health/Primary Care Integration." *HMO Practice* 8(4):75-9, Dec. 1994.

29. Zwillich, T. "Mental Health HMO Keeps Primary Care Physicians Involved." *Clinical Psychiatry News* 25(6):28, June 1997.

30. Personal communication, Michael Quirk, PhD, Director of Behavioral Health, Group Health Cooperative of Puget Sound, Seattle, Wash., July 31, 1997.

31. Hammer, M., and Noetzel, T. "How to Survive and Prosper in the Health Care Revolution." *HMO Practice* 11(2):83-7, June 1997.

32. Robertson, P. *The Book of Firsts.* New York, N.Y.: Bramhall House, NY, 1982.

33. Jones, E. "Telepsychiatry Programs Abet Lasting Healing." *Telemedicine and Telehealth Networks* 2(5):4-6, June 1996.

34. Chhibber, S. "Telepsychiatry and the Role of Residents". *Psychiatric News* 31(23):26-40, Dec. 6, 1996.

35. Preston, J. *The Telemedicine Handbook.* Austin, Tex.: Telemedical Interactive Consultative Services, Inc., 1993.

36. "Nearly One-Third of Rural Hospitals Use Telemedicine." *Physician Executive* 22(4):3, April 1996.

37. Dakins, D. "Utopian Home Healthcare Vision Lacks Social Reality." *Telemedicine and Telehealth Networks.* 3(1):7-9, Feb. 1997.

38. Burrus, D., and Gittines. *Techno Trends.* New York, N.Y.: Harper Business/Harper Collins Publishers, 1993, p. 55.

39. "Altered Crops in Landscape." *Hartford Courant*, Section E, Tuesday, June 10, 1997, p. E1.

40. Kendler, K., and others. "Evidence for a Schizophrenia Vulnerability Locus on Chromosome 8P in the Irish Study of High-Density Schizophrenia Families." *American Journal of Psychiatry* 153(12):1534-40, Dec. 1996.

41. Wright, P., and others. "Genetic Association of the HLA DRB1 Gene Locus on Chromosome 6p21.3 with Schizophrenia." *American Journal of Psychiatry* 153(12):1530-3, Dec. 1996.

42. Papolos, D., and others. "Bipolar Spectrum Disorders in Patients Diagnosed with Velo-Cardio-Facial Syndrome: Does a Hemizygous Deletion of Chromosome 22q11 Result in Bipolar Affective Disorder?" *American Journal of Psychiatry* 153(12):1541-7, Dec. 1996.

43. Rao, P. "Review of Gene Mapping and Molecular Genetic Studies of Schizophrenia." *Psychiatric Annals* 24(4):279-84, April 1997.

44. Joyce, T. "Gene Therapy for Huntington's Disease." *Brattleboro Retreat Psychiatry Review* 6(1):1-3, Nov. 1997.

45. Nash, J. "The Personality Genes." *Time*, April 27, 1998, pp. 60-1.

46. Gillis, J., and Weiss, R. "Private Group Plans Rush to Genetic Finale." *Hartford Courant*, May 12, 1998, p. A9.

47. Duman, R., and others. "A Molecular and Cellular Theory of Depression." *Archives of General Psychiatry* 54(7):597-606, July 1997.

48. "Monkeys Cloned in Oregon." *Hartford Courant*, March 2, 1997, p. 1.

Frank Boruch, MD, a board-certified psychiatrist with almost 25 years' experience as a physician executive who has helped mold and direct both public and private health services. He is also an international speaker and consultant on a variety of health care, human potential, and management issues. Currently, he and his wife operate a unique enterprise assisting health care professionals, and others around the nation, to diversify and improve their streams of income.

Chapter 3

Legal Issues in Mental Health Care

by Ernest J. Mattei, Esq., and Mary B. Cardin, Esq.

Mental health care professionals cannot avoid the impact that law in our society has had on their daily work. The legal issues affecting mental health care are seemingly endless. Awareness of how the law affects the provision of mental health care can help the mental health care professional avoid legal problems. The discussion here is not intended to be a complete review of all the legal issues that may confront mental health care professionals, nor is it intended to be an exhaustive source on the issues it addresses. Rather, it is an overview of issues most likely to affect the mental health care professional.

Confidentiality

Many observers see confidentiality as the essential element of the treatment relationship in mental health care.[1] The patient expects that his or her communications to the mental health care professional will remain private. Confidentiality issues arise when someone other than the patient seeks information about the patient's care and treatment. Often family members, other health care providers, and lawyers attempt to obtain information about a patient from his or her mental health care professional. The growth of managed care has greatly affected the mental health care provider's relationship with patients, as more information must be disclosed to managed care review groups and to insurers. Mandated reporting and research situations also raise important confidentiality issues. Finally, the mental health care professional may be called on to testify about a patient in judicial, quasi-judicial, or administrative forums.

The law seeks to preserve the confidentiality of communications between the mental health professional and the patient. Case law and statutes recognize that a mental health professional has a duty not to disclose information about a patient without the patient's consent. Judicial decisions and statutes also recognize that some communications between health care professionals and a patient are privileged and are therefore protected from disclosure in judicial, quasi-judicial, and administrative settings.

Liability for Unauthorized Disclosure of Confidential Patient Information

The law recognizes several bases of liability for unauthorized disclosure of confidential patient information. Invasion of privacy, breach of the physician-patient confidential relationship, violation of statutory law, malpractice, and prima facie tort are all legal theories upon which patients may recover.[2]

In jurisdictions recognizing the right to privacy, courts examine factors such as the nature and content of the disclosure, the person to whom the information was disclosed, and the person who made the disclosure.[3] Other jurisdictions recognize a cause of action for breach of a confidential relationship.[4] In determining whether there has been a breach of a confidential relationship, courts consider similar factors.[5] Disclosure of confidential patient information has also been held to be a violation of statutes governing physician licensing and therefore a basis for liability.[6] At least one court, however, has found that violation of statutory licensing provisions that govern physicians' conduct are solely violations of administrative provisions and do not give rise to a right of recovery against the physician.[7] Some courts have recognized malpractice tort actions brought for disclosure of confidential information.[8] Other courts have held that, while a physician's unauthorized disclosure of confidential patient information may be a violation of the physician's professional responsibility, it does not create a basis for a private action in malpractice or prima facie tort.[9] Finally, unauthorized disclosure of certain protected information may expose the mental health professional to fines.[10]

Statutory Protection of Specific Patient Information

Many jurisdictions have enacted statutes aimed at preventing disclosure of confidential patient information by health care providers.[11] Often, statutes protect, as privileged or confidential, records containing sensitive patient information. Statutory protection is frequently afforded information related to alcohol and drug abuse treatment, counseling, or rehabilitation,[12] sexually transmitted diseases,[13] pregnancy, abortion counseling,[14] mental health treatment or psychiatric or psychological information,[15] HIV-related information,[16] and sexual assault counseling.1[7] However, statutes often contain exceptions that permit disclosure of confidential information in particular circumstances.

Some jurisdictions may require that a patient give specific consent for the release of certain categories of information. For example, with the rising number of AIDS and HIV cases, many states have passed regulations that govern the disclosure of HIV-related information. Statutes may specify the circumstances under which HIV information can be disclosed.[18] Some laws impose fines for negligent or willful disclosure of the results of HIV tests.[19] Rape or sexual assault, abortion counseling, and venereal disease may also be governed by confidentiality statutes. Some state statutes protect information related to the care and treatment of minors from being disclosed even to the minor's parent or guardian.[20] Federal law also gives special protection to certain patient information.[21]

Mental health care providers can best protect themselves against claims of unauthorized disclosure of confidential information by obtaining the patient's consent, in writing, to the disclosure of information regarding his or her care and treatment. The provider should be careful to use a written consent form that protects him or her under applicable law. The form authorizing release of confidential information may have to include special language that may be required by the statutory law in the provider's jurisdiction. The consent form should address the release of all types of information and, if required by the law of the jurisdiction, should address why and under what circumstances the information sought will be released. The consent form authorizing disclosure of information should be prepared in such a manner that a partial consent to the disclosure of information will not by its nature reveal information that a patient has not specifically authorized for disclosure.[22] Finally, the mental health care provider should be aware of the existence of state and federal legislation that may affect disclosure in specific instances.

Sources Requesting Confidential Patient Information

The mental health professional can expect to receive requests for confidential patient information from several different sources.

Subpoenas

Mental health care providers are frequently served with subpoenas, a form of legal process that commands a witness to appear before a specified court or court officer at a specified time and give testimony. A subpoena *duces tecum* is a subpoena that requires the attendance of a witness and commands the witness to produce and permit inspection and copying of designated books, papers, documents, or tangible things that are within the witness' possession or control. Different jurisdictions may have different names for a subpoena. Many jurisdictions have procedures by which a resident can be subpoenaed by someone in another jurisdiction. Records and the testimony of mental health care providers can also be obtained by a court or judicial order.

A subpoena or court order should be responded to promptly. However, if the patient is not a named party, the health care provider must not release the requested information without an authorization from the patient. In any case, a mental health care provider cannot release information that is protected by confidentiality statutes and that requires specific authorization for disclosure without first obtaining such authorization. If confidential information is sought by a subpoena, the health care provider should respond to the subpoena by indicating that a consent or authorization for release is required. In order to protect oneself, a health care provider may wish to tailor his or her own authorization form, making it as detailed as possible in order to avoid any problems that may arise from unauthorized disclosure.

Family Members

As part of family or group therapy, family members are frequently involved in the therapeutic relationship. It is not uncommon for family members to play an active role in the treatment being given to the patient. Mental health care professionals must be cautious, however, not to disclose confidential information to family members without the patient's consent. Some jurisdictions have statutes that indicate who has confidentiality rights to medical records from family or marital therapy sessions.[23]

While disclosure of medical information to a spouse may be justified, it may not always be appropriate. Because counseling is often sought in response to problems arising out of a marital relationship, disclosure might deter treatment. At least one court has held that disclosure should be made only where there might be a danger to the patient or spouse.[24]

Parents of Minors Undergoing Treatment

A mental health care provider must not assume that a parent always has the right to his or her child's mental health records. Many statutes require that information related to the care and treatment of minors be kept confidential.

In California, for example, a guardian or adult representative of a minor may not be entitled to the patient's mental health records if the health care provider has determined that parental access would be detrimental to his or her professional relationship with the minor or to the minor's physical and psychological well-being.[25] A mental health care provider may also refuse to allow the patient to see his or her records if the provider determines there could be a detrimental impact on the patient. However, the patient may request that the records be revealed to a licensed physician, surgeon, or psychologist acting on his or her behalf.[26] The mental health care provider must follow careful procedures that document his or her refusal to include parents in the treatment process.[27]

In Connecticut, minors may be treated on an outpatient basis without parental consent if notification of a parent or guardian would cause the minor to reject the treatment, if provision of the treatment is clinically indicated, if failure to provide treatment would be detrimental to the patient's well-being, if the minor knowingly and willingly sought treatment, or if the minor is mature enough to participate in the treatment.[28] The mental health care provider must document the reasons for determining parental consent is not necessary, and the patient must sign a statement attesting in part that he or she is a willful participant in the treatment and has discussed with the health care provider the possibility of involving an adult in the treatment process.[29] After the initial determination not to disclose treatment to the minor's parent or guardian, the mental health care provider must reassess whether parental involvement remains a detriment to the minor's well-being at every sixth session. If this is not done, disclosure must be made.[30] In conclusion, mental health providers should be aware of the special problems that confront minors seeking treatment for mental health problems and of the applicable jurisdictional law.[31]

Other Providers

Requests from other health care providers for disclosure of records or information regarding a patient must not be treated casually. Often, mental health care providers share records and information when it will benefit the patient's treatment.[32] However, providers no longer involved with a patient's care have no right to confidential information without the patient's consent. Statutes may require records that are to be shared to be stamped with language prohibiting further disclosure without the patient's consent.[33]

Managed Care Insurers/Third Parties

In the age of managed care, the question of a managed care review group and its insurer's or a patient's insurer's right to a patient's health care information creates new confidentiality problems. Decisions to treat or to shorten or extend a patient's treatment are no longer made solely by that patient's psychotherapist. Managed care group reviews make crucial decisions that may lead to liability.[34] While managed care programs and their insurers may be found partially liable, so may the therapist.

The mental health care professional's liability for breach of confidentiality in fact may be increased substantially if he or she discloses confidential patient information to managed care review groups or to the patient's insurer. Mental health care providers should therefore be sure to procure specific authorization from the patient allowing them to share their patient records with the insurer. Blanket forms signed by the patient when consenting to the terms of insurance coverage are considered insufficient. Often, persons signing insurance authorizations may not know what kind of information may be disclosed and to whom they are authorizing disclosure. Further, the person signing the forms for initial coverage may not be the eventual patient.[35] Because the patient must provide permission to release information or risk the insurer's refusing payment for all services, it has been argued that the patient's informed consent is not truly obtained in such situations.

Last, because of the stigma that attaches to patients seeking treatment for mental health problems, a patient not assured complete confidentiality may choose to not seek treatment at all.[36]

Defenses To Disclosure Without Consent

There are situations in which a mental health care provider may disclose patient information without the patient's consent. For example, very often mental health practitioners are required to report confidential patient information pursuant to what are known as "reporting" statutes.[37] These statutes exist because the state has identified a compelling interest in disclosure of information that should otherwise be confidential. All 50 states, the District of Columbia, and the U.S. Virgin Islands have enacted statutes that require physicians, including psychiatrists, to report instances of child abuse or suspected child abuse to governmental authorities.[38] Similar statutes require reporting of elderly abuse[39] and instances of certain communicable diseases.[40] Reporting of elderly abuse does not usually require disclosure of the patient's identity or other personal patient information.

Mental health professionals are shielded from liability if a specific statute calls for disclosure. For example, under Connecticut law, a patient need not consent when disclosure is made pursuant to a statute, regulation, or rule of court; by a health care provider against whom a claim has been made; to a physician's attorney or a professional liability insurer; or in abuse cases involving children, the elderly, the physically disabled, the mentally retarded, or incompetent persons. Moreover, a patient's consent to disclosure may not be necessary when disclosure is being made to others engaged in the patient's diagnosis or treatment and is necessary to accomplish the objectives of the diagnosis and treatment. Finally, some statutes provide that consent to disclosure need not be obtained when there is substantial risk of physical injury to the patient or other persons and property, or when disclosure is necessary for placing a patient in a mental health care facility.[41]

In California, similar provisions exist. Disclosure without patient authorization is permitted when it is compelled by law, including court order, or pursuant to an administrative agency, a subpoena, or a search warrant; when made to other health care providers for the purposes of diagnosis and treatment, including emergency situations; or when made to an employer, insurer, or holder of a benefit or service plan to the extent that disclosure is necessary to determine responsibility for payment.[42] If a patient is comatose, incompetent, or otherwise unable to consent because of a medical condition and no other arrangements for payment have been made, disclosure can be made to the government to the extent necessary to determine eligibility for government aid.[43]

Some states have provisions dealing specifically with disclosure of psychological communications. In Connecticut, for example, psychiatric communications can be disclosed without a patient's consent when the psychiatrist determines that disclosure to others involved in the patient's care is necessary to accomplish the objectives of the treatment and the patient is informed[44]; when the psychiatrist determines the patient poses a substantial risk of imminent physical injury to self or to others; if disclosure is necessary to place a patient in a mental care facility[45]; for collection of fees[46]; or when the record or communication is made by a psychiatrist in the course of an examination ordered by a court or made in connection with an application for appointment of a conservator by the probate court.[47]

Disclosure of communications about a patient's mental condition is also permitted where good cause is shown in judicial or administrative proceedings in which the patient is a party or in which the question of incompetence is an issue, provided the patient has been informed before making the communications or records that they will not be confidential.[47] Disclosure may also be made in a civil proceeding in which the patient puts his mental condition into issue, or after his or her death when the patient's condition is introduced by a party making a claim through or as a beneficiary of the patient.[48] Finally, Connecticut law allows for disclosure to be made to the Commissioner of Health Services in connection with any inspection, investigation, or examination of an institution[49]; to a homicide victim's immediate family or legal representative if the killing was committed by the patient[50]; and for specific research purposes, with limitations set forth in the statute.[51]

New York also has very specific guidelines governing the release of clinical records for mental patients in state facilities. Information may only be released pursuant to court order, upon a finding that the "interests of justice significantly outweigh the need for confidentiality," or to agencies such as the Mental Hygiene Legal Service, the Commission on the Quality of Care for the Mentally Disabled, and similar medical review boards.[52] If a patient presents a serious and imminent danger, disclosure may be made to endangered individuals or to law enforcement agencies.[53] Disclosure is also appropriate with the consent of the patient to someone authorized to act on the patient's behalf.[54] Patient information may also be released with the consent of the Commissioner of Mental Health to government agencies and insurance companies to determine payment for services, to prevent imminent harm to the patient, and in other specified situations.[55]

Psychotherapist-Patient Privilege

All 50 states have adopted statutes that provide for therapist-patient privilege in some form. Most commonly, the statutory privilege is invoked by the patient to prevent disclosure of communications between the patient and the therapist.[56] Connecticut's psychologist-patient privilege prohibits disclosure of oral and written communications related to diagnosis and treatment in civil and criminal actions; in juvenile, probate, commitment, and arbitration proceedings; and in legislative and administrative proceedings.[57] Other statutes give a psychotherapist the right to refuse to disclose communications made during examination and treatment of the patient.

In some jurisdictions, there may be specific types of communications protected from disclosure by statute. For example, under federal statutes, a Veterans Administration patient's records of specific treatment[58] and the records of a narcotics addict's voluntary psychiatric treatment for drug withdrawal at a federal hospital are privileged.[59]

While state statutes recognize psychotherapist-patient privilege, because of public policy concerns, exceptions are often so numerous that the statutes render little protection. Some jurisdictions may not allow a patient to assert a testimonial privilege in litigation where he or she has brought a legal action that puts his or her mental condition into issue; where the patient has sued the mental health professional for malpractice, relating to billing or fraud; or where the mental health professional is seeking to recover for unpaid bills. The privilege may not be invoked, for example, when a mental health examination has been ordered by a court to assess a patient's competence to stand trial or to apply criminal responsibility; when the mental health care provider has been asked by the patient to assist in criminal activity; when the patient has died or poses a danger to him- or herself or to others; or in criminal cases and child custody cases.[60]

Adding to state statutory protection, the Supreme Court recently held that communications between psychotherapists and licensed social workers and their patients are privileged in federal litigation.[61] The Court, in *Jaffe v. Redmond*, resolved a split in federal circuit courts as to the existence of a psychotherapist-patient privilege that arose out of Rule 501 of the Federal Rules of Evidence.[62] Prior to the Supreme Court's ruling, other circuits had defined the privilege only narrowly.[63]

In conclusion, the extent of the communications to which state and federal statutory privilege extends protection is generally very limited. Even though the Supreme Court in *Jaffe* interpreted patient-psychotherapist relationship very broadly, communications are protected only if they arise in the course of treatment or out of the professional relationship. The mental health care provider must also be aware that statutes often specify the particular type of mental health professional to whom the privilege applies.

Malpractice

In addition to having knowledge of liability for breach of confidentiality, mental health care professionals should have a general awareness of the law of negligence in order to avoid liability for malpractice.

Patients commonly file malpractice claims alleging that a mental health care professional has acted in a negligent manner or failed to act in a manner in keeping with the standard of care recognized by similar mental health care providers in the field or with the same training.[64] Liability for negligence can be based on a duty that the mental health care provider owes his or her patients and in some instances may be based on a duty that is owed to third parties.[65]

Duty to Patients

A mental health professional has a duty to his or her patients and can be found negligent if he or she breaches the required duty of care. To establish a case for negligence, a patient must first establish the duty and the standard of care that are required. This usually calls for the testimony of an "expert witness," someone who has the qualifications to testify as to the applicable standard of care. Once duty and standard of care are established, a patient must prove that the negligence of the provider caused the specific harm that he or she suffered. A patient must establish that the professional's conduct is both the legal cause and the proximate cause of the alleged injury.

Different types of malpractice claims, including misdiagnosis of psychiatric disorders, negligent use of somatic treatments or psychotherapy, negligent failure to prevent patients from harming themselves, sexual activity between a therapist and his or her patients, negligent supervision, and abandonment, have all been brought by patients. Failure to obtain informed consent is another negligence claim sought under a malpractice theory.[66]

In recent years, the number of cases brought against mental health care providers for patient suicides has increased. To avoid liability, mental health care providers must exercise the degree of care that other mental health care providers in their field would exercise when treating patients with possible suicidal tendencies. To determine if a plaintiff should recover for a therapist's failure to prevent a suicide, courts ask whether the defendant health care provider reasonably should have anticipated the possible danger that the patient would attempt suicide.[67] Liability is imposed if the risk was foreseeable and the therapist did not exercise the necessary degree of care. Courts are less likely to impose liability when a patient is treated as an outpatient, because the risk is less foreseeable and the therapist is not in a position to control the patient.

Because mental health care providers often make subjective determinations based on patient histories and because human behavior often is unpredictable, some jurisdictions have adopted an objective standard for judging the mental health care provider's conduct. New York, for example, uses a professional medical judgment rule that protects psychiatrists from any liability resulting from a patient's suicide after the therapist has carefully examined and evaluated the patient.[68] Under the New York standard, a therapist is liable only when the decision to release or not to treat the patient is based on "something less than a medical determination."[69] Liability cannot be based on a difference in medical opinion as to the standard of care.

When faced with patients who have suicidal tendencies, mental health care professionals must seriously consider the risk that the patient may attempt to harm him- or herself. The mental health care provider must also be aware of the standard for liability in his or her jurisdiction.

Duty to Third Parties

The mental health care provider may owe a duty of care to third parties, the breach of which forms a basis for liability. Generally, the law recognizes only a limited duty to unknown third parties. In some cases, however, a patient's disclosure to his or her mental health care provider creates an affirmative obligation to protect third parties against a hazard created by the patient. For mental health professionals, psychiatric dangerousness commonly creates such an obligation. In a long line of cases extending back to the well-known *Tarasoff v. Regents of the Univ. of California* case, psychotherapists have risked liability for failure to take action to warn a third party of a patient's potential danger.[70] In *Tarasoff*, a mentally disturbed patient made specific threats of bodily harm toward his former girlfriend while undergoing psychiatric treatment. The patient ultimately killed the girl, and her parent brought suit against the patient's doctors. The California Supreme Court held that a therapist treating a mentally ill patient owed a duty of reasonable care to warn threatened individuals of foreseeable danger created by the patient's condition, and the patient's doctors were found liable for failure to warn the victim.[71]

In response to situations such as *Tarasoff*, some states have adopted statutes that create an affirmative duty for mental health professionals to warn third parties.[72] Jurisdictions differ on the extent to which such a duty is owed to a third party. Very recently, the Connecticut Supreme Court was asked by the Second Circuit to answer the question of whether or not a psychotherapist has the duty to control his or her outpatients in order to prevent harm to third persons.[73] In *Fraser v. United States*, the family of a victim killed by a psychiatric patient brought suit against the veteran's hospital and staff who were treating him. The plaintiffs alleged that the hospital failed to warn third parties of the potential danger the patient presented and to take reasonable precautions to control the patient. The court reasoned that current state negligence law imposed no duty to unidentifiable victims and, for public policy reasons (protection of the psychotherapeutic relationship and of the mental patient's due process rights), weighed against imposing expansive duties on therapists to control the behavior of outpatients.[74] Therefore, the medical center had no duty to control its patient.[73] As a result of this ruling, the Federal District Court of Connecticut dismissed plaintiff's claim, and that dismissal was upheld by the Second Circuit. See 83 F.3d 591 (1996).

Before the ruling in *Fraser*, the Federal District Court of Connecticut in *Almonte v. New York Medical College* addressed the same issue.[75] In *Almonte*, a psychology resident admitted to his professor, during a mandatory analysis session, that he was a pedophile and that he wished to become a child psychologist. The court held in part that the professor's knowledge of these factors created a duty to warn or control the resident, who later assaulted a minor.[76] The court distinguished the case from *Fraser* because a special relationship existed between the student and his professor that gave rise to a duty. Further, the court found that the risk of harm to foreseeable victims was sufficient to impose liability.[77]

In addition to instances in which patients have made specific threats of physical harm, some courts have imposed liability for failure to warn patients about the side-effects of medication. In a Michigan case, *Welke v. Kuzilla*, the plaintiff's wife was killed in a car collision after the defendant's physician prescribed medication for which driving was contraindicated.[78] The court found that a doctor owed a duty to unknown third parties when he determined that his patient posed a serious threat of danger to third persons and that he was required to take steps to protect his patient and any third parties from foreseeable injuries.[79] Precautions should have included warning the patient about the effects of the medication or even refusing to prescribe the medication if he knew that the patient might still drive.[80]

Case law continues to develop in the area of HIV/AIDS and the duty to warn. In a recent California case, *Reisner v. Regents of the Univ. of California*, physicians failed to warn a young patient that she had received HIV-contaminated blood.[81] The patient's boyfriend brought suit against the girl's physicians, alleging they had a duty to warn the patient of risks that her conduct might later have on third persons. The court held that the possibility of foreseeable harm to a third person required the defendant physician to control his patient's conduct or to warn of the risks involved in sexual conduct. Where the risk was foreseeable, the physician's duty extended to unforeseeable third persons, including the plaintiff.[82]

It is unclear what impact *Reisner* will have in jurisdictions such as Connecticut, where disclosure of confidential HIV-related information is prohibited by state as well as federal statutes.[83] However, *Reisner* raises serious questions for mental health care providers who may be counseling HIV patients and who possess knowledge that their patients may pose significant risks to others. Accordingly, mental health care providers should be aware of state legislation and developing case law that would impose a duty on them to warn or inform third parties of risks.

Informed Consent

Failure to obtain consent for medical and surgical treatment, as well as for the administration of psychotropic medications, can result in professional liability for malpractice.[84] The principle of informed consent presumes that every competent adult has the right to determine what shall be done to his or her body.[85] Surgeons and other health care providers are therefore required to disclose sufficient information to the patient to enable him or her to make an intelligent and informed decision with respect to the proposed surgery or treatment.[86] In very limited circumstances, however, informed consent may not apply. In cases of emergencies or when it is in the mental patient's best interest that he or she not to be told of a treatment's side-effects, for example in the case of a schizophrenic individual, informed consent is not desirable. Additionally, when informed consent has been waived by the patient or when the patient is incompetent, informed consent requirements may be relaxed.[87]

The doctrine of informed consent has three components that are generally agreed on by most jurisdictions and must be present if the patient is said to have properly consented—information, voluntariness, and competence.[88] The amount of information considered to be sufficient varies by jurisdiction, but a majority of courts have adopted one of two standards.[88] The professional standard mandates disclosure of information that other professionals in the therapist's position would disclose. The second standard is disclosure of information that a reasonable person in the plaintiff's position would require to make his or her treatment decision. The health care provider should be aware of the applicable standard in his or her jurisdiction so that appropriate information is disclosed.

The patient must make his or her decision voluntarily and must not be coerced into making treatment decisions. The patient must be competent to give consent. Although competence is not universally defined, the patient must have sufficient mental abilities to engage in the informed consent process. Therefore, children, the mentally impaired, and psychotic individuals are not considered competent to consent, and necessary consent must be obtained from an appropriate guardian. Specific types of treatment may also require a separate consent under statutes or regulations.[89]

While, ideally, informed consent should be obtained each time a treatment decision is made, failure to obtain adequate informed consent does not automatically constitute malpractice. In order to establish that a lack of informed consent has risen to the level of malpractice, a patient must establish a prima facie case of malpractice. He or she must first establish a duty of care and that the health care provider breached that duty, usually through negligent failure to obtain informed consent. The plaintiff must also show that the harm that occurred was the result of the procedure in question and that a reasonable person in the patient's position would not have consented to the procedure had he or she been fully informed.[90]

To protect against a claim of failure to provide informed consent, it is imperative that the health care professional document discussions regarding consent as well as refusal to consent. Information provided to the patient ordinarily should include the provider's diagnosis and prognosis; the suggested procedure and/or treatment and its purpose; a description of what is involved; and a discussion of benefits, material risks, and alternatives.[90] Material risks are those a reasonable physician would customarily disclose under the circumstances.[91] The option of nontreatment and its prognosis should also be discussed by the health care provider.

A health care provider should not be lulled into reliance on a signed standardized form as proof of informed medical consent.[92] Often technical forms are beyond the understanding of the average patient.[93] The focus instead should be on what actually occurs between the patient and the provider. Documentation of what transpires protects the health care professional against a patient who later forgets what he or she was told or, worse, claims that consent was given under coercion.

In addition to liability based on failure to gain informed consent, most courts have adopted the view that extending treatment beyond what is expressly or by implication consented to by the patient may expose the health care provider to liability for battery based on unpermitted touching of the patient's body. Consent allows the health care provider to treat or perform surgery only to the extent of the consent granted. The health care provider's privilege is limited only to the conduct to which the patient consents or to acts "similar" in nature.[94] The typical defenses to allegations of battery are consent and the emergency privilege.[95]

Competence

The competence of a patient will affect the manner in which care and treatment are given. Competence can frequently be an issue that precipitates the need for treatment and yet requires the practitioner to take particular steps before beginning such treatment.

Competence arises both generally, when determining a patient's ability to handle his or her affairs, and specifically, when determining whether the patient is competent to consent to an operation or treatment. Most jurisdictions have either statutory or case law that defines competence. Typically, standards for competence are broadly defined, leaving the courts with sufficient flexibility to make a determination. The mental health care provider should be familiar with the jurisdiction's definition of competence. Most legal standards incorporate one or more of the following four elements:

■ The ability to communicate choice.

■ The ability to understand the facts relevant to the proposed decision.

■ The ability to understand what consequences the information has for the person's situation.

■ The ability to rationally process information to arrive at an outcome.[96]

A patient must be competent to consent to treatment or surgery. Informed consent cannot be given in the case of an incompetent person. The law presumes sanity rather than insanity and competence rather than incompetence.[97] Therefore, to protect themselves and their patients, mental health providers must make individual functional assessments of competence or of their patients' functional capacity to understand and consent.[98] The mere presence of psychosis, dementia, or other mental condition is not sufficient in and of itself to constitute incompetence.[98] The mental health care provider must be aware of the jurisdiction's definition of a minor and any statutes specifically dealing with consent for care and treatment of minors.[99]

After making his or her determination of competence or incompetence, the mental health care provider should investigate whether the jurisdiction allows the provider to make decisions on behalf of a patient. If there are no legal provisions for such action, the provider must be certain that consent to treat a patient is obtained from someone who has legal authority to make decisions on behalf of the patient.[100] Guardianship grants a designated person the power to make a legally binding decision on behalf of an incompetent person.

If the mental health care provider thinks the patient lacks competence and the patient has no legal guardian to make a decision on his or her behalf, a judicial determination of competence should be made. Judicial determinations protect the mental health care provider from charges of abuse and malpractice and protect the patient's liberty interests. In cases of "extraordinary" treatments, such as sterilization, psychosurgery, and electroconvulsive therapy (ECT), guardians are not authorized to make decisions on behalf of the incompetent patient, and judicial determinations are mandatory.[101]

Treatment Rights

A patient's right to refuse treatment or medication has been recognized in a majority of juris-dictions. Recent decisions from the United States Supreme Court note that strong due process safeguards surround the right not to have one's body invaded by the unwanted administration of medication, absent an overriding justification and medical necessity.[102]

The issue of the right to refuse treatment arises most often with involuntarily committed men-tal patients. While earlier cases dealt with the patient's right to refuse "intrusive" treatment, such as psychosurgery or ECT, recent cases deal with the right to refuse treatments such as antipsy-chotic medications.[103] Most states have enacted statutes or regulations detailing a patient's right to refuse treatment with medication.[104] In jurisdictions without such laws or regulations, case law may be the source of such a right.[105]

Statutory and case law recognize that both voluntarily and involuntarily committed patients have privacy rights, as well as due process and equal protection rights. The mental health care provider must be aware of any recent state legislation that may govern informed consent and competence determinations as they relate to treatment rights. Connecticut, for example, has enacted a statute to ensure that informed consent is achieved before treatment is given.[106] The statute provides that no medication shall be given to a patient without his or her informed con-sent, unless it is determined that the condition of the inpatient "will rapidly deteriorate," in which case such medication as is necessary may be given for 90 days.[107] If it is determined by the head of a hospital and two qualified physicians that a patient is unable to give informed consent to medication and that the medication is necessary to treatment, a facility must apply to the pro-bate court for a determination of the patient's ability to give informed consent.[108] If the patient is unable to consent, a conservator is appointed to determine whether medication should be administered.[109] No medical or surgical procedures may be performed without the patient's written informed consent or the written consent of a conservator.[110]

To ensure that a mental patient's rights are not violated, most jurisdictions have enacted laws requiring judicial review of proposed involuntary treatment of a mental patient.[111] Typically, jurisdictions recognize one or two approaches to the right to refuse treatment with medica-tion. One approach focuses on the treatment and requires review of the patient's refusal of treatment by the physician or an independent person.[112] The other common approach gives the greatest regard to the patient's rights. Typically, patients' competence is evaluated, and only those determined incompetent can be treated despite their objections.[113] It is therefore incum-bent on the mental health care provider to be aware of the law and of his or her jurisdiction's approach to involuntary treatment to avoid liability for nonconsensual treatment. As long as the patient's due process rights are not violated, applicable statutes are followed, and treat-ment is deemed necessary for the patient and is not against public policy, treatment may be administered according to the law. Claims may arise under theories of malpractice (for devi-ating from the standard of care), failure to obtain informed consent, battery (civil and crimi-nal), and violation of civil rights.[114]

Conclusion

Health care providers, especially those working in the area of mental health, are faced with complex issues and situations involving their patients that may have significant legal ramification Health care providers who are generally informed about emerging legal issues in mental healt care and have an understanding of the law in their jurisdictions are in a better position to pro tect their patients and to avoid potential legal claims.

References and Footnotes

1. The historical development of a patient's right to have his or her health care information remain pr vate has been explained as having roots in the "formulation of a right to privacy" and in the medic professional's "ethical proscription against the needless divulgence of patients' confidences Appelbaum, P., and Gutheil, T. *Clinical Handbook of Psychiatry and the Law*, Second Editio Baltimore, Md.: Williams and Wilkins, 1991, pp. 4-5.

2. Judy E. Zelin, Annotation, *Physician's Tort Liability for Unauthorized Disclosure of Confidentia Information about Patient*, 48 A.L.R. 4th 668, 674-78 (1986 & Supp. 1996).

3. *Ibid.*, pp. 674-5. See also Leger v. Spurlock, 589 So. 2d 40, 42 (La. Ct. App. 1991), recognizing action able invasion of privacy.

4. *Physician's Tort*, 48 A.L.R. 4th at 675-76. See *Alberts v. Devine*, 395 Mass. 59, 479 N.E.2d 113, 119-2(*cert. denied*, 474 U.S. 1013 (1985), finding that a psychiatrist violated the duty of confidentiality to hi patient by disclosing confidential communications to the patient's superiors. As a result of such dis closure, the patient, who was a minister, was not reappointed to his position. See also, *Schwartz Goldstein*, 400 Mass. 152, 508 N.E.2d 97, 98-99 (1987), recognizing that the remedy for a breach of physician's duty of confidentiality is an action for damages for invasion of privacy and breach of th duty of confidentiality.

5. In *Horne v. Patton*, 291 Ala. 701, 287 So. 2d 824, 830 (1973), where a physician disclosed confidentia information to an employer, contrary to the employee's wishes, there was a breach of confidential rela tionship. In *Hague v. Williams*, 37 N.J. 328, 181 A.2d 345, 349 (1962), the court held that a physician patient relationship gave rise to a general duty not to make nontestimonial disclosures. In *McDonal v. Clinger*, 84 A.D.2d 482, 446 N.Y.S.2d 801, 804-05 (1982), where a patient disclosed intimacies abou himself during the course of treatment, and his psychiatrist later divulged specific details to th patient's wife, without the patient's consent, the court found a breach of fiduciary duty of confiden tiality. Damages arose in tort.

6. The court in *Abelson's, Inc. v. New Jersey State Bd. of Optometrists*, 5 N.J. 412, 75 A.2d 867, 872-7 (1950) upheld a licensing statute that required that patient information be kept confidential. The por tion of the statute that provided for civil damages was found to be valid.

7. In *Quarles v. Sutherland*, 215 Tenn. 651, 389 S.W.2d 249, 251 (1965), the court held that standards se forth in a statute providing for revocation of a physician's license were merely administrative provi sions concerning the licensure of physicians and did not give rise to a right of recovery for the wrong ful disclosure of a medical report.

8. *Watts v. Cumberland County Hosp. Sys., Inc.,* 75 N.C. App. 1, 330 S.E.2d 242, 249-50 (1985), rev'd in part, 317, N.C. 321, 345 S.E.2d 201 (1986).

9. *Hammer v. Polsky,* 36 Misc.2d 482, 233 N.Y.S.2d 110, 111 (1962), and *Moses v. McWilliams,* 379 Pa. Super 150, 549 A.2d 950, 953-54 (1988), appeal denied, 521 Pa. 630, 631, 588 A.2d 532, in which the court noted a patient's right to confidentiality is less than absolute. In order to be actionable, the disclosure must be made without legal justification or cause.

10. In Massachusetts, for example, violation of a statute protecting records relating to venereal disease is punishable by a fine of up to $50 for the first offense and $100 for each subsequent offense. Mass. Gen. Laws Ann. ch. 11, §119 (West 1986 & Supp. 1996). In Connecticut, physicians are required to disclose cases of specific communicable diseases and corresponding laboratory results to the Commissioner of Public Health within 12 hours of an outbreak. However, personal information about people who are infected is strictly confidential. Failure to report and/or failure to keep information confidential results in fines of $500 per violation. Conn. Gen. Stat. §19a-215 (West 1991 & Supp. 1996). See also Conn. Gen. Stat. §19-216a, which imposes fines of $1,000 for disclosure of information related to patients being treated at communicable disease control clinics. Conn. Gen. Stat. § 19-216a (West 1991 & Supp. 1996). See also 38 U.S.C.A. §7332 (West 1991 & Supp. 1996). Violation of this federal statute protecting records relating to alcohol and drug abuse treatment of veterans is punishable by a fine of up to $5,000 for the first offense and $20,000 for each subsequent offense.

11. Mass. Gen. Laws Ann. ch. 233, §20B (West 1986 & Supp. 1996) relating to psychotherapists; Mass. Gen. Laws Ann. ch. 112, §129A, (West 1996) relating to psychologists; Mass. Gen. Laws Ann. ch. 112, §§ 135A, 135B, relating to social workers; Conn. Gen. Stat. §§52-146d-52-146j; (1995), relating to psychiatrists; and Conn. Gen. Stat. §52-146c (1995), relating to psychologists.

12. Conn. Gen. Stat. §l9a-126h (West 1991 & Supp. 1996); 42 U.S.C. §290dd-2(a) (1991 & Supp. 1996); and 38 U.S.C.A. §7332 (West 1991 & Supp. 1996).

13. Conn. Gen. Stat. §19a-216.

14. Conn. Gen. Stat. §§19a-600-l9a-602 (1995) with respect to minors.

15. Conn. Gen. Stat. §§52-146e, 52-146c (1995).

16. Conn. Gen. Stat. §§19a-581-19a-592 (1995); see also, State Statutes or Regulations Expressly Governing Disclosure of Fact That Person Has Tested Positive For Human Immunodeficiency Virus (HIV) or Acquired Immunodeficiency Syndrome (AIDS), 12 A.L.R. 5th 149 (1993).

17. Conn. Gen. Stat. §52-146 (1995).

18. For example, Conn. Gen. Stat. §§19a-581-l9a-592 (1995) details 12 entities to whom confidential HIV-related information can be disclosed and the circumstances under which a physician can disclose information to a known partner of an infected individual. The statute proscribes a written statement to accompany any disclosure. Similarly, a California statute shields physicians from civil and criminal liability for "disclosing to a person reasonably believed to be the spouse, or to a person reasonably believed to be a sexual partner or a person with whom the patient has shared the use of hypodermic needles", that the patient has tested positive for the HIV virus. Cal. Health & Safety Code §121015(a) (West 1996). Also note 16, 12 A.L.R. 5th 149 (1993).

19. In California for example, anyone who negligently discloses the results of an HIV test to a third party is subject to a $1,000 penalty. Willful disclosure will result in a $1,000 to $5,000 penalty; and disclosure that results in economic, bodily, or psychological harm to the test subject is a misdemeanor punishable by one year and/or a $10,000 fine. Cal. Health & Safety Code §120980 (West 1996). See also Conn. Gen. Stat. §19a-583 and §19a-590 (1995), imposing penalties for willful violation of the statutes.

20. For example in Connecticut, the fact that a minor has sought or is receiving alcohol or drug dependence treatment or rehabilitation cannot be released or discussed without the minor's consent. Conn. Gen. Stat. §19a-126h; see also Cal Health & Safety Code §123115 (West 1996).

21. 42 U.S.C. §290dd-2, a statute protecting the confidentiality of patient records maintained in connection with any program or activity relating to substance abuse education, prevention, training, treatment, rehabilitation, or research that is conducted, regulated, or assisted by any department or agency of the United States; and 38 U.S.C. §7332, a law that protects the confidentiality of patient records maintained in connection with any program or activity relating to drug abuse, alcoholism or alcohol abuse, HIV infection, or sickle cell anemia carried out by the Department of Veteran Affairs.

22. Often, medical associations and hospitals have developed consent forms that may be useful to individual practitioners.

23. For example, under Conn. Gen. Stat. §52-146p, family and marital therapy records are considered the records of each person involved in the therapy session. Therefore, prior to release of such records, the family or marital therapist should obtain authorization from each participant in the therapy. Jurisdictions may address the rights of noncustodial parents to their child's health records. For example, Conn. Gen. Stat. §46B-56(e) provides that the noncustodial parent "shall not be denied the right of access" to his or her minor child's academic or health records unless ordered by the court.

24. *McDonald v. Clinger*, 446 N.Y.S.2d at 805.

25. Cal. Health & Safety Code §123115(a)(2), as added by, 1995 Cal. Stat. 415, §8.

26. Cal. Health & Safety Code §123115(b)(2).

27. Cal. Health & Safety Code §123115(b)(1).

28. Conn. Gen. Stat. §19a-14c (1995), as amended by 1995 Conn. Acts 289, §8 (Reg. Sess.).

29. Conn. Gen. Stat. §19a-14c(b).

30. Conn. Gen. Stat. §19a-14c(c).

31. In addition to mental health treatment, abortion counseling, HIV/AIDS information, alcohol/drug abuse counseling or rehabilitation, sexual assault/rape counseling, and venereal disease information related to minors is often specially protected from disclosure by statute.

32. Consent of the patient is not required when the communications or records are disclosed to others engaged in the patient's diagnosis or treatment, as long as the disclosing psychiatrist determines that disclosure is necessary to accomplish the objectives of diagnosis or treatment. Conn. Gen. Stat. §52-146f(1).

33. See, for example Conn. Gen. Stat. §19a-583 on disclosure of HIV/AIDS information.

34. In *Wilson v, Blue Cross of So. California,* 271 Cal. Rptr. 876, 883 (1990), the mother of a patient being treated for major depression, drug dependency, and anorexia brought a wrongful death action against a managed care group and its insurer after the decision was made to stop treatment of her son. The patient's physician recommended a hospital stay of 3-4 weeks, but a managed care review shortened the treatment time to 10 days. Upon his release, the patient committed suicide. The court found there was sufficient evidence to infer liability on behalf of the managed care program and its insurers.

35. Corcoran, K., and Winslade, W. "Eavesdropping on the 50-Minute Hour: Managed Mental Health Care and Confidentiality." In 12 Behavioral Sciences & the Law, New York, N.Y.: John Wiley and Sons, pp. 351, 359, 1994.

36. *Ibid.,* p. 354.

37. Danny R. Veilleux, Annotation, *Validity. Construction. and Application of State Statute Requiring Doctor or Other Person to Report Child Abuse,* 73 A.L.R. 4th 782 (1989 & Supp. 1995).

38. *Ibid.,* pp. 789-90. See also Conn. Gen. Stat. §17a-101 (1995), as amended by 1995 Conn. Acts 287, §7 (Reg. Sess), 1995 Conn Acts 103 (Reg. Sess.); 42 U.S.C. §13031 (1995).

39. Conn. Gen. Stat. §17b-451 (1995).

40. Conn. Gen. Stat. §l9a-2a (1995).

41 Conn. Gen. Stat. §§52-146c, 52-146f. Another statute allows a physician to report to the department of motor vehicles the name of any patient diagnosed with a chronic health problem that the physician believes significantly affects the patient's ability to safely operate a motor vehicle. Conn. Gen. Stat. §14-46 (1995).

42. Cal. Civ. Code §56.10(b)-(c) (Deering 1990 & Supp. 1995).

43. Cal. Civ. Code §56.10(c)(2).

44. Conn. Gen. Stat. §52-146f(1).

45. Conn. Gen. Stat. §52-146f(2).

46. Conn. Gen. Stat. §52-146f(3).

47. Conn. Gen. Stat. §52-146f(4).

48. Conn. Gen. Stat. §52-146f(5).

49. Conn. Gen. Stat. §52-146f(6).

50. Conn. Gen. Stat. §52-146f(7).

51. Conn. Gen. Stat. §52-146g.

52. N.Y. Mental Hyg. Law §33.13(a)-(c) (McKinney's 1996).

53. N.Y. Mental Hyg. Law §33.13(c)(6).

54. N.Y. Mental Hyg. Law §33.13(c)(7).

55. N.Y. Mental Hyg. Law §33.13(c)(9).

56. In Connecticut, for example, statutes provide that oral and written communications (including records relating to diagnosis or treatment of a patient's medical condition) between a patient or a member of the patient's family and a psychiatrist, or someone under the supervision of the psychiatrist, are confidential and cannot be disclosed without the consent of the patient or the patient's authorized representative. Conn. Gen. Stat. §52-146e. Also, consent is not required when there is substantial risk of physical injury to the patient or others, or when necessary for placing a patient in a mental health facility. Other situations in which the patient's consent is not necessary for disclosure of psychiatric communications or records are listed in Conn. Gen. Stat. §52-146f. A patient may, however, consent to disclosure. Consent is not required in situations in which child abuse is known or in good faith suspected or where there is a good faith belief that there is risk of personal injury to the patient, to others, or to the property of others. Other situations in which a patient's consent is not required for disclosure of psychologist-patient communications are listed at Conn. Gen. Stat. §52-146(c).

57. Conn. Gen. Stat. §52-146c.

58. See 38 U.S.C. §7332.

59. 42 U.S.C. §260(d) (1991 & Supp. 1996).

60. Appelbaum, P., and Gutheil, T., op. cit., p. 16.

61. In *Jaffee v. Redmond,* the court reviewed the 7th Circuit's opinion in, 51 F.3d 1346, 1357 (7th Cir. 1995), cert. Granted _U.S._, 116 S. Ct. 334 (1995), aff'd, _U.S.~ 116 S. Ct. 1923 (1996). The test articulated by the 7th Circuit was similar to that expressed in the other circuits; "whether, in the interests of justice, the *Jaffee v. Redmond* evidentiary need for disclosure of a patient's counseling sessions outweighed the patient's privacy interests." (citations omitted).

62. Rule 501 states in pertinent part, "the privilege of a witness shall be governed by the principles of the common law as they may be interpreted by the Courts of the United States in the light of reason and experience." Fed. R. Evid. 501. Courts that recognize the privilege read Rule 501 broadly, whereas the 4th, 5th, 9th, 10th, & 11th circuits refused to expand the common law doctor-patient privilege any further than it already was. See, e.g. *Slaken v. Porter,* 737 F.2d 368, 377 (4th Cir. 1984), cert. denied, 470 U.S. 1035 (1985); United States v. Moore, 970 F.2d 48, 49-50 (5th Cir. 1992); *In re Grand Jury Proceedings,* 867 F.2d 562, 564-65 (9th Cir.), *cert. denied,* 493 U.S. 906 (1989) rejecting a defendant's assertion of privilege in a grand jury murder investigation; *United States v. Burkum,* 17 F.3d 1299, 1302 (10th Cir.), *cert. denied,* 115 S. Ct. 176 (1994), refusing to recognize a privilege in a criminal child sexual abuse case; and *Hancock v. Hobbs,* 967 F.2d 462, 466-67 (11th Cir. 1992). However, the Second Circuit in *In re Doe,* 964 F.2d 1325, 1328-29 (2d. Cir. 1992) recognized the privilege where the plaintiff sought production of psychiatric history. The Sixth Circuit recognized the privilege in *In re Zuniga,* 714 F.2d 632, 637 (6th Cir.), where the defendants' psychotherapists were issued grand jury subpoenas, *cert. denied* 464 U.S. 983 (1983).

63. The Second Circuit privilege required an examination of a witness' privacy interests as an important factor to be weighed when considering the admissibility of psychiatric histories or diagnoses. *In re Doe,* 964 F.2d at 1329. The Sixth Circuit privilege protected only the patient's "innermost thoughts" and did not shield a patient from disclosure of basic information, such as his or her name and the type of treatment he or she received. *In re Zuniga,* 714 F.2d at 640. In determining the existence of the

privilege, both circuits balanced whether the need for privacy outweighed the need for disclosure of a witnesses' psychiatric history.

64. Because of the constraints imposed on physicians by managed care organizations, the mental health care provider may find that restrictions on authorized services conflict with treatment he or she deems necessary for his or her patient. Practitioners must be extremely cautious to avoid suits by not allowing the quality of their treatment to fall below the requisite standard of care because of managed care decisions. Following the changes brought by managed care, legal actions have been initiated by patients against providers because of decisions made regarding treatment. See Corcoran, K., and Winslade, W., *op. cit.*, pp. 353-4.

65. Note that claims of malpractice may also be asserted for disclosure of confidential information. See note 2.

66. Appelbaum, P., and Gutheil, T., *op cit.*, pp. 145-65. Other forms of liability discussed by Appelbaum and Gutheil include false imprisonment (unjust deprivation of privacy), breach of privacy, (including appropriation of a likeness or name, intrusion or seclusion, false light, public disclosure of embarrassing facts). *Ibid.*, pp. 166-7. Also discussed by the authors are defamation (communication harming one's reputation in the community); interference with advantageous relations (causing financial or personal loss); civil rights actions; and fraud (civil or criminal). *Ibid.*, pp. 167-70.67.

67. *Pisel v. Stamford Hospital,* 100 Conn. 314, 430 A.2d 1 (1980). See also J.L. Rigelhaupt, Jr., Annotation, *Liability of Doctor, Psychiatrist, or Psychologist for Failure to Take Steps to Prevent Patient's Suicide,* 17 A.L.R. 4th 1128 (1986 & Supp. 1995).

68. *Vera v. Beth Israel Medical Hosp.,* 214 A.D.2d 384, 625 N.Y.S. 2d, 499, 500-02, *appeal denied,* 87 N.Y 2d 802, 661 N.E. 2d. 999, 638 N.Y.S. 2d 425 (1995), holding a physician is not liable for his patient's self-inflicted injuries after he was released from the hospital following an injection of psychotropic drug. See also *Bell v. New York Citv Health & Hosp. Corp.*, 90 A. D.2d 270 456 N.Y.S. 2d 787, 795-6 (1982), holding there is no liability for erroneous professional judgment. The court in Bell did, however, impose liability, because the psychiatrist did not conduct the proper inquiry into the patient's past history and medical records.

69. *Bell v. New York City Health & Hosp. Corp.,* at 795.

70. *Tarasoff v. Regents of the Univ. of California,* 17 Cal. 3d. 425,551 P.2d334, 131 Cal. Rptr. 14 (1976).

71. *Ibid.,* at 342-3.

72. For example, in Massachusetts, statutes relating to psychologists (Mass. Gen. Laws Ann. ch. 112, §129A (West 1996)), social workers (Mass. Gen. Laws Ann. ch. 112, §135A (West 1996)), and mental health professionals (Mass. Gen. Laws Ann. ch. 123, §36B (West Supp. 1996)) require disclosure if the rights and safety of others require protection:

- When a patient has communicated an explicit threat to kill or inflict serious bodily injury upon a reasonably identified person and the patient has the apparent ability and intent to carry out the threat, a mental health professional has a duty to take reasonable precautions by communicating the threat to the reasonably identified person, by notifying an appropriate law enforcement agency, and by arranging for voluntary hospitalization of the patient or initiating procedures for involuntary hospitalization.

- If the patient has a history of physical violence and it is known to the mental health professional and the mental health professional has a reasonable basis to believe that there is a danger that the patient will attempt to kill or inflict serious bodily injury upon a reasonably identified person, the mental health professional has a duty to take reasonable precautions, including notifying the person of the threat, notifying the appropriate law enforcement agency, arranging for voluntary hospitalization, or initiating procedures for involuntary hospitalization. A reference to a "reasonable basis to believe that there is a clear and present danger...against a clearly identified or reasonably identifiable victim" means that "the patient's words or behavior strongly suggest that there is a 'reasonable' possibility that the client will attempt to kill or inflict serious bodily injury on a reasonably identified victim or victims whom...words or behavior or history have clearly identified as a likely target of such behavior." Mass. Regs. Code tit. 251, §3.11(4)(1996).

Nothing within the statutes requires a mental health professional to take any action that, in the exercise of reasonable professional judgment, would endanger the mental health professional or increase the danger to a potential victim. Only information that is essential to protect the rights and safety of others should be disclosed. As long as reasonable precautions are taken, no cause of action will be allowed by the patient for disclosure of otherwise confidential communications. See also N.Y. Mental Hyg. Law §33.13(c)(6).

73. *Fraser v. United States,* 236 Conn. 625, 634-37, 674 A.2d 811 (1996).

74. *Ibid.* at 632.

75. *Almonte v. New York Medical College,* 851 F.Supp. 34 (D. Conn. 1994).

76. *Ibid.* at 40.

77. *Ibid.* at 41. Mental health care providers should be aware that case law varies dramatically, as do the facts surrounding the treatment of patients. Nonetheless, mental health care providers must be aware of judicial standards established in their jurisdictions to avoid liability.

78. *Welke v. Kuzilla,* 114 Mich. App. 245, 375 N.W.2d 403 (1985).

79. *Ibid.* at 406.

80. *Gooden v. Tips,* 651 S.W. 2d 364 (Text Ct. App. 1983), where a physician failed to warn a patient of dangers while taking tranquilizers. See also *Watkins v. United States,* 589 F.2d 214, 216-18 (5th Cir. 1979), where a physician was held liable when his patient collided into the plaintiff's car. The physician failed to check the patient's psychiatric history before prescribing a 50-day supply of Valium, on which the patient overdosed before hitting the plaintiff.

81. *Reisner v. Regents of the Univ. of California,* 31 Cal. App. 4th 1195, 37 Cal. Rptr. 2d 518, 519 (1995).

82. *Ibid.* at 1196.

83. Conn. Gen. Stat. §19a-583-590 and 38 U.S.C.A. §7332.

84. Legal standards relating to the doctrine of informed consent have evolved over the past two decades. Before that time, a physician could be held liable for assault or battery if he or she performed a treatment or procedure in the absence of any consent by the patient. See, e.g., *Schmeltz v. Tracey,* 119 Conn. 492, 494-97, 177 A. 520 (1935). A patient's consent to a procedure vitiated any liability on the part of

the surgeon, as long as the physician gave the patient sufficient information to make an intelligent decision. What was sufficient information was judged by a physician or professional standard, that is what the average health care provider would have told the patient. In the early seventies, states began to adopt a patient-oriented standard, that is, what was material and necessary for a patient's determination of whether or not to undergo a particular medical treatment. In Massachusetts, a physician reasonably should disclose what is material to an intelligent decision by the patient as to whether or not to consent to a proposed procedure. See *Harnish v. Children's Hosp. Medical Ctr.,* 387 Mass. 152, 439 N.E.2d 240, 242-44 (1982); *Martin v. Lowney,* 401 Mass. 1006, 517 N.E.2d 162 (1988).

85. Keeton, W., and others. *Prosser & Keeton on the Law of Torts,* §32 at 190 (5th Ed., 1984).

86. Appelbaum, P., and Gutheil, T., *op. cit.* The doctrine of informed consent has been criticized by health care providers because it presumes perhaps wrongly that the patient listens to all his doctor tells him and makes treatment decisions based on what he is told.

87. *Ibid.,* pp. 160-1.

88. *Ibid.,* pp. 156-60.

89. In Mass. Gen. Laws Ann., Department of Mental Health regulations require a specific consent, pursuant to ch. 123, §23, before electroconvulsive treatment or lobotomy is given. See Mass. Regs. Code tit. 104, §3.08(2) (1995). Regulations relevant to the mentally retarded also delineate particular consent procedures. See Mass Regs. Code tit. 104, §20.13(2). Consent shall be in writing and filed in the client's record; a written record should be made that details the procedure utilized to obtain the consent, identifies the individual securing the consent, and summarizes the information provided to the person. The person securing consent shall explain the intended outcome, nature, and procedures involved; explain the risks, including side-effects, of the proposed treatment or activity; explain the alternatives to the proposed treatment or activity; and explain that consent may be withheld or withdrawn at any time, with no punitive action.

90. *Demers v. Gerety,* 87 N.M. 52, 529 P.2d 278, 280 (1974), holding inadequate disclosure to be malpractice and that consent agreement is invalid when a party is incompetent or under sedation that would destroy competency, *cert. denied,* 87 N.M. 47, 529 P.2d 273 (1974).

91. *Ibid.* at 190-91.

92. *Hondroulis v. Schumacher,* 553 So.2d 398, 420 (La. 1989), holding that a written, informed consent form that listed broad categories of possible risks related to surgery did not necessarily require a conclusion that a patient who signed it gave informed consent to surgery. On rehearing, the Louisiana Supreme Court determined that disclosure must be made where the risk is material. Absent proof of material risk, the question of whether the magnitude of the risk would have convinced the patient not to undergo treatment is a factual inquiry. Very minor risks, however, are insufficient. *Parikh v. Cuningham,* 493 So. 2d 999, 1001-02 (Flat Ct. App. 1986), holding conclusive statutory presumption that signed informed consent form constitutes valid consent violates due process of law.

93. Grundner, T. "On the Readability of Surgical Consent Forms." *New England Journal of Medicine* 302(16):900-2, April 17, 1980.

94. Keeton, W., *op. cit.*, §18 at 118; see also, W. E. Shipley, Annotation, *Liability of Physician or Surgeon for Extending Operation or Treatment Beyond That Expressly Authorized,* 56 A.L.R. 2d 695 (1957 & Supp. 1995).

95. *Ibid.* at 114-115. The touching of another that would be battery in the absence of consent by either the person touched or that person's guardian may be justified in the case of an emergency. For the emergency doctrine to apply, the patient or his guardian must be unable to consent, time must be of the essence, and it must be determined that under the circumstances a reasonable person would have consented.

96. Appelbaum, P., and Gutheil, T., *op. cit.,* pp. 222-3.

97. R.H. Lockwood, Annotation, *Mental Competency of Patient to Consent to Surgical Operation or Medical Treatment,* 25 A.L.R. 3d. 1439 (1969 & Supp. 1995).

98. Appelbaum, P., and Gutheil, T., *op. cit.,* p. 220.

99. Mass. Gen. Laws. Ann., ch. 112 §12F (1994) outlines statutory guidelines for determination of when a minor is able to consent.

100. *Aponte v. United States,* 582 F. Supp. 65, 71-72 (D.P.R. 1984), holding that the Veteran's Administration could not rely on a schizophrenic patient's consent to an operation removing a testicle. Where the patient's wife had been appointed his executrix and fiduciary, she should have been consulted and given consent or denial to the operation.

101. Appelbaum, P., and Gutheil, T., *op. cit.,* p. 226.

102. *Doe v. Hunter,* 44 Conn. Supp. 53, 58, 667 A.2d 90 (1995), holding that, in order to protect a patient's rights to refuse treatment, the defendants were restrained from administering medication until the patient consented or until there was a duly noticed hearing in the Probate Court; *Riggins v. Nevada,* 504 U.S. 127, 134, 112 S. Ct. 1810 (1992), holding that forcible injection of antipsychotic drugs into a mentally ill inmate is a violation of the Due Process Clause of the Constitution because it is a substantial interference with that person's liberty, but is not a violation if it has been determined that the inmate is a danger to himself and others. See also *Washington v. Harper,* 494 U.S. 210, 211, 110 S. Ct. 1028 (1990), holding that the Due Process Clause does not prohibit treatment of a mentally ill inmate with antipsychotic medication against his will if the inmate is dangerous to himself and others and treatment is in his best medical interest.

103. Appelbaum, P., and Gutheil, T., *op. cit.,* p. 98; Michael R. Flaherty, Annotation, *Nonconsensual Treatment of Involuntarily Committed Mentally Ill Persons with Neuroleptic or Antipsvchotic Drugs as Violative of State Constitutional Guaranty,* 74 A.LR.4th 1099, 1102 (1984). See also, Brooks, "The Right to Refuse Antipsvchotic Medications Law and Policy; 39 *Rutgers Law Review* 339 (Winter/Spring 1987), and *Jarvis v. Levine,* 418 N.W.2d 139 (Minn. 1988), holding in part that administration of antipsychotic drugs is considered intrusive therapy. Later proceeding, 433 N.W.2d 120 (Minn. App. 1988). See also, *Riggins v. Nevada,* 504 U.S. 127, 112 S. Ct. 1810 and *Washington v. Harper,* 494 U.S. 210, 110 S. Ct. 1028, supra note 102.

104. Mass. Gen. Laws ch. 123, §12 (1995). See also *Opinion of the Justices*, 123 N.H. 554, 465 A.2d 484, 488-89 (N.H. 1983), where the New Hampshire Supreme Court held that a state statute that protected an involuntarily committed mental patient's right to refuse treatment could be superseded by compelling state interest when the patient presented a real potential to do harm and was unable to make an informed treatment decision.

105. Appelbaum, P., and Gutheil, T., *op. cit.*, p. 100; see also *Rivers v. Katz*. 67 N.Y.2d 485, 495 N.E.2d 337, 504 N.Y. S.2d 74, 79 (1986), holding the right of involuntarily committed patient to refuse treatment of antipsychotic medication is not absolute and under certain circumstances may yield to compelling state interests or to the protection of others. Because the schizophrenic patient's symptoms would be greatly reduced through medication, allowing her to return home to live independently within months, the court reasoned that treatment did not interfere with the patient's liberty interests. See also *Eleanor R. v. South Oaks Hosp.*, 123 A.D.2d 460, 506 N.Y.S.2d 763, 764-65, *appeal denied*, 69 N.Y.D. 602, 504 N.E.2d 395, 512 N.Y.S.2d 1025 (1986), where the court upheld an order permitting a mental hospital to administer antipsychotic drugs to a patient unable to give consent, after finding administration of the medication to be "narrowly tailored to give substantial effect to the patient's liberty interests." (citation omitted).

106. Conn. Gen. Stat. §17-543 (West 1996), as amended by 1996 Conn. Acts 180, §47; 1996 Conn. Acts 202, §2; 1996 Conn. Acts 215, §1 (Reg. Sess.).

107. Conn. Gen. Stat. §17a-543(a), (d).

108. Conn. Gen. Stat. §17a-543; see also *Doe v. Hunter*, 44 Conn. Supp. at 59, holding that the defendants were restrained from administering medication until the patient had consented or until there was a duly noticed hearing in the Probate Court resulting in a finding that he was unable to give informed consent but that the newly appointed conservator had consented.

109. Conn. Gen. Stat. §17a-543(e), (d).

110. Conn. Gen. Stat. §17a-543(b).

111. *In re Bilie*, 414 N.W.2d 877, Minn. 1993, holding that even where state hospital staff prescribed medication and a publicly appointed guardian approved it, the patient's right to privacy was adequately protected. See also, In re Guardianship of Willis, 74 Ohio App. 3d 554, 599 N.E. 2d 745 (1991), where the court properly ordered guardianship for the administration of psychotropic drugs when the patient's condition was manageable but she occasionally refused to take her medication.

112. Appelbaum, P., and Gutheil, T., *op. cit.*, pp. 98-99.

113. *Ibid.*, pp. 99-100.

114. *Ibid.*, pp. 101-02.

Ernest J. Mattei, Esq., and Mary B. Cardin, Esq., are attorneys with Day, Berry and Howard, Hartford, Connecticut. They extend their thanks to Jessica J. Mitchell for her assistance with this chapter.

Chapter 4

Some Metaphysical Quandaries

by Eric D. Lister, MD

A matrix of interrelated forces have revolutionized health care delivery in the United States during the past 10 years. Although the primary forces have been extrinsic to our work—issues such as the demands of large employers for reduced health care costs—the effects of these pressures have touched every aspect of clinical medicine in the Unites States, and there is reason to suspect that the pace of change will only increase over the next decade.

Organizations funding the delivery of health care services—primarily employers and various branches of government—have shifted dramatically from their traditional role as conduits of funding into a much more active position. Funding sources at this juncture set operational policies for health care delivery that, in some cases, amount to directing the delivery of clinical care; they describe "benchmarks" (statistics on cost and outcome that become explicit expectations); and they have assumed the prerogative to question clinical decisions—in individual cases and in general. This chapter will focus on a series of "quandaries"—questions that demand discussion but escape resolution—quandaries that must be addressed by each of us and by each organization that is affected by the managed care revolution.

The Quandary of Reactivity

As erudite or intellectualized as we may be about managed care, as logical and precise as we can be in studying the realities, analyzing the costs, and analyzing the benefits, we cannot help but feel the jarring shock of change. Many therapists feel invalidated and devalued, as services that have been given successfully and in good faith are deemed "outside the boundaries of medical necessity." Long-established treatments for which insurance reimbursement has been regular and unquestioned are suddenly unreimbursed. Patterns of practice are jeopardized. Personal security has become uncertain. The institutions in which we work, struggling to survive with almost frantic urgency, have become unpredictable and are rapidly redefining themselves in a process of contraction, alliance formation, and partnership.

We know from our clinical work that tumult of this degree cannot help but stir anxiety, apprehension, and the experience of loss. Anger and indignation follow in short order. Some of us veer in the direction of denial, some toward feeling victimized, some toward righteousness and indignation. Some, more or less consciously prepared for the wave of change, see opportunity and feel excited.

In fact, the pressure to examine traditional patterns of care delivery opens the door to progress on a number of fronts. We are mobilized to study, for the first time, efficiency as well as effectiveness. We are becoming attentive to the need for outcome studies. We are directed to look at what, in quality improvement terms, might be called "process variation" in our clinical work. In the most successful systems, the best aspects of traditional private practice are being blended with the most sophisticated methodologies of community mental health.

Our professional associations have, by and large, been confused and inconsistent in their reactions, fueled often by the collective affects of large and prominent constituent groups. Initiatives to "combat" managed care have been launched by many of the mental health professional associations, while prominent individuals in some of these same organizations have moved to positions of leadership in managed care organizations.

Here is the quandary: We cannot avoid an emotional response and accompanying reactive reflexes, but we must—for our own sake and the sake of our patients—step back to simultaneously analyze and plan. The analysis and planning must be conducted in the most balanced and reasoned manner possible.

In my experience, consulting to a large number of health care organizations, this necessary tension between dealing with affect and thinking through a reasoned response is rarely well maintained. Either the affect overruns the need for rational planning or rational planning is attempted in denial of affective undercurrents that make clear thinking, clear planning, and effective implementation virtually impossible.

The Quandary of Perspective: Guild vs. Profession

Our membership in professional societies—whether we are marriage and family counselors, social workers, nurses, psychiatrists, or psychologists—is an essential aspect of professional identity. These societies play crucial roles in our early training, our induction into the practice of clinical work, our continuing education, and our certification or licensure. We look to our professional societies for support, leadership, advocacy, promulgation of knowledge, and maintenance of our humanitarian mission.

Yet we often forget that these same societies occupy a confusing place at the intersection of guild and professional interests. The guild interest focuses on protection of guild members—their access to a livelihood, freedom from competition, access to appropriate working conditions, and need for "public relations."

In fact, our professional societies usually do a reasonable job of serving both of these agendas—professional identity and guild advocacy. However, the current climate of rapid change has elicited responses from our professional societies that confuse guild and professional issues.

For instance, although managed care may indeed be a threat to the practice preference of many (or even most) established outpatient providers and hence elicit a "battle plan" from the guild representing these providers, it may simultaneously present an enormous opportunity to expand the efficiency of resource utilization and bring basic mental health services to a far wider section of the population—a cause for celebration at the level of the profession's humanitarian mission. Those of us with leadership responsibility in our professional societies will need to address this inevitable tension quite clearly and explicitly.

The Conundrum of an Expanded Frame

Although many of us have worked for years in complex systems, we have, by and large, been tenacious in our attempts to frame the clinical encounter as a dyadic one. There is a therapist, with a task of being helpful, and a patient or client whose role is to participate in receiving the professional services of the therapist. Although third parties have long participated in this arrangement by processing funds, it has been reasonably possible to define their relevance in such a way that they were excluded from the dyadic encounter where "real therapy" takes place.

At this juncture, the complexities of health care delivery systems are such that this frame of reference no longer applies, and clinging to it runs the risk of denial, providing a disservice to our patients. Certainly, outside of the world of insurance reimbursement, where patients are paying out-of-pocket for private psychiatric services, the old model still has some applicability. However, less and less of our work takes place in such settings.

What, then, is the current frame of reference? We need to explicitly appreciate that our patients have a primary relationship with their insurance carriers. They have contracts with insurance carriers that often predate their contacts with us, and the contracts are negotiated in the world of business, according to the parameters of business, not those of healing. The adequacy of this contract, its extent and limitations, are, from this perspective, reality factors open to exploration and understanding, but not open to negotiation. We need to see ourselves as clarifiers, as educators, who can explain these realities to our patients and help them advocate and lobby effectively for changes in the contracting system when it is inadequate. Contracts for health care services are not primarily "about us" or about the clinical decision making that we, obviously, need to undertake with our patients.

Simultaneously, we have very complicated contractual relationships ourselves with health care organizations that pay for our services and, increasingly, act as our employers. We have complicated contracts, and our work is overseen from a variety of perspectives, including patterns of utilization, quality of care, and patient satisfaction. Our records are open to various types of review, and our behavior with our patients is in this sense "public" to our overseeing or employing organizations more than ever before.

In the midst of this matrix of relationships, the clinical relationship endures, where we as professionals have decisions to make and recommendations to share and where complex judgments need to be exercised. And here is the quandary: How can we continue to develop our ability to make effective clinical decisions without blinding ourselves to the reality of other relationships—the patient's relationship with his or her insurance company, our relationship with the institutions in which we work. There are tensions to be balanced and realities extrinsic to the clinical encounter that need to be accommodated without capitulation, which would involve allowing external forces to completely dictate clinical decision making. This is not ethically (or legally) acceptable. Nor, however, is it acceptable to act inside the clinical encounter as though these other realities were irrelevant or nonexistent.

The Conundrum of Confidentiality

Related to the changing frame of reference within which therapy takes place is a dramatic change in the nature of confidentiality. Confidentiality has been a watchword of the healing professions since the days of Hippocrates, but its meaning is more and more confusing in contemporary practice. On the one hand, we have grown to appreciate the importance of multidisciplinary treatment, which involves the act of communication of clinical details among a group of involved practitioners. This, by and large, feels comfortable, and it is a breach of confidentiality limited enough and tangible enough that patients can, and for the most part will, give informed consent to it. Nonetheless, even this redefinition of confidentiality becomes complicated when patients ask us to keep secrets from our collaborators. This not infrequent experience has resulted in more than one sleepless therapist.

Confidentiality is further eroded by the legal system, which has delineated a growing set of circumstances wherein we are legally obliged to do what our professional traditions forbid—to speak out to the authorities.

Then there is the waiver of confidentiality that insurers increasingly require of insured members and that is rarely accompanied by anything approaching fully informed consent. Funding is contingent on our releasing information used in the process of utilization review, quality assurance, quality improvement, provider profiling, and peer review. The move toward electronic records allows for an efficiency in this process that further compromises confidentiality. Again, patients are often unaware of just how "porous" is the membrane that protects personal details from public scrutiny.

We cannot abandon our commitment to confidentiality, but we cannot at this juncture ensure it. We are forced to live in the gray zone of unclarity and ambiguity, helping our patients to be more informed and active politically, working inside our professional organizations to lobby for record-keeping guidelines that provide necessary oversight at minimum cost to privacy, and working with the institutions that reimburse us toward ever-increasing levels of professionalism in accessing and handling private information.

The Conundrum of Quality vs. Cost: Treating with Populations in Mind

For many of us, training in the helping professions was attended by very little attention to matters of cost. We were taught to do "what the patient needed" and were rarely even told the cost. Effectiveness was the watchword, even though our embarrassing failure to rigorously look at outcomes meant that we were always driving toward what we thought was most effective. In any case, issues of efficiency were nonexistent. We were after the maximal effect, and the idea of a cost-benefit analysis had little relevance. Many of us were trained to treat individual patients as though resources were limitless, even when we knew from the setting in which we practiced that resources might be quite limited. Those whose early professional experiences took place in the inner city, the Indian Health Service, or some other resource-deprived arena did not, perhaps, experience this peculiar acculturation, but I know that many of us did.

At this juncture, the institutions in which we work are increasingly responsible for treating entire populations and do so with fixed resources. Institutional survival depends on success at this practice, and so the pressure to be efficient as well as effective is quickly transmitted to each and every practicing clinician. At the extreme, the need to balance effectiveness and efficiency results in rationing, but that is a concept that we in this country avoid with a passion. Only in Oregon has it been frankly and courageously confronted.

We need, therefore, to make treatment plans that continue to strive for maximum effectiveness while responding to the requirement of resource stewardship—saving enough resources for the next patient—by addressing efficiency as we attend to effectiveness. This struggle, to find solid ground between concern for efficiency and concern for effectiveness, requires all of our clinical wisdom and drives us toward outcome studies and processes of quality improvement. The application of outcome studies and quality improvement methodologies offers us our only chance of improving efficiency and effectiveness simultaneously.

No matter how successful we are in this regard, however, some of the issues involved are inescapably issues of public policy rather than clinical decision making. We need to try to frame the necessary public policy debates in ways that are informed by our expertise and guided by our principles, for we in turn are going to be guided by the results of these discussions in the public arena.

The Quandary of Standardization

Psychotherapy is one of the most intrinsically personal of all healing processes. To do our work well, even if we are prescribing and monitoring psychotropic medications, we need at some level to know our patients deeply, intimately, three-dimensionally. We need to understand their symptoms, the meanings of these symptoms, their hopes and fears, their secrets and shames. It is the opportunity to engage at this level of intimacy, the honor that is extended to us in the process, that allows us to be helpful and that provides an important source of gratification for many of us.

Given this, how can we think about clinical approaches driven by standardized protocols without cringing. At one level, we can answer this question by reassuring ourselves that individualized assessments always need to precede standardized protocols and that even standardized protocols can be delivered in individualized ways. Those reassurances are true, but they do not entirely satisfy. Reflexively, many of us feel that working "by the numbers" somehow dehumanizes what we believe must be essentially personal and human. Yet those who have worked in public health settings tell us very clearly that we can extend our clinical resources much more effectively by using clinical protocols, and epidemiologists are just as clear in teaching us that we cannot gather meaningful outcome data that can be useful to us in our attempts at self-improvement without standardizing our practice.

And so, once again, we must try to reconcile yet another dramatic and dynamic tension. Somehow, we need not only to accommodate protocols, but also to invest in inventing the best possible protocols for psychotherapeutic encounters. At the same time, we must work to maintain consciousness of the unique human encounter and its importance, training those who enter our professions to work in a way that is simultaneously "by the numbers," from the mind, and from the heart.

The Quandary of Medical Necessity

Training in psychotherapy for decades has blurred the distinction between "clinically useful" and "medically necessary." Patients first seek our services in times of crisis, but we try to use that crisis to move beyond immediate symptoms, to help people grow or change in ways that would speak to preexisting difficulties, to maladaptive patterns, psychological vulnerabilities, and to unrecognized traumas. I think that much good has been done by our practice of not simply stopping with symptom reduction, but working steadily to maximize growth and health. This approach has been criticized as having fostered dependency or, at worst, perpetuated relationships for the benefit of the therapist's psychological or financial gain. Although there are irrefutable examples of such duplicity, we have, for the most part, done well by doing more.

Nonetheless, at this juncture, the insurance contract—whether public or private—defines itself as serving medical necessity rather than personal betterment. This forces us to make a distinction that we have in the past actively and intentionally avoided. It feels enormously uncomfortable. It is often quite arbitrary. It runs the risk of confusing patients, and we see a "two-tiered system" developing in which more affluent patients can pay for the helpful but "not necessary" treatment that less affluent patients must do without.

We can certainly do a better job at steering patients toward self-help groups, give them books to read, offer low-fee group therapies, etc. Nonetheless, as we expand our repertoire of interventions in these directions, we know full well that there was a time when we would be reimbursed for doing more, and our inability to do so at this juncture feels like a loss for us as well as for our patients.

Conundrums of Payment

Current funding mechanisms and the tangled rules of reimbursement for health care create terrible binds for us. When "medically necessary" treatment has been funded by insurance and we terminate patients but refer them to ourselves or to colleagues for out-of-pocket treatment, are we "double dipping?" Are we engaging in something shady or fraudulent? Do we need to get informed consent for charging patients?

When we enter into capitated arrangements, there may seem to be a short-term or immediate incentive to undertreat. How do we protect ourselves from being subtly influenced or, frankly, seduced? Even outside capitated arrangements, how do we deal with the pressure to "please" managed care organizations that are engaged in "provider profiling"—in seeing how efficiently we utilize resources. Are we at risk of having this need to please impinge on clinical decision making? Of course we are. We are only human. At this juncture, it suffices to underline the issue.

We need to be rigorous, scrupulous, and conscientious in dealing with a variety of payment-related issues that run the risk of compromising the treatment relationship, our ability to provide treatment, and even ourselves legally.

The Quandary of Personal Choice

So what do we do? For each of us this question arises. Do I stay in the field, do I look for another way of making a living, do I retire early, do I look to be hired and leave private practice, or do I join a group in lieu of solo practice? Do I try to develop a "niche" out-of-pocket practice where I can do my work and make a living outside the "medical-industrial complex?" These are not questions that any one person or group can decide for another, although the process of addressing these questions is often best done with the support of peers and colleagues.

We know, again, from our clinical work and our understanding of adult development that several things are necessary. The affective crisis referred to earlier needs to find some resolution or we will be unhappy. We need to find enough comfort with the inevitable tensions and ambiguities raised by all of these conundrums that we can practice without denial on the one hand or anxiety on the other. We need to find a setting for professional work that offers support and a frame of reference that allows us to be excited by something—even if it is very different from whatever it was that excited us 10 or 20 years ago. If we cannot do these things, we are at great risk of "burning out," of going through the motions of doing the work, a process from which no one is likely to benefit greatly.

Some of us will change the nature or the setting of our work dramatically. Some will embark on exciting and creative enterprises. Others will make only a minor adjustment. Some will leave the field entirely, and I think that this needs to be seen as a healthy step for those who choose it rather than as failure or resignation. But no matter what our personal experience is with this revolution in health care, some personal resolution is necessary for each and every one of us.

Eric D. Lister, MD, is a practicing psychiatrist and a partner of Ki Associates, and organizational consulting firm in Portsmouth, New Hampshire, that specializes in helping health care organizations with major change initiatives.

Section II

Systems

Chapter 5

Staffing of Behavioral Health Programs: Development and Analysis of a Computer-Based Algorithm

by Robert M. Atkins, MD, MPH

Behavioral health programs must allocate resources prudently with regard to both cost and quality. To meet program requirements within available clinical resources, administrative psychiatrists must justify clinical staffing in terms of expected performance. This chapter describes initial development and analysis of a computerized algorithm that derives nonnursing staffing requirements from quantifiable performance expectations. The algorithm is used to examine the effects of managed care on a hypothetical adult inpatient program. Results show the validity of the algorithm as a prototype capable of being customized to many different settings by changing the values of the variables. In addition, the algorithm is able to predict staffing requirements as average length of stay and daily census vary. System characteristics quantified by the algorithm suggest possibilities to improve clinical processes. Using the algorithm to model proposed changes in advance will permit program leadership to modify clinical services on the basis of quantifiable and testable assumptions.

Introduction

The staffing required in any behavioral health program is a complex function of the program's average daily census, the rate at which patients move through the program, and the amount and type of clinical services patients receive. A tool that predicts clinical staffing as a function of these variables would have many uses. Clinical administrators could assess the adequacy of current staffing, plan program start-up, analyze financial viability, and forecast the effects of possible scenarios. In particular, they could examine the growing influence of managed care.

To be applicable across various treatment sites, this tool must be able to reflect the requirements of different treatment philosophies, the availability of different staffing resources, and the constraints of different marketplace conditions. It must also accommodate varying intensities of service as patients move among inpatient, partial hospitalization, and intensive outpatient programs. Finally, it must allow for programs tailored to different clinical populations, ranging from acute units to specialized treatment programs to long-term state hospitals.

Development of the Algorithm

While patient acuity-based nurse staffing models are in common use, overall staffing of the interdisciplinary treatment program has eluded practical analysis. Patient classification systems determine the nursing staff required for core nursing practice, which is highly dependent on patient acuity.[1,2] Other approaches integrate categories of patient behaviors with levels of nursing interventions to determine nursing care hours.[3] The algorithm shown in figure 1, pages 74 and 75, focuses on the interdisciplinary treatment program. It reflects the assumption that therapist staffing is not dependent solely on patient acuity, but rather depends on the overall program being designed to meet the needs of the variety of patients being served. The algorithm integrates a comprehensive set of input variables (A-G) that quantify program features that predict staffing. Output variables of the algorithm (H-J) include numbers of staff members needed, weekly productivity ratios, and hours of structured therapy per day per patient.

The algorithm predicts staffing levels for "structured therapy," which includes the variety of psychotherapies that make up a treatment program, with a distinction between behavioral rehabilitation (occupational, recreational, and expressive therapies) and the other psychotherapies. Because several disciplines prepare clinicians to provide a variety of structured therapies, each program must decide the categories of clinicians who may treat patients. A "therapist," then, is any clinician who meets program criteria for delivering structured therapy of one or more types. To the extent that nurses provide services described in the algorithm, they should be counted in the "number of therapists needed" predicted by the algorithm.

Each variable in the algorithm depends on one or more assumptions. High-lighted elements in figure 1 identify assumptions made by program leadership. (This example uses values coming from the author's clinical experience.) All other elements are derived from these assumptions.

Treatment Mode (A) is the type of therapy staff members provide. Patients at lower functional levels often cannot tolerate longer therapy sessions. This is the rationale for distinguishing between full-length and brief individual therapies and between high and low functioning groups. The group therapy sizes represent average attendance. The community meeting, set at 25 patients in this example, will vary with the size of the unit.

Full-Time Equivalent (FTE) (B) reflects expectations regarding predictable time staff members spend away from the program. This is the actual number of weeks each therapist is available to treat patients.

Staff/Patient Contact Hours (C) reflects the number of contact hours per day that program leadership expects of staff members. The ratio of supervisees to supervisor is also set by the program. Most programs include staff members who are at different levels of clinical sophistication. Some are senior experts in the field who can clinically supervise other staff. Others are fully educated but require supervision during the clinical phase of their training. Most are fully qualified to practice without direct supervision, but they may need help with difficult, unusual, or treatment-resistant patients.

Patient Volume (D) reflects the program's capacity, average daily census, and average length of stay (ALOS). Program experience establishes the percentage of patients who function at lower levels, which influences the intensity of their treatment.

Hours of Structured Therapy/Week (E) presents a mix of services sufficient to meet an operational definition of "active treatment" of at least two structured therapy sessions per day, one of which is not rehabilitation. With a seven-day-per-week program, every patient receives two individual and five group sessions, stratified according to functional level. Half the patients receive one family therapy session during the week. All patients receive two rehabilitation group therapies per day, with low-functioning patients also receiving an individual rehabilitation session once a week. Finally, all patients participate in a community meeting every day. As shown later in the algorithm, this program provides about five hours of structured therapy daily for high-functioning patients and about four hours daily for low-functioning patients. The mix of treatment services can vary in almost any combination to optimize the amount of treatment patients receive at any particular staffing level.

Assessments/Discharge (F) addresses the work of admitting and discharging patients. Program policies define the professionals responsible for specific assessments of all patients. Other assessments are useful only for a percentage of patients (e.g., psychological testing). The time required for each assessment reflects processes in place in the program. The process begins with notification that a patient needs assessment and ends with the final signature on the completed document. For physicians, this would include writing orders. For any clinician, it could involve reviewing old records. Changing these variables in the model might reveal opportunities to make programs more cost-efficient through computerization and process reengineering. Also, variations in the relationship of any private practicing clinicians to the program can be modeled here, e.g., private practicing vs. employed psychiatrists.

Ancillary Activities (G) are necessary tasks for clinical staff that are outside the scope of direct patient contact hours. They include the variety of meetings and indirect activities related to patient care and the milieu. These hours do not include activities required by the institution, such as service on medical staff committees, administrative functions, etc.

Staff Needed [H] is derived from the assumptions specified in this example. Program leadership defines distribution of various levels of staff expertise (and expense) in response to financial and human resource constraints.

Weekly Productivity Ratios (I) are derived from the previous assumptions and conclusions. The idea, analogous to financial ratios,[4] is that there is a variety of ways to assess staff productivity.[5-8] For example, during a full individual therapy session, one hour of therapy is provided and one hour of therapy is received. During a high-functioning group therapy session, there are one and one-half hours of therapy provided and 15 hours of therapy received (assuming 10 group members). These ratios permit assessment of various programming decisions to determine their effects on productivity.

Figure 1. Program Staffing Algorithm (Non-Nursing)

A. Treatment Mode	Patients/Session	Hour(s)/Session	Therapists/ Session	
Individual: FULL	1	1	1	*The shaded fields are input areas for user variables. The unshaded fields are derived from the user input.*
Individual: BRIEF	1	0.5	1	
Family/Couples	1	1	1	
Group: Low Fxn	10	1	1	
High Fxn	10	1.5	1	The amount of time allocated to each treatment mode is inclusive of time for documentation. This implies a "50-minute hour" and "75-minute hour and a half."
RehaB: Low Fxn	10	1	1	
High Fxn	10	1.5	1	
Individual	1	.5	1	
Community Mtg	25	.75	6	

B. Full Time Equiv			
Vacation Days	15	**Total Weeks**	
Holidays	7	**44.8**	
Personal Leave Days	3		
Cont Educ Days	5		
Sick Day	6		

C. Contact Hours	Contact hrs/day	Days/week	Weeks/year	Contact hrs/week	Hrs/wk supervis
Therapist (Autonomous)	5.5	5	44.8	26.5	1
With Supervision	5.5	5	44.8	26.5	1
Supervisor	5.5	5	44.8	22.5	5
Rehab (Autonomous)	5.5	5	44.8	26.5	1
With Supervision	5.5	5	44.8	26.5	1
Supervisor	5.5	5	44.8	22.5	5
Supervisee/ Supervisor	2.5				

D. Patient Volume	Average Daily Census	Capacity	ALOS (Tx Days)	Admission Rate (per day)	Occupancy %
High-Functioning	30				
Low-Functioning	8				
TOTAL	38	50	12	3.2	75

E. Hours of Structured Therapy/ week	Sessions/ Day/ Patient	Sessions/ week/ patient	Therapy session provided	Hours of Therapy provided	Therapist Hours
Individual: FULL	"Active Treatment implies at least one non-Rehab structured therapy per day"	2	60	60	60
Individual: BRIEF		2	16	8	8
Family/Couples		0.5	19	19	19
Group: Low Fxn		5	5	5	5
High Fxn		5	15	22.5	22.5
Total Non-Rehab	1		115	114.5	114.5
Rehab					
Individual		1	8	4	4
Low-functioning	2	14	14	14	14
High-functioning	2	14	42	63	63
Total Rehab			64	81	81
Community Mtg		7	14	10.5	63

Figure 1. Program Staffing Algorithm (Non-Nursing) *continued*

F. Assessments/ Disch	Proportion of admits	Hours/ Assessment	Hours/ Discharge	Total hours/ Discipline/week
Psychiatry	1	1.5	.75	50.4
Social Work	1	1.5	.5	44.8
Rehab	1	1	.5	33.6
Psych Testing	.05	1.5	.5	2.24
Allied MH Prof/ MSN	1	1.5	.5	44.8

G. Ancillary Activities	Hours/ professional/ week	# participants	Total prof hrs/week	Average cost/ prof hour	Total Cost/ Week
Treatment	1.5	17.1	25.65	$17.00	$436.05
Planning		17.1			
Staff Meeting	1.5	17.1	25.65	$17.00	$436.05
Daily	5	17.1	85.5	$17.00	$1,453.50
Communication		17.1			
Admin Meetings	1		17.1	$17.00	$290.70
Phone/Mail/etc	3.5		59.85	$17.00	$1,017.45
Total	**12.5**		**213.75**	**$17.00**	**$3,633.75**

H. Staff Needed	Total Number	Distribution	Annual Contact Hrs/FTE	Total Annual Contact Hrs
Therapists	10.6	1		12367.68
With Supervision	3.2	.3	1187.2	356.16
Autonomous	6.4	.6	1187.2	712.32
Expert	1.1	.1	1008	100.8
Rehab Therapists	6.5	1	1187.2	7597.2
With Supervision	2	.3	1187.2	356.16
Autonomous	3.9	.6	1008	712.32
Expert	.6	.1		100.8

I. Weekly Productivity Ratios	
Hrs Direct Service/FTE	22.5
Hrs Tx Provided/FTE	12
Hrs Tx Received/FTE	81.8
New Pts Served/FTE	1.3
Daily Census/FTE	2.2

J. Hrs Strux'd Tx/day/Pt	
High Fxn	5.2
Low Fxn	3.8

Analysis Using the Algorithm

Initial validation of this model compared projected staffing to predictions derived from the literature, based on staffing ratios.[9-12] This model generated a staffing profile in the middle of the range derived from the literature when applied to a program of a given size. The second step in validating the model was to use it to analyze current programs in the host institution. After the assumptions were standardized, the model accurately predicted actual staffing. For example, the model predicted that the detoxification program needs 3.9 FTEs. The program director, using "productivity expectations," decided that the program needs 4.1 FTEs. Productivity management, using a staffing analysis based on labor standards, derived a need for 4.0 FTEs.

Methods

In order to examine the effects of managed care on staffing, hypothetical operating assumptions (reflecting the author's clinical experience) were entered into the algorithm. ALOS and average daily census (ADC) were varied independently, with the number of nonrehabilitation therapists as the output variable. Holding ADC constant, the number of therapists was recorded as ALOS varied from five to 60 days. This process was repeated at small increments in ADC from 15 to 50 patients. The results reveal the performance characteristics of the model.

Results

Overall Model

Figure 2, page 77, shows the number of therapists needed to deliver the program. When ALOS is longer than 30 days, staffing is driven almost entirely by ADC. ALOS exerts no significant effect. As ALOS decreases, however, its contribution to staffing becomes increasingly significant.

Scenario 1: Assume a 25-bed unit running at 80 percent capacity (ADC = 20) with an ALOS of 30 days. The unit requires 4.3 therapists to deliver the program. As ALOS drops to 10 days, the unit drops the number of beds in service to 20 and runs at 75 percent capacity, resulting in an ADC of 15. Declining ALOS leads to falling ADC. The pressure to admit increases as the system attempts to compensate for the change. The number of therapists required to do the additional assessments and discharges goes up to 4.5, offsetting the drop resulting from the decrease in the number of patients being treated at one time. Revenue has decreased, however, because every day the program operates at five fewer patient-days.

Scenario 2: Assume a 50-bed service running at full capacity with an ALOS of 15 days. The service requires 12.3 therapists to deliver the program as designed. As ALOS drops to nine days, the service runs at only 80 percent capacity, requiring the same number of FTEs but losing 10 patient-days of revenue per day of operation. As ALOS continues to drop to five days, ADC drops to 30 patients, still requiring the same number of staff to deliver the program.

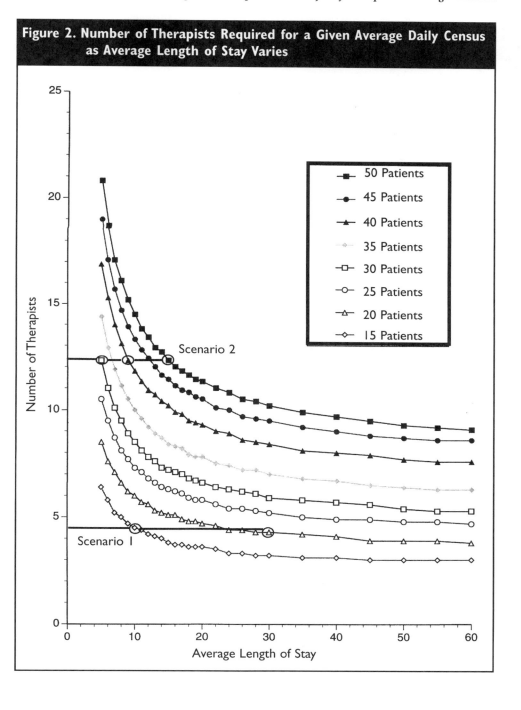

Figure 2. Number of Therapists Required for a Given Average Daily Census as Average Length of Stay Varies

Staff-Patient Ratios

Figure 3, below, displays the effect of ALOS on staff-patient ratios. The average staff-patient ratio is calculated from the number of therapists per average daily census, averaged over the range of ADC at a given ALOS. At any ALOS, the ratio is consistent regardless of ADC. At longer ALOSs, the ratios are comparable across a broad range of ALOSs. At shorter ALOSs, however, not only are the ratios dramatically different from those at longer ALOSs, but also they vary significantly with small changes in ALOS.

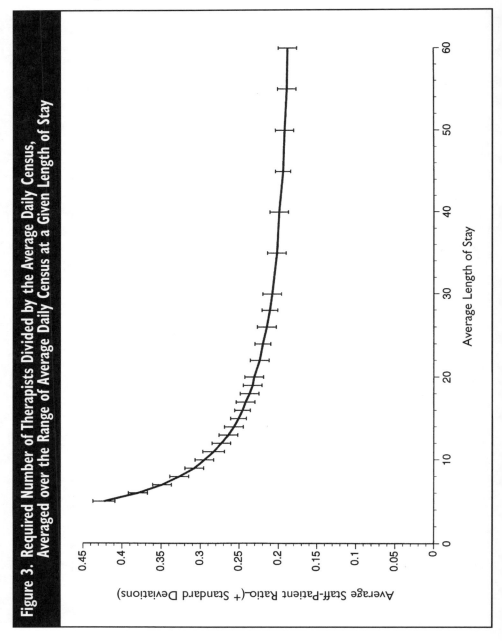

Figure 3. Required Number of Therapists Divided by the Average Daily Census, Averaged over the Range of Average Daily Census at a Given Length of Stay

Discussion

A rapidly changing environment makes many demands on treatment programs. For the delivery system to provide care that routinely and reliably meets requirements, it cannot depend on "heroic" efforts from staff members. System performance should meet requirements by design.[13] This requires a treatment program to have adequate staff to care for patients. The question is, "What is 'adequate' and who defines it?"

Staff-patient ratios are a traditional approach to program staffing. Others have noted that "the utility of staff-patient ratios is very limited, and the ratios can create much confusion."[11] Designing programs for different clinical populations without clarifying the relationship between staffing and quality contributes to this confusion.[11] Until recently, the relatively long ALOS that was the norm had a negligible impact on staffing (see figure 2). The main factor influencing service demand was the number of patients in treatment at one time. Small differences contributed by ALOS were obscured by variation in clinical population, type of institution, and program design. As ALOS has declined, programs attempt to maintain ADC by increasing admission rates. This results in a higher flow of patients through the program, which dramatically increases the number of staff required at very brief ALOS. ALOS has become a more important variable than ADC in effecting staffing.[5,14]

This reveals a paradoxical effect of managed care on the costs of delivering behavioral health services. As managed care drives ALOS down, cost to the payer falls for an inpatient stay (assuming per-diem reimbursement). Costs of providing that treatment go up substantially, however. Programs with the shortest ALOS need the highest staff-patient ratio, and so will have the highest cost per day of service, everything else being equal. The impact of costs associated with admitting and discharging patients had been minimized by spreading them across the entire ALOS. Now, as admitting and discharging patients assumes a greater proportion of staff time, those costs increase in parallel with the increasing number of assessments and discharges. Under current reimbursement incentives, however, revenues are related almost entirely to the number of patients served at one time rather than to the number of patients served over a period of time. This creates a financial double-bind for program providers.

As the scenarios described earlier show, reimbursement based on a per-diem rate cannot sustain the staffing demanded by a high flow of patients through a program. Programs will need more staff to handle the increased flow of patients but will have shrinking resources because of decreases in ADC. Even in a capitated arrangement, the higher staff-patient ratio at lower ALOS represents a financial challenge to the program provider. Designing an inpatient program as a crisis stabilization and assessment unit with very brief ALOS has emerged as one response to managed care. This algorithm shows that such programs will be very expensive if the assessments are done to current professional standards and use processes now in place. Even if program capacity shrinks in response to decreased ALOS, the reduction is largely offset by the rapidly increasing service demands for very short stays. Inevitably, treatment time will shift to assessment and discharge planning, while the quality of assessments and discharge planning will suffer as staff members devote less time to each patient.

This analysis suggests several possible responses. Information technology, by linking data sources and minimizing redundancy, has the potential to decrease dramatically the time spent on an assessment. In a continuum of care built on a coordinated network of community providers, data linkage creates an opportunity to reengineer the entire process of assessment.[15] A medical record that moves with the patient becomes possible if the network is integrated both clinically and at the level of information transfer.

Continuity of the treatment team across the continuum of care would enhance these effects. The duration of an episode of treatment, equivalent to the cumulative ALOS at each step of the continuum, would move the delivery system to the right on the curves of figures 2 and 3. This decreases the overall staff-patient ratio and, therefore, decreases the cost per patient served. Such economies of scale are consistent with broad business experience, further demonstrating the validity of the algorithm.

System integration would enable another process redesign. The clinical assessment process could be a distinct operation, rather than part of the routine operations of a treatment program.[16] This would make it possible to assess peoples' needs and resources initially and to match each person with the appropriate provider and level of service. Treatment program staff would not devote time to the assessment process. This algorithm makes it possible to evaluate the cost-benefit of any of these actions prior to implementation.

Perhaps the most viable solution to the financial dilemma demonstrated above is providers' accepting financial risk for the entire episode of illness. In mature managed care markets, it is not unusual for acute inpatient average lengths of stay to fall between three and five days, which makes the financial pressures even more burdensome. The behavioral inpatient unit becomes analogous to the medical/surgical intensive care unit, with interdisciplinary treatment relocated to the partial hospital program. Assessment, stabilization, and engagement become the goals of inpatient treatment, followed by rapid movement down the continuum. The cost per day of this intensive inpatient care will not be reimbursable using a fee-for-service per diem. These costs would be incorporated in the overall capitation rate as a predicted number of inpatient bed-days per thousand capitated lives. Financial viability would result from decreasing the overall reliance on inpatient treatment, rather than covering the actual costs of an inpatient day.

Future enhancements of the algorithm should incorporate any activities related to patient care that influence the number of therapists a program needs to meet requirements routinely. These might include involuntary commitment hearings or emergency situations. Another area for improvement is the model's reliance on averages, which ignores the operational challenges that arise from the normal variation inherent in any process. Probability functions related to statistical process control charts may provide a way to quantify the effects of normal variation on program staffing.

Application of this algorithm must consider the amount of time clinical staff devote to institutional and administrative responsibilities. Other issues for development include the relationship between therapists and nursing staff; the "physical environment;...level of staff skill or talent unrelated to professional training; role of nonprofessional personnel, volunteers, and family; number and severity of untoward incidents on the unit; and ethical and humanitarian expectations."[17] At a formal level, this will call for fairly specific staff privileging methodologies. At an implicit level, issues of professional autonomy, self-esteem, and turf require resolution.

The algorithm itself might be considered a "second-generation" staffing model. First-generation approaches are empirical, sometimes use work-load analysis,[9,11] and are only applicable to consistent program descriptions within a single sector of behavioral health care. Sectors studied include state hospitals,[9,11] units of general hospitals,[10] and private psychiatric hospitals.[12] Drawing data from only one sector helps to control many variables with the potential to influence staffing. While this may allow conclusions regarding the sector studied, it has not been possible to generalize across sectors.

This algorithm builds upon the first-generation by proposing quantifiable relationships among key factors influencing staffing. Moreover, the model moves the analysis from the institutional and programmatic level to the delivery of specific services to specific patients. This is consistent with national standards for mental health data, which specify "Who receives What, from Whom, at what Cost, and with what Outcome?"[18] Staffing is "adequate" if it is capable of providing specific services that meet identifiable and measurable patient needs. Comparing empirically determined (and possibly sector-specific) standards for productivity ratios, contact hours/day, etc. will shed light on the relationship between staffing levels and the services provided to patients. Combining this with outcomes measurement would contribute to understanding the relationship between costs and outcomes. Using a computerized algorithm to study the efficiency and effectiveness of behavioral health services will enable people to express opinions as quantifiable assumptions and to test assumptions against measurable results.

References

1. Eklof, M., and Qu, W. "Validating a Psychiatric Patient Classification System." *Journal of Nursing Administration* 16(5):10-17, May 1986.

2. Schroder, P., and Washington, W. "Administrative Decision Making: Staff-Patient Ratios." *Perspectives in Psychiatric Care* 20(3):111-23, July-Sept. 1982

3. Dee, V., and Randall, B. "NPH Patient Classification System: A Theory-Based Nursing Practice Model for Staffing Nursing Department." UCLA Neuropsychiatric Institute and Hospital, Los Angeles, Calif., 1989.

4. Cleverley, W. "Analyzing Financial Statements." *In Essentials of Health Care Finance,* Second Edition. Rockville, Md.: Aspen Publishers, Inc., 1986.

5. Binner, P. "Needed for Mental Health Management: A New Measurement Paradigm." *Administration and Policy in Mental Health* 17(4):235-45, April 1990.

6. Buckner, M., and Larcen, S. "Strategies for Increasing Productivity and Revenues in Community Mental Health Centers." *Community Mental Health Journal* 21(4):237-51, Winter 1985.

7. Schinnar, A., and others. Organizational Determinants of Efficiency and Effectiveness in Mental Health Partial Care Programs." *Health Services Research* 25(2):387-420, June 1990.

8. Taubman, S. "Developing Productivity in Mental Health Organizations." *Administration in Mental Health* 13(4):260-74, April 1986.

9. "Staffing Standards: A Clinical Study of Maryland's State Mental Health Hospitals and Residential Treatment Centers." Baltimore, Md.: Department of Health and Mental Hygiene, 1986.

10. Goplerud, E. "Effects of Proprietary Management in General Hospital Psychiatry Units." *Hospital and Community Psychiatry* 37(8):832-6, Aug. 1986.

11. Treanor, J., and Cotch, K. "Staffing of Adult Inpatient Facilities." *Hospital and Community Psychiatry* 41(5):545-9, May 1990.

12. Gibson, R., and Levenson, "Private Psychiatric Hospitals." In *Psychiatric Administration: A Comprehensive Text for the Clinician-Executive.* Talbott, J., and Kaplan, S., Editors. Orlando, Fla.: Grune & Stratton, Inc., 1983.

13. *Quality Management and Applied Statistical Process Control: A Guide to Process Improvement, Unit 7: Process Capability.* Palm Beach Gardens, Fla.: Philip Crosby Associates, Inc., 1990.

14. Goldratt, E., and Cox, J. *The Goal: A Process of Ongoing Improvement,* Second Revised Edition. Croton-on-Hudson, N.Y.: North River Press, 1992.

15. Hammer, M., and Champy, J. *Reengineering the Corporation: A Manifesto for Business Revolution.* New York, N.Y.: Harper Collins Publishers, Inc., 1993.

16. Dennison, R., Editor. *Access Center Resource Manual.* Littleton, Colo.: Psychiatric Integrated Services, Inc., 1992.

17. Sacks, M. "Taking Issue: Considerations in Determining Staff-Patient Ratios." *Hospital and Community Psychiatry* 43(4):309, April 1992.

18. Leginski, W. "Data Standards for Mental Health Decision Support Systems," Series FN Number 10. Bethesda, Md.: National Institute of Mental Health, 1989.

Robert M. Atkins, MD, MPH, is President, Patient-Centered Partnership, Inc., Louisville, Kentucky. He was Chief Executive Officer and Medical Director, ClearSprings Health Partnership, Louisville, Kentucky. The model described in this chapter, which is available from the author on computer disk, was first reported in the December 1995 issue of Psychiatric Services. The chapter borrows on the original report and adds information on developments since that time.

Chapter 6

Developing a Continuum of Care

by William R. Dubin, MD, and Shivkumar Hatti, MD

T he mid-1980s brought increasing concern in corporate America that the cost of psychiatric care was rising at a rate greater than that of the rest of the health care sector. In the 1980s, mental health costs doubled for the average large employer. Of the nation's $900 billion health bill, it was estimated that between 10 and 30 percent was spent on mental health.[1,2] Behavioral health managed care evolved out of the need to control and contain the rising cost of psychiatric care and other mental health and substance abuse treatment services. With the advent of managed care, the delivery of health care has undergone profound and permanent changes. Nowhere have these changes been as dramatic or as widespread as in the delivery of behavioral health care. The use of inpatient services has diminished dramatically, methodologies and rationales for outpatient therapy have changed, and the use of crisis services for rapid stabilization has increased. Determining the appropriate level of care for the patient's illness based on severity is now one of the most important aspects of managing care. There is no standard length of stay under managed care, and every treatment is individually tailored. Treatment has shifted to a focus on problem resolution and symptom relief rather than assessment of personality and psychological development with the goal of restructuring the patient's personality.

Ideally, "genuine managed care is a practice pattern that psychiatrists and other mental health professionals can employ in the delivery of quality care. The practice emphasizes outpatient treatment and extensive use of shorter term interventions as a first treatment. Hospitalization is used primarily for stabilizing acute situations. The basis for genuine care is scientific management principles, i.e., integration of services, collaboration among psychiatrists and providers, and the use of provider teams....[A]lthough the short term therapies are necessary they are not sufficient, and longer term and specialized treatments and programs need to be available for selected patients."[3] Goldstein further notes that managed care is not an access or benefit barrier. It is a practice that psychiatrists and other mental health professionals employ in the delivery of high-quality care. In a managed care environment, clinical responsibility is as important as fiscal responsibility. Cost control is always balanced with quality of treatment, as well as with access to care. Patterson argues that cost-effective mental health care utilizing the principles of managed care is possible.[4] His model includes assignment of clinical functioning by clinical expertise (e.g., psychiatrists do medical management while psychologists and social workers do psychotherapy and family therapy), fiscal responsibility, direct patient access, incentives for prevention, choice of services, and outcomes assessment.

Effective managed care as described by Goldstein and Patterson[3,4] requires shifting clinical services to a continuum of care model. Such a model offers alternatives to inpatient care in that patients no longer have to remain in a hospital until they recover. In a continuum of care, a variety of clinical services, or levels of care, are available to the patient during the various stages of his or her illness. The patient is admitted to treatment at the level of care that is most clinically appropriate. The patient is then gradually moved to lesser levels of care as he or she begins to improve The core clinical services in the continuum of care model include inpatient, residential, step-down, partial hospitalization, intensive outpatient, outpatient, crisis intervention, and evaluation/triage services.

This chapter will describe the various clinical programs in a continuum of care model. It will also address changes in treatments and examine impediments to making a successful transition to this model. The continuum of care model discussed in this chapter can evolve from a hospital base, a private practice model, or affiliation and collaboration of several systems. One of the authors [Dubin] has developed such a model in a hospital setting while the other author [Hatti] has developed a continuum of care in a private practice group model.

Evaluation/Triage

A cornerstone of a continuum of care model is the evaluation/triage program for the system. The evaluation/triage service is the gateway to all other treatment programs. Skilled clinical evaluation and appropriate triage are necessary to ensure that patients are initially diagnosed correctly, prescribed the correct treatment, and receive treatment at the appropriate level of care. Inappropriate evaluation and triage can lead to potentially serious morbidity; possibly to mortality; or to inefficient, unnecessary, or excessively expensive care. Despite the fundamental role of this service, many programs are staffed with the least experienced staff. Efforts to save money by staffing the evaluation/triage service with less experienced clinicians may ultimately lead to more expensive care because of misdiagnosis, undertreatment, or overtreatment. The authors believe that an evaluation/triage service should be staffed by experienced clinicians because of the central role this service has in the continuum of care.

The Crisis Service

The crisis service has a major role as the service dedicated to averting unnecessary hospitalization.[5] It is the service to which acutely ill patients are referred for intensive short-term treatment, including medication, crisis psychotherapy, and family/couples therapy. When necessary, psychosocial resources (e.g., housing, medical assistance checks, food stamps, family support, and friends) may also be mobilized to further support the patient during the crisis. Crisis intervention may last as long as 12-24 hours. The crisis service should also have the capacity to follow the discharged patient for several consecutive days to further stabilize and consolidate the therapeutic gains. An alternative for the intensive follow up is to have follow-up visits occur in an associated outpatient department. The failure to have a crisis service can be costly to a hospital system attempting to manage patients in a capitated contract.[6]

An expanded model for a crisis service would include a 23-hour holding or observation bed. The availability of crisis beds can help decrease or eliminate the need for hospitalization for patients with drug- or alcohol-induced behavior problems, situational stress, or adjustment reactions. The holding bed is especially useful for patients with personality disorders who need a brief period of containment and support following persistent threats of suicide or suicidal gestures. Patients can be quickly stabilized with medication-intense psychotherapy and family therapy.

Schneider and Ross describe a four-bed crisis unit with a targeted length of stay of three days.[7] The program treated 405 patients over a two-year period and had a 2.9 day average length of stay. Outcome, as measured by the 30-day readmission rate (14.6 percent), compared favorably with the readmission rate (15 percent) for patients in traditional inpatient services and for other patient samples in the community.

In one author's [Dubin] program, the crisis service is part of an evaluation/triage service called Entry Point, i.e., the entry point for the treatment system. The rationale for combining the two services is that many patients who are referred or call for an evaluation are often in a crisis and require more than a 45-90 minute evaluation. However, the acuity of the problem may not be known until the patient comes in for the evaluation. When a patient requires more than an evaluation, he or she is easily transferred to the crisis service. Because the triage and evaluation staff also function as crisis staff, the change involves a simple computer entry. The Entry Point staff is a multidisciplinary team that has a staff psychiatrist assigned to it each day on a rotating schedule. A patient who requires overnight observation sleeps in a bed on a unit in the hospital that has been designated the crisis bed. Hospital nurses who have been cross-trained to work on the crisis unit provide treatment and coverage at night and on weekends.

Unlike the crisis service, a psychiatric emergency service (PES) treats more acutely ill patients and is usually located in or next to a hospital emergency department. Patients treated in the PES usually pose an imminent risk of either self-directed or other-directed harm. Patients who are in medical danger from an overdose or from drug/alcohol withdrawal, who have medical complications or illness, or who are involuntarily committed are referred to the PES for initial evaluation and treatment. Some psychiatric emergency services combine the functions of a PES and a crisis service. Other systems have a separate crisis service and a PES. Ideally, staffing is most cost-effective when the two services can be combined.

Outpatient Treatment

The model for delivery of outpatient care is also undergoing significant change. The team concept of patient care is gaining increasing importance.[8] In developing a program of care, assignment of clinical responsibilities occurs in collaboration with other mental health professionals.[9] A team consisting of a psychiatrist, psychologists, clinical nurse specialists, and social workers provides care for the patient. Individual clinical roles and resource dedication may vary in intensity from day to day and from week to week, depending on illness severity and acuteness. For example, once the patient is stabilized, he or she can be transferred from a psychiatrist to a social worker for family therapy, to a psychologist for psychotherapy, or to a clinical nurse specialist under the supervision of a psychiatrist for medical management. Most patients will be in "joint custody" with a psychiatrist and another clinician, such as a psychologist, nurse or social worker. In such an arrangement, the psychiatrist will supervise the treatment team. This model contrasts with the previous model in which one clinician provided all of the treatment.

Case management will become a very important aspect of outpatient care. The main function of case management is to ensure that the patient is at an appropriate level of care and moves smoothly from one level of care to another depending on the severity of illness. The case manager assesses all of the patient's clinical and psychosocial needs and ensures that needed services occur in a timely fashion and that the patient does not "slip through the cracks." Case management cannot be done with resources only from the outside; case management needs to be an internalized initiative of every provider who believes in managed care.

Psychiatric outpatient treatment is shifting from 45- to 50-minute sessions with psychiatrists to an interdisciplinary team approach in which therapy is provided for variable encounter durations by licensed doctorate-level psychologists, licensed social workers, clinical nurse specialists, advanced practice registered nurses, or master's-level counselors working in collaboration with a psychiatrist. Therapy in some outpatient settings may continue to make provision for longer term individual psychoanalytic-oriented psychotherapy, but most today focus on briefer therapies (that may be short-term), e.g., cognitive, behavioral, interpersonal, while employing a mix of modalities, e.g., family, couples, individual, or group therapy. There is increasing emphasis on time-effective therapy that emphasizes how the treatment time is utilized and how the time between treatment sessions can be used therapeutically.[10] Group therapy is experiencing renewed interest as a clinically efficacious and cost-effective treatment modality. Saying the same thing to 10 patients at one time rather than the same thing to 10 patients at 10 different times is more efficient use of therapists' time.

Outpatient services also should provide a continuum of care. In addition to therapy, outpatient programs should include the capacity to provide crisis intervention, immediate patient access, the capacity to evaluate and treat walk-in cases, and intensive outpatient services. Ideally, outpatient care is offered in several different geographical locations for easier access by patients.

Partial Hospitalization

Partial hospitalization is an ambulatory treatment program that includes the major diagnostic, medical, psychiatric, psychosocial, and prevocational treatment modalities designed for patients with serious mental disorders who require coordinated intensive, comprehensive, and multidisciplinary treatment not provided in an outpatient clinic setting.[11] Partial hospitalization offers an alternative to inpatient treatment and can be utilized by patients who are able to function in the community, present no imminent potential for harm to themselves or others, and possess an ability to maintain a consistent place of residence. Partial hospitalization is a generic term embracing day, night, evening, and weekend treatment programs that employ an integrated, comprehensive, and complementary schedule of recognized psychiatric treatments.[11] A variety of patient populations, including adolescents, adults, geriatric patients, substance abuse patients, or patients with chronic mental illness, can be successfully treated through partial hospitalization.[11,12] The clinical structure offered by partial hospitalization is effective not only in treating acutely ill patients but also in preventing or minimizing hospitalization for patients with chronic mental illness or severe character disorders.[12,13] Most programs operate four to six hours a day and provide a structured treatment milieu. Until recently, partial hospitalizations may have been used to treat a patient for months or even for years. Currently, partial hospitalization lengths of stay are more brief, i.e., only long enough for appropriate clinical transition of a patient to a treatment program of lesser intensity.

Intensive Outpatient Programs

There has been significant interest in the development of intensive outpatient programs (IOP), which are seen by some as an alternative to partial hospitalization. IOPs can be provided in an outpatient department for two to three hours a day and generally consist of some combination of therapy, education, support, and social activities. Intensive outpatient programs are gaining popularity and are seen as an adjunct to a crisis program to stabilize a patient and avert unnecessary hospitalization. The IOP is also considered a less resource intense but clinically effective alternative to partial hospitalization for appropriate patients. From a provider perspective, an IOP is less costly to operate and staffing requirements are easier to manage. Staff members who treat patients in an IOP are usually part of the outpatient staff. When they are not treating patients in the IOP, staff members can treat outpatients. From a staff efficiency standpoint, IOPs offer an advantage over partial hospitalization. However, no known research demonstrates the effectiveness of an IOP compared to other treatment modalities.

Residential/Step-Down Programs

Residential treatment centers were originally developed as an intermediate-level medical institution designed to provide psychosocial and/or educational rehabilitation for child and adolescent patients with major psychiatric behavioral or personality disorders.[14] With the evolution of managed care, residential programs have expanded to include adult populations and are now used as an alternative to hospitalization for patients who are not suicidal, who have no significant medical problems, and who do not require the intense supervision of a hospital setting. Residential programs are located in vacant wings of hospitals; in converted hospital buildings, such as old student dormitories, or in homes in residential neighborhoods. Staffing requirements are lower than in a hospital and usually consist of a registered nurse during the day and the evening and psychiatric aides making up the rest of the staff. Treatment can be provided by staff members who are contracted to work only the hours that they are providing therapy.

A step-down unit is similar to a residential setting but is found in a hospital. Like residential programs, the step-down unit can be used either as a transition from inpatient treatment or as a treatment setting to avert hospitalization for outpatients who require 24-hour monitoring or structure.

In the author's (Dubin) institution, the step-down unit is a 12-bed program staffed by one registered nurse and one psychiatric technician during the day. In the evening and the night, one psychiatric technician is on the unit. If a nurse is needed, the nurse from the adjacent inpatient unit provides the coverage. Patients admitted to this unit are adults with mostly Axis I and/or Axis II disorders. Most treatment takes place in an adult partial hospital that is located on the same campus. Patients with substance abuse problems are treated in the substance abuse partial hospital program. By receiving treatment in the partial hospital, a patient is better prepared for outpatient treatment because he or she establishes a therapeutic relationship with clinicians in the next program in the continuum of treatment. A staff physician and a case manager from an inpatient unit are assigned to each patient admitted to the step-down unit The same psychiatrist will continue to treat the patient in the partial hospital and in outpatient treatment. At discharge from the step-down unit, the patient is transferred to a case manager in the partial hospital. Ideally, the same case manager would follow the patient in the partial hospital and then as a case manager and/or therapist in the outpatient department. However, this is not practical, because case managers could quickly accumulate large and unmanageable caseloads.

Inpatient

One profound impact of managed care has been the dramatic decrease in the lengths of inpatient hospitalizations. In contrast to previous 28-to-30-day average lengths of stay, most hospitalizations are now five to 10 days. Hospitals now function more as a crisis service, with the goal of stabilizing and then referring patients to lower levels of care. As a result of this change, the entire nature of hospital care has changed. Process-oriented therapy is usually not possible in this rapid turnover, high-volume atmosphere. Therapy now has an educational focus. Family evaluations and involvement start immediately, preferably at the time of admission. There are rarely drug-free intervals "to clarify the diagnosis." Nonemergency medical care that used to routinely occur in the hospital now takes place after patients are discharged. Laboratory and other studies that are directly related to patients' illnesses and current hospital treatments are done. Unnecessary testing of any sort has been curtailed or discontinued. Patients now return home more rapidly, are integrated more rapidly into their environments, and can return to work sooner while still receiving needed treatment.

Significant changes in staffing patterns have also occurred. Many hospitals, for example, have reduced or eliminated departments of psychology and rehabilitative services, which are now often contracted out on an hourly or fee-for-service basis. The number of registered nurses has been reduced, and psychiatric technicians are given more responsibility under the supervision of nurses. Supervised psychiatric technicians are trained to provide activities for lower functioning, more regressed patients.

In the changed role of the hospital, case managers and physician extenders are important new positions in the provision of efficient hospital care. Case managers act as primary therapists, provide support/education to families, are responsible for discharge planning and ensure timely dispositions, act as liaison with aftercare providers and managed care companies, and provide most of the chart documentation. Nurse case managers can evaluate patients for medication side-effects, coordinate and monitor necessary medical care, provide drug education, and evaluate and monitor patients who are on drug detoxification regimens. All of these clinical activities are carried out under the direction and supervision of the attending psychiatrist. In the case management model, the job description rather than the professional discipline is primary. In the authors' programs, social workers, rehabilitative therapists, and nurses all work primarily as case managers or physician extenders.

In the case management model, the considerable time physicians save allows them the flexibility to treat patients in other parts of the system, e.g., outpatient, nursing homes, partial hospital, etc. The utilization review department finds it extremely efficient and helpful to have one person (i.e., the case manager) always available for exchange of information regarding individual patients. Initially, case managers did phone reviews with managed care companies. However, it was time-consuming and inefficient to review 15 cases with six different case managers. As a result, the system reverted to using utilization review department staff assigned to specific companies. Families and patients are pleased with the daily availability of a case manager to meet and spend high-quality time with them. The case managers themselves feel quite positive about this new position. They enjoy the added responsibility, the greater involvement with patient care, and the ability to have a greater direct therapeutic impact on the patient.

Finally, psychiatrists no longer have the luxury of being employed to work only on an inpatient unit. Shrinking reimbursement for inpatient care makes it difficult for a psychiatrist to earn adequate compensation for inpatient work alone, and health care systems cannot afford to hire psychiatrists each time they start new programs. As a result, psychiatrists are being asked to supervise and provide care at several clinical sites in the course of a day. A psychiatrist might spend the morning in the hospital and the afternoon in a partial program, outpatient program, or crisis service or doing consultation and follow up in a nursing home. A psychiatrist can only cover these services if he or she can collaborate with a case manager and/or a physician extender to share responsibilities for the treatment plan.

Other Services in the Continuum

Home health care is attracting increasing attention. Many patients are unable to come to an office because of their illnesses, lack of family support, or lack of transportation. Home visiting nurses or therapists can oversee medication compliance, give medications, and conduct therapy with the patient and/or family. Often, a potential hospitalization or increased morbidity and dysfunction can be averted with timely home treatment. Patient satisfaction with home treatment is high.

A service that may have an important role in the continuum of care is a mobile crisis service that evaluates or treats a patient in his or her home. The crisis team may return to the patient's home several days in a row to stabilize the patient and avert hospitalization. A patient can be evaluated and treated in his or her home and family can be supported in their efforts to manage a patient's illness. While this is theoretically an important treatment intervention, there is little evidence in the literature that actually demonstrates that a mobile crisis team is cost-effective.[15] The ultimate role of a mobile crisis team remains to be determined and requires further research to evaluate its efficacy and cost-effectiveness.

Electroconvulsive therapy (ECT) is one procedure receiving more attention in some outpatient programs. With significant advances in the delivery of this treatment, outpatient ECT has enjoyed a major revival and can avert hospitalization.[16] Outpatient ECT becomes a very important part of the continuum of care, especially in hospitals that treat large numbers of geriatric patients.

School-based psychiatric outpatient services are another area of increasing interest. Problems can be identified and treated early and effectively. Treatment programs are being set up in schools to ensure that students receive needed evaluation and treatment in a timely way. An active school treatment program is also an opportunity for mental health professionals to educate teachers and parents regarding child and adolescent behavior and to offer appropriate strategies to manage such problems as hyperactivity, attention deficit disorder, and learning disability.

One important area of collaborative care is the integration of behavioral health with primary care. Cooperation between behavioral medicine practitioners and primary care physicians will receive increasing emphasis and importance over the next several years. Applying timely and appropriate treatment to avoid more costly treatment in the future will increasingly be touted as a means to reduce medical costs of patients who inappropriately use medical/surgical services. An example is the anxious patient who frequently goes to the emergency department for chest pain and overutilizes emergency department and cardiology services. Until this patient is appropriately treated for anxiety disorder, he or she is going to unnecessarily consume medical resources.

Nursing homes are other important points of service in the continuum of care. With appropriate evaluation and clinical intervention, many elderly patients who are suffering from organic mental disorder, psychosis, and depression can be treated successfully in nursing homes. Successful treatment can avert both psychiatric and medical hospitalization and can dramatically increase a patient's quality of life. In capitated models of reimbursement, aggressive and timely intervention and treatment in nursing homes is essential to avoid more costly treatments.

Quarterway and halfway houses can also be an important part of a continuum of care. A quarterway house is similar to a residential treatment program and is a 24-hour supervised living arrangement that includes an in-house treatment program for patients who are not in a day treatment program or in a community psychosocial rehabilitation program.[17] Patients may spend several hours a day away from the facility and return in the evening. A halfway house provides temporary living arrangements for patients who need professional supervision or who need help in making the transition from the hospital back into the community.[17] Unlike a quarterway house, a halfway house generally does not have an in-house treatment program, and patients generally have less supervision. Some halfway houses provide residents with daytime supervision and telephone contact at night. Others offer supervised employment or volunteer work.

Preventive psychiatry and wellness programs are gaining increasing importance. Such programs stress education of the community at large as well as education of patient and family. Education can occur in a school-based health clinic or through lectures, presentations, and screening clinics in churches, schools, or neighborhood shopping centers. Kaiser asserts that self care will play a prominent role in the future and has the potential to reduce visits to primary care physicians by as much a 50 percent. He predicts that nurses with well-designed primary care computer programs will be able to educate family members at home and on the job site.[18]

Computer-assisted treatment programs that can be used in the home are already in the early stages of development.[19,20]

Impediments to Development of a New Delivery System

A major impediment to development of a resource-efficient continuum of care model is staff resistance. Some staff members are still wedded to the concept of longer inpatient treatment, despite data that underscore the efficacy of short-term hospitalization.[21,22] Similarly, resistance can be found to "brief" modes of ambulatory care. Some clinicians still harbor the prejudice that short hospital stays and short-term outpatient therapies are inferior and ineffective.

The most contentious issue, however, is clinician resentment over their perceived loss of control of patient care. These feelings are further exacerbated by the perceived intrusiveness and intensity of some utilization management concurrent reviews and the continued need for clinical justification of inpatient or outpatient care. Other changes compound the anxiety and the discontent of staff with the transition to managed care. Staff must not only adapt to change, but also cope with changes in job descriptions that challenge their professional identity. As was discussed with regard to case mangers, the job description is now more important then the professional discipline. Staff members also have to cope with the impact of these changes on their personal lives, as they may now be required to work weekends and evenings. These issues, coupled with the reality or threat of downsizing, create stress and anxiety among staff that can lead to morale problems that can adversely affect the delivery of care.

Clinical and administrative leaders must first acknowledge that they will not be able to relieve all stress and anxiety as long as the health care environment remains volatile and rapidly changing. However, if staff members are given some sense of control over and involvement in planning for their future, they usually respond in a constructive and positive manner. Development of new clinical programming, staff scheduling, and treatment strategies is most effective when multidisciplinary committees are given the responsibility to help create a new treatment model.

Staff should be informed of the national financial picture that led to the development of managed care, of the theoretical orientation of managed care, and of the implications of successful managed care. They should understand that many of the treatment elements in a managed care model have existed for more than 30 years in community mental health. Ultimately, this model may be preferred by patients and staff, because it has the potential to offer more treatment choices. Staff education should also include bringing in people from managed care companies to help problem solve around issues specific to companies. These types of meetings put a human face on a managed care company, and, as personal relationships develop, working relationships can improve.

It is also important for hospital administration to share with managers of the various departments the fiscal health of the program. Volume data, case mix data, as well as general information about income and expenses should be shared at least quarterly and preferably monthly. This approach is most effective as a scheduled meeting between department managers and clinical and administrative leaders of the hospital. While it could be argued that this will increase anxiety, the staff's anxiety is usually greatest concerning the unknown. Staff members appreciate the sharing of information and feel more empowered, as if they are partners in the change. The authors' experience has been that staff members are creative and energetic and help facilitate change when they understand the reason for and have a role in the change.

Finally, there will be staff members, including physicians, who are so hostile to the managed care model or so unable to adapt that they will be disruptive to any effort to change. Ultimately, these clinicians may have to leave the system.

Some psychiatrists may resent clinical utilization reviews if they feel their clinical work and judgment are being second-guessed, especially when the reviewer is not a physician. Often problematic for the treating psychiatrist is his or her anger at the review and the reviewer and the failure to concisely give the clinical information that the reviewers require to certify more care. Venting anger or refusing to cooperate can lead to inappropriate decisions or waste more time by requiring that the review be passed on to a supervisor or to another physician. Adversarial professional relationships can prolong the review and impede the treatment process. This process will eventually affect patient care. A patient is best served when practitioners, reviewers, and payers work cooperatively for optimal patient care.

A second important issue is the technique of reviewing the case with the managed care reviewer. It is always helpful if the clinician has the same review criteria, and many companies will provide this information on request. In general, most reviewers want to know why the patient needs continued care in a given program and what the clinician will do to resolve the patient's problems in order to move the patient to the next level of care. Psychiatrists should present opinions or conclusions with supporting data.[23] Reviewers are looking for concrete behavior or symptoms with supporting data, such as: "The patient is suicidal, has overdosed three times in the past, has an unknown quantity of pills at home, and continues to state 'life is not worth living, and I am going to kill myself if I have a chance.'"

Similarly, obtaining approval for additional outpatient treatment can pose difficulties if the clinician cannot succinctly and concretely describe the need for continued treatment. For example, for a patient with a borderline personality disorder, the treating psychiatrist might refer to psychodynamic theory and say, "The patient has suffered severe narcissistic injury, uses extensive splitting, and is not able to cope with his disappointment with idealized objects. The goal of therapy is to help him explore the developmental antecedents of his anger, his poor self-esteem, and his chronic cycle of idealization/devaluation." A reviewer might find this presentation too difficult to assess and too vague to endorse. In contrast, the psychiatrist might present the same case as follows: "This patient is chronically suicidal and has not been able to hold a job for more than six months. The therapy is going to focus on helping him recognize his unrealistic expectations of other people, how these expectations lead to angry responses that lead to the end of the relationship or employment or to self-destructive behavior. I will help him develop alternative strategies to cope with his anger by recognizing these cognitive distortions. The treatment plan is to help him keep his current employment for longer than three months by helping him understand his distortions of interpersonal relationships as they occur." The treating psychiatrist is describing the same clinical phenomena but, by being more concrete and specific, is helping the reviewer to understand so that all participants in treatment planning can move forward with appropriate decisions.

Development of Clinical Outcomes

There is an increasing demand for health service providers to demonstrate the effectiveness of treatment by assessing clinical outcomes. Health plans and employers are also very concerned about, and monitor, patient satisfaction. Evaluation of clinical outcomes is becoming an integral part of performance improvement activities and can be used to improve clinical services and deliver a better health care product.[24] Although some hospital administrators may be reluctant to commit scarce resources to the development of outcome programs, no mental health system will be able to successfully compete in the future without a clinical outcomes program. Waxman describes in detail how an inexpensive outcome program can be developed and tailored to a hospital's needs and is a less expensive alternative to evaluation by an external contractor.[24,25]

Conclusion

Managed care has brought profound change to the delivery of psychiatric care. At the core of this change is the evolution of a continuum of care that de-emphasizes inpatient treatment and offers a variety of treatments at less expensive levels of care. Early evidence indicates savings of 15 to 40 percent using a continuum of care compared with traditional approaches.[17] A new health care delivery order is evolving that redefines health professional roles, emphasizes community treatment and wellness, and offers patients a greater variety of treatments and treatment settings. The transition to this new model remains turbulent. Despite the complexities and stress of this change, a continuum of care model can improve quality, be cost-effective, and bring high patient satisfaction. Health care systems that can make the transition to this model will thrive and flourish well into the next century.

References

1. Hamilton, J., and Galen, M. "A Furor over Mental Health." *Business Week*, Aug. 8, 1994, pp.66-9.

2. Kenkel, P. "Reining in Mental Health Costs." *Modern Healthcare* 20(19):60, May 14, 1990.

3. Goldstein, L. "Genuine Managed Care in Psychiatry: A Proposed Practice Model." *General Hospital Psychiatry* 11(4):271-7, July 1989.

4. Patterson, D. "Managed Care: An Approach to Rational Psychiatric Treatment." *Hospital and Community Psychiatry* 41(10):1092-5, Oct. 1990.

5. Gillig, P., and others. "The Psychiatric Emergency Service Holding Area: Effect on Utilization of Inpatient Resources." *American Journal of Psychiatry* 146(3):369-72, March 1989.

6. Fink, J., and Dubin, W. "No Free Lunch: Limitations on Psychiatric Care in HMOs." *Hospital and Community Psychiatry* 42(4):363-5, April 1991.

7. Schneider, S., and Ross, I. "Ultra-Short Hospitalization for Severely Mentally Ill Patients." *Psychiatric Services* 47(2):137-8, Feb. 1996.

8. Olsen, D., and others. "A Treatment-Team Model of Managed Mental Health Care." *Psychiatric Services* 46(3):252-6, March 1995.

9. Pomerantz, J., and others. "The Professional Affiliation Group: A New Model for Managed Mental Health Care." *Hospital and Community Psychiatry* 45(4):308-10, April 1994.

10. Budman, S. and Gurman, A. *Theory and Practice of Brief Therapy.* New York, N.Y.: Guilford Press, 1988.

11. Casarino, J., and others. "American Association for Partial Hospitalization (AAPH) Standards and Guidelines for Partial Hospitalization." *International Journal of Partial Hospitalization* 1(1):5-20, Jan. 1982.

12. Weiss, K., and Dubin, W. "Partial Hospitalization: State of the Art." *Hospital and Community Psychiatry* 33(11):923-8, Nov. 1982.

13. Miller, B. "Characteristics of Effective Day Treatment Programming for Persons with Borderline Personality Disorders." *Psychiatric Services* 46(6):605-8, June 1995.

14. Wilson, G., and Phillips, K. "Residential Treatment Centers: Quality Assurance and Utilization Review Guidelines." In *Manual of Psychiatric Quality Assurance*, Mattson, M., Editor. Washington, D.C.: American Psychiatric Association, 1992, pp.173-180.

15. Geller, J., and others. "A National Survey of Mobile Crisis Services and Their Evaluation." *Psychiatric Services* 46(9):893-7, Sept. 1995.

16. Jaffe, R., and others. "Outpatient Electroconvulsive Therapy: Efficacy and Safety." *Convulsive Therapy* 6(3):231-8, Sept. 1990.

17. Bhatia, G., and Moss, K. "Psychiatric Delivery Systems Are Changing for the Better." *Business and Health Special Report.* Montvale, N.J.: Medical Economics Publishing, 1993, pp.1-22.

18. Kaiser, L. "Health Care in the 21st Century." *Physician Executive* 22(1):12-5, Jan. 1996.

19. Kirkby, K. "Computer-Assisted Treatment of Phobias." *Psychiatric Services* 47(2):139-40,142, Feb. 1996.

20. Selmi, P., and others. "Computer-Administered Cognitive-Behavioral Therapy for Depression." *American Journal of Psychiatry* 147(1):51-6, Jan. 1990.

21. Baker, N., and Giese, M. "Reorganization of a Private Psychiatric Unit to Promote Collaboration with Managed Care." *Hospital and Community Psychiatry* 43(11):1126-9, Nov. 1992.

22. Olden, K., and Johnson, M. "A 'Facilitated Model' of Inpatient Psychiatric Care." *Hospital and Community Psychiatry* 44(9):879-82, Sept. 1993.

23. Mohl, P. "Confessions of a Concurrent Reviewer." *Psychiatric Services* 47(1):35-40, Jan. 1996.

24. Waxman, H. "Using Outcomes Assessment for Quality Improvement." In *Outcomes Assessment in Clinical Practice*, Sederer, L., and Dickey, B., Editors. Baltimore, Md.: Williams & Wilkins, 1996, pp. 25-33.

25. Waxman, H. "An Inexpensive Hospital-Based Program for Outcome Evaluation." *Hospital and Community Psychiatry* 45(2):160-2, Feb. 1994.

William R. Dubin, MD, was Director of Clinical Services, Belmont Behavioral Health; Associate Chairman, Department of Psychiatry, Albert Einstein Medical Center; and Professor of Psychiatry, Temple University School of Medicine, Philadelphia, Pennsylvania. He now is Medical Director, AmeriChoice Behavioral Health, Philadelphia, Pennsylvania. Shivkumar Hatti, MD, is Chief Executive Officer, Suburban Psychiatric Associates, and Clinical Assistant Professor of Psychiatry, Jefferson Medical College, Philadelphia. The authors would like to thank Alicia J. Dubin for her help in the preparation of the manuscript for this chapter.

Chapter 7

Integrating Clinical and Professional Services in an Era of Public Managed Care

by M. Annette Hanson, MD, and Raymond B. Flannery, Jr., PhD

Thereisacrisis in health care in the United States: needs are increasing even as resources become more limited and costs continue to rise. Indeed, many citizens remain without any form of health care coverage at all.

Traditional health care services have emphasized the role of the physician who determines the diagnosis, the type and course of treatment, and usual and customary fees.[1] Less attention was paid to the service delivery system as a whole and to its need for ongoing monitoring of quality of care, cost-effectiveness, and ease of access. In this view, physician executives either developed policy directly, without input from nonphysician personnel, or left policy planning entirely in the hands of others, approaches that usually satisfied few. These traditional approaches to service delivery and management have not been helpful in the current crisis. Difficult times have demanded new solutions.

One behavioral health care approach to this emerging national need has been managed care,[1-3] which emphasizes goal-directed, easily accessed, high-quality, and time-limited distribution of treatment resources.[1-10] Early empirical findings of mental health service systems have demonstrated the efficacy of this approach, including shorter hospital stays,[11] fewer readmissions,[12] cost-effective aftercare services in the community,[13] and apparent consumer satisfaction.[14]

Several state mental health authorities (SMHAs), particularly those faced with severe fiscal crises, have begun to explore the applicability of private managed care approaches for public-sector mental health needs, and early papers have begun to explore capitation approaches[15] and a comprehensive, organized system of care.[14]

In response to its fiscal crisis, the Massachusetts SMHA has been in the forefront of developing an organized system of public managed care (PMC). Restructuring of its system of care required a corresponding reorganization of the role of Division of Clinical and Professional Services (CPS). The SMHA reorganization included building an infrastructure to support the provision of high-quality care in an era of rapid change. As the system of care evolved, CPS underwent a corresponding modification of its role and function. This chapter documents these changes and suggests one possible model for SMHA clinical and professional services in an era of behavioral health care reform. The chapter also outlines newer roles for physician executives within this approach.

Massachusetts Approach to Public Managed Care

In the period preceding the rise and implementation of managed care, health care providers were largely autonomous and services were neither integrated nor consumer-driven.[14] Organization was needed to manage the care of persons with persistent illness, including serious mental illness (SMI).[4] The Massachusetts SMHA designed and fielded the Comprehensive Community Support System (CCSS) model as one approach to an organized system of care. Development of the CCSS model was guided by core values that included primacy of services for persons with SMI, active consumer and family participation, an interdisciplinary biopsychosocial rehabilitation approach, and a continuum of hospital-based and community care, including generic, community-based services. CCSS was intended to provide all of the medical, rehabilitative, and social services needed to ensure high-quality, accessible, cost-effective care, enabling persons with SMI to function at the highest possible level in the least restrictive environment, the desired standard of care for any chronic illness.

Policy and planning, quality management, utilization management, training, and research and evaluation provided the infrastructure that institutionalizes the values of CCSS and enhances the quality, effectiveness, and accessibility of this system of care. However, even with the establishment of this infrastructure, the challenge remained to inculcate the value of continuous assessment and improvement and to integrate these components within the CPS division, and, ultimately, into the service delivery functions of the SMHA. In designing a system of care for people with serious mental illness, the crucial tasks are to define the array and definition of programs; models, services, practice, and interventions that are most effective for each subgroup of the population served; clinical criteria and standards of care; methods of delivering care that work best; expected outcomes; training and training models that helped service deliverers learn best practices; and, finally, in the context of a strategic plan for the SMHA, the policies that were needed to support the plan. Successful implementation depended on an agreed-upon method of problem identification and a mechanism to take corrective action.

Prior to 1991, the SMHA's CPS division was organized on a specialist or consultant model, headed by the agency's deputy commissioner, a psychiatrist. CPS staff were responsible for issues that arose within their areas of expertise: AIDS education, clozapine administration, disaster preparedness, health policy, licensing, program evaluation, and quality management. Early efforts in quality management and program evaluation were addressed by designating quality managers in each SMHA field office to evaluate patient care as a function of consumer need.

The arrival of a new deputy commissioner in 1991 led to a basic reorganization of the CPS structure that was more consistent with managed care initiatives adapted for the public sector and the mission of the SMHA. Whereas the earlier structure emphasized individual specialists, the new structure focused on the establishment of the infrastructure noted earlier (policy and planning, quality management, utilization management, training, and research/evaluation). Attention to cultural diversity and human rights was also highly valued in the reconfigured division.

Policy and Planning

An internal policy and planning committee was established as a forum in which 18 senior managers from the agency's various divisions, including the Office of Consumer and Ex-patient Relations, met biweekly to discuss and make recommendations regarding the development of SMHA policy and standards that were consistent with public managed care principles. The committee, cochaired by the deputy commissioner of CPS and a senior manager in her division, was responsible for ensuring that legislation, regulations, training, research, and programs were integrated at the policy level and for systematically reviewing and revising all SMHA policies. In addition, the committee convened on an as-needed basis as a statewide quality council to evaluate the results and effectiveness of quality improvement activities. The deputy commissioner was expected to provide the link between the committee and the SMHA's executive staff.

The committee considered issues brought to its attention by other standing or ad hoc groups within the agency (e.g., area quality councils, area directors, area medical directors, critical incident committees, human rights committees) that affected the SMHA's ability to provide or ensure the provision of high-quality, accessible, cost-effective services to its consumers. In its role as the statewide quality council, the committee was charged with ensuring communication and coordination of all quality improvement activities within the SMHA; reviewed and evaluated aggregate data and trends specific to SMHA's missions, goals and values; and set goals for statewide training to further the public managed care agenda. The quality council role has been the most difficult to integrate, primarily because of lack of a refined mechanism for communication between the field and the SMHA central office.

In addition to promulgating new policies on such topics as HIV/AIDS, mandatory forensic reviews, smoking, patient rights and responsibilities, patient privileges, informed consent, and human rights, the committee also reviewed and approved agencywide standards, clinical criteria, and protocols related to adult and child/adolescent inpatient care; emergency and partial hospitalization programs; crisis stabilization and respite care; clubhouse (an organized program that provides social and vocational services for mentally disabled adults); residential, education, employment, and home-based programs; utilization management; research; and psychiatric training. Adoption and acceptance of uniform standards and clinical criteria, in conjunction with a commitment to pursue accreditation of its eligible programs and facilities from nationally recognized bodies, such as the Joint Commission on Accreditation of Healthcare Organizations (JCAHO), positioned the SMHA to be a competitive *public* player in the new world of managed care.

The importance of this accomplishment was evidenced by a unique collaboration between the SMHA and the state's Medicaid agency. Because Medicaid is the largest purchaser of mental health services in the state and the majority of SMHA consumers are Medicaid recipients, the agencies entered into an interagency service agreement designed to create a unified system of care in which Medicaid, through a contract with a behavioral health managed care organization

(BHMCO), oversaw the entire system of acute mental health care. In this arrangement, the SMHA's statutory role was maintained. This joint venture entailed the transfer of SMHA funds for acute care to Medicaid, which purchased acute care for SMHA consumers through a private managed care organization. Medicaid and its BHMCO were held accountable by the SMHA for adhering to its purchasing specifications, which included standards, clinical criteria, etc.

Quality Management

One of the most important functions of CPS is to ensure the highest level of quality of care for its consumers. Based on recent advances in quality assurance, and with a specific focus on the Deming approach to total quality management,[16] CPS instituted a statewide system of continuous quality management that emphasized standards and performance indicators, provider self-monitoring, data collection and analysis, and problem identification and correction. Standards and performance-based indicators defined what services were to be provided, and clinical practice guidelines defined best practices for how those services were to be provided.

For example, standards needed to be written for clubhouses. With the presence of several different clubhouse models in operation statewide, the SMHA needed to arrive at a consensus on basic standards regardless of approach. A group of all interested stakeholders was convened to seek input and write draft standards to address clubhouse needs. When the draft standards had been written and reviewed in a variety of contexts, they were sent to the policy and planning committee for review and, ultimately, for promulgation by the Commissioner.

The standards, indicators, and guidelines were the vehicle for programs to monitor their performance. Corrective action planning and implementation provided the vehicle for revising programs, specific services, or service delivery aspects identified as being problematic by stakeholders.

Standards and performance indicators were developed that complemented, expanded, or added to quality management standards used by nationally recognized organizations for emergency services, inpatient services, partial hospital programs, day treatment and day rehabilitation settings, residential housing placements, and social club houses and that supported employment and education programs. Human rights, HIV/AIDS and infection control, licensing, requests for proposals, performance-based contracts, and other monitoring activities were also integrated into the process.

An infrastructure of quality councils was developed at all levels of this organized system of care (see figure, page 101). This included councils for quality assessment and improvement at all SMHA state and provider agencies, at all SMHA field offices, and at the SMHA central office. Quality management specialists were appointed at all levels and received training in standards development, monitoring, and improvement skills.

In this way, an ongoing process was created that continually examined every program and function to ensure that performance standards were being maintained.

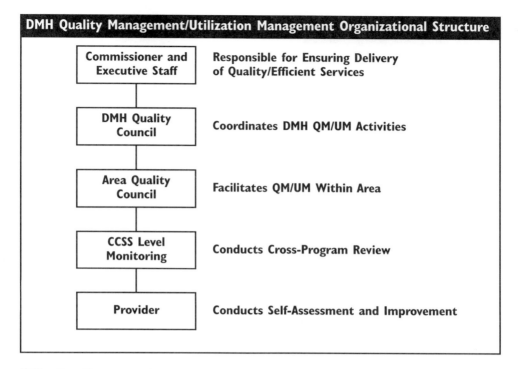

DMH Quality Management/Utilization Management Organizational Structure

Commissioner and Executive Staff	Responsible for Ensuring Delivery of Quality/Efficient Services
DMH Quality Council	Coordinates DMH QM/UM Activities
Area Quality Council	Facilitates QM/UM Within Area
CCSS Level Monitoring	Conducts Cross-Program Review
Provider	Conducts Self-Assessment and Improvement

Utilization Management

An important component of the quality management approach was creation of a utilization program to provide, monitor, and improve access as well as ensure appropriate and cost-effective use of health care dollars. Utilization management standards were developed in conjunction with a statewide group of appointed utilization management staff and included clinical criteria for all levels of care and for other specific expectations, for example, structures and processes needed to enhance dimensions of care required by accrediting bodies. These standards were shared with a broad set of constituents and were ultimately approved and fielded. Ongoing utilization management data were collected, reported, and used by management to continually assess and improve performance.

Among the more important utilization management standards were the clinical criteria and protocols developed by the SMHA and Medicaid and its BHMCO, as noted earlier. Protocols outlined the criteria and procedures that emergency service programs would follow in triage of mental health consumers. For example, clinical criteria and protocols were delineated so that emergency teams could decide whether to admit a consumer to the SMHA-funded acute replacement unit (DMH-contracted psychiatric inpatient beds in general or private psychiatric hospitals that replace SMHA acute inpatient services), to a BHMCO network hospital, or to a state hospital. These expectations were based on the consumer's clinical profile and on the different programs' abilities to meet the consumer's needs. The protocol may have served its most important function in defining the boundary between acute, medically necessary care provided by the BHMCO and subacute, rehabilitative, and social support services administered by the SMHA. These protocols were necessary to ensure a clinically focused and integrated system of care that suits consumers' needs and to help define the responsibilities of both the private sector BHMCO hospital network and the SMHA. Protocols defining the interface between the SMHA and the BHMCO were also helpful to the field in promoting dialogue, negotiation, and coordination concerning clinical care for consumers.

Because data management and analysis are critical for effective utilization management, a series of utilization management reports were instituted. For example, in delivering inpatient care, performance with respect to five indicators—inpatient admission rate per 100,000 population, inpatient bed days per 100,000 population, transfer from acute care to continuing inpatient care, length of stay, and readmission rates—was examined statewide, across areas, and for similar facilities. Control charts were used to identify variants in performance. Using this methodology, it was easy to identify significant outliers that prompted further review. In like manner, data management approaches were developed to accomplish additional utilization management tasks. For example, a statewide standardized inpatient census software program was developed to track length of stay in various facilities.

Clinical Training
The success of the new initiatives in public managed care rested in large part on a workforce able to understand the new SMHA culture and to implement its clinical practice guidelines. The process began with the development of a core curriculum that was expected to be mastered by every SMHA state and provider employee. Statewide focus groups comprised of all stakeholders identified nine areas in need of immediate clinical practice guidelines—consumer empowerment, human rights, public managed care (an overview of policy, quality management, utilization management, training, and research), dual diagnosis (SMI/substance abuse), role of the family, alternatives to restraint and seclusion, cultural diversity, rehabilitation, and care for the elderly with SMI. These nine areas were judged to be of particular importance in the success of the restructuring process. Statewide committees of specialists in each topic area were convened. Each group wrote a training manual in its area of expertise that included state-of-the-art clinical content and clinical practice guidelines. Each group then held a "train-the-trainer" day on its topic to which each SMHA state and provider agency was invited to send representatives. Each work group's training day was required to be a program that qualified by content for continuing education credits from Harvard Medical School. Over time, these nine training topics were coupled with other offerings in major mental illness, violence, psychological trauma, psychopharmacology, quality management, utilization management, HIV/AIDS, risk management, forensics, and the like.

To provide additional support to SMHA state and provider agencies during the transition to community-based services, the SMHA, in conjunction with the state's medical schools, offered difficult-to-treat case conferences and the SMHA Speakers Bureau.

The difficult-to-treat case conferences were held statewide every other week and were staffed by the faculties of Harvard Medical School/Massachusetts Mental Health Center and the University of Massachusetts Medical Center. Faculty experts volunteered to conduct case consultations on difficult-to-manage clinical issues in field settings. In a similar manner, the SMHA Speakers Bureau, comprising medical school faculty from Boston University, Harvard University, Tufts University, and the University of Massachusetts, volunteered to provide lectures in their areas of expertise at statewide field sites.

A child-oriented core curriculum was developed, with clinical practice guidelines for the role of the family and for cultural diversity issues in working with families. A core curriculum for residential house staff was also written and fielded. An annual conference jointly sponsored by the SMHA and the Alliance for the Mentally Ill of Massachusetts focused specifically on pre-service training issues for graduate school faculty in local universities. Finally, all of the Massachusetts Mental Health Center's Continuing Education Summer Courses on Cape Cod were offered to all SMHA state and provider employees at a substantial discount.

With time, an area training director was appointed in each SMHA field office to repeat training that had already been offered and to provide training requested at the local level. As the program grew, a Training Advisory Committee, comprising representatives from all of the basic constituent groups, was created to coordinate training and to conduct yearly needs assessments so that the policy and planning committee could integrate training needs with the overall needs, policies, and directions of the SMHA.

As training proceeded for the general workforce, a special program was developed to redefine traditional approaches for the training of psychiatric residents and psychology interns. Based on a request for proposals (RFP) that included goals, objectives, standards, and performance indicators relevant to the newly emerging SMHA public managed care culture, interested psychiatric residency and psychology internship training programs were required to educate trainees about treatment of persons with serious mental illness, including recovery and rehabilitation.

The process of funding training programs was based on responses to RFPs, as noted, and provided stipends for education rather than stipends for service. The SMHA assumed that direct funding of education and training would be a more powerful mechanism to ensure that training programs supported the new SMHA culture. While the SMHA awarded its highest rating to programs whose demonstrated missions were most consistent with that of the SMHA, all training programs that responded to the RFP were funded to some extent so that all programs were provided with opportunities to change, using funding as leverage. Funding was contingent on a program's willingness to develop a corrective action plan for issues associated with consumer empowerment, family education, and rehabilitation. Maintenance of each program's funding level was contingent on its adherence to the SMHA goals, objectives, standards, and performance-based indicators for residency training.

An advisory committee of members of all the funded training programs was convened to field this new initiative and to work collaboratively to ensure the highest levels of training in the most cost-effective approaches.

Research and Evaluation

Research into the nature and causes of SMI as well as evaluation of services provided are important components of a high-quality system of care. Better management usually emerges from better measurement, and the SMHA, through CPS, fielded a variety of initiatives to meet these needs.

To ensure strong public-academic linkages, CPS created two research "centers of excellence," one in neuroscience and one in behavioral and forensic science, including service system delivery. The centers were to focus on SMI in adults and on serious emotional disturbances in children. An RFP with appropriate research goals, objectives, standards, and performance indicators was issued, with the expectation that the funding of these centers would act as seed money to create a research infrastructure that would attract other research resources and external funding. In addition to attracting grant support, both centers were also expected to provide training opportunities for new researchers and to present their findings to the general workforce at suitable forums. The neuroscience center was awarded to Harvard Medical School/Commonwealth Research Center at Massachusetts Mental Health Center and the behavioral and forensic science center to the University of Massachusetts Medical Center.

At the same time, CPS also provided an internal research structure to coordinate all research activities, including the centers of excellence, and to provide more immediate internal support for SMHA managers. The SMHA internal research group monitored centers of excellence research efforts to ensure relevance to the SMHA mission and applied for additional research monies in areas of importance to the SMHA that were not addressed by the centers.

In addition to a mandated institutional review board that provides oversight of all research activity and of two research internship placements, special emphasis was placed on development of reliable internal databases for evaluation purposes. Outcomes assessment protocols were designed to assess the impact on level of consumer functioning and effectiveness of services. The protocols included utilization management reports, tracking of consumers receiving clozapine, special analyses of Medicaid data, and the like and have provided critical information support for SMHA managers in developing policies and procedures that directly address consumer needs.

Implications

Preliminary Outcomes

From 1991 to 1996, these PMC initiatives by CPS and the other divisions within the SMHA resulted in a reshaped community-based behavioral health care system. Four traditional inpatient facilities were closed, with a significant proportion of the savings redirected to expand community-based services. Acute care services are now provided in general and private psychiatric hospitals in the community; 1,400 new community residential beds were created; and case management and other community support services were expanded to meet consumer needs. These services have maintained quality of care, expanded accessibility, and improved cost-effectiveness dramatically and were accomplished with no increase in tax dollars. These preliminary outcomes suggest that establishing an integrated infrastructure of clinical and professional services, in accordance with principles of managed care, can be successfully adapted for the public-sector.[1-15]

Implications for Behavioral Health Care

Instead of the former CPS model of individual specialized consultants, the new CPS behavioral health care approach emphasizes a team of senior managers guided by a common set of health care principles and structures as well as products that are integrated into the SMHA's overall mission and policy directives. This integrated approach provides a stable yet flexible structure in an era of constant change. The statewide CPS infrastructure and the processes outlined here provide the SMHA with a stable vehicle for effecting ongoing cultural modifications in the face of new research findings, new policy initiatives, collaboration with other agencies, or changes in health care funding at the state or national level. The CPS model noted here serves a regulatory function with regard to care for all of the SMHA's services for its priority population (persons with SMI) to ensure continued high quality and sustained cost-effective approaches.

An important component in the success of this new model was the inclusion of all significant stakeholders in each step of the process. In an era of scarce fiscal resources, it is important that each constituent voice is heard, understood, and respected. CPS stakeholders were many and varied, including consumers and families, state and private provider employees, unions, public officials, regulatory agencies, advocates, advisory boards, and representatives of the academic communities. Focus groups for various tasks provided forums in which to grieve the passing of the existing system,[17] to voice differences of opinion about components of the emerging order, and to work toward consensus in a fair and reasonable partnership with other stakeholders. This group process enhanced acceptance of, and compliance with, the new CPS model.

Implications for Medicine

This new CPS approach has implications for medicine in at least two spheres: maintenance of strong public-academic linkages in an era of privatized services and continuing education of physician executives.

Because training and research were services purchased by the SMHA, it was reasonable to privatize these services through an RFP process. The challenge was to maintain the long tradition of strong and productive public-academic liaisons. Massachusetts is rich in medical resources, with four medical schools and a great many teaching hospitals. The RFP processes noted earlier for residency training and the development of two research centers have involved the state's medical community in continuing the distinguished public-academic linkages developed in more traditional health care models. The quality of traditional residency training programs has been maintained, as each SMHA residency training program still adheres closely to accreditation guidelines for its general residency training. In addition, residents in the SMHA programs learn about SMI and its treatments as well as the quality/utilization management processes of health care that are emerging as a national trend. Similarly, researchers are free to pursue their academic research interests, but within a framework that meets the needs of the SMHA. In each case, the SMHA has been able to insert its values to direct the general culture. This ensures accountability for tax dollars spent, without interfering with academic intellectual freedom. The approaches noted here permit trainees and researchers interested in SMHA issues to pursue those goals, while medical schools are free to spend their other monies on faculty and trainees with other interests.

A second implication from the CPS model involves the roles and ongoing education of physician executives. Because of advances in the technology and the funding bases of medicine, the management role of the senior group manager is being developed. In this role, physicians need to be fully conversant with principles of behavioral health care and with management of systems of care. Physicians need to refine their skills in establishing a team of competent specialists for the tasks at hand; to learn how to manage a team most likely comprising members from several disciplines in addition to medicine; and to be well versed in conflict resolution among the highly educated members of that team. Physician executives also need to be instructed on how to change team structures as health care organizations continue to evolve and on how to guide a system through a radical transformation of its service delivery approach.

These are not traditional medical school skills, but they are needed for medicine to retain its preeminence in an era of rapidly changing behavioral health care models. The CPS model noted here, other behavioral health care models currently in place, and those that are yet to evolve are crucial if high-quality care is to be maintained and the percentage of the gross domestic product spent on health care is to be lowered. Such approaches will strengthen medicine and the country's economy. Such approaches also provide the physician executive with a variety of career opportunities that can truly make a difference in health care. The stakes are very high, but outcomes can be very great for physicians wishing to undertake these tasks.

References

1. Schwartz, B. *The Costs of Living: How Market Freedom Erodes the Best Things in Life.* New York, N.Y.: Basic Books, 1994.

2. Broskowski, A. "Current Mental Health Care Environments: Why Managed Care Is Necessary." *Professional Psychology: Research and Practice* 22(1):6-14, Spring 1991.

3. Bennett, M. "View from the Bridge: Reflections of a Covering Staff Model HMO Psychiatrist." *Psychiatric Quarterly* 64(1):45-75, Spring 1993.

4. Bevilacqua, J. "New Paradigms, Old Pitfalls." *New Directions in Mental Health Services* (66):19-30, Summer 1995.

5. England, M., and Goff, V. "Health Reform and Organized Systems of Care." *New Directions in Mental Health Services* (59):5-12, Fall 1993.

6. Hollingsworth, E. "Issues of Politics, Boundaries, and Technology Choice." *New Directions in Mental Health Services* (66):31-42, Summer 1995.

7. Sabin, J. "Clinical Skills for the 1990s: Six Lessons from HMO Practice." *Hospital and Community Psychiatry* 42(6):605-8, June 1991.

8. Schreter, R. "Ten Trends in Managed Care and Their Impact on the Biopsychosocial Model." *Hospital and Community Psychiatry* 44(4):325-7, April 1993.

9. Schuster, J. "Ensuring Highest-Quality Care for the Cost: Coping Strategies for Mental Health Providers." *Hospital and Community Psychiatry* 42(8):774-6, Aug. 1991.

10. Reinhardt, U. "Managed Competition in Health Care Reform: Just Another American Dream or the Perfect Solution?" *Journal of Law and Medical Ethics* 22(2):106-20, Summer 1994.

11. Criscione, T., and others. "Managed Health Care Services for People with Mental Retardation: Impact on Inpatient Utilization." *Mental Retardation* 31(5):297-306, Oct. 1993.

12. Baker, N., and Giese, A. "Reorganization of a Private Psychiatric Unit to Promote Collaboration with Managed Care." *Hospital and Community Psychiatry* 43(11):1126-9, Nov. 1992.

13. Moore, R., and others. "Hospital-Based HMO: An Outpatient Study." *Psychiatric Hospital* 23(3-4):79-82, Summer-Fall 1992.

14. Leadholm, B., and Kerzner, J. "Public Managed Care: Developing Comprehensive Community Support Systems in Massachusetts." *Managed Care Quarterly* 2(2):25-30, Spring 1994.

15. Mauch, D. "Rhode Island: An Early Effort at Managed Care." *New Directions in Mental Health Services* (43):55-64, Fall 1989.

16. Walton, M. *The Deming Management Method.* New York, N.Y.: Perigree, 1986.

17. Duck, J. "Managing Change: The Art of Balancing." *Harvard Business Review* 71(6):109-18, Nov./Dec. 1993.

M. Annette Hanson, MD, is Medical Director for the Massachusetts Department of Medical Assistance and was formerly Deputy Commissioner for Clinical and Professional Services in the Massachusetts Department of Mental Health. Dr. Hanson is Instructor in Psychiatry, Department of Psychiatry, Harvard Medical School. Raymond B. Flannery Jr., PhD, is Director of Training for the Massachusetts Department of Mental Health and Associate Clinical Professor of Psychology, Department of Psychiatry, Harvard Medical School. The authors would like to express their gratitude to the former members of the Division of Clinical and Professional Services: Frederick Altaffer, PhD, Director of Research; William Crane, Esq, Special Assistant for Human Rights; Mary Egan, RN, Clinical Specialist; Joan Kerzner, MSPA, Director of Policy and Planning; Margery Kravitz, EdD, Director of Monitoring and Evaluation; Marc Navon, LICSW, Director of Utilization Management; Eugene Nigro, MSW, Licensing; Gary Pastva, MSW, Assistant Commissioner of Quality Management; Walter Penk, PhD, Director of Evaluation Research; Marian Reynolds, RN, AIDS Coordinator; Esta-Lee Stone, MS, OTR/L, Director of Special Projects; and Michael Weeks, Licensing.

Chapter 8

Urban Assertive Community Treatment for Adults with Severe Mental Illness

by Ranga N. Ram, MD, Lisa Dixon, MD, MPH, and Jack E. Scott, ScD

Programs for Assertive Community Treatment (PACT) have demonstrated considerable success in the care of persons with severe and persistent mental illness (SPMI). There is an emerging consensus that groups of patients with special needs can be effectively served by PACT models. Treatment recommendations developed by the federally funded Schizophrenia Client Outcomes Research Team include the recommendation that PACT be part of systems of care for persons with schizophrenia. The effectiveness and efficiency of the PACT model for high utilizers of services has led to its increasing implementation around the country.

PACT, which is frequently shortened to ACT, provides a comprehensive range of treatment, rehabilitation, and supportive services through a multidisciplinary team based in the community. Basic characteristics of ACT programs include assertive engagement, *in vivo* delivery of services, a multidisciplinary team approach, continuous responsibility and staff continuity over time, caseloads with high staff-to-client ratios, and brief but frequent contacts (high service intensity). Assertive engagement refers to the process of outreach and establishing a treatment relationship with the client on the basis of his or her individual preference and autonomy. All skills of daily living are learned in the community—e.g., team members will shop with the patient to help develop budgeting skills ("in vivo"). The team assumes continuous responsibility, working closely with the client even when he or she may be hospitalized, in conjunction with the inpatient treatment team. ACT teams also provide close liaison with the client's support system and a treatment focus on alternate activities.[1] The original PACT model was developed for persons with acute symptoms of mental illness who were thought to be appropriate for hospitalization and had some level of family/community support. During the past decade, PACT principles have been modified and applied in different settings, including inner-city and rural environments, and to other client groups, for example, dual diagnosis patients and outpatients with high levels of service utilization.[2]

Overview of Research on Programs of Assertive Community Treatment

The effectiveness of PACT models has been extensively reviewed elsewhere.[3] The most important research findings concerning service utilization and effectiveness of this model of care delivery are summarized here. The research evidence points out that assertive community treatment reduces the rate and duration of psychiatric hospitalization. In a meta analysis including nine studies involving the assertive outreach approach, Bond et al. concluded that, "as a rule of thumb, providing assertive outreach programs for frequent users of hospitals can be expected to reduce inpatient days by about 50 percent."[4] Assertive outreach represents an adaptation of the assertive community treatment model developed at Thresholds, a large psychosocial agency in Chicago.[3]

In this context, however, three points must be noted. First, reduction in the use of psychiatric hospitalization may be at least partially offset by increased use of other community-based alternative services, such as 24-hour crisis intervention and residential services. Therefore, reductions in the use of inpatient services may not be as pronounced without the availability of the full continuum of care. Second, control of hospital admissions, length of stay, and discharge may be necessary to reduce hospitalization. Third, reductions in hospital use have tended to cease after ACT treatment is discontinued.[5-7]

McGrew and colleagues assessed the impact of program fidelity for assertive outreach on reductions in psychiatric hospital days in a sample of 18 programs employing this model.[8] They found a significant association between the total fidelity index score and two fidelity index sub-scale scores (staffing and organization) and reductions in hospital days. That is, the greater the program fidelity to ACT, the greater the reduction in hospitalization.

The impact of assertive community treatment programs on the costs of treatment has been addressed in several economic analyses. A comprehensive cost-benefit analysis of the original PACT model, called Training in Community Living (TCL), found that the average direct treatment costs per client for one year after admission to the study were higher for TCL subjects than for controls.[9] These increased direct treatment costs were offset by a higher level of benefits (including a doubling of work productivity) accruing to the experimental subjects, resulting in a small but significant positive cost-benefit ratio that favored the TCL program. Hoult and colleagues found that the average annual direct and indirect treatment costs for persons receiving ACT services were substantially less than for persons receiving standard services in a randomized clinical trial ($4,489 versus $5,669 per client).[10] In addition, there were significant differences in the sources of these costs. For the experimental subjects, 81 percent of the costs were incurred in the community, while 79 percent of the costs for control subjects resulted from the costs of inpatient treatment. In a study of an ACT model called Daily Living Program (DLP) in London, Knapp et al. concluded that the DLP treatment was significantly less costly in the short and medium term than standard hospital-based inpatient and outpatient care at Bethlem-Maudsley Hospital.[11] Cost-effectiveness was achieved without shifting the costs of care from the National Health Service to other agencies or to families.

Evidence for cost savings from assertive outreach programs, an adaptation of assertive community treatment, is less consistent. The original evaluation at Thresholds and a subsequent replication showed that costs for service recipients were significantly reduced.[12] In a third study involving three separate replications of the assertive outreach model in community mental health centers in Indiana, the findings were highly inconsistent (i.e., in one case, assertive outreach costs were higher than standard community mental health center care; in another they were equivalent, while in the third they were less costly).[13] Bond et al. suggested that program fidelity may be an important factor in the realization of any potential savings.[14]

Several factors complicate comparisons of the results from these studies, including variation in adherence to the program model, the ways in which the cost analyses were conducted, and differences in study design (e.g., random assignment versus pre-post designs). Nevertheless, the evidence for cost savings from TCL-type programs appears stronger and more consistent than for the assertive outreach adaptation of PACT. Past studies have shown that TCL programs are either less costly than comparison conditions, or, when more costly, the higher costs may be offset by an increased earning capacity on the part of service recipients. In addition, several studies have shown that sources of treatment costs change as a result of TCL programming, with a reduction in costs attributable to inpatient care and an increase in structured residential and/or outpatient costs.

Providing Care to Persons with Mental Illness in Urban Settings

Access to high-quality mental health care for urban indigent and homeless persons, especially those with severe mental health problems, is a significant public health problem. Urban homeless adults with severe and persistent mental illness present with special needs. We choose to focus on homeless persons here because of the general risk for homelessness experienced by persons with severe mental illness.[15] Further, they represent one of the greatest challenges to an urban system of care. The Department of Health and Human Services recently created the Access to Community Care and Effective Services (ACCESS) program for homeless mentally ill adults, which uses PACT principles. If a system can meet the needs of these individuals, it can probably successfully treat less difficult groups of persons with severe mental illness.

Mental health problems and homelessness have a complex interaction. Homelessness is a major stressor that can easily precipitate a relapse of major mental illness or worsening of symptoms and/or disability. Further, homelessness is a complicating factor in the treatment of individuals with severe mental illness. Not having a home and an address makes it difficult for these persons to access care in traditional settings that serve on the basis of notions of "urban catchment areas." These persons are less able to negotiate bureaucratic systems in accessing benefits, housing, and supportive community services. As a result, they go largely untreated or undertreated.

The most common health care resource available to homeless mentally ill persons is hospital emergency departments. Hospital stays serve the dual purpose of treating symptoms that are intolerable and of providing temporary housing. Multiple admissions with no continuity of care may be one result of the homeless condition for some of these people. Their general separation from society and their distrust of authority create further barriers to care. Because this population needs a targeted approach that is aggressive in seeking them out for care rather than passively waiting for them to appear, the PACT model lends itself well to providing care for these persons.

Treatment of homeless persons with severe mental illnesses in an inner-city area poses several problems. Homelessness is only one presenting aspect for persons with severe mental illness. These persons may have multiple problems, including lack of social support, lack of day-time structure, severe alcohol and or substance use, and concomitant medical illnesses. While the trajectory to homelessness varies, there are some similarities in presentation and service needs that may be addressed in a comprehensive manner using the PACT approach, as is being done in Baltimore. One such program, a modified PACT model targeting severely mentally ill clients, is discussed in detail here.

The Baltimore ACT Team

The mission of the ACT team is to provide comprehensive services to homeless persons with severe mental illnesses who have been unable to make use of traditional outpatient mental health services. The package of services includes direct clinical case management, medical and psychiatric care, social work services, as well as some housing options. The immmediate treatment team consists of psychiatrists, therapists, psychiatric nurses, counselors, and consumer advocates. The team philosophy is that, by engaging individuals in a nonthreatening and non-intrusive way; assisting them to secure housing, entitlements (public assistance, Medicaid, and other federal benefits), and psychiatric and medical care; and helping them to function in the community, their quality of life will improve. The team's philosophy is that this can only be achieved if the autonomy and preferences of individuals are respected.

Working with Clients

Working with clients of the ACT team has been conceptualized in a framework of four phases of treatment:

- Engagement
- Stabilization
- Ongoing Treatment and Maintenance
- Discharge

Not all individuals referred to the program pass through each of these phases, nor are these phases necessarily always connected in a linear fashion. Nevertheless, this framework helps to conceptualize where individuals have been and where they may go with respect to their work with the program.

Engagement

Many homeless people with severe mental illness have had negative experiences with established agencies and care providers. The goal of the engagement phase is to develop a trusting relationship between the treatment team and the client. Engagement is successful when clients identify the team as their service provider. An essential ingredient of this process is determining what the

112

client wants. The team helps clients meet basic needs and provides material support, such as meals, bus tokens, laundry money, and, perhaps most important, shelter. The team does not stay in the office, but goes into the community—to street corners, restaurants, missions, and shelters—spending time simply talking to and getting to know the client. Treatment and medication may be offered, but they are not required. The team is persistent and supportive, often following clients through psychiatric hospitalizations, episodes of substance use, arrests, and disappearances. For some, this phase takes an entire year. Others engage quickly, particularly if they have a specific need that ACT can help them to meet, such as housing or psychiatric care.

Stabilization

During this phase, clients develop and enhance skills necessary to maintain themselves in the community. Long-term housing, income, daily activities, chronic medical problems, substance abuse, family and relationship issues, and psychiatric care are addressed. Generally, each client is willing or interested in working on some, if not all, of these issues. Critical to identification of goals is active participation of clients in the process. If preferences and desires of clients are not integral to the development of goals, they often leave treatment. Strategies used in this phase are discussed in more detail below.

Ongoing Treatment/Maintenance

The goal of this phase is to help clients maintain progress they have achieved. The life-styles and circumstances of clients often change dramatically over a year or two; people who have lived on the streets for 20 years now have an independent apartment. Maintaining stability is itself a goal, and clients may have difficulty creating a new social structure and way of living. Clients in this phase often require a lower intensity of services but are not yet ready for discharge from ACT.

Discharge

All ACT clients are reviewed annually for eligibility to continue in the program. This aspect of the Baltimore ACT team is a significant departure from the traditional PACT model. It is a necessary adaptation to continue a targeted approach to dealing with homeless adults with mental illness, "graduating" them to less intense care when they are stable. It creates an opportunity to recruit new clients. It also helps focus on a tangible outcome that may be seen as desirable for clients and the team staff.

However, discharge to a less intensive mental health program has proved to be as difficult as engagement in some instances. Integration of services at a local systems level has led to formation of a mobile outreach team that provides care for patients who need less intensive services.

Day-to-Day Operations

Each person referred to the ACT team is assigned to a "mini-team" composed of a clinical case manager, a psychiatrist and a consumer advocate. A clinical case manager may be a nurse, a social worker, or a rehabilitation aide. Consumer advocates have histories of homelessness and/or mental illness. The family consultant works with all of the clients as indicated. However, the entire team works together in decision making, and each staff member is knowledgeable about most of the patients. This teamwork is fostered through twice weekly team meetings in which treatment plans are developed and through daily "morning reports" at which the day's activity is planned for all staff and all clients to be seen that day. At the end of the day, the day's work is reviewed and the next day's work is reported and planned in "sign-out" meetings.

All team members who are therapists divide call responsibilities for evenings, weekends, and holidays. Thus, ACT staff members are accessible 24 hours a day. The on-call therapist is expected to be available for crisis intervention counseling by telephone. All patients are given a laminated card identifying them as part of the ACT program. An emergency telephone number appears on the card.

Problem Areas and Interventions

Mental Illness

The majority of ACT clients suffer from severe and persistent psychiatric disorders. Conceptual departures from the traditional PACT model have been necessary in dealing with this population, because homeless persons do not always have the extensive treatment history available for persons in the original PACT study. Further, homeless persons are more suspicious of treatment, treatment settings, and providers. Third, they have dealt with a different type of adversity (life on the streets) and have different coping mechanisms compared to long-term institutional patients. These differences are important to understand in the ACT services for homeless persons with severe mental illness.

Interventions begin at the time of the engagement phase with a focus on building trust between the client and the team. Psychotropic medications, psychoeducation, hospitalization, and psychotherapy with behavioral, cognitive, and psychological approaches are employed. In general, the challenge is to find the right balance of flexibility and structure.

Homelessness

Because all patients referred to the ACT team are homeless, many for more than five years, the team immediately develops a short-term and a long-term housing plan. Plans are developed in conjunction with clients, balancing their wants and needs, their clinical status, and available resources. Short-term housing options include motels (often paid for by ACT client assistance funds), psychiatric or medical hospitalization (if necessary), residential crisis beds, and transitional shelter beds or missions. Clients may also stay with their families or friends.

Long-term housing plans are made after engagement is successful. Long-term housing options include board and care homes, single-room occupancy dwellings, and independent apartments, including Section 8 housing. (Section 8 housing is a federally funded, locally administered rental assistance program for low-income individuals and families. Under the program, recipients pay 30 percent of their income to rent and utilities; the local housing authority pays the remainder directly to the landlord.) The decision about which option to pursue is developed collaboratively with the client as part of the treatment plan. For example, if the client is pursuing independent living in an apartment, staff will work with the client on skills of independent living, such as shopping, keeping an apartment clean, and budgeting.

Clients with substance abuse problems and mental illness pose other problems related to housing. Many shelters will not accept clients who are dually diagnosed or are currently using substances. Shelters accepting people with addiction histories often have strict rules. Clients may be required to attend Alcoholics Anonymous (AA) or Narcotics Anonymous (NA) meetings or to submit to urine screens. Clients who deny that they have a substance abuse problem may object to these measures. In these cases, the team does its best to determine what is most therapeutic for the client. Some clients are motivated by rules and need firm limits. However, others will continue to flounder on the streets if they are only given housing options that have a requirement of abstinence. We have found that there is a fine line between "enabling" substance abuse and providing a suitable environment with housing in which patients can begin to struggle with their addictions.

Money/Income

Many ACT clients either have no income at the time of referral or have been unable to manage their income to provide for their basic needs. The team makes an immediate assessment of clients' entitlements and, if appropriate, either initiates or continues the process of obtaining benefits. Most clients are disabled and qualify for Social Security Insurance or Disability Insurance (SSI/SSDI). However, many have been unable to negotiate the process of applying for SSI/SSDI or have not been in one place long enough to complete an application. If a client already receives income, the team will assess the need for a representative payee and will become the representative payee, if necessary. The use of a representative payee is particularly appropriate for those using drugs or alcohol and is mandated by federal law at this time.

As the representative payee, the team makes a budget with the client and pay rents and utility bills and purchases food and clothing. Allowances are given to some clients on a daily basis and to others on a weekly or monthly basis. Clients who abuse substances will often not receive any cash; their therapist or consumer advocate will shop with them and purchase what they need.

Medical Illness

Acute and chronic medical problems are common among homeless people. Staff members work with clients, providing health education and motivating them to keep medical appointments. Team psychiatrists coordinate prescriptions for medical problems, and all client medications are dispensed by the ACT team, regardless of treatment phase. Team nurses monitor medications closely. HIV and AIDS have been major health problems, as are infections, chronic illnesses such as diabetes and hypertension, and other acute problems. The team takes a comprehensive approach to providing care that keeps medical problems in focus in the treatment plan.

Activities of Daily Living/Rehabilitation

In addition to being able to obtain income and manage it appropriately, many ACT clients lack skills in basic areas, such as shopping, budgeting, and hygiene. For some, simply being provided with the resources, such as money or showers, solves the problem. However, others need more assistance. ACT team members accompany patients to shop for clothes, furniture, food, and the like and help with budgeting and paying bills. These skills are learned in "real-life" situations.

Rehabilitation in this context means helping individuals to regain (or gain for the first time) the living skills they need to function in the community, as well as to achieve vocational and social goals. The tasks of rehabilitation generally do not become relevant until the individual has engaged with and trusts the team, when their basic needs have been met and the client and the team can turn their attention to the future. The ACT program is currently participating in a multisite, randomized study of vocational rehabilitation that compares a focused approach using vocational rehabilitation professionals as team members with community programs to find out if a targeted approach is more effective.

Family

A high proportion of ACT clients have no or minimal family contact at referral. Anger, guilt, and grief characterize the feelings clients express when talking about their families. The ACT team encourages patients on an individual basis to improve their family relationships. A family outreach consultant has proved to be a unique and valuable member of the team. The consultant participates in the intake and treatment planning process, helping the team to understand the family perspective. The family consultant also runs a group for family psychoeducation. She has helped families increase their understanding of patients' illnesses, behavior, and need for, and side-effects of, medication.

Substance Abuse

Inner-city programs providing care for severe mental illness have to contend with a very high prevalence of substance use in the people they treat. Traditional administrative approaches to mental illness and substance abuse have left a number of persons who are dually diagnosed untreated, as if they do not belong to either treatment system. We have adopted a model for treatment of people with dual diagnoses advanced by Osher and Kofoed, which defines four phases: engagement, persuasion, active treatment, and relapse prevention.[16] We try to persuade patients to enter treatment by pointing out, repetitively if necessary, how their addictions are causing them problems. Their homelessness is often powerful evidence of the consequences of addiction. The team has a dual diagnosis treatment group that meets twice a week for one hour. We encourage the use of AA and NA where appropriate and have had staff members attend meetings with patients. Integrating treatment for substance abuse with money management, medical and psychiatric care, and housing is critical.

Daily Structure

Some clients attend day treatment or psychosocial programs, attend job training sessions, or are employed. Others spend time walking, interacting with peers, window shopping, or just coming into the ACT office. Daily structure is frequently more a need of the treatment team than a stated need of clients. More focus is necessary to assist these persons in finding jobs.

Documentation

The ACT team keeps records in a manner consistent with Maryland rules and regulations for mobile treatment units. This includes monthly therapist progress notes, at least quarterly psychiatric notes on medication, and treatment plans with long-term and short-term goals and interventions (outlined within four client contacts and renewed every 90 days thereafter).

Records of medication are maintained in a medication order book, and psychiatrists must document medication changes, the rationale for such changes, and that risks and benefits of medications have been explained to patients. Therapists must record patients' progress toward goals outlined in treatment plans. Patients must be aware of their rights and documentation of their being informed must appear in the chart. Individual charts are reviewed randomly on a monthly basis by the ACT quality assurance committee for adherence to these requirements. Staff members are given feedback and improvements are initiated.

Conclusion

PACT models are increasingly being adopted by provider systems nationwide. For example, there are at least four states (Delaware, Michigan, Rhode Island, and Wisconsin) where state standards have been established to promote the development and expansion of ACT programs.[17,18] Within the VA health care system, interest in the PACT model led to a recent multisite trial with successful results.[19] The effectiveness of this approach and the ingredients of its success need to be monitored through further outcomes research. Managed care approaches may have to tailor their techniques to address the unique needs of PACT programs. Capitation projects that target clients with specific needs may be one useful approach to cost savings. PACT models can be modified in this manner because they provide comprehensive services in one organizational program. Treatment can be modified to meet clients' needs in a flexible, individualized manner.

References

1. Taube, C., and others. "New Directions in Research on Assertive Community Treatment." *Hospital and Community Psychiatry* 41(6):642-7, June 1990.

2. Olfson, M. "Assertive Community Treatment: An Evaluation of the Experimental Evidence." *Hospital and Community Psychiatry* 41(6):634-41, June 1990.

3. Scott, J., and Dixon, L. "Assertive Community Treatment and Case Management for Schizophrenia." *Schizophrenia Bulletin*, 21(4):657-68, 1995.

4. Bond, G., and others. "Assertive Outreach for Frequent Users of Psychiatric Hospitals: A Meta-Analysis. *Journal of Mental Health Administration* 22(1):4-16, Winter 1995.

5. Audini, B., and others. "Home-Based Versus Outpatient/Inpatient Care for People with Serious Mental Illness—Phase II of a Controlled Study." *British Journal of Psychiatry* 165(2):204-10, Aug. 1994.

6. Test, M., and Stein, L. "Alternative to Mental Hospital Treatment. III. Social Cost." *Archives of General Psychiatry* 37(4):409-12, April 1980.

7. Test, M., and others. "The Long-Term Treatment of Young Schizophrenics in a Community Support Program." *New Directions for Mental Health Services* (26):17-27, June 1985.

8. McGrew, J., and others. "Measuring the Fidelity of Implementation of a Mental Health Program Model." *Journal of Consulting and Clinical Psychology* 62(4):670-8, Aug. 1994.

9. Weisbrod, B., and others. "Alternative to Mental Hospital Treatment. II. Economic Benefit-Cost Analysis." *Archives of General Psychiatry* 37(4): 400-5, April 1980.

10. Hoult, J., and others. "Psychiatric Hospital Versus Community Treatment: The Results of a Randomized Trial." *Australian and New Zealand Journal of Psychiatry* 17(2):160-7, June 1983.

11. Knapp, M., and others. "Service Use and Costs of Home-Based Versus Hospital-Based Care for People with Serious Mental Illness." *British Journal of Psychiatry* 165(2):195-203, Aug. 1994.

12. Bond, G. "An Economic Analysis of Psychosocial Rehabilitation." *Hospital and Community Psychiatry* 35(4):356-62, April 1984.

13. Bond, G., and others. "Assertive Case Management in Three CMHCs: A Controlled Study." *Hospital and Community Psychiatry* 39(4):411-8, April 1988.

14. Bond, G., and others. "A Comparison of Two Crisis Housing Alternatives to Psychiatric Hospitalization." *Hospital and Community Psychiatry* 40(2):177-83, Feb. 1989.

15. Dixon, L., and Osher, F. "Housing for Persons with Mental Illness and Substance Use Disorders." In Lehman, A., and Dixon, L., *Double Jeopardy: Chronic Mental Illness and Substance Use Disorders*. Chur, Switzerland: Harwood Academic Publishers, 1995.

16. Osher, F., and Kofoed, L. "Treatment of Patients with Both Psychiatric and Psychoactive Substance Use Disorders." *Hospital and Community Psychiatry* 40(10):1025-30, Oct. 1989.

17. Meisler, N., and others. "Statewide Dissemination of the Training in Community Living Program." *Administration and Policy in Mental Health* 23(1):71-6, Sept. 1994.

18. Meisler, N., and Santos, A. "Case Management of Persons with Schizophrenia and Other Severe Mental Illnesses in the U.S.A." In *Handbook of Mental Health Economics and Health Policy,* Moscarelli, M., and others, Editors. New York, N.Y.: John Wiley and Sons, 1996.

19. Rosenheck, R., and others. "Multisite Experimental Cost Study of Intensive Psychiatric Community Care." *Schizophrenia Bulletin* 21(1):129-40, 1995.

Ranga N. Ram, MD, is an Assistant Professor; Lisa Dixon, MD, MPH, is an Associate Professor; and Jack Scott, ScD, is an Assistant Professor, Department of Psychiatry, School of Medicine, University of Maryland, Baltimore.

Chapter 9

The Honeycomb Model

by Brian E. Tugana, MD, MBA, CTP, FACPE

T he model offered in this chapter sits squarely on a caisson, a foundation belief, that efficient, effective availability of behavioral health services will contribute to the well-being of the population and will significantly contribute in a cost-effective fashion to reducing health care expenditures.

Before getting to the proposed model, however, it is necessary to consider some of the many problems facing behavioral health as it is presently delivered to help bring the model and the expectations of its impact into more realistic perspective.

The problems of the present system are broad. Why are services that hold such potential promise so poorly utilized? A major difficulty lies with the stigma that continues to persist regarding behavioral health intervention. Until the public becomes better educated on psychology and until media portrayals become more balanced and realistic, individuals needing or considering outside counsel will continue to procrastinate in seeking help, if they get it at all.

Often the wide talent diversity among providers coupled with the perceived difficulty in quantification of both illness and progression toward greater well-being are offered as reasons for underutilization of mental health services. Community mental health centers, the great hope of the '60s, unfortunately have not delivered on either the hope or their promise.

Psychiatric providers often have been isolated or solitary in their relationships with fellow physicians, tending to follow an individual treatment model and contributing to poor integration and application of the knowledge of the field into workplaces, schools, and general health care.

The model that is described here is not proposed as a "save the profession" program or as a "jobs program for endangered psychiatrists." Instead, the model will address some of the significant problems facing our citizens regarding their psychiatric wellness.

A recurrent theme appears in the litany of problems—isolation and lack of integration. Behavioral health disciplines in general are poorly integrated into the health care system and into communities in general. Some of this isolation has been imposed upon behavioral health clinicians; some of it has been self-imposed.

Honeycomb Model

Background

A central concept of the Honeycomb Model is its organizational structure and the shared professional philosophy of its members. The staffing configuration consists of a psychiatrist and a mixture of 5-6 psychiatric social workers and psychiatric nurses. The operational structure of the team is organic as opposed to hierarchical (figure 1, below).

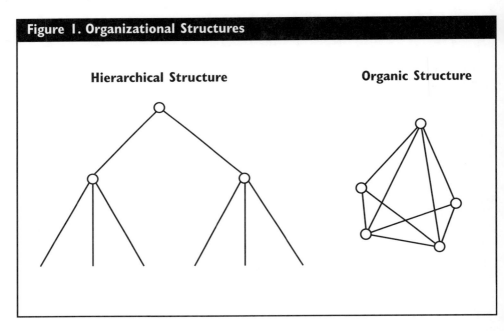

Figure 1. Organizational Structures

Hierarchical Structure

Organic Structure

The members of the Honeycomb work together and coordinate their actions to find the best way of performing their tasks. There are high levels of delegation of authority and high levels of lateral communication. While individual professionals are assigned specific tasks, there is a high level of sharing of their skills with others, which leads to a blurring of authority and responsibility as the team gels and matures. Although some organizations purport to operate in such an interdisciplinary framework, closer examination usually shows significant disparity between what exists on paper and what occurs during day-to-day operations.

Organizational Values

Many organizational theorists argue that an organization is reflected much more by its philosophical core than by its structural shape. Core organizational beliefs in the Honeycomb Model include the following:

■ A systems approach is intrinsically important in effective treatment. At times, this involves not only appropriate pharmacological and other biological interventions but also any number of therapeutic interventions.

■ Embracing a systems approach means more than simply focusing on the "identified patient." It means considering, and in many instances intervening in, the system from which the patient came.

■ Honeycomb Model providers are wellness-oriented in their approach. Patients' areas of dysfunction are braced and shored up, and their existing strengths are identified and strengthened. The broad goal of treatment is to help people achieve healthier adaptive independence. The purpose of treatment is to help patients identify areas in which adaptive work needs to be done and to motivate and assist patients in pursuing therapeutic goals.

■ Finally, there is a shared belief in the economic and societal benefits—beyond those to the patient—that occur when intervention is early as opposed to late. This belief translates into a strong belief in preventive care. The practical impact is that the professionals who practice this model are committed to early response and to being integrated into various aspects of their communities so that they can act on behalf of their patients.

Professional Roles

A psychiatrist functions as the chief team facilitator and coach. His or her role is central as a diagnostician when a patient is in the evaluation stage of intervention and as a team leader as the team formulates and implements a treatment plan. The psychiatrist, in addition to carrying a caseload in which he is the primary therapist, is active in consultative activities of the team.

A psychiatric social worker carries a therapeutic caseload but also has primary interface responsibilities between the team and community and business organizations. On occasion, he or she is the patients' advocate and assistant in moving through any bureaucratic mazes encountered.

The psychiatric nurse, like all the other professionals on the team, carries a primary treatment caseload and has major responsibilities as an interface between the team and other health care organizations and professionals. He or she often works in conjunction with personnel of business organizations to facilitate reintegration and progress of patients into the work world.

This model calls for regular, not simply problem-focused, treatment case review among the psychiatrist and other professionals on the team. Regular clinical conferences centering around troublesome cases in which patients fail to thrive are held. This type of case conference format alternates with conferences that illustrate issues to keep clinical team members fresh and up to date in their knowledge.

Beyond being primary providers of care, team members provide a substantial amount of service as consultants and trainers. They work to form complementary rather than competing relationships with other primary care practitioners and health care specialists. The team promotes the concept of providing evaluations and treatment plan formation in which minimal direct care is provided by Honeycomb Team members. Because some services are on the prevention or wellness side of the continuum of care, the team will provide these services while wearing the professional hats of teacher and trainer.

Entering the Honeycomb

In some traditional models, a patient seeking treatment is interviewed over several sessions by either a professional practicing in isolation or by a junior team member in settings where multiple professionals coexist. The initial interview often occurs several weeks after the patient has initiated contact. Because the Honeycomb cell interfaces with multiple audiences, there are many ways to receive services. Its members are committed to being a rapidly responding unit. That means they are prepared to begin the evaluation process almost immediately and have an evaluation process in place that facilitates treatment (figure 2, below).

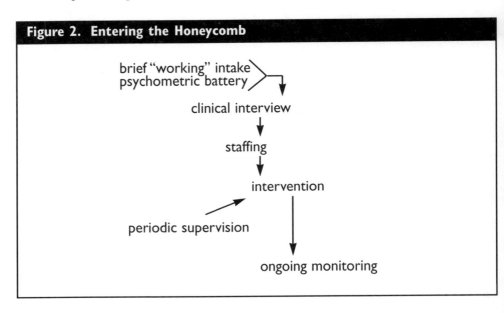

Figure 2. Entering the Honeycomb

The initial contact with a Honeycomb Team member centers around a brief interview, followed by a battery of paper and pencil (self-administrated) exercises that take most people 1½ to 2 hours to complete. Coupling the battery with a brief interview promotes setting an appointment time for a more traditional clinical interview that is sensitive to the patient's needs rather than offering a uniform nonresponsive initial appointment from the reception desk when a request for service comes in.

Broadening the information sampling approaches used offers several important benefits. The most skilled interviewer is vulnerable to the effects of availability bias as one pursues the threads that the patient presents during the initial interview. As information piles up, there is a shaping of professional perspective that affects clinical decision making. The psychometric battery provides the professional with adjunctive, system information about the patient in addition to offering a different perspective on the initial chief complaints for which the patient is seeking assistance.

Counter-transference issues or experiential bias is particularly destructive of good clinical judgment in the behavioral sciences. Again, the broader sampling of information and the sampling by clinical interview and self-administered batteries helps to alleviate this difficulty by eliciting information that might not otherwise be obtained.

This approach also is more cost-effective. Treatment plans can be formulated more readily and treatment instituted more quickly. Experience has shown that there is a significant reduction in the number of clinical interviews needed to arrive at the point when treatment begins by using the multifaceted approach.

Despite the rarity of this approach in the behavioral health field, a trip to the emergency department with a surgical colleague to examine a patient with stomach pain will illustrate that this approach is routinely taken by our nonpsychiatric colleagues.

We meet our colleague in the emergency department. The patient is lying on a gurney, recounting the history of his abdominal pain. An exploration of the patient's chief complaint is elicited by our empathetic colleague. Often some laboratory studies are ordered and a laying on of hands occurs—visual observation, auscultation, palpation of the area in question, followed often by a more generalized physical assessment of the patient.

Both patient and physician want treatment to begin in a responsible and expedient fashion. The physician generally observes the following sequence in a search for a clinical conclusion to the patient's dilemma.

Information gathered directly from a clinical interview and a physical examination leads the physician to engage in some possibility thinking. A preliminary mental list of differential diagnoses is formulated. Our colleague is a psychologically mature individual with a healthy attitude about the intertwining role of laboratory data in the treatment equation. Based on the information gathered by interview and physical examination, a priority list of possibilities has been developed for the patient's state. When the laboratory studies are reviewed, the physician examines them with an eye for the consistency or lack thereof that they offer to the preliminary working diagnosis. If the physician finds consistency between these two broad pieces of information, our colleague proceeds with a reasonable sense of confidence to discuss and to implement a course of treatment with the patient.

If, on the other hand, our colleague finds disparity and inconsistency between the information gathered by interview and examination and the laboratory results, the physician disparages neither. Ever mindful that the origin of the word diagnosis means thorough understanding, the physician moves the diagnostic microscope to a higher level. The physician may well return to the emergency cubicle to make further inquiry and to examine the patient further. Laboratory personnel may well be summoned to obtain additional "higher level" studies. The search continues until the information is internally consistent. As that point occurs, therapy becomes the focus of both the patient and the physician.

More than 20 years' experience with the Honeycomb Model has demonstrated numerous advantages to clinicians, patients, and third-party payers. Patients at times of need appreciate being able to access care rapidly. This process, which has a strong triage approach, facilitates more appropriate scheduling according to acuity needs. Another important aspect of the philosophy of the Honeycomb Team is members' respect and recognition of the role of availability for the services they provide. They appreciate that working patients have significant transaction costs when inconvenient appointment times force them to miss work. A customer-focused, value-added philosophy leads to intervention times being available to meet the needs of the team's patient base.

This process has also been associated with a very high rate (greater than 95 percent) of patients who keep their first appointments with clinicians. A broader information sweep leads to faster implementation of a comprehensive treatment plan, which, in turn, leads to more timely resolution of problems. The overall result is less direct and indirect costs for the patient, the third-party payer, and the patient's employer.

Once the clinician has completed the information gathering phase in the Honeycomb Model, a staffing meeting is held. A broad treatment plan is developed and, often, a nonpsychiatrist professional becomes the primary therapist. Subsequently, regular supervisory sessions are held to review progress and to serve as troubleshooting opportunities concerning therapeutic impasses.

Support the Honeycomb Team

Each Honeycomb team has available to it the services of both a Psychological Assessment Center and a Living Resource Center. Each of these resources is able to comfortably support four to eight Honeycomb Teams. The Psychological Assessment Center is staffed by a clinical psychologist and testing psychometricians. It functions as a pathology laboratory functions, serving as a site where more sophisticated psychometric and psychological testing can be obtained. The testing team is mobile in its immediate service area and is connected by computer to serve more remote locations.

The Living Resource Center is an information resource to assist Honeycomb Teams with the psycho-educational part of their missions. Reflecting an acknowledgment that people learn in different ways, information is available in various forms: print, video, on-line, collaborative exercise, etc. An information search specialist is an essential ingredient of the Center and is available to assist clients in finding information about current problems of living.

Service Bundle and Site of Delivery

Honeycomb Team members believe that services need to be continuously examined regarding their relevance in meeting the needs of patients. The goals are to offer services in nontraditional sites so that services are available to people when their needs arise and to help reduce the walls of suspicion and myth surrounding behavioral health services and behavioral health professionals. Team members are proactive, which leads them into areas of applied psychiatry and psychology, offering some services on the pre-symptom, pre-conflict part of the continuum (figure 3, below). Earlier intervention means reduced costs.

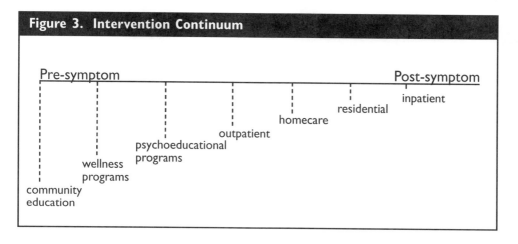

Figure 3. Intervention Continuum

Although the team functions in traditional settings—outpatient clinics and inpatient units of behavioral health units—it also maintains an active presence on general medical and surgical units. The Honeycomb Model is well suited to delivery of behavioral health services in other health care organizations (figure 4, below).

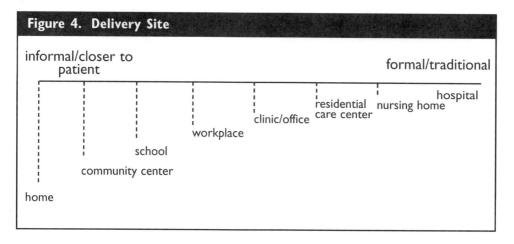

Figure 4. Delivery Site

Because team members maintain an open attitude toward technical advances, the group moves comfortably into participating in videotherapy and telemonitoring. Both of these technology areas will open up broad horizons that will benefit patients and society by making care and intervention much more effortless, effective, and early.

The Honeycomb Team, with its strong drive toward inclusion, seeks an active role in occupational arenas. Its ability to respond quickly to requests for assistance bodes well for its ability as a provider of employee assistance program services. Providing these type of services can be the bridge to providing additional, more prevention-oriented services as business clients become comfortable with Honeycomb Team members. Business organizations often welcome the opportunity to host wellness-oriented continuing education programs. Such business partnering can lead to leadership development and executive coaching projects for the Honeycomb Team.

Schools are another area in which the team can provide clinical and consultative services. Student assistance programs and problem-oriented consultation services for the counseling staff of the education system are common services that can be provided. Again, the team's ability hinges on its rapid, more complete assessment and diagnosis. On the wellness end of the continuum, self-esteem and life skill-building programs can be offered to students and train-the-trainer programs to the staff. Skill-building psycho-educational programs can be made available to the community in general through other community sites.

Today, we are in the midst of change unprecedented in terms of both its speed and its pervasiveness. Change breeds fear and insecurity, which are ideal breeding conditions for conflict and isolationary behaviors. The Honeycomb Team, activist and proactive as it is, is on the threshold of providing conflict resolution and collaboration services. Presently, nonbehavioral health providers of an array of backgrounds have begun to fill the growing demand for conflict resolution and collaborative services. A careful examination of the mediation process leads many to the conclusion that this area is most appropriately in the purview of behavioral health clinicians.

The conflict management continuum consists of postconflict services such as mediation and divorce education programs. Mediation programs are beginning to crop up in educational settings as peer mediation programs and in occupational settings as conflict resolution programs. Stand-alone mediation centers, generally community-based, are beginning to show up in some communities, most commonly offering services to individuals to help resolve minor business and neighborhood disputes.

The Honeycomb Team is ideally suited to providing these services by virtue of its members' professional knowledge and experience. Resolution of conflict services involve helping people to identify and express issues in greater depth and to develop a broader perspective of options available to them to close the gap between the issues and their initial needs and wants. Honeycomb Team members find this in many ways identical to brief problem-oriented therapy.

Active provision of change management services is another appropriate area for the team. This commonly occurs occupationally in assisting those who have been caught in the downsizing, rightsizing net, but it can also be offered to organizations and individuals as they seek to be more prospective in planning organizational changes.

Finally, while the topic may at first blush seem far afield, enhancing economic literacy is another area for the Honeycomb Team to include in its service bundle. Economic issues are major factors behind the stresses and conflicts experienced by individuals and groups. The Honeycomb Team enhances its members' basic professional training and their ability to assist patients and clients by developing their working knowledge of economic and financial disciplines. With their appreciation of learning style differences and of advances in the area of accelerated learning, team members participate in the development of economic literacy programs for elementary and secondary students.

Payment Method

This model is able to participate in a variety of payment systems. Espousing a dually responsible patient-professional partnership in the intervention process leads the Honeycomb Team to be active promoters of payment programs that require and promote ongoing, responsible choices on the part of the patient. This means that deductibles and copayments are welcomed and encouraged. Irresponsibility on the part of the patient, such as missing appointments, becomes the patient's responsibility and not that of either the provider or the payer. The approach encourages the patient to seek help early and with minimal hesitation, yet helps to avoid provider exploitation and interminable treatment. As patients seek intervention for situations that move from the medically necessary to the more personally enhancing, payment responsibility increasingly switches to the consumer.

Because of the array of services that are "pre-problem" and "pre-symptom," a significant amount of the revenue generated by the Honeycomb Team falls outside of traditional health care funding mechanisms. Some of the revenue comes from organizations using teams' consultative and development services, such as schools and business organizations, or from individuals who seek services such as mediation and psycho-educational skill building.

Monitoring

Behavioral health services can be reasonably quantified to assist decision makers in distinguishing both the need for service and the effectiveness of intervention. Most of the initial battery of clinical information was developed around a system of quantification. This initial battery can serve as a benchmark against which the impact of intervention may be compared.

Quantitative statistics can be gathered, such as cost of treatment per diagnostic episode, as they are for other medical conditions. Additional considerations should be given to future health care costs and recidivism costs. Now there is focus on the present episode, which short-circuits a strong educational focus for the patient and family. While an educational focus increases the cost of treatment for the present episode, it significantly reduces costs for conditions that tend to be recurrent.

Professionals need to change their attitude regarding comparative statistics of performance. Professional performance summaries should be welcomed so that patients and payers can make more informed decisions in selecting providers. With such information on comparative performance, team members would be affected by the performance of fellow colleagues, which would help motivate them to shore up areas of weakness. In addition, in instances of professional impairment, there would be significantly increased motivation for those around the impaired professional to deal with the situation head on and early on.

We should always remember that there is another party in this equation—the patient. Voluntary patient behavior has significant impact on treatment outcomes and on the costs of health care delivery. Nonconstructive behaviors on the part of patients need to be monitored and should have an impact on an individual's cost of participating in a health plan.

Summary

The potential benefits that the behavioral disciplines can bring to individuals and to broader audiences of organizations, community, and public policy formation have not yet been harnessed. The Honeycomb Model, by bringing together professionals from several behavioral health disciplines, offers interventions to varied audiences in a fashion that is cost-effective and convenient. The Honeycomb Team offers services to meet the evolving needs of an individual, a business, a school, or a community.

An overarching goal of this model is to achieve inclusion, broad availability of behavioral health professionals who actively seek to be involved throughout a community to make available their services and the benefits of their knowledge and experience. The Honeycomb Model is not so much a structural model as it is an organizational value structure.

Brian E. Tugana, MD, MBA, CTP, FACPE, is President of Phoenix Associates, Clinton, Iowa.

Chapter 10

Application of the Human Service Matrix Model to the Treatment of Mental Illness: The Targeted Services Paradigm

by Michael D. McGee, MD

This chapter presents the Human Service Matrix, a conceptual service delivery model, and describes its practical application to the treatment of mental illness. The Human Service Matrix model distinguishes clinical from social needs and stresses the integrated provision of clinical and social services to achieve optimal clinical and fiscal outcomes. This model discourages meeting social needs implicitly via the clinical setting and encourages clinicians and administrators to expand the scope of services to include both clinical and social service realms. The chapter concludes with a presentation of the initial results of the application of the Human Service Matrix model to a statewide managed provider network.

Introduction

Skillful mental health administrators understand the need to create structures and processes that most effectively mirror patients' needs. If our goal is to provide the highest quality care as efficiently as possible, we must ask ourselves which aspects of our health care delivery system we can most effectively manage to achieve this goal. To date, the health care industry has focused on quality assurance, utilization review, and benefits management strategies.[1] The field has also elaborated the concept of the health care continuum, allowing for different levels of service intensity according to need as defined by medical necessity criteria. These different levels of service intensity have been coined "levels of care."[2,3] Defined by both site of care and intensity of care, they generally include inpatient, residential, intensive outpatient, and routine outpatient levels.

Although the level of care paradigm does move us away from an inefficient, "one size fits all" approach to service delivery, it has limitations. In particular, by defining both the intensity and site of care, this approach to psychiatric treatment simultaneously addresses both clinical and social needs (the setting of care) in a rigidly linked manner, preventing a more flexible matching of services and settings.[4] We have yet to develop an approach to treatment matching that delinks clinical and social services (settings) and then directs the coordinated provision of a broader range of clinical and social services, including appropriate treatment settings.[4-8]

Some health care system strategists understand the need to delink services from settings and to provide adjunctive social services. It is this understanding that drives the current elaboration of "alternative" services, such as home-based treatment, outpatient detoxification, respite care, child care, transportation, peer support services, and assertive community treatment approaches.[9-12] These enhancements modify the setting or provide necessary social services to improve both fiscal efficiencies and clinical outcomes.

The issue of clinical versus social services actually stems from a more fundamental question of what people suffering from mental illnesses need to heal. We have evolved a sophisticated and broad repertoire of clinical approaches, such as cognitive-behavioral, psychodynamic, and psychopharmacological treatments. Yet these clinical approaches only help if provided in a setting in which patients can benefit from them. Like Maslow's concept of a hierarchy of needs, patients first need the appropriate combination of social ingredients to benefit from clinical services.[13-15] A service matching model should therefore attend explicitly to both the social and the clinical service needs of patients and provide for their integration in the delivery of patient care.

We have yet to develop a new conceptual approach that addresses the inefficiencies of the level of care paradigm and brings clarity to the question of how to most effectively meet patients' needs.[16-19] This chapter describes the Human Service Matrix model for service matching and reviews the literature that supports the validity of the model. Finally, the application of this model in the form of the Targeted Services Paradigm, a managed care network delivery model, is described.

The Human Service Matrix

Figure 1, page 131, represents the Human Service Matrix model developed by McGee and Mee-Lee.[20] Licensed clinicians with professional clinical training provide clinical services to alleviate symptomatic and functional impairment. Social services include both professional services and community resources.

Community resources include the patient's existing network of supportive relationships, family ties, mutual-help groups, community service organizations such as YMCA, religious groups, transportation, social clubs, and other social-dating relationship services. Volunteers, community activists, paraprofessionals, and recovering alumnae sometimes provide services in this realm. Professional social services include vocational training, legal services, child care services, residential services, occupational services, family and youth services, and social service entitlements such as Social Security and Medicaid. Together, professional services and community resources provide the sustenance and support patients require to benefit from treatment.

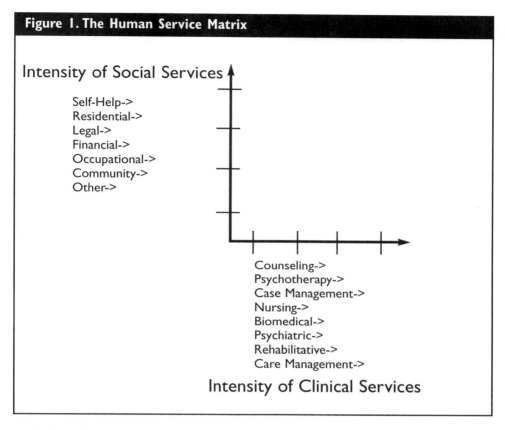

Figure 1. The Human Service Matrix

Intensity of Social Services

Self-Help->
Residential->
Legal->
Financial->
Occupational->
Community->
Other->

Counseling->
Psychotherapy->
Case Management->
Nursing->
Biomedical->
Psychiatric->
Rehabilitative->
Care Management->

Intensity of Clinical Services

By placing clinical services along the horizontal axis, the Human Service Matrix allocates these resources independently of a patient's social service needs. Non-health care professionals provide necessary social services, such as a safe, supportive, and supervised place to sleep; transportation; and child care. This model delinks clinical services from settings and from other social services, thereby eliminating the need to use clinical treatment settings to meet social needs. Clinicians can conceptualize and ultimately provide treatment independently of setting in a system that provides a variety of health care and social services in multiple settings, including home-based, outpatient, residential, and inpatient. For example, a patient recovering from a schizophrenic episode who would otherwise be hospitalized may be better served through support and monitoring by nonclinicians in a foster care setting while attending a day treatment program.

The vertical axis encourages the clinician to pay explicit attention to social services and supports. It makes explicit the need for treatment planning to produce a biopsychosocial solution that details both the social and the clinical elements required for a patient's recovery. It encourages clinicians to think carefully about what each patient requires to receive and benefit from treatment. A patient with alcohol dependence who chronically relapses because of a lack of meaningful daytime structures, for example, may benefit from a vocational rehabilitation program in addition to weekly psychotherapy.

Clinical services include arrangement or referral for necessary social services. Coordinating and managing the treatment plan is an additional clinical function in this model. A clinician performing these functions serves as a "bridging professional" who integrates and coordinates the often separate worlds of clinical and social service providers. This becomes more important as necessary social services are no longer implicitly provided as part of a treatment program.

Several authors have noted that future improvements in clinical and fiscal outcomes will begin with innovations in conceptual approaches to assessment, treatment planning, and treatment.[16,21] The Human Service Matrix may represent such an innovation by delinking social from clinical services and then providing for their reintegration to meet the broader range of each patient's needs.

Social Supports and Services

The wide array of both natural and professional social services and supports, upon which we all rely for our well being and survival, exist as a necessary repository of resources to support a patient's healing and recovery.

Good clinicians instinctively attend to the social requirements for healing and change. These include safety, structure, support, supervision, stability, optimal stress, therapeutic sequelae, and sobriety. Together, these eight factors make up what may be called the "eight-S environment" (table 1, below), components of which have been noted by others as important prerequisites for healing.[13,22-24] In fact, much of the work of clinicians, especially in social work and case management roles, involves helping patients obtain needed social services.[14] In this way, clinicians become bridging agents between the clinical and the social realms. Mental health administrators and policy makers face the challenge of how they will create clinical and administrative structures that allow ready access to appropriate housing, support, supervision, and daytime occupational services for their patients.

Just as there are continuums in clinical care, there are continuums in the social services realm. These include the degree of structure and support in a patient's living situation, ranging from living alone to living in a highly structured residential setting. There is also a continuum in

Table I. Social Structures and Supports: The "Eight-S" Environment
• Safety
• Structure
• Support
• Supervision
• Stability
• Sobriety
• Optimal Stress
• Sequelae

terms of family relationships, from those living solitary lives to those who are imbedded in an extended family matrix. There is a continuum of community relationships from those who have no community ties to those who live in very close-knit communities. There is also a continuum of economic resources and a continuum of available social services, which vary from remote rural settings to wealthy urban centers.

The available range, or continuum, of social services and supports has a significant impact on clinical outcomes.[25-27] The provision of safe and sober housing, food, or access to money via entitlements, for example, may make the difference for a chronically relapsing heroin addict, who would otherwise not benefit from any amount of psychotherapy.[28] Several studies have shown that combining social services with clinical services improves outcomes for homeless substance abusers.[27,29-31] These findings call for a shift from "treatment matching" to "service matching" and the combined provision of clinical and social services.

Making the Human Service Matrix a Reality

Creating a functional Human Service Matrix requires several steps (table 2, below). The first step involves separating social services embodied in the current level of care paradigm (i.e., the necessary "Eight-S" environment) from actual clinical services needed, such as psychotherapy or nursing monitoring. Next, one must identify necessary social and clinical services (including where patients will live while receiving treatment) that patients require for successful treatment. Finally, the continuum of both social and clinical services must be developed. Treatment systems accomplish this last step with varying degrees of success through a combination of direct service provision and interagency collaboration arrangements.

Because no one organization can be all things to all people, interagency collaboration becomes crucial to an organization's success in creating a Human Service Matrix.[14,32] Barriers to collaboration need to be overcome, including excessive boundaries, exclusion and territoriality, rigid funding streams, lack of a strong shared constituency, mistrust, differing philosophies and beliefs, and fragility of collaborative relationships.[14,32,33] Because of these barriers, health care and social service professions have yet to address the polarization and redundancy of services that now exist.[34,35]

The clinical service continuum would include the range of biopsychiatric modalities, including medical evaluations and treatment; psychiatric evaluation and treatment; individual, group and

---

Table 2. Strategies for Creating the Human Service Matrix

- Define practice under the current level of care paradigm.
- Identify implicit social services that can be provided separately from clinical services.
- Ascertain social and clinical services required to facilitate healing.
- Create the necessary clinical and social service continuums.

couples psychotherapies; dynamic behavioral supportive psychotherapies; crisis intervention and stabilization services; intensive outpatient services, including day treatment; evening and partial hospitalization services; and 24-hour intensive treatment in residential and hospital settings. This range of services represents what some have traditionally called the horizontal and vertical continuums in mental health care delivery.

The continuum of social services provided during either acute or subacute care might include:

■ Supportive residential and other housing services

■ Home-based support and supervision

■ Vocational supervision and training

■ Transportation services

■ Care-tracking services

■ Companion services

■ Child care

■ Mutual-help groups

■ Meals

■ Legal assistance

■ Financial assistance

Health care organizations need to decide which of these services they will provide, either directly or through collaboration, on the basis of existing contingencies, priorities, resources, and opportunities. Najavits and Weiss enhanced the engagement of patients by providing needed food, money, and housing.[28] Some programs provide adolescents with positive role models through social service programs such as the Big Brother program.[36] Programs exist that allow women recovering from cocaine addiction to have their children stay with them.[37] The Addiction Treatment and Research Corporation provides job placement services and tutoring as a part of its substance abuse treatment program.[5] Several studies describe other treatment programs that provide a variety of social services for homeless substance abusers.[29-31,38]

Perhaps the most well-known application of the Human Service Matrix model comes from the work of Gudeman et al., who created the Fenwood Inn System at Massachusetts Mental Health Hospital in Boston in the early 1980s.[39] In this model, patients requiring 24-hour residential support and supervision live in an inn staffed and monitored by mental health counselors with bachelor's degrees. Patients simultaneously attend a day hospital program in the same building. For many patients, provision of these two services together obviates the need for 24-hour nursing and thus greatly reduces costs. This model has operated successfully for more than a decade now and serves as perhaps the best example of the combination of supportive residential and intensive clinical services.

Targeted Services Paradigm (TSP)

TSP Service Delivery Design
In late 1993, Merit Behavioral Care (MBC) began to contract in Massachusetts for supportive residential services as part of a continuum of services (table 3, page 136). Patients receive supportive residential services in combination with mental health or substance abuse intensive outpatient programs and medically supervised (outpatient) detoxification services. In this way, unnecessary treatment in settings providing 24-hour biopsychiatric services is avoided for patients who do not need these services but who require a safe, structured, supportive, and supervised setting for successful treatment. This might include depressed patients who are not suicidal but need help to ensure they get dressed, eat, go to their treatment program, and take their medications, or patients who are disorganized and psychotic, unable to function independently, and yet cooperative and nondestructive. Many substance abusing patients can be safely detoxified with medical supervision once daily, yet do not have a structured and drug-free environment in which they can be monitored. Supportive residential services for these patients allows them to safely receive a medically supervised detoxification with or without other intensive outpatient services, such as day treatment (figure 2, page 137).

In the TSP model, supportive residential services are a social service rather than a clinical service and are always provided in combination with intensive treatment. MBC thus maintains its mission of certifying clinical services to reduce acute psychiatric impairment and risk. Paraprofessionals or counselors staff supportive residential settings. They provide support and supervision, provide informal teaching, and alert the patient's current treaters when they detect variance from the treatment plan or changes in a patient's status that require immediate clinical attention.

The modular service components of TSP allow for several possible service combinations (table 4, page 137). As of 1995, only 29 percent of MBC network facilities had contracted for all or most of these service combinations for mental health or substance abuse (table 5, page 137).

Effectively Managing Service Certification
The increased complexity of service options requires careful utilization management by well-trained clinical staff. As with any tool, TSP is only as good as the skill with which it is used. Care managers need good service criteria to certify services that are targeted to clinical and social need so that patients receive exactly what they need, no more and no less.

For addiction services, MBC created a criteria crosswalk modified from the American Society of Addiction Medicine (ASAM) criteria as shown in table 6, pages 138 and 139. This crosswalk guides clinicians and care managers in their matching of services to needs.

Impact of TSP on Service Delivery
Certification for acute clinical and social (i.e., supportive residential) services according to TSP has decreased the rate of inpatient treatment (table 7, page 140). Prior to implementation of TSP, the great majority of addictions patients who were appropriate for medically supervised detoxification were unable to receive this treatment because of the lack of highly structured,

Table 3. MBC Massachusetts Services

Service	Service Elements	Service Criteria
Crisis Services(crisis evaluations, crisis stabilization, and crisis intervention	Crisis evaluation: 1-3 hour evaluation by independently licensed crisis specialist. Crisis intervention: 1-3 meetings/week with patient, providers, and family, together with case management. Crisis stabilization: Containment for safety, evaluation and treatment up to 24 hours in a crisis bed. Complete assessment of patient, system, and current treatment, formulation of case, and articulation of case, and articulation of a treatment plan.	Imminent life-threatening risk and impairment requiring immediate assessment and stabilization.
Medically Managed Inpatient	24-hour biopsychiatric management by psychiatrists and multidisciplinary team.	Imminent life-threatening risk and/or impairment requiring 24 hour management by a psychiatrist.
Medically Monitored Residential	24-hour biopsychiatric monitoring by nurses and a multidisciplinary team, with psychiatrist consultation.	Imminent risk and/or impairment requiring 24 hour monitoring by nursing staff.
Intensive Nonresidential (day/evening treatment, partial hospitalization, medically supervised detoxification, intensive outpatient services)	3 hours/week to 8 hours/day biopsychosocial treatments, including psychopharmacology; individual, group, couples, and family psychotherapy; medical screening, and case management.	Risk and/or impairment requiring intensive (>2 hours/week) multidisciplinary clinical services.
Low-Intensity Outpatient Services	1-2 hours/week outpatient psychiatric services. Risk and/or impairment	Requiring low-intensity psychiatric services.
Supportive Residential Services	Meals, sleeping quarters, and supervision by a counselor.	Lack of necessary natural supports to facilitate safe and effective treatment.

Figure 2. Targeted Services Paradigm for Addictions Services

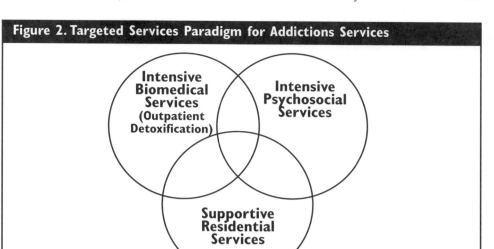

Table 4. Service Combinations in the MBC Targeted Services Paradigm

▌ Crisis Evaluation

▌ Crisis Intervention (up to 1 week)

▌ Crisis Stabilization (up to 24 hours)

▌ Psychiatrically Managed Inpatient

▌ Psychiatrically Monitored Residential

▌ Supportive Residential + Intensive Nonresidential (e.g., Day Treatment, Medically Supervised Detoxification)

▌ Intensive Nonresidential

▌ Low-Intensity Outpatient Treatment

Table 5. MBC Massachusetts Network Facility Type

Facility Type	Number	Percentage of Network
Traditional	22	71%
TSP Mental Health and Substance Abuse	3	10
TSP Substance Abuse Only	6	19
TSP Total	9	29
Total All Facilities	**31**	**100%**

Table 6. MBC Massachusetts Addictions Service Criteria

Services	I. Acute Intoxication Withdrawal	II. Biomedical	III. Emotions/ Behavioral	IV. Change Readiness	V. Dependence Severity	VI. Recovery Environment
Psychiatrically Managed Inpatient (e.g., Level IV)	Severe withdrawal risk: H/O, DTs, Szs, pregnancy, require 24-hour management by psychiatrist and intensive nursing care.	Medical problems require 24-hour management by psychiatrist and intensive nursing care.	Psychiatric problems require 24-hour psychiatric management and intensive nursing care.	N/A	N/A	N/A
Psychiatrically Monitored Residential (e.g., Level III)	History or probability of severe withdrawal Sxs require 24-hour Medical problems require 24-hour nursing monitoring and management.	Medical problems require 24-hour nursing monitoring and management.	Psychiatric problems require 24-hour nursing monitoring and management.	N/A	N/A	N/A
Medically Supervised (e.g. outpatient detoxification)	History or probability of severe withdrawal Sxs require 24-hour nursing monitoring and management.	Medical problems require daily nursing monitoring and management.	N/A	N/A	N/A	N/A

Intensive Psychosocial (daily psychotherapy up to partial hospitalization	N/A	N/A	Intensive Rx required to manage emotional/behavioral Sxs.	Intensive Rx required for engagement and for motivational interventions.	Intensive Rx required to build relapse management and prevention skills.	Intensive Rx required to address barriers to recovery and build Recovery supports.
Low-Intensity Psychosocial (e.g., weekly psychotherapy)	N/A	N/A	Low-intensity Rx required to manage emotional/behavioral Sxs.	Intensive Rx required for engagement and persuasion work and for motivational intentions.	Low-intensity Rx required to build relapse management skills or to monitor recovery.	Low-intensity Rx required to address barriers to recovery and build recovery supports.
Intensive Psychosocial (daily psychotherapy up to partial hospitalization	N/A	N/A	Intensive Rx required to manage emotional/behavioral Sxs.	Intensive Rx required for engagement and for motivational interventions.	Intensive Rx required to build relapse management and prevention skills.	Intensive Rx required to address barriers to recovery and build Recovery supports.
Supportive Residential (e.g., Sober House)	N/A	N/A	24-hour structure and support required to manage emotional/behavioral problems.	24-hour structure and support required for engagement and motivational interventions.	24-hour structure and support required to support practice of relapse management skills.	24-hour structure and support required for patient to safely and effectively pursue intensive.

Table 7. Service Profile Comparison for Four TSP Facilities and Four Traditional Facilities for the Period from 9/94 to 6/95.

Service	Traditional Facility	TSP Facility
Crisis Stabilization	2%	5%
Psychiatrically Managed Inpatient	65%	5%
Psychiatrically Monitored Residential	14%	57%
Supportive Residential + Intensive Treatment	3%	13%
Intensive Outpatient	16%	23%

Table 8. Percentage of Network Patients Treated at TSP Facilities

Year	Percentage of Patients
1992	34%
1993	36
1994	38
1995	46

Table 9. Six-Month Readmission Rates to TSP and Traditional Facilities, 8/94-6/95

Facility Type	Readmission Rate
Traditional	42%
TSP	17%

Table 10. Average Length of Treatment (ALOT) by Year and Program Type

Program Type	Year			
	1992	1993	1994	1995
Traditional	7.95	8.27	7.79	8.27
Total TSP	8.44	7.31	8.79	7.00
Total Network	8.12	7.93	8.17	7.68

supportive, supervised, and sober environments. Mental health patients who had no options for returning to safe community environments while completing their intensive treatment now may receive supportive residential services instead of psychiatrically managed or psychiatrically monitored services. Provision of supportive residential services has allowed safe diversion of patients from 24-hour biopsychiatric settings.

MBC gradually increased the number of patients treated at TSP facilities from 34 percent in 1992 to almost 46 percent in 1995 (table 8, page 140). During 1995, the first full year after implementation of this model, 1,171 patients, or 46 percent of all patients, received treatment at the 29 percent of our facilities that were TSP facilities.

Impact on Quality of Care
Initial analysis of readmission rates for addictions patients showed a striking decrease at TSP facilities (table 9, page 140), alleviating concerns that this model might adversely affect the quality of clinical care. The lower readmission rate at TSP facilities is likely due to our contracting with facilities with recognized expertise in the field of substance abuse. It may also be that the need in the TSP model to more precisely define a patient's needs leads to better formulations and treatment matching. The anti-regressive nature of the model, which avoids hospitalization unless it is necessary for biomedical or biopsychiatric reasons, may also be of benefit to patients.

As of 1995, there were no adverse clinical incidents related to certifying a TSP service in place of a 24-hour biopsychiatric service. Preliminary data suggest the TSP is both safe and effective as compared to the traditional level of care model.

Fiscal Outcomes
We began contracting for TSP services late in 1993 and had several new arrangements for facilities to provide supportive residential services by the end of 1994. Different facilities provided these services for our patients in different ways. One facility subcontracts with a sober home. Another converted a house on its grounds. Another took advantage of an underused wing of the hospital. Several of our substance abuse facilities have residential treatment programs that essentially combine supportive residential and partial hospital services in one package.

Table 10, page 140, shows the average length of treatment (ALOT) by year and program type. One concern with expansion of our range of service options was that there would be increased utilization of new service options, with a resultant increase in the length of treatment and treatment costs. The data actually show a small decline in ALOT at TSP facilities in 1995.

Table 11, page 142, shows the cost per patient by year and program type. Cost per patient was calculated for each network facility by dividing the number of patients treated during the year by the total annual costs. A patient retreated one or more times at the same facility was counted once, so the cost per treatment may include one or more episodes of treatment at a facility. Average costs were then calculated by program type.

Table 11. Average Annual Cost per Patient by Year and Program Type

Program Type	1992	1993	1994	1995
TSP SA	$1,500	$1,034	$ 942	$ 984
TSP MH AND SA	1,990	1,920	1,971	1,352
TSP Overall	1,711	1,699	1,781	1,258
Traditional Overall	3,191	3,310	2,778	3,119

Table 12. Total Average Annual Cost per Treated Patient by Year

Year	Cost
1992	$2,684
1993	$2,733
1994	$2,397
1995	$2,257

Table 13. Total Average Cost per Treatment Day

Year	Cost
1992	$331
1993	$345
1994	$293
1995	$294

Table 14. Estimated Savings due to TSP Contracting

	Year		
	1993	1994	1995
Annual Costs	$3,367,629	$4,904,828	$5,703,108
Costs based on 1993 Cost/Patient	$3,367,629	$5,592,670	$6,907,466
Savings		$ 687,842	$1,204,358

These data reveal a significant reduction in 1995 in average annual cost per treated patient after TSP was implemented at several of our combined mental health/substance abuse facilities. Similar reductions were achieved in 1993 for substance abuse facilities when we initially contracted for supportive residential combined with intensive treatment and for psychiatrically monitored treatment. The average cost per patient at substance abuse facilities remained steady through 1995 as MBC expanded contracts for supportive residential and medically supervised detoxification services.

Table 12, page 142, shows the impact of our contracting efforts on total average annual cost per treated patient. Table 13, page 142, shows the average cost per treatment day for our network by year. The combination of reduced average cost per treated patient at TSP facilities combined with an increase in patient volume directed to TSP facilities resulted in a 17 percent reduction in average cost per treated patient and a 15 percent reduction in average cost per day for our overall network.

Table 14, page 142, summarizes estimated cost savings based on 1993 costs per treated patient. Our shift to the TSP model has resulted in almost $2 million saved over a two-year period.

Together, these preliminary data from our initial efforts to implement TSP show a significant improvement in fiscal quality without sacrificing clinical quality, despite only partial implementation of TSP by the end of 1995.

Discussion and Conclusions

Sharfstein and Beigel framed the challenge of the current health care crisis as finding ways to do more with less.[21] The Human Service Matrix meets this challenge by opening the door to integration of clinical and social services, a frontier that remains largely undeveloped. TSP represents one example of the Human Service Matrix in operation and demonstrates the clinical and fiscal efficacy of this model.

Many more opportunities exist for providing care according to this model. Outcomes can be improved by treating patients in their homes rather than in facilities[9-12] Some managed care organizations now pay for home health aides, companions, case managers, care trackers, and other personnel who provide support and supervision. These personnel can track medication compliance, provide support in dealing with daily stresses and negative affect states, and assist with daily tasks. The availability of such services, for example, can make the difference between one patient's ability to receive electroconvulsive therapy (ECT) in an outpatient setting versus in the hospital, or another isolated patient's ability to recover from a depression with support in the home versus in a hospital setting.

The community mental health system has long been a pioneer in the development of social and rehabilitative services, including social day treatment programs and social clubs. These services currently remain largely within the purview of the public sector. This may change as public-private distinctions gradually dissolve and health care systems assume more risk and responsibility for the more severely ill.

Ultimately, new agencies may evolve, on both local and national levels, that integrate clinical and social services. Such a reorganization could help reduce redundancies, fill needed service gaps, and promote integration of clinical and social service worlds.

Systems, like people, tend to resist change unless strong pressures make change desirable. Such strong pressures now exist for greater cost- and outcome-effective treatment. They represent an opportunity for evolution of new treatment models that improve patients' care.

These pressures will be essential for making the Human Service Matrix a standard model for service delivery. Clinical services will need to be less linked to a particular setting. There will need to be much greater interagency collaboration. The range of available social services and supports, including appropriate treatment settings, will also need to be expanded.

Several sources of resistance to these changes may explain in part why the application of the Human Service Matrix model is not more prevalent, especially given the data supporting its validity. They include conceptual barriers such as the "medical paradigm," which tends to look upon illness as something to be cured with a clinical service, as opposed to the "interdependent paradigm," which also looks to the patient's world to provide supports and accommodations that minimize disability.[13] Unlike the interdependent paradigm, the medical paradigm tends to see the social service world as more peripheral to the problem of healing.

Another source of resistance lies in systems issues that create barriers to effective treatment, including:

■ Excessive boundaries, exclusion, and territoriality

■ Inadequate assessment and diagnosis

■ Lack of trained staff

■ Inadequate array of services

■ Rigid funding streams

■ Lack of a strong shared constituency

■ Limited dissemination of effective program models

■ Fragility of collaborative relationships[33]

To date, incentives for collaboration and coordination have been insufficient to bring together the traditionally autonomous clinical and social service worlds. Developing coordinated treatment systems is a slow, evolutionary process that requires consensus-building, strong leadership, funding incentives, a clear mandate, and a clear perception of benefit.[34] Increased competition and pressures for efficient, effective care, along with further outcomes data from projects such as TSP, should facilitate more widespread adoption of the Human Service Matrix model. This would promote continued reengineering of our service delivery systems to fit this model, a move from "treatment matching" to "service matching," and development of new service criteria sets. If skillfully executed, these changes should benefit both patients and society and help us to meet our challenge to do "more with less."

References

1. Kongstvedt, P. *Essentials of Managed Care.* Gaithersburg, Md.: Aspen Publication, 1995.

2. Mee-Lee, D. *Matching in Addictions Treatment: How Do We Get There from Here?* New York, N.Y.: The Haworth Press, Inc., 1995.

3. Sederer, L., and Summergrad, P. "Criteria for Hospital Admission." *Hospital and Community Psychiatry,* 44(2):116-8, Feb. 1993.

4. Garter, L., and Mee-Lee, D. *The Role and Current Status of Patient Placement Criteria In the Treatment of Substance Use Disorders.* Rockville, Md.: The Center for Substance Abuse Treatment, 1995.

5. Batson, H., and others. "A Multicomponent Model for Substance Abuse Treatment." *Journal for Substance Abuse Treatment* 9(2):177-81, 1992.

6. Joe, G., and others. "Treatment Process and Relapse to Opioid Use during Methadone Maintenance." *American Journal of Drug and Alcohol Abuse* 20(2):173-97, 1994.

7. McLellan, A., and Alterman, A.. "Patient Treatment Matching: A Conceptual and Methodological Review with Suggestions for Future Research." *NIDA Research Monograph* 106:114-35, 1991.

8. Moos, R., and others. *Alcoholism Treatment: Context. Process, and Outcome.* New York, N.Y.: Oxford University Press, 1990.

9. McGrew, J. "Critical Ingredients of Assertive Community Treatment: Judgments of the Experts." *Journal of Mental Health Administration* 22(2):113-25, Spring 1995.

10. Olfson, M. "Assertive Community Treatment: An Evaluation of the Experimental Evidence." *Hospital and Community Psychiatry* 41(6):634-41, June 1990.

11. Teague, G., and others. "Evaluating Use of Continuous Treatment Teams for Persons with Mental Illness and Substance Abuse." *Psychiatric Services* 46(7):689-95, July 1995.

12. Test, M. "Training in Community Living." In Liberman, R., Editor, *Handbook of Psychiatric Rehabilitation.* Boston, Mass.: Allyn and Bacon, 1992, pp. 153-170.

13. Condeluci, A. *Interdependence: The Route to Community.* Winter Park, Fla.: GR Press, Inc., 1995.

14. Crimando, W., and Rigger, T., Editors. *Utilizing Community Resources: An Overview of Human Services.* Delray Beach, Fla.: St. Lucie Press, 1996.

15. Maslow, A., Editor. *Motivation and Personality.* New York, N.Y.: Harper and Row, 1970.

16. Ball, J.. "Why Has It Proved So Difficult to Match Drug Abuse Patients to Appropriate Treatment?" *Addiction* 89(3):263-5, March 1994.

17. Havens, L. *Approaches to the Mind.* Boston, Mass.: Little Brown and Company, 1973.

18. Schon, D. *The Reflective Practitioner.* New York, N.Y.: Basic Books, 1983.

19. Shaffer, H. "Assessment of Addictive Disorders. the Use of Clinical Reflection and Hypotheses Testing." *Psychiatric Clinics of North America* 9(3):385-98, Sept. 1986.

20. McGee, M., and Mee-Lee, D. "Rethinking Patient Placement: The Human Service Matrix Model for Matching Services to Needs." *Journal for Substance Abuse Treatment* 14(2):141-8, 1997.

21. Sharfstein, S., and Beigel, A. "Less Is More? Today's Economics and Its Challenge to Psychiatry." American Journal of Psychiatry 141(11):1403-8, Nov. 1984.

22. Anthony, W. "Psychological Rehabilitation: A Concept in Need of a Method." *American Psychologist* 32(8):658-62, Aug. 1977.

23. Anthony, W., and Liberman, R. "Principles of Psychiatric Rehabilitation." In Liberman, R., Editor, *Handbook of Psychiatric Rehabilitation.* Needham Heights, Mass.: Allyn and Bacon, 1992, pp. 1-25.

24. Lamb, H. "Structure: The Unspoken Word in Community Treatment." *Psychiatric Services* 46(7):647, July 1995.

25. Ford, J., and others. "Needs Assessment for Persons with Severe Mental Illness: What Services Are Needed for Successful Community Living?" *Community Mental Health Journal* 28(6):491-503, Dec. 1992.

26. Mirin, S., and others. "Practice Guideline for the Treatment of Patients with Substance Use Disorders: Alcohol, Cocaine, Opioids." *American Journal of Psychiatry* 152(11 Suppl):1-59, Nov. 1995.

27. Stahler, G., and others. "Evaluating Alternative Treatments for Homeless Substance-Abusing Men: Outcomes and Predictors of Success." *Journal of Addictive Diseases* 14(4):151-68, 1995.

28. Najavits, L., and Weiss, R. "The Role of Psychotherapy in the Treatment of Substance-Use Disorders." *Harvard Review of Psychiatry* 2(2):84-96, March-April 1994.

29. Braucht, G., and others. "Effective Services for Homeless Substance Abusers." *Journal of Addictive Diseases* 14(4):87-109, 1995.

30. Smith, E., and others. "Eighteen Month Follow-Up Data on a Treatment Program for Homeless Substance Abusing Mothers." *Journal of Addictive Diseases* 14(4):57-72, 1995.

31. Sosin, M., and others. "Paths and Impacts in the Progressive Independence Model: A Homeless and Substance Abuse Intervention in Chicago." *Journal of Addictive Diseases* 14(1):1-19, 1995.

32. McGee, M. "Interagency Collaboration: Improving Outcomes in the Treatment of Addictions." In *The Hatherleigh Guide to Treating Substance Abuse*, Part 1, Lansdale, J., Editor. New York, N.Y.: Hatherleigh Press, 1996, pp. 243-58.

33. Thacker, W., and Tremaine, L. "Systems Issues in Serving the Mentally Ill Substance Abuser: Virginia's Experience." *Hospital and Community Psychiatry* 40(10):1046-9, Oct. 1989.

34. Baker, F. *Coordination of Alcohol, Drug Abuse and Mental Health Services*(4). Rockville, Md.: Center for Substance Abuse Treatment, U.S. Department of Health and Human Services, 1991.

35. Baker, F., and Intagliata, J. "Case Management." In Liberman, R., Editor, *Handbook of Psychiatric Rehabilitation.* Boston, Mass.: Allyn and Bacon, 1992, pp. 213-39.

36. Epstein, J., and others. "The Role of Social Factors and Individual Characteristics in Promoting Alcohol Use Among Inner-City Minority Youths." *Journal of Studies on Alcohol* 56(1):39-46, Jan. 1995.

37. Hughes, P., and others. "Retaining Cocaine-Abusing Women in a Therapeutic Community: The Effect of a Child Live-in Program." *American Journal of Public Health* 85(8 Pt 1):1149-52, Aug. 1995.

38. Stahler, G. "Social Interventions for Homeless Substance Abusers: Evaluating Treatment Outcomes." *Journal of Addictive Diseases* 14(4):xv-xxvi, 1995.

39. Gudeman, J., and others. "Four-Year Assessment of a Day Hospital-Inn Program as an Alternative to Inpatient Hospitalization." *American Journal of Psychiatry* 142(11):1330-3, Nov. 1985.

Michael D. McGee, MD, is President and CEO, Psych Solutions, Inc., Wenham, Massachusetts.

Chapter 11

Behavioral Health Care in Academic Institutions

by David T. Feinberg, MD, and James McGough, MD

A cademic Medical Centers (AMCs) face unique challenges as the health care marketplace demands delivery of services in more efficient and less costly modes. Academic institutions must satisfy their missions of research and teaching in addition to clinical service delivery. This unique position creates specific advantages and disadvantages as these institutions enter the competitive marketplace. This chapter will address how academic centers can provide and manage health services while at the same time performing research and providing training. The chapter will conclude with a description of a rapid stabilization unit for psychiatrically hospitalized children and adolescents in an AMC.

Historically, academic institutions survived and, in fact, prospered in direct proportion to the quality of the research they did. High-quality research brought in grant money and other high-quality researchers. As a result of ongoing research and researchers, these institutions became high-quality training sites. Additionally, in behavioral health, some training programs flourished because of the particular theoretical background of the faculty. Known for being biologic, psychodynamic, eclectic, etc., programs developed their own reputations, which, in turn, drove training missions. Clinical care neatly fell under the umbrella of research at most institutions. Patients were needed for clinical research. At other institutions, patients provided the vehicle for training. A good patient mix and good clinical supervision would make for good clinical training. Many programs did, and still do, provide clinical services to patients and families who would be unable to access care if it were not for these teaching institutions and their affiliations.

The present state of behavioral health care delivery is very different from just a few years ago. Such changes, outlined elsewhere in this book, have affected academic medical centers. Behavioral health care has undergone a dramatic shift in utilization management that has paralleled the changes in medicine and that, in some instances, has taken an accelerated course. In short, many AMCs must now compete with private organizations for patients. This may seem rather simple to those accustomed to the private sector, but it is very challenging to institutions that have not had to do so previously. Additionally, there are obstacles inherent in the academic arena that make this new element of competition quite challenging.

Contrasts between academic medical centers and managed care organizations (MCOs) have created an environment in which change becomes crucial for survival. AMCs have provided tertiary care and have been specialty-based, while managed care emphasizes primary care and is population-based. In behavioral health care, this results in two outcomes. First, the AMC must become involved in primary mental health services. This can be accomplished via network development in which AMCs partner with primary providers of behavioral health services. Alternatively, AMCs can directly expand their services into the primary care market. From a teaching perspective, this requires faculty to be versed in brief, time-limited treatment. The second outcome that results from MCOs' focus on primary care is AMCs transitions into becoming regional specialty centers. The network of primary care services can funnel difficult or complicated cases to AMCs, because economies of scale can be reached by regionalizing tertiary care. Obviously, this creates a competitive market when more than one AMC exists in a given market area. Examples of tertiary behavioral health care are seen in such areas as severe eating disorders, electroconvulsive therapy, and medically compromised psychiatric patients.

Another area of contrast is that AMCs have traditionally stood alone, while MCOs have fostered integrated health systems. This presents significant difficulty in behavioral health, as many departments of psychiatry at various AMCs have held very differing philosophical approaches to treatments. These differences can add another complexity to integration.

Additionally, AMCs have been hospital-based and would utilize relatively long lengths of stay as a way to teach continuity of care. The most complicated or difficult cases are sought out because of their teaching potential. On the other hand, MCOs are population-based and avoid adverse selection of patients. This creates a problem for AMCs, which need difficult patients to meet their training missions. Specialty clinics in departments of psychiatry bring status to the institutions. They provide training and research and are run by faculty members devoted to the specialty. However, because of other responsibilities, such as research, these faculty members may be available in clinics only once or twice a week. In psychiatry, this occurs in clinics for many of the major mental disorders as well as most of the other diagnosable mental disorders. These clinics are not based on a gatekeeper model, and utilization management is not a priority. Consequently, patient accessibility is not optimized, costs are not controlled, and specialists provide ongoing, albeit limited, care.

The orientation of AMCs has been to the intellectual challenge of medicine, while MCOs have been focused more on the business of medicine, even as both aim to provide high-quality care. AMCs might see service as revenue-generating activity, while MCOs might see service as cost.

With all these differences, what are the solutions? Most likely, this question will be answered over time and will also change with time, but there appear to be guiding principles that can help with the inevitable change. The first is acceptance of the concept of medically necessary care. The other is the need to integrate care in primary care settings. The best way to accomplish the cultural change that is needed is for AMCs to form strategic business units devoted to managed care. Staff can be hired or existing staff can be retrained in a "managed care friendly" way. This must include easy access to care, a focus on medically necessary care, an understanding of revenue flow from MCOs, and creation of incentives for clinicians based on efficient, high-quality care. Additionally, AMCs have to explore nonphysician clinicians as providers of care. If patient flow is going to shift to population-based from hospital-based, social workers, psychologists, nurses, and physician assistants become needed providers.

Yet another area of needed change would have psychiatry enter medical aspects of treatment. Many AMCs have freestanding psychiatric hospitals. Even when psychiatry exists within the walls of academic medical centers, there are still many boundaries that need to be examined. In many institutions, psychiatry is focused on specific mental disorders and does not contribute to the management of many medical disorders where behavioral health intervention would be appropriate. Consultation-liaison psychiatry attempts to address this need, but, in many instances, it only sees patients with major mental disorders, as the gravity of psychiatric disorders of other medical patients is either unappreciated or unknown. This boundary also exists at the industry level. Many insurance companies have "carved out" mental health care. The result usually is that some patients have fewer resources for treatment of mental disorders. Additionally, reimbursement for behavioral care of medical patients may not exist in some systems.

Departments of psychiatry should explore innovative ways of reintegrating service delivery into the medical arena. This can be accomplished by establishing programs on the medical side, wherein behavioral interventions add value by decreasing total medical costs. Medication compliance, high utilizer clinics, and psychoeducation are examples of ways in which behavioral health can reintegrate into medicine. The industrialization of medicine can enhance this reintegration. When people's lives are fully capitated in AMCs, psychiatric intervention has the potential of decreasing total costs. The question of medical cost offsetting is not yet resolved, but psychiatric departments in AMCs can take the lead in examining the issue.

Innovations in the conceptualization of patient care are essential to the financial viability of academic institutions and their subsequent ability to sustain research and teaching functions. Many academic departments have supported research and teaching activities with revenues generated by inpatient services. Inpatient rotations have provided the most focused and intensive training experiences for psychiatric residents, including opportunities to master skills in assessment, medication management, case coordination, family work, and individual therapies. Trainees in tertiary care centers rarely followed patients into outpatient settings and depended on extended lengths of stay to develop an awareness of patient course and response to treatment.

As recently as the mid-1980s, inpatient psychiatric treatment was viewed as an opportunity for thorough, multidisciplinary assessment and intensive, long-term treatment. It was not uncommon, particularly with children and adolescents, for patients to remain in the hospital for six or more months. Psychodynamic theory provided the rationale for "therapeutic milieus" in which a safe holding environment was deemed essential to facilitate patient regression and to work through core conflicts. Hospitalization and institutional therapies were viewed as long-term settings for "corrective emotional experience" designed to free patients from neurotic conflict and to restore them to full function. At academic centers, the emphasis in training was on provision of intensive, long-term, psychodynamically oriented therapies. Trainees maintained relatively low case loads and often competed for assignment to new cases. Research generally remained at the level of anecdotal reports and theoretical speculation, with little emphasis given to rigorous diagnosis or objective outcome assessment.

Advances in psychopharmacology, reemergence of the medical model in psychiatry, and increasing economic constraints contributed to a reconceptualization of inpatient psychiatric care. By the late 1980s, the trend was to "brief hospitalizations," viewed at the time as three-to-four-week lengths of stay. This shift had a discernible impact on psychiatric training. Increased patient turnover increased the types and numbers of patients to whom residents gained direct exposure. Following publication of updated editions of the *Diagnostic and Statistical Mannual* (DSM) of Mental Disorders, i.e., DSM III and DSM III-R, renewed training emphasis was given to diagnostic assessment. Hospitalization was viewed as the appropriate venue for medication trials and other somatic therapies, such as electroconvulsive therapy. Collection of research data and training in specialized treatment modalities was enhanced by creation of specialized treatment units. Some attention was paid to "justification for hospital admission," but this was often viewed as a technicality and was addressed with only minor increases in documentation. The prevailing view was that inpatient treatment was justified by the need for comprehensive evaluation and multidisciplinary interventions.

The tenets of managed care that emerged in the 1990s challenged the necessity of many costly tests and procedures. There has been a dramatic shift in the conceptualization of need for inpatient care in all medical specialties. Preoperative work-ups, simple surgeries, and electroconvulsive therapy are now routinely performed on an outpatient basis. Development of clinical pathways has challenged the need for and cost-effectiveness of diagnostic studies and treatment interventions that had been considered routine. New models of inpatient psychiatric care, including the concept of rapid stabilization, have emerged to replace use of inpatient services as venues for comprehensive, multidisciplinary interventions.

Traditional Inpatient Models

Inpatient units in academic settings have typically been organized around a physician/attending unit director who supervises work performed by psychiatric residents and other trainees. Trainees serve as case coordinators. Treatment teams are multidisciplinary and consist of members from psychiatry, psychology, nursing, social work, school, occupational therapy, and recreational therapy.

Length of stay in this model is generally two to three weeks. The focus of intervention includes comprehensive assessment and significant resolution of symptoms with return to full functioning. Laboratory studies, psychological testing, EEGs, and neuro-imaging studies are frequently performed for comprehensive assessment and trainee education.

Patient programming in these settings is designed to facilitate comprehensive evaluation, treatment, and educational needs. In a typical program, patients may be restricted to the unit for one to several days before beginning intensive programming as a means for the staff to "get to know" patients. Daily schedules in adolescent programs often revolve around time actually spent attending school. Patients spend large periods in semi-structured general activities, such as recreational and occupational therapy. Families of patients participate in once or twice weekly family sessions. Psychiatric trainees often participate in family therapy with the social work staff as a learning experience. Psychiatric trainees also provide medication management and daily individual therapy under the supervision of the unit director. The entire treatment team generally meets on a weekly basis to discuss patient progress and to set treatment goals for the ensuing week. Trainees might occasionally continue to see a patient after discharge, but generally the intense demands of inpatient service preclude continued contact with patients.

Rapid Stabilization Model

"Imminent risk of harm to self or others" could soon be the only acceptable justification for inpatient admission. Rapid stabilization implies efficient step-down of patients to less restrictive, and less costly, treatment settings as soon as clinically appropriate. It challenges the conception that inpatient venues are appropriate settings for comprehensive evaluations and resolution of symptoms. Some faculty and staff have developed the misconception that only patients with straightforward problems are suitable for the "rapid" service and that more difficult patients should be admitted to the traditional model. The underlying philosophy of rapid stabilization is the expressed commitment by the treatment team to provide appropriate, cost-effective levels of clinical service. It is not an assurance that patients will be discharged in three to four days. A nine-day average length of stay represents an institutional target, and but it does not preclude longer stays when they are clinically required. No patient is discharged from the service sooner than clinically indicated.

Clinical interventions in the rapid stabilization model specifically and vigorously address three primary goals: containment, evaluation, and initiation of treatment. Staff resources are most appropriately utilized in service of these three goals. Containment applies both to removal of the patient from the situation where harm is likely to occur and to facilitation of an acceptable holding environment for subsequent outpatient management. It is recognized that diagnostic clarity and full treatment response require a continuum of patient care that extends beyond the inpatient stay. Treatment interventions are directed toward problems that preclude management at a lower level of care. In most cases, resolution of core difficulties is deferred to outpatient follow-up.

Payers have an expectation that inpatient care utilizes highly integrated, well-scheduled, organized, problem-specific treatment interventions. They expect a majority of a patient's time to be spent in evaluation or in individual, group, and family therapies. Payers do not view school or other nonspecific activities as justification for inpatient admission.

Limited reimbursement for physician time necessitates a more focused and streamlined effort in patient management. Much duplication of effort among various disciplines occurs in the traditional treatment model. Administrative demands for increased patient turnover limit the amount of work some staff members can realistically accomplish. Successful management of patients in the rapid stabilization mode requires a clearer elucidation of responsibilities by discipline. Trainees gain comprehensive understanding of patient pathology and response to treatment by following cases across inpatient, intensive outpatient, and outpatient settings.

Program time under a rapid stabilization model needs to address specifically the clinical problems that necessitate inpatient care. There is little therapeutic impact from dedicating time to nonspecific program activities, such as school, unstructured process groups, and occupational therapy.

A needs-review of patients initially treated under the rapid stabilization mode revealed the types of programmatic needs most typically demonstrated by the patient population (see figure on page 155). This needs assessment serves as the basis for continued program planning and for development of appropriate activity modules designed to address specific patient problems. Treatment modules are contained in manuals that specifically instruct therapists on how to conduct both the process and the content of the sessions and can be designed for use as individual or group exercises. There should be no restraints as to which discipline has responsibility for any given program. Outcome measures are built into programmatic activities to promote general research and assessment of intervention efficacy.

Most programs could be created with a moderate shifting of resources and a commitment by some staff to develop certain modalities. The goal should be the development of a series of treatment interventions, described in manuals, that are adaptable either as group or as individual activities. Outcomes measures are used to assess the effectiveness of the intervention.

Management of the rapid stabilization team follows a traditional model in which daily patient rounds and team meetings substitute for weekly treatment planning. Trainees continue to serve as case coordinators under the supervision of attending physicians. Treatment goals and interventions are determined and assessed on a daily basis.

The rapid stabilization team has worked to define optimal functioning of our interdisciplinary efforts. The following is a brief description of the team members and their individual functions.

Case Management
Provides liaison with managed care payers and hospital administrative functions. Obtains all authorizations for services. Advises team of available benefits. Helps coordinate post discharge referral. The case manager in the rapid stabilization model serves as a key resource on the treatment team. He or she is not viewed as being imposed externally to monitor clinician activity, but works with clinicians to ensure efficient clinical care and payment for services.

Attending Physician/Case Coordinator
Coordinates assessment, treatment, and disposition of the patient. Coordinates daily rounds and treatment plan. Provides for medication management. Coordinates final feedback and recommendation to patient's family. Completes admission and discharge paperwork. In this model, the physician is not seen as a primary therapist, but instead assigns individual and family therapy to other members of the treatment team.

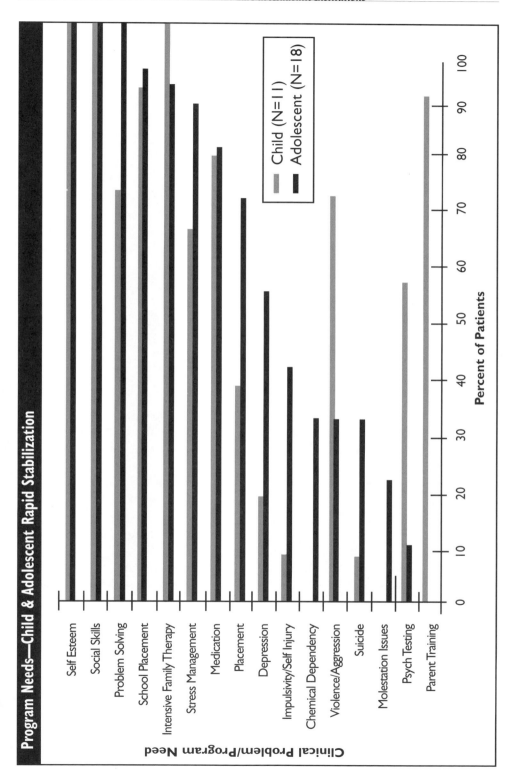

Attending Nurse

The nursing staff has primary responsibility for management and safety of the milieu. They are responsible for administration of medications. The attending nurse has additional responsibility for providing individual supportive therapy and for managing the individual patient's daily schedule.

Social Work

Social workers currently complete family assessments and coordinate discharge planning. The ability to provide a high level of family intervention is crucial to the success of the rapid stabilization model in child and adolescent patients. Most managed care companies have an expectation of two family sessions minimally for each week of treatment. Many patients require more intensive, even daily, family sessions for rapid discharge. Social workers have been precluded by time constraints from committing significant effort to the intensive family interventions required by many patients. Discharge planners now carry the load for discharge, and social workers can spend more time in intensive family work.

School

Time spent in school should be utilized in preparing patients to leave the hospital. It has become evident that school functioning is a core problem exhibited by many rapid stabilization patients. The most useful function of school staff is provision of a comprehensive school assessment and coordination of information with the home school district.

Psychology

Psychological testing has been obtained in approximately 50 percent of rapid stabilization cases. Psychological testing is performed on an as-needed basis and requires preauthorization. In the ideal rapid stabilization model, all significant evaluation should be completed within two to three days of admission. Testing that cannot be completed in this time will have little impact on clinical treatment. Efforts should be made to ensure adequate resources to complete this testing when it is required. Cases of less than three days length of stay are omitted from testing or are started and then completed at a lower level of care.

Occupational and Recreational Therapies (OT and RT)

The OT and RT staffs have been useful in providing comprehensive information about patient functioning. They also provide activities that enhance social interaction and physical functioning. Some opportunity for daily physical activity is important for patient well-being and should be provided for.

Summary

The industrialization of medicine and the emergence of managed care has brought about necessary change and reexamination on the part of academic medical centers as to the clinical- and cost-efficiency of the traditional long-term treatment model. The rapid stabilization model offers a specific treatment milieu in which patient care and treatment decisions are well managed and well utilized. The switch from tertiary and specialty-based care to primary and population-based care signals a reevaluation of inpatient care efficacy. The rapid stabilization model allows for this transition but still maintains the AMC missions of research and training and provides more focused patient care.

David T. Feinberg, MD, is Associate Medical Director of Behavioral Health Services, and James McGough, MD, is Medical Director, Access Center, UCLA Neuropsychiatric Institute and Hospital, Los Angeles, California.

Chapter 12

A Patient-Centered Continuum of Care System Model*

by Robert M. Atkins, MD, MPH

Historically, hospitals have been the exclusive providers of intensive psychiatric treatment. In a delivery system shaped by reimbursement rules, anyone too sick for outpatient care had only one option: admission to inpatient care. No other alternatives were widely available. From this perspective, the number of hospital beds became the critical indicator of a community's intensive treatment capacity.

This linkage of intensive psychiatric treatment with inpatient admission is not viable in today's health care environment. Inpatient services combine 24-hour nursing care, room and board, and intensive interdisciplinary assessment and treatment. Intensive assessment and treatment do not necessarily require 24-hour care or room and board services. Decoupling these three components will permit patients to receive the full range of clinically required services without their being packaged with services that do not increase the likelihood of a desirable clinical outcome.

A patient-centered delivery system reflects the diverse needs of the people and communities it serves. It offers quality, richness, and diversity of treatment at varying intensity levels along a continuum of care. This permits the system to assume both clinical and financial accountability for a given population over a given period (i.e., denominator accountability). Inpatient beds then become an ancillary service, used only when they add specific value to treatment.

Continuity of the therapeutic relationship throughout the episode of illness is a robust contributor to good clinical outcomes. Setting up the components of a continuum of care without providing continuity of care across the continuum fragments care. This is a response to immediate financial pressures with short-term solutions that contradict clinical effectiveness studies. The successful delivery system will find ways to provide superb quality that do not equate duration, comprehensiveness, and intensity of treatment with high cost.

---

* Much of the material in this chapter has been implemented to a large degree. In the author's prior role as Medical Director of a behavioral health service line at a large community teaching hospital in Pennsylvania, the delivery system described was designed and operationalized. When the author moved to a behavioral managed care organization, the entire operation was reengineered to reflect the principles described in this chapter. The one aspect the author has not personally participated in operationalizing is the behavioral integrated delivery system, which is adapted from the organizational approach to services at Sheppard Pratt Hospital, Baltimore, Maryland.

Coverage: Eligibility

Strategic Question: Who Should Be Covered?

Access to behavioral health care must reflect patient needs rather than the source of reimbursement for the care. Payer classification (commercial insurance, capitation, Medical Assistance/Medicaid, Medicare, state mental health authority/public sector, and self-pay) alone does not define clinical need.

The clinically distinct populations present in a market service area form the basis for organizing cross-functional service lines. Each service line provides the full continuum of services that will meet the diverse needs of its target population. This replaces the traditional functional organization and operational divisions present in many health systems/hospitals. Distinct departments, such as nursing services, social work services, and the organized medical staff, become secondary to interdisciplinary treatment programs. Operationally separate inpatient and outpatient services become integrated within a single administrative structure.

Development of clinical service lines first distinguishes between two broad diagnostic categories: addictive and psychiatric disorders. The primary diagnosis determines program requirements and clinician qualifications and identifies which insurance benefits provide coverage for treatment. These two large disease groups are further segmented into age categories, which further specify program requirements and clinician qualifications. A variety of developmental issues influence whether an individual is best treated as a child, an adolescent, or a young adult. To the extent information is available, this is a clinical decision. Otherwise, age categories are child (0-11 years), adolescent (12-17 years), and adult (18+ years).

A second programming distinction addresses whether the patient suffers from a severe and persisting mental illness or one that is acute and/or intermittent. These two groups of patients are clinically distinct in many ways. People with severe and persisting mental illness suffer substantial functional disability between acute episodes of illness. They require long-term treatment and specific rehabilitation and residential services. People who suffer acute or intermittent psychiatric and/or addictive disorders show little functional disability between acute episodes. They have a different set of clinical needs.

There is no necessary correlation between the clinical population to which a person belongs and the source of reimbursement for the services he or she receives (table 1, page 161). Treatment programs that meet the clinical needs of a distinct clinical population are likely to have patients with varied sources of payment. Some people with acute, nondisabling mental illnesses have commercial insurance or pay privately, while others have Medical Assistance or Medicaid. People who are medically indigent and have acute or intermittent behavioral disorders without persistent functional disability need the same treatment services as people with similar problems who have commercial coverage.

Table 1. Clinical Populations and Payer Classifications

Clinical population	Characteristics of treatment program	Sources of payment for services
People with acute and intermittent, nondisabling mental illness	Rapid stabilization and short term treatment with little psychosocial support	1. Commercial insurance 2. Medicaid/Medical Assistance
People with severe and persisting mental illness	Long term, community based supportive treatment and rehabilitation services	1. Medicaid/Medical Assistance 2. State Mental Health authority 3. Medicaid

In contrast, many states have identified adults with severe and persisting mental illness as a high priority. They direct state funds through some variety of mental health funding authority to programs designed to meet the needs of those patients rather than of patients with acute nondisabling illnesses. People with severe and persisting mental illness who qualify for Medical Assistance or Medicaid also attend these programs.

While these observations may be self evident, it is not unusual for programs to use payer classification as a key inclusion or exclusion criterion for deciding whether to admit a patient. A person with commercial insurance may be admitted regardless of whether the program is designed to meet his or her needs. A person with Medical Assistance may be excluded, even though in all other respects he or she meets program admission criteria.

Payer classification in and of itself identifies a clinically heterogeneous population. Medical Assistance is the reimbursement vehicle for indigent health care. People who are both mentally ill and medically indigent are not clinically homogeneous. Some people with Medical Assistance are best treated in programs designed to meet the needs of people with acute nondisabling disorders. Others are best treated in programs designed to meet the needs of people with severe and persisting mental illnesses. Treatment programs that primarily serve patients receiving Medical Assistance need to provide services that meet the needs of both groups of patients. Likewise, patients with commercial insurance who have severe and persisting mental disorders require the appropriate clinical services. If public sector mental health programs are the best providers of those services, these patients should be referred there even though their insurance would pay for private sector treatment.

Coverage: Benefits

Strategic Question: What Should Be Covered?
Basic benefits should be determined through physicians and behavioral health professionals' decision making aimed at optimizing the lifelong behavioral health status of individuals.

The challenge of designing a delivery system in today's market is to expand access to health care and contain costs while promoting improvement in quality. One way of achieving this is to design a continuum of care from preventive through long-term care. While this range of benefits may seem "rich," access to appropriate services early in the course of illness preserves functional strengths and productivity, thereby decreasing costs. Reducing unnecessary or marginal care; eliminating heavy bureaucratic overhead burdens; and providing care in the most appropriate, cost-effective setting will adequately address issues of cost.

Clinical service lines operationalize a continuum of care for each patient population, addressing crisis management services, treatment services, and residential services (table 2, below). While there clearly is overlap among these three services, it appears practical to make this distinction.

The treatment continuum probably represents the greatest departure from traditional delivery system design. Clinically driven level-of-care criteria reflect a fundamental assumption that the traditional role of inpatient care has changed. Partial hospital and intensive outpatient care are intermediate steps between traditional inpatient and traditional outpatient treatment. While

Table 2. Level-of-Care Continua

Crisis management continuum	Treatment continuum	Residential continuum
Mobile outreach	Home-based	In-home services
Telephonic crisis intervention	Outpatient	Supervised community living
Outpatient crisis intervention	Intensive outpatient	Therapeutic housing
Emergency services (ambulance services and emergency departments)	Partial hospital	Inpatient (24 hour nursing supervision and external structural controls)
23-hour observation and stabilization	Inpatient	Residential care

patients who need 24-hour nursing care and external controls require inpatient admission, partial hospital now provides the intensity of traditional inpatient treatment programs. Acute partial hospitalization is a substitute for inpatient treatment and has the mix of modalities and intensity of services characteristic of traditional inpatient treatment programs. Treatment occurs five to seven days a week, with four to eight hours of structured therapy per day. Because of the amount of time and the intensity of interaction with patients, acute partial programs are able to manage the milieu therapeutically (table 3, page 164).

Intensive outpatient services (IOP) are an extension of traditional outpatient treatment. Treatment generally occurs no more than five days a week, for no more than three hours a day, resulting in a maximum of 15 hours per week. Frequently IOP is less intensive. Because patient interaction is often intermittent, IOP addresses the daily context of patients lives rather than the issues of a therapeutic milieu. As always, the needs of the individual patient determine frequency, intensity, and duration of service.

Financing and Payment Systems

Strategic Question: How Should Payments To Providers Be Made?
Financing and payment need to align incentives for all participants: patients, providers, health systems, and payers. Payment mechanisms must be flexible enough to support improvements in system design and practice patterns over time and to address the specific needs of the community.

The current payment system creates perverse incentives for behavioral health care providers. Paying for units of service rather than for outcomes rewards busy-ness rather than effectiveness. A population-based capitated payment system fosters more reasonable incentives. Capitation demands denominator accountability for the outcomes of treatment decisions for a defined population over a given period. Rewarding clinical decision makers who direct patients to the least restrictive level of care as expeditiously as possible will improve access to services without increasing costs. Patients gain access to a more responsive, interactive and cost-effective range of service options when they face no economic barriers to moving among levels of care.

Providers change their practice patterns to use the full continuum of care and minimize their use of expensive inpatient treatment when financial incentives reward desired practice patterns.* This prepares providers for financial risk-sharing, including case rates; regular reconciliation with provider systems on the basis of quantifiable performance indicators that address cost, utilization, and quality/outcomes; and full-risk capitation. Providers accept increasing financial risk and outcome accountability in order to obtain increased clinical control.

Operational redundancies that add costs without improving the performance of the system demand key process redesign. Costly consequences of fragmented delivery services include disconnected and incompatible information systems, multiple performance measurement systems

---

* This change has been demonstrated at the behavioral MCO where the author was CEO and Medical Director.

Table 3. Distinctions between Inpatient and Acute Partial		
Level of Care	**Inpatient**	**Acute Partial**
Goal	To provide essential services for patients who either are dangerous to themselves or to others, or who are gravely disabled	To provide "definitive treatment" for patients who meet admission criteria.
Tasks	Comprehensive multidisciplinary assessment. Crisis stabilization Discharge planning	Comprehensive multi-disciplinary assessment (Direct admits). Crisis stabilization (lesser acuity than inpatient). Interdisciplinary treatment. Psycho-education. Discharge planning.
Outcomes	Assessment and stabilization. Clarification of patient/family decision: ▌ To commit to continuing treatment or ▌ To stop treatment at this time. Discharge: ▌ Refer to less intensive level of care or ▌ Clinical transition to long-term care.	Discharge to less intensive level of care with demonstrable lasting changes in functional capacity.

that only measure results at a single level of care, and multiple parallel committees that all address similar issues and often depend on the same participants. Perhaps the most obvious example is the repetitive patient assessment process. In most delivery systems, patients who receive treatment at more than one level of care must go through a separate clinical evaluation as they move through the continuum. There is limited linkage of clinical information. Likewise, each admission to each distinct level of care generally requires repeating the admission process. All of this is burdensome to the patient, who wonders, "Does anyone talk with anyone else around here?" Repetition creates the opportunity for errors in data entry and adds significant operational cost in the staffing and support needed to do all the rework.

Operational integration means building a delivery system and its processes around the needs of the patient/client. When a person enters treatment, providers gather a variety of data. The person forms a therapeutic alliance with his or her primary therapists. Whenever treatment entails moving up or down the continuum of care, the data should remain with the person in treatment. Likewise, the patient should be able to maintain continuity of the therapeutic relationship across the continuum of care. Traditional boundaries between inpatient, partial hospital, IOP, outpatient, etc. fragment care, require rework, and so add cost, while interfering with the ability of the patient/client to achieve desirable outcomes. This decreases the value of the care.

$$\text{Value} = \frac{\text{Desired Outcomes - Adverse Outcomes}}{\text{Total Costs}}$$

where total costs include money, time, patient inconvenience, etc.

Creating such an integrated delivery system faces substantial political challenges within and between organizations and between delivery systems and their medical/clinical staffs. In markets in which there is an oversupply of hospital beds and psychiatrists, the question is, Who will remain standing after the dust settles? Continuing market consolidation (a smaller number of larger participants: purchasers, payers, and providers) and downward price pressures create an apparent conflict for many providers. At the same time that more powerful customers are demanding lower prices, they are also are demanding a higher level of performance accountability. Provider systems prepared to meet performance requirements and able to manage financial risk have the competitive advantage. The requirements for financial survival under a capitated payment system include minimizing administrative and staffing costs without limiting access to care or compromising quality. When all participants share financial risk through aligned incentives, it behooves them to contribute to the least costly ways to get the job done. To the extent that systems remain fragmented and continue redundant processes, they are less likely to maintain financial viability.

Providers who can spread the fixed costs of their administrative infrastructure over a broader range of services will create economies of scale. Under fee-for-service arrangements, providers would try to increase the volume of their traditional services (more inpatient days, more outpatient visits, etc.). This doesn't work under capitation, however, where increasing the number of covered lives produces economies of scale. The national consolidation of managed care organizations demonstrates this process.

The next step providers might consider is full administrative, economic, and operational integration among health systems, physicians and other clinicians, and payers. The Medicare Preservation Act of 1995 describes this arrangement as a Provider Service Network (PSN), which would allow physicians and hospitals to contract directly and collaboratively with Medicare. In some markets, employers have formed large purchasing alliances that contract directly with providers instead of going through the HMO (disintermediation). The PSN must provide all of the administrative services needed to manage financial risk, create and maintain a provider network, ensure timely access to care, address and resolve members' concerns, measure and report performance, and measure and improve the quality of care and the quality of service. At the same time, it must reduce overhead costs, including profits, to no more than 10-15 percent of premiums. Holding administrative costs to less than 10 percent is necessary to create a net gain.

The performance specifications for full administrative, economic, and operational integration among health systems, physicians and other clinicians, and payers could result in a regional behavioral services system, or behavioral integrated delivery system (figure 1, below). Implementation challenges for the system include:

■ Who will choose to participate?

—Which clinicians?

—Which health systems?

■ Legal issues

■ Political issues

■ Power and control issues: Manage What?

■ Market segmentation issues

■ Staff issues: Who *won't* be employed?

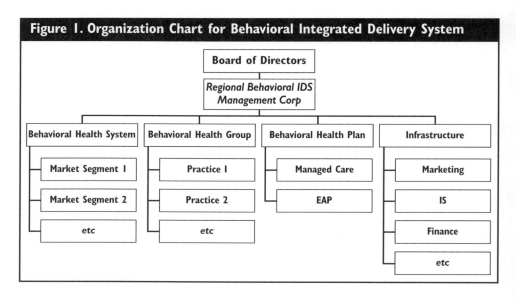

Figure 1. Organization Chart for Behavioral Integrated Delivery System

166

Maintaining a network that is dynamic and responsive to changes in patients needs will align economic incentives for all network providers. Efficiencies gained in one treatment modality will translate into more available resources for other modalities in the network. This degree of risk-sharing calls for a phased-in implementation. Networks could limit losses while they gain necessary utilization experience with newly aggregated service populations. Conversely, reward-sharing opportunities during the phase-in will encourage more efficient collaboration, such as elimination of redundant administrative costs that add no value to patient care. Finally, relating behavioral health care costs and services to those associated with general acute health care might make it possible to quantify possible cost-offset effects. This could result in additional resource allocation to behavioral care, thus optimizing the overall health status of the population being served.

Delivery System

Strategic Question: How Should the Health Care Delivery System Be Restructured?

The behavioral health care system will be characterized by a "seamless network" of services based on continuity of treatment relationships and organized as an integrated continuum of care to respond in a flexible and timely manner to peoples' needs. The system will provide the organizational and clinical expertise to develop and adhere to criteria that define the intensity and mix of services, from intensive inpatient care through partial and day treatment, intensive outpatient, outpatient, home-based, therapeutic housing, and other nontraditional services.

The proposed delivery system reflects the belief that consumer needs can be met in several legitimate ways in several alternative delivery sites. A community behavioral health care network chooses which of those needs to meet. It then develops the means to meet them in the least restrictive, least expensive, least regressive setting compatible with effective care. While some of these needs mandate a locked inpatient setting, most do not. While many of the latter needs historically have been met in an inpatient setting, it is necessary to challenge the assumptions that continue to lead clinicians to sustain this practice. Today, this challenge arises from managed care. In the future, changed reimbursement incentives will address the total cost of care and will reward the system for long-term improvement in community health status.

Figures 2-4, pages 168-170, show the overall matrix of consumer needs and alternative delivery sites applicable to specifically defined populations. Showing which needs are met at which sites, for which populations, describes the continuum of care within a community. (Note that these matrices will need to change as practice patterns evolve and different forms of service delivery take shape.) A "+" shows that a consumer need is commonly met at that alternative delivery site. A "+/-" means that there is no consensus about the appropriateness of meeting that need at that site. A blank cell shows that a consumer need is generally not met, or by definition cannot be met, at that site. The completed matrix serves as a visual depiction of the continuum of care, with clearly described step-down functions at each level of care.

Within a given mental health continuum of care, "Primary Mental Health Services" (see the shaded cells in figure 2) are elaborated on in figure 3. Addictions services are organized differently, reflecting the different historical development of those services from those for mental health.

Figure 2. Mental Health Services Continuum of Care: Adult/Adolescent/Child

CONSUMER NEEDS	Crisis Intervention	Emergency Department	Crisis Stabilization	Outpatient Med/Surg Clinics	Inpatient Med/Surg Units	Special Inpatient Psych Units	Discrete Psychiatric Program in General Hospital	Free-Standing Psychiatric Facility	University/Research Psychiatric Facility	Residential 24-hour Non-Hospital	State Hospital	Nursing Facility	Structured/Supervised Housing
Hotline	+												
Emergency Services	+	+											
Brief Crisis Stabilization		+	+										
Psychiatric Consultations to Nonpsychiatric Patients		+	+	+	+	+							
Medical/Psychiatric Liaison				+	+	+							
Primary Mental Health Services							+	+	+				
Extended Intensive Interdisciplinary Treatment								+	+				
Specialized Treatment Programs							+/-	+/-	+				
Specialized Diagnostic Assessment									+				
Long-Term Care: Active Treatment								+/-	+/-	+	+		
Long-Term Care: Maintenance										+	+	+	+
ALTERNATIVE DELIVERY SITES	Emergency Psychiatric Services			General Hospital Psychiatry			Primary	Secondary	Tertiary	Long-Term Care			

Figure 3. Primary Mental Health Services

CONSUMER NEEDS

	High Security Psychiatric Unit	Psychiatric Inpatient Locked	Psychiatric Inpatient Open	Therapeutic Housing	Hi-Acuity Partial	Long-Term Partial/ Rehabilitation	Psychiatric Intensive Outpatient	Psychiatric Outpatient Clinic	Outpatient Private Providers	Primary Care Setting	Workplace or School	Home
Close Staff Observation	+											
External Controls	+	+										
24-Hour Supervision	+	+	+									
Safe Secure Environment	+	+	+	+								
Extended Interdisciplinary Treatment						+	+/-					
Intensive Interdisciplinary Treatment	+/-	+	+		+	+	+					
Multidisciplinary Assessment	+	+	+		+	+	+	+/-				
Psychiatric Assessment	+	+	+		+	+	+	+	+			
Medication/ECT	+	+	+		+	+	+	+	+	+		
Rehabilitation/Education		+	+	+/-	+	+	+	+	+	+	+	+/-
Financial/Social Case Management	+/-	+	+	+	+	+	+	+	+/-	+/-	+/-	+/-
Psychotherapy	+/-	+	+		+	+	+	+	+	+/-	+	+
Community Education/Prevention						+	+	+	+	+	+	+

ALTERNATIVE DELIVERY SITES

169

Figure 4. Addictions Services Continuum of Care

CONSUMER NEEDS	Hospital ICU	Hospital Detox	Hospital Rehabilitation	Residential Detox	Residential Rehabilitation	Structured Supervised Housing	Addictions Partial Program	Addictions Outpatient Clinic	Addictions Outpatient Prvate	Psychiatric & Med/Surg Services	Employee Assistance Programs	Emergency Dept/Crisis Intervention	Community Outreach
Detox Complicated	+												
Detox Medical Risk		+											
Detox No Medical Risk			+	+									
Rehabilitation		+	+		+		+						
Intensive Interdisciplinary Treatment		+	+	+	+								
Extended Interdisciplinary Treatment					+/-	+/-	+/-						
Safe, Secure Environment	+	+		+	+	+							
Multidisciplinary Assessment	+/-	+	+	+	+		+	+/-	+/-				
Addictions Consultations to Non-Addictions Patients										+			
Case Management	+/-	+	+	+	+	+	+	+	+/-	+/-	+	+/-	
Psychotherapy/Counseling		+	+	+	+	+/-	+	+	+	+	+		
Medication	+	+	+	+	+		+	+	+	+/-			
Diagnosis	+	+	+	+	+	+	+	+	+	+	+/-	+/-	
Education/Information & Prevention											+		+
Hotline												+	
ALTERNATIVE DELIVERY SITES													

Figure 5. Model of Continuum of Care

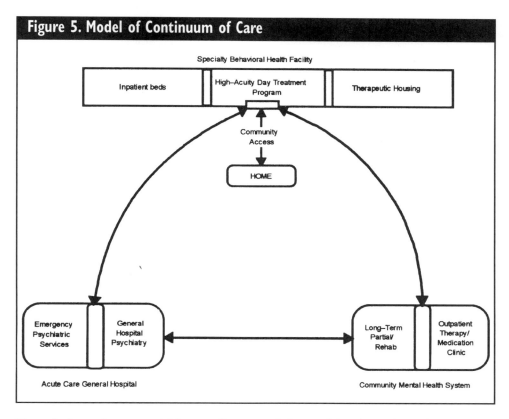

Figure 5, above, shows a model for overall systems design applying the analysis of services presented in figures 2-4. Certain consumer needs are best met in acute care general hospitals. These services include: differential diagnosis and treatment of behavioral emergencies, treatment of patients with coexisting psychiatric and somatic problems, and detoxification of patients with severe medical acuity. These services generally require ready access to the resources of the general hospital.

In contrast, community mental health provides community-based services to adults with severe and persisting mental disorders and to children and adolescents with severe emotional disabilities. Such disorders are long-lasting and are complicated by a high level of residual or baseline disability. This population requires substantial rehabilitative services, especially during the times between acute exacerbations of their underlying disorder. Inpatient treatment should be brief, with the goal being to restabilize the patient in the community as quickly as possible.

Finally, specialty behavioral health facilities provide primary mental health services and the analogous addictions services to meet the needs of patients and the community. Each program service line includes a full continuum of care. Access to these treatment programs may be from the inpatient unit, from therapeutic housing alternatives, or from home, depending on the individual patient's needs (figure 6, page 172).

Figure 6. Access to Specialty Facilities

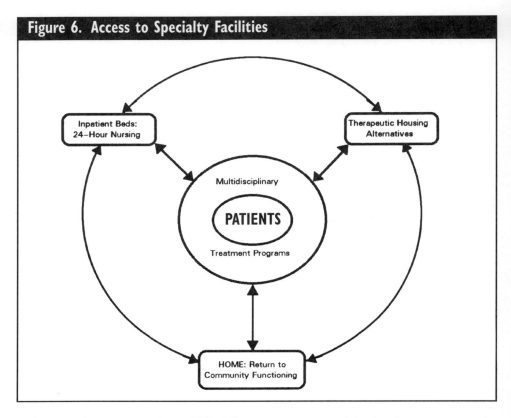

Patients receive treatment in multidisciplinary programs. Participation in treatment varies according to patients' clinical needs and may vary independently of their residential settings. Conversely, patients may move through the range of residential options (e.g., from being an inpatient, to living in hospital-provided or sanctioned therapeutic housing, to living at home) without interrupting their treatment. The same treatment team would remain involved with the patient throughout the episode of illness (and ideally across repeated episodes, if necessary) whatever their residential circumstance. The seamless continuum offers coordinated and easily accessible services to the patient, rather than the patient jumping from provider to provider and from organization to organization as the need for different services emerges. Continuity of the treatment relationship supports the patient as he or she negotiates the variety of services available within the continuum.

Patients move through the residential continuum according to their needs for specific services. While related to level-of-care criteria for treatment, independent consideration of residential alternatives will best match the patient with the appropriate mix of resources. Figure 7, page 173, shows the residential services corresponding to the clinical/functional status of the patient. It also shows the degree of overlap with treatment appropriateness criteria. For example, patients who meet the dangerousness criterion need to reside in an inpatient unit, receive 24-hour nursing care, and receive treatment in an inpatient setting. Patients who are severely ill might require inpatient 24-hour nursing care, but they might also live in a residential alternative if they are

Figure 7. Residential Continuum

INPATIENT	THERAPEUTIC HOUSING	HOME
Patient requires assistance with ADLs and IADLs	Patient performs ADLs acceptably; requires assistance with IADLs	Patient performs ADLs and IADLs 90% of the time
24-Hour Nursing Care	Room and Board	Self-Care with Family

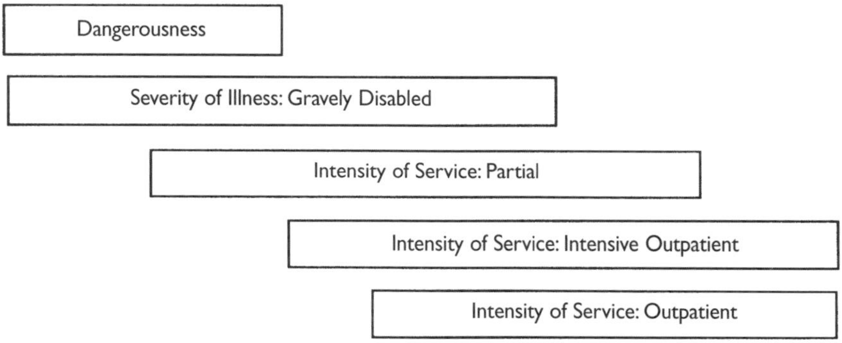

Dangerousness

Severity of Illness: Gravely Disabled

Intensity of Service: Partial

Intensity of Service: Intensive Outpatient

Intensity of Service: Outpatient

Activities of Daily Living [ADL's]: A combination of skills that enable individuals to meet their basic human needs for survival in regard to food, shelter, and self-preservation. These skills tend to be more concrete and instinctual when an indicvidual is functioning normally, and is not impaired by major illness or disability; *eg*, feeding, hygiene, grooming, awareness of needing and finding food and shelter, *etc*
Instrumental Activities of Daily Living [IADL's]: More complex functions requiring integration of multiple skills, promoting greater independence. These skills tend to utilize abstract reasoning, problem-solving, judgment, and integration of information; *eg*, functional communication, social interaction, shopping, cooking, money management, vocational skills, *etc*

functioning well enough in that setting. Finally, patients who need an intensity of service that historically required inpatient admission might continue in a treatment program while moving among the three types of settings.

Only to the extent that clinicians are free to decouple beds from the programs will they be able to allocate resources to match patient needs. This degree of individualized treatment planning will enable the clinical staff to be effective in terms of both clinical outcomes and cost containment. The therapeutic relationship will endure as patients move through a range of treatment intensities, reducing cost while addressing the long-term health status of the patient.

The requirement that residential services be decoupled from treatment services in all respects is much less difficult to carry out clinically than it is operationally. Clinicians readily understand the distinction and view it positively because it allows more treatment at lower cost without compromising continuity of care. The operational implications prove more difficult, however. Staffing models generally look at staff:patient ratios for a given program. Medical records are rarely continuous from one level of care to the next. Regulatory and licensing constraints only recognize elements of the traditional delivery system. Success requires substantial changes of the infrastructure to be consistent with the desired delivery system and clinical practice patterns.

Accountability

Strategic Question: How Can Appropriate Accountability for All Participants in the Health Care System Be Ensured?
All parties in the health care system have a responsibility to manage resources efficiently and effectively, thereby increasing the value of those services to all parties.

Accountability of the behavioral health care system includes issues of quality, access, and cost-effectiveness. The system needs to address the disparate needs, both acute and long-term, of different groups of people in the community. Emphasis should be on culturally competent services, tailored to patients' needs, delivered in the least restrictive setting possible, that promote family preservation. Ultimately, services are accountable for creating value in the marketplace.

Evaluation and outcome standards will address both the effectiveness of the entire health care system and the individual performance of specific service providers. Two major challenges are lack of consensus regarding which standardized outcome criteria to use and the inability of many service providers to determine the actual costs incurred in the provision of services.

Outcome Evaluation
Behavioral health services should produce lasting changes in the lives of the people who receive care. While specific measures have not achieved universal acceptance, it has become clear that the outcomes desired are multidimensional and require several different measures. Classes of outcome are:

Changes in Clinical Symptoms

■ Decrease in acute signs and symptoms in terms of intensity, frequency, and duration.

■ Improved cognitive and ego-adaptive functioning in terms of capacity to respond adaptively to stressors precipitating admission.

■ Decreased demoralization.

Behavioral Changes Related to Social Role Performance

■ Occupational/vocational performance, whether in competitive workplace, as a homemaker, in scholastic performance or in noncompetitive workplace such as vocational rehabilitation.

■ Social and leisure activities, with respect to the frequency and quality of social contacts and the capacity to make rewarding use of unstructured time rather than to regress and become symptomatic.

- Improved family adjustment in terms of parental/family role, quality of intimate relationships in or out of marriage, and relationships with extended family.

- Disability days, in which a person spends all or part of the day in bed because of illness, is kept from usual activities, misses work, or is late to work because of feeling ill.

Health Care Resource Consumption

- Mental health, chemical dependency, and general health care resource utilization after treatment.

- Recidivism, readmission rates, total time living in community in contrast to time as inpatient.

- Maintenance of prescribed medication regimen.

- Extent to which treatment plan is implemented and followed (continuity of care).

- Patients' understanding of their illnesses, their medications, and their treatment programs enables them to share responsibility with the treatment team.

Changes in Quality of Life

- Self-sufficiency (ability to meet ones own basic needs).

- Capacity to attain goals specified by the patient.

- Self-esteem.

- Life satisfaction.

- Fullness of life.

Patient and Family Satisfaction

- Broad-based survey.

- Would patient/family recommend program?

- Strength of therapeutic alliance.

- Decreased AMA (against medical advice) discharge rate.

While there are many research/study programs in progress to establish outcome criteria for mental health services, there are no universally accepted standards. Outcome assessments will need to be performed using local standards. In this regard, it is important that providers of services, purchasers of services, and consumers participate in the development of outcome criteria. The financial incentives under managed care need to be balanced by clinically informed performance expectations that specify the needs of both consumers and payers. Comparative data relating cost, conformity with performance criteria, and outcome will establish a consistent level of accountability.

Determination of Costs and Services

Historically, service providers have managed costs departmentally rather than relating costs to the particular services a patient receives through an entire episode of care. Inpatient utilization has been the financial foundation that supported the treatment programs. The inpatient day has been the unit cost for pricing and accounting purposes.

When providers are both clinically and financially accountable, they must measure the unit costs for each component of the mix of services each patient receives. This produces a total cost for the episode of illness. Case rates must cover this total cost for treatment to be financially self-sustaining. Full-risk capitation must cover the utilization rate of each component of care per member per month at its unit cost. While the inpatient daily rate may not cover the fully allocated cost of an inpatient day, the case rate or capitated payment will reward systems based on a continuum of care that minimizes clinical rework and administrative overhead.

Outcomes of treatment will be weighed against the health care resources expended in producing those outcomes. Providers who prove that they are economically disciplined in the delivery of their services and that their services are effective in achieving desired outcomes will have a competitive advantage.

Conclusion

The new role for organized behavioral health delivery systems builds on the strengths of high-quality psychiatric providers, namely, interdisciplinary treatment services staffed by experienced professionals who are accomplished at multidisciplinary assessment, interdisciplinary treatment, and clinical case management. Patients can more easily use an array of services when it is coordinated, convenient, and accessible. Delivery systems that organize a complex array of providers to address the medical, psychiatric, and psychosocial needs of patients will not emphasize bed capacity. Successful delivery systems will be those that organize treatment programs into an effective and efficient continuum of care.

Delivery systems that survive consolidation of the marketplace will meet a variety of customer specifications. To the extent that operational and clinical decision makers must change their behaviors, the whole delivery system must change. The traditional infrastructure does not support new organizational processes and patterns of behavior. Integrity of design will produce a system organized to meet the new performance requirements of the market. When the desired changes become the path of least resistance for each decision maker, the likelihood of success in a turbulent era increases.

Robert M. Atkins, MD, MPH, is President, Patient-Centered Partnership, Inc., Louisvile, Kentucky. He was Chief Executive Officer and Medical Director, ClearSprings Health Partnership, Louisville, Kentucky.

Section III

Networks

Chapter 13

Managed Behavioral Health Care Network Development

by Ian A. Shaffer, MD, and Michael E. Glasser, MD

Introduction

Managed behavioral health care organizations (MBHCOs) provide access to care through contractual relationships with providers and/or through the use of employed clinicians. In many managed plans, a point of service option also exists that permits beneficiaries to seek treatment outside the network with a higher copayment, lower benefits, and additional paperwork. This chapter will focus on the development of contractual relationships between MBHCOs and their providers.

With the initiation of managed behavioral health care, employer groups required networks of sufficient size to ensure ready access to a contracted provider for all covered employees. Managed care organizations were required to develop networks in new areas of employee populations, making network development a significant component of any contract implementation. More recently, computer technology has become an important enhancement in the ability to match beneficiary location to provider availability.

Network Development

Network development has several components, including identification of providers for contracting, use of credentialing criteria, application procedures to determine appropriateness for the network, and, finally, execution of a contract.

Managed care organizations have used several techniques to identify providers for their networks. Initially, when a health plan or an employer group enters into a contract with the managed behavioral health care organization (MBHCO), it will express some of its own interest in network development based on experience with providers utilized prior to the managed care contract. Moreover, when possible, there is a strong effort to maintain continuity of care. Specifically, health plans often have had their own networks in place and request that the managed care organization incorporate those individuals into its network. Employer groups often ask that providers currently seeing their beneficiaries be offered an opportunity to enter the network. As networks were developed, these two methods provided an opportunity for managed care organizations to identify a significant component of an area's provider population. Some organizations joining managed behavioral health care had internal or external employee assistance professionals working with their beneficiaries as part of employee assistance programs (EAPs). These EAPs have a history of referral patterns that is also incorporated into network development.

There are times when the methods described above are not sufficient for the development of an adequate network. The MBHCO would then utilize a more hands-on method for identifying providers. In some cases, this includes members of the network development department of the MBHCO going to a specific area and identifying providers directly. Meetings are held with providers to explain managed behavioral health care and to ascertain providers' interest. Expectations and implications of contracting are discussed, and providers decide on their interest in joining a network. National and local organizations (e.g., American Psychiatric Association, American Psychological Association, National Alliance for the Mentally III, American Society of Addiction Medicine) are also consulted regarding their membership in an area undergoing network development. Finally, contracted providers from other areas who have national exposure are asked for recommendations for individuals to be approached regarding network development.

Once a significant number of providers are identified, the application process is explained and applications are made available. The information obtained about a provider is reviewed against credentialing criteria, which will be explained later, and qualified providers are offered contracts. The credentialing process has continued to evolve with increasing specificity of information. This provider network data offers greater reliability regarding a provider's area of expertise and practice patterns. Moreover, a more detailed series of questions are now asked regarding a clinician's practice. Specifically, practitioners are asked about types of treatment provided, demographics of patients treated, and diseases in which providers may have particular expertise. This information is requested at a minimum on a biannual basis, with updates to licensure and malpractice coverage required at all points of expiration. History of malpractice cases or questions raised by any licensing board about an individual's practice are researched carefully. These data are utilized, along with credentialing criteria, to determine the appropriateness of offering an individual practitioner a contract.

Credential Criteria

MBHCOs developed credentialing criteria to determine the basic requirements for participation in a network. In their initial stages, networks were limited to psychiatrists, psychologists, social workers, and master's degree-prepared nurse practitioners. As other disciplines have evolved and areas of expertise have been defined, other categories of practitioner credentialing have developed. Basic standards for practitioner involvement in a network are consistent from one MBHCO to another. However, depending on the type of managed care organization, the types of products sold to employers, and account-specific (employer) expectations, there are unique characteristics for each MBHCO's provider network. While providers are required to meet the MBHCO's credentialing criteria for consideration, it is not sufficient to ensure a contract offer. Additional critical factors, such as licensure concerns and history of malpractice claims, must be reviewed.

Credentialing criteria are developed in most cases utilizing a workgroup made up of senior members of the provider relations staff, the clinical and medical departments of MBHCOs. While licensure requirements for psychiatrists and, for the most part, psychologists are similar throughout the country, there is variability in requirements for the training and licensure of master's degree-prepared clinicians. Moreover, a number of states do not provide licensure for master's degree-prepared clinicians in some disciplines. As a result, it is necessary for credentialing criteria to include both training and licensure requirements. Practice experience is also a requirement before providers are accepted into many networks. The degree of experience required to join a network is another characteristic that is unique for each MBHCO.

In many MBHCOs a practitioner has to be in practice for a minimum number of hours per week in order to meet credentialing standards for the network and to minimize issues of access. Client companies are very concerned about access to care, and MBHCOs must ensure access for individuals requiring emergency, urgent, and routine care. Providers are also required to have a specified level of malpractice insurance. In some disciplines, additional requirements, such as a Drug Enforcement Administration (DEA) license for psychiatrists, are used in credentialing.

Credentialing criteria for facilities and programs are developed in the same manner as described for clinician credentialing. Appropriate licensure and certification is required, as is a specific period for the program to have been in operation. Many MBHCOs initially developed credentialing criteria for acute inpatient programs, residential treatment centers, and partial hospitalization programs. With encouragement from managed care organizations, programs have developed additional alternatives to traditional inpatient and outpatient sites. As new levels of care are more clearly defined, such as structured outpatient programs for chemical dependency and mental health disorders, home health services, and the 23-hour bed, new program-specific credentialing criteria are developed and refined. As new programs develop and their clinical use is validated, there will be a continual evolution of credentialing criteria, enabling these newer programs to become part of MBHCO networks.

Credentialing Process

The credentialing process begins with submission by a provider of an application for network participation. Along with the application, providers are asked for copies of licensure, education and training credentials, and evidence of malpractice insurance. Frequently, MBHCOs will also request a current curriculum vitae. Primary source verification is requested for training, licensure, and malpractice history. Many contracts between MBHCOs and employers include network development performance standards such as time frames required for action by an MBHCO on an application and the density of a network (number of providers per covered lives) at the time of contract initiation. While efforts are made to streamline the credentialing process, providers have become frustrated with MBHCOs because of the time it takes to complete the process. However, MBHCOs do not control all of the required data elements; for example, a number of states require 6 to 10 weeks for completion of primary source verification material. Information regarding prior malpractice actions can also take an extended period to receive.

Once all of the credentialing data have been received, they are reviewed by network specialists who apply the MBHCOs credentialing criteria and make a recommendation to the credentialing committee for acceptance or further review. Some applications require further review because of the presence of a history of malpractice or licensure actions. The credentialing committee or its designee reviews the material provided, seeking consultation from appropriate departments in the MBHCO. A determination is then made, and the results are forwarded to the practitioner. In the case of facilities and programs, most MBHCOs make an onsite visit to the facility or program as a component of the credentialing process. Many MBHCOs use specific facility/program evaluation protocols during site visits to maintain consistency in the evaluation process.

Reimbursement Methodology

For the most part, the marketplace determines the prices in the health care system. Reimbursement rates also reflect demand for services, local levels of fees, and how care is managed.

Practitioner Reimbursement

Practitioners are reimbursed almost exclusively on either a discounted fee-for-service or a capitation basis. The method for determining the discounted fee for service varies by MBHCO. Most frequently, service fees are determined by Current Procedural Terminology (CPT) codes and by the specialty of the clinician. The fees are set either by state or by region within a state. This method allows for recognition of the variability that currently exists across the country. Discounted fee for service allows the MBHCO to contain the cost per unit of service. Discounted fee for service with utilization management and the requirement of precertification of services were significant components in the early containment mechanisms to control rapidly increasing behavioral healthcare costs. This methodology presented two significant problems for clinicians. Precertification signaled a major shift in the decision-making processes to include a third party, the clinical arm of the MBHCO. Providers were required to present focused, targeted treatment plans specific to the individual's functional impairments. This accountability created the second problem for providers in that they were often not trained and accustomed to presenting such plans and found their development difficult. Along with the heightened level of accountability experienced by providers, there was a decrease in the length of time for treatment because of the expectation that treatment was to be more focused. These changes often resulted in frustration and resentment for both providers and MBHCO. The publication of medical necessity and clinical criteria upon which MBHCOs base their decisions has eased some of the stress between providers and managed behavioral health care organizations. Discounted fee for service, along with utilization review, precertification, concurrent review, copayments, deductibles, and other methods, has not resulted in the expected control over utilization and cost. As with the traditional fee-for-service model, discounted fee for service continued to foster a provider mindset of doing more. However, "more" care is neither necessarily appropriate nor clinically indicated.

Capitation reimbursement arrangements have been developed as a way of managing limited health resources available while maximizing the likelihood that those who need care have reliable access to services. When the clinician who provides care for an individual also has control of the finances available to pay for care, there is clear responsibility for resource management and accountability for outcomes. Too much care can financially destroy a system; too little or inappropriate care can affect the provider's or group's reputation and status. Both are clinically inappropriate and could raise questions of ethics and malpractice. In a capitation environment, treatment must be targeted at the individual's specific impairments, and have the appropriate follow up, given that many mental health and substance abuse problems are recurrent and life-long. For a capitation program to be successful in maintaining appropriate access and quality outcomes, it is essential for the MBHCO to have a strong quality improvement program to address these issues.

With capitation, providers are reimbursed on a per member per month basis, and the services that are expected to be provided for a particular population are defined. Capitation programs are designed in a variety of ways. In one model, clinicians receive a capitation payment to cover all professional services required by the covered population. In this model, facility and program services are kept separate from capitation and are paid directly by the MBHCO. Other models include the facility and program component in the capitation and require clinicians to reimburse facilities and programs when they are utilized. A variation of this model involves payment of a capitation fee for professional services and a shared risk pool for facility and program utilization. The MBHCO will set the shared pool aside and pay all facilities and programs from it. Following a specified period, often 6 to 12 months, the amount of money within the pool is analyzed. Any money remaining in the pool is shared between providers and the MBHCO, while any shortfall in the pool will be made up by providers and the MBHCO.

In entering into these capitation agreements, providers must clearly understand the assumptions that have been made in establishing capitation rates. The provider or group must understand such things as expected services, who is eligible, and their ability to manage and deliver expected services. While a discussion of how to develop successful capitation rates is beyond the scope of this chapter, there are a number of useful references on the subject.[1,2] In addition to the clinical and economic aspects of capitation, there are ethical considerations. Providers should never be put in a position of limiting appropriate and medically necessary care. Providers entering into capitation arrangements must have an ability to carefully monitor utilization and outcomes; to utilize state-of-the-art, cost-effective treatment interventions; to understand the basic principles of total quality management; and to develop expertise in multidisciplinary teamwork and communication.

Depending on the MBHCO, there are various requirements expected of contracted groups, such as the ability to share financially in the risk of capitation; an infrastructure for effective monitoring of utilization; the ability to use case management techniques; a quality improvement program; and a cooperative, collegial interaction among group members and with the MBHCO. In a capitated environment, group practice is the rule and individual practice the exception. Additionally, teamwork and a willingness to enter into the role of "clinical economist" are promoted. Because there are limited resources, providers are being asked to manage both the care of individual patients and the health and well-being of a defined population. Capitated groups need leadership, individuals who understand the changes taking place in the delivery of high-quality, cost-effective health care. Leaders must develop and effectively communicate to other group members the goals of the group, the principles of quality management, the importance of understanding and managing organized systems of care, and the importance of the health status of the population for which they are responsible. A group's leadership is the moral and ethical backbone of its providers and has the ability to empower its members to make clinically appropriate and medically necessary treatment decisions.

In a capitation model, there is a shift from a focus on individuals to an understanding that consumers of health care are a part of a community. With this shift, groups tend to become more creative in their planning and more aware of community needs and resources. An example of this creativity involves a capitated group in an area in which a natural disaster occurred. The group, recognizing the risk of significant post-traumatic stress disorder (PTSD) to its population, immediately put in place no-cost group sessions for its membership. This process allowed the group to proactively intervene in an effort to minimize the development of PTSD, which would be more difficult and costly to treat and, more important, would result in more human suffering than necessary. Understanding the health status of the defined population, the group was able to develop treatments that were more timely, were clinically and cost effective, and played a role in prevention. Because capitation provides an economic base, a group can begin to develop prevention and early detection programs and can learn the prevalence of diseases within its defined population.

The major area of concern with respect to capitation is underutilization. Because groups receive a prepayment to fund all care, it is clear that withholding of services provides a larger profit. Therefore, a critical component for any capitation program involves monitoring for underutilization. In a prospective payment system, the utilization management component of the program will frequently shift from a managed care organization to the provider group. Monitoring of the group practice by the MBHCO must, therefore, shift to a macromanagement quality system by which the MBHCO not only can monitor levels of appropriate utilization, but also receive more detailed quality of care and outcomes data. The group and the MBHCO must have a method to work together to improve the delivery of care to the membership.

Frequently, MBHCOs will put in place a bonus program that is based on utilization information and is heavily weighted with quality of care indicators and outcomes data, including patient and provider satisfaction surveys. This detailed level of accountability is not present in the fee-for-service model. Because of early abuses in the capitation system, there is still strong emotional reaction by many people to this method of reimbursement. However, as quality and outcomes monitoring evolve, employers and beneficiaries are likely to become more comfortable with the care received in a capitated environment and more willing to enter into programs with this reimbursement methodology.

Facility and Program Reimbursement
In the initial stages of managed behavioral health care, discounted fee for service was also present in programs and facilities. In this method, a daily or program rate, as well as rates for various services, was negotiated. There was an increasing amount of service unbundling as a

method to increase revenue because of the cost containment efforts of MBHCOs. The negative financial impact of unbundling led to alternative methods of reimbursement.

The most common reimbursement program for facilities and programs at present is an all-inclusive per diem rate. These rates are individually negotiated by facilities and programs. The rate includes not only the hospital bed but also therapies, medical services, and laboratory services required, with the one exception being the provision of attending clinician services. In most hospitals with voluntary attending staffs, the professional fee remains separated from the all-inclusive per diem rate. The clinician is reimbursed by one of the methods described in the previous section. In an alternative facility and program model, the staff that provides the care is employed, thus providing all the services required for that level of care. In these cases, the professional component of the service is included in the negotiated per diem. From the MBHCO perspective, an all-inclusive per diem provides a set rate for services and avoids the a la carte costs seen previously. It is recognized that not all services within the all-inclusive per diem rate are going to be required by all patients. The MBHCO will expect the services required by each individual to be provided by the program. With the program determining the necessary services for an individual, it can individualize treatment plans for beneficiaries without seeking certification for each component. The absence of the need to request each specific service within a program diminishes the tension between the program and the MBHCO.

It is important to understand the impact of the attending clinician in the per diem reimbursement system. When the attending clinician is a member of the program staff, the MBHCO frequently deals exclusively with the program, working to ensure that appropriate clinical services are provided and that the medically appropriate number of days are utilized. There is a similar review by the MBHCO when the attending clinician is a discounted fee-for-service provider. However, in this situation the managed care organization will frequently interact with both the staff of the program and the attending clinician in order to obtain information needed to determine medical necessity certifications. The situation changes when the attending clinician is a member of a group receiving capitation. In this scenario, the group will most frequently decide the clinically appropriate length of hospitalization and the transition to alternative levels of care. Managed care organizations need to ensure that the appropriate transition from higher to lower levels of care takes place. Specifically, within the quality monitoring program, MBHCOs must be satisfied that patients are not being discharged from programs prematurely. Readmission rates and measures of continuity of care become a component of the quality management program.

A variant of the per diem program involves reduction in the reimbursement rate over time. Thus, while a program may receive one level of reimbursement when a patient is admitted, the rate decreases as the stay continues. This type of per diem reimbursement recognizes the higher costs incurred during the admission and evaluation process compared to later in the hospital stay. While there is an understandable desire on the part of some programs to have patients remain, this type of financial incentive decreases some of the trend toward overutilization while decreasing the risk of underutilization.

Another form of program reimbursement is the program rate, which is most commonly seen in substance abuse treatment. In this model, a program receives a specific fee to complete detoxification, rehabilitation, or both for each individual referred to it. Frequently, this model uses a modified per diem rate, with the facility receiving a per diem rate up to a certain point and then a program rate for the remainder of the patient's time in the program. Within this reimbursement structure, the program requires MBHCO certification for the medical appropriateness of the patient's stay, but the program generally controls the length of stay. The MBHCO monitors the case initially for appropriateness and at intervals to validate that an effective treatment plan is in process. Any length-of-stay tensions between programs and the managed care organization are significantly diminished. The use of clinical indicators such as readmission and relapse rates helps monitor issues of underutilization, premature discharge, or absence of adequate follow-up care.

An alternative reimbursement model uses case rates. Programs receive a specific fee to manage an individual's care over a specified period. In substance abuse, for example, treatment involves detoxification, rehabilitation, and aftercare services. For the reimbursement received, the program agrees to manage not only the program and aftercare, but also any relapse treatment for the specified period. Case rates are similar to capitation, except that it is not the potential for care in a population, but only for care actually provided that is being reimbursed. Programs recognize the need for proactive support for individuals under their care and are very aggressive in ensuring that comorbid conditions are addressed promptly and effectively. Here again, the MBHCO and the program can monitor for quality rather than for utilization.

These changes in the reimbursement methodology alters the interaction between the MBHCO and the facility or program and provides a more positive experience for both. The quality management program must not only focus on quality of care and outcomes of treatment, but also address any concerns regarding underutilization. MBHCOs must be assured that providers are delivering necessary services to maximize functional improvement. Further, program services require ongoing monitoring to ensure that individualized treatment plans are being developed as clinically indicated and that a "one size fits all" program methodology is not being applied.

Integrated System
Clinician groups, facilities, and programs are banding together to develop integrated systems of care. These systems are relatively new and only beginning to contract with managed care organizations. Capitation and case rate reimbursement methods are most likely to occur in this environment. The governance of the integrated system takes responsibility for ensuring appropriate interaction between all components of care delivery. The financial incentive for all will be to provide appropriately required services for each beneficiary. An efficient integrated system with its components working in concert recognizes that the group as a whole will be significantly stronger if each program is utilized when appropriate and that the interface between programs is effective.

Conclusions

Initial contracts focused on decreasing costs and utilization and were based on discounted fee for service with strong utilization controls retained by managed care organizations. With the maturing of managed care and an enhanced level of participation by many providers, MBHCOs recognize that they must move away from micromanagement of cases to network management of provider communities. Quality of care issues and reimbursement methods are becoming aligned to encourage improved treatment for individuals along with needed cost containment. These methodological changes are returning the locus of clinical decision making to the provider of care. Managed behavioral health care organizations monitor quality of care and utilization through quality improvement programs that assist provider groups in developing and managing data to understand their practice patterns from administrative, clinical delivery, and outcomes perspectives. With the assistance of managed behavioral health care organizations, providers are becoming more adept at collecting and interpreting data. Moreover, they are able to use data to improve delivery of care to beneficiaries on the one hand and the outcomes of that care on the other. The reimbursement structure must be aligned to promote these processes.

Health care has clearly become a team effort. No single provider has the skills and expertise to treat the multiplicity of issues that occur in the delivery, monitoring, and outcomes analysis now expected. The composition of the MBHCO network and the reimbursement methodology must support the provider's ability to deliver care.

References

1. American Psychiatric Association. *Capitation Handbook.* Washington, D.C.: American Psychiatric Association, 1995.

2. Zieman, G., and Freeman, M., Editors. *The Complete Capitation Handbook.* Tiburon, Calif.: CentraLink Publications, 1995.

Bibliography

American Psychiatric Committee on Managed Care and the American Psychiatric Association Ethics Committee. "Report on Managed Care." *APA Ethics Newsletter* 8(1):1-12, 1992.

Bixler, J., and others. *Managed Healthcare Organizational Readiness Guide and Checklist.* Rockville, Md.: U.S. Department of Health and Human Services. Public Health Service, Substance Abuse & Mental Health Services Administration, July 1994.

Boland, P. *Making Managed Healthcare Work.* Gaithersburg, Md.: Aspen Publications, 1993.

Coile, R. "The Future of American Health Care in the 'Post Reform' Era." *Physician Executive* 21(1):3-6, January 1995.

Feldman, J., and Fitzpatrick, R. *Managed Mental Health Care.* Washington, D.C.: American Psychiatric Press. Inc., 1992.

Lee, F. "What Is the Future for Providers in Managed Care?" *Journal of Practical Psychiatry and Behavioral Health* 1(2):77-82, July 1995.

Talbott, J., and Kaplan, S. *Psychiatric Administration*. New York, N.Y.: Grune Stratton, 1983.

Younger, P., and others. *Managed Care Law Manual*. Gaithersburg, Md.: Aspen Publications, 1994.

Zieman, G. "Information Systems and Capitation Contracting." *Behavioral Healthcare Tomorrow* Jan.-Feb. 1993.

Ian A. Shaffer, MD, is Executive Vice President and Chief Medical Officer, ValueOptions, Falls Church, Virginia. Michael E. Glasser, MD, was Regional Medical Director, Value Behavioral Health, Inc., Long Beach, California at the time this chapter was written. He now is Medical Director, MCC Behavioral Health of California, Glendale.

Chapter 14

Independent Practice Association: Contracting with Regional HMOs, Preferred Provider Organizations, and Similar Organizations

by Charles Haddock Hendry, MD

A ll service organizations exist to broker work done by someone else; ergo, all managed care organizations came into existence to broker your services as a provider. If you want to market your own services, you must emulate some of the services they provide. You must be able to sell your organization on the basis of value added. To do so, you must create an organization that will resemble other managed care organizations to potential clients. Whether or not you create an entity to contract with an HMO, a PPO, or a point-of-service product, you probably need to be part of creating a network. Setting up a network can create a "virtual" organization.[1,2] As a virtual organization, you can exist with minimal need for infrastructure, such as office rent, full-time staff, or insurance expenses. To begin, you will exist as a set of agreements and organization on paper and in computer files.

Getting Started
The construction of an independent practice association (IPA) is a multidimensional process, requiring a complex paper structure that can contain processes that can be quickly implemented. This complexity has become multiplied by increased regulations and requirements such as processes to comply with NCQA requirements. Fortunately, you do not have to offer a full range of services to get started.

Many excellent providers do not want to be part of a business venture and are content to see patients. Many are risk-averse and/or believe that payment mechanisms such as capitation represent an unacceptable choice ethically or financially. You do not necessarily have more cost-effective or cooperative providers by making them owners. Generally, being an owner has some positive effect but utilization by psychiatrists seems to be based primarily on other factors.

Some decisions have to be made at the outset and involve, to some extent, guessing what the future will be. You must assess your own personal strengths and weaknesses. Talk to your business advisor. An organization is a coming together of specialists in various activities. You cannot expect to do everything yourself. Talk to other physicians in terms of what they would want as providers or possible owner/participants and of their objections to any participation. Forms of ownership can be changed if conditions change at some later time.

You will need to decide on your ownership structure as a business. The alternatives to the usual corporation should be discussed with an attorney. Alternatives worth considering are limited partnerships or Subchapter S or "S" corporations. An alternative form may avoid the double taxation of the usual corporation, assuming there are any profits.

Initial Financing

The initial money will need to come from providers who wish to retain market share. You can elect to treat the medical providers differently from the nonmedical providers in terms of sharing ownership. Typical of such arrangements is the sale of some form of ownership to medical providers and the use of access fees or credentialing fees plus an annual access fee to nonmedical providers. Ideally, this would cover all start up costs.

What about financing through venture capital? Venture capital for partially financing behavioral health is likely to be scarce. This form of financing would be especially helpful when it would add business expertise to your venture. The current business prospects in the behavioral health area are unlikely to tempt venture capital.

What about partnering with a hospital or hospital chain? This approach may make very good sense in some situations and should be explored. If true partnering could be structured, with the physician group sharing in the rewards of better management, it might be a reasonable choice. Clearly, improved quality and the accompanying improved utilization should reward those who bring this about as well as those who enroll new business. The natural tendency of full-time administrators to dominate such organizations has to be recognized. If the hospital profits from efficient care, this might overcome its opposition to the increased support that is required to produce superior clinical performance and document superior outcomes.

Structure

Two concerns have to be addressed in the structure of the organization:

■ Who will make the day-to-day decisions?

■ What will the governing process be?

A typical governance structure is a small elected board representing a majority portion of the shareholders. The CEO of the company reports to the board. In a small company, the CEO could be the medical director. As the company grows, the CEO would be an administrator of some kind.

To distinguish between day-to-day decisions and strategy, the board might listen to a presentation of a marketing strategy from a marketing consultant and decide on the overall strategy. You might market your group as an IPA of preferred providers to insurance companies or as a capitated organization to an HMO or both but favor one over another to start. Thinking about marketing focuses you on what business you want to be in. Once the strategy is decided, the CEO would probably review the progress of the marketing, be present at some presentations, choose some organizations to pursue over others, and track the efforts of the marketing person. These day-to-day decisions would be presented back to the board for further consideration. The board should be expected to make strategic decisions, not detailed decisions. An administrator would need to make day-to-day decisions without consulting the board.

The structure of the group must contain the following:

■ A board of directors wherein the medical director would be separate from other officers. In a small single-specialty group, the assumption would be that the medical director would oversee a number of functions. Other officers would be a secretary, a treasurer, or a combination position. The administrator, if any, would be a director, and another member of the board would usually be at least one stockholder/shareholder physician.

■ Policy decisions would be set with board approval. The board should not make day-to-day decisions about the operation of the organization. This is a surprisingly common mistake.

■ Provision should be made for the addition of stockholders (alternately, these individuals could be termed partners, share holders, or limited partners, the choice reflecting ownership structure).

■ Provision should be made for terminating providers, including those with ownership, for cause, not for cause, or both. Start with this understanding written into agreements. Current advice in this area is to always say that decisions are made for "business" reasons. In the type of organization described here, this is not likely to be acceptable. The organization should have reasonable standards for all providers. For example, some causes for removal are:

— Loss of medical license

— Patient complaints set at a predetermined number preceded by a warning about behaviors that generate complaints.

— Undue familiarity with patients proven even with retention of licensure.

— Failure to cooperate with utilization guidelines, treatment guidelines, or formulary requirements; medical records below NCQA standards; or failure to cooperate with quality initiatives such as standard outcome studies. These requirements should not be so onerous as to be unreasonable. Some due process of notification, warning, deadline for compliance, etc. might be determined.

— Failure to notify when going on vacation so that referrals become inconvenienced, failure to be on call when agreed upon, refusal to be on call for emergencies, availability limited compared to other providers.

— Member satisfaction falling below the norm by a statistical standard.

— Impairment.

— Criticizes the organization repeatedly and without reasonable detail. You can differentiate reasonable complaints about changes, requirements, and so forth from diatribes directed at your organization. You want providers to be able to disagree without being disagreeable. If these criticisms are made to patients, this is more serious and should be subject to disciplinary steps and the process for termination. This is not a "gag" rule but an acknowledgment that, if you have individuals who say they do not like your organization, they should not participate in it.

— A combination of these events that causes the board to determine an unsatisfactory status without a precisely stated standard except for a pattern of unsatisfactory behavior; an inability to function in a collegial manner. The closest you might come to this would be a statement that an annual review would be made of all providers. If any provider has required warnings or been below standard in two or more areas, the board may terminate at its discretion.

Some provision should be made for compensation for a stockholder in the event of termination of provider status. The company may have a provision to repurchase the stock at the original price, a portion of the price, or not at all if the removal is for cause. This is a messy business at best, but providing for the eventuality before the fact will reduce the inevitable headaches. Generally, you must plan as though a number of things can go wrong at some future point.

■ Compensation should be provided for administrative time and board attendance. If compensation is not available initially, a record can be kept of time expended and compensation can be deferred until such time as profits are available. The time investment then becomes a type of sweat equity.

How Many Providers Do You Need?

The number of providers varies with the geographical area being covered. If you are talking about a typical health maintenance organization population, one full-time psychiatrist per 25,000-30,000 members is adequate. Because this membership is likely to be spread over a number of psychiatrists, you can estimate the impact on the panel of patients for any one psychiatrist. If you are marketing a list of preferred providers, you can have a much larger number than you will actually need for years to come.

For nonphysician providers, you want to have a selection that is geographically widespread and have individuals who can offer some specialized services and skills. No clear rules of thumb exist for this. If you had a closed HMO and members were captive, you would need one provider for about 5,000 members. In an IPA context, you cannot translate staffing easily into membership. From one perspective, you want as few providers as possible to still be able to market your network. If the network is a preferred provider organization and providers pay a fee to belong, you may want as many providers as you can properly credential.

If you have a capitated contract and your group must do crisis intervention in the hospital, you probably need a close relationship with someone who is highly skilled at high-quality crisis intervention in a hospital context. The trend toward hospital intensivists will include behavioral health—the current term appears to be "hospitalist." If you have an increase in hospital demand for services, you might consider hiring a nurse practitioner part time to assist the hospital intensivist rather than a second psychiatrist. The details of how this would be set up would vary with local conditions.

What Services Do You Offer?

Provider Listing

The offering of a provider listing for a company will not be a remunerative process unless your providers actually pay you a fee for the listing. You will need to provide marketing services, credentialing services, and some overhead costs. If the listing is a foot in the door, however, there would be an incentive for the third party to turn to you for other services. The strategy would be for the third party to use more of your services so that you become a de facto "carve-out" provider for behavioral health.

Central Referral Number

This service would be of the most immediate interest to a third party. You would have one number that members can have printed on their cards to call for referrals. This would be a local number and a toll free number if you anticipate many long-distance calls. This number should be served by an individual with some ability to triage. The tendency to use gatekeepers to make all psychiatric referrals is decreasing and will be unmarketable in the near future. This was a barrier to utilization, and employers and patients will not continue to tolerate the practice. You will need to be able to guarantee accessibility standards for routine and urgent appointments.

The trend nationally has been for referral personnel to have master's degree level training in social work or counseling. This is probably unnecessary as long as adequate backup exists by similarly trained individuals. In a small membership, this would be easily outsourced to a master's degree level person for a nominal fee. This should be coupled with procedures for handling emergency calls, after hours back up, and clear triage procedures. In a small IPA-type HMO with only 10,000-40,000 members, these referrals can be accomplished with one or two people. The advantage in having a master's degree level person for referrals is that not all callers need to be seen in person. Some members want information about community services. Some calls are similar to those for member services and want an explanation of benefits. Many individuals who are referred to providers never call and schedule an appointment. Emergency call procedures should be in place so that triage can be done quickly, although the number of such calls is surprisingly small.

Entering all contacts into an encounter database allows for the following:

■ If a referral is generated, the referral can be sent to the appropriate provider with any information gathered. You can directly fax or send it as an e-mail attachment to the designated provider. If you have specified a predetermined number of visits, this is noted, although requesting a brief treatment plan probably makes more administrative sense. The process in your office thus far will have been electronic. Your minimal expectation for providers will be their availability to communicate by fax. Because e-mail and intranets are becoming widely available, their cost can be quite low, and security software is readily available. The time on line would be quite minimal, and ease of communication for the group would be enhanced.

■ Basic information is ready for later claims processing. The savings in avoiding duplicate data processing is remarkable.

■ The necessity to communicate rapidly about policy changes, interpretations, new clients, etc. will fit with this central authorization process.

■ Sampling of referrals for follow up will provide information as to whether appointments were made and kept. "No Shows" are a major headache for providers and plans.

■ A central referral process allows for efficient utilization of providers with specialization expertise.

■ A central referral process allows for maximizing the involvement of providers with appropriate utilization and high-quality care and service patterns.

Utilization Review and Quality Improvement

Marketing your organization for utilization review is a natural product to increase your value to a third-party payer. Simple quality improvement work by hospitals probably will do more in the short term. The "borrowing" of these studies for your organization might produce credible work, and you may want to collaborate with hospitals in producing useful studies. In the long run, the added value that local organization and leadership brings will be greater. In the short run, this is not what is "selling." NCQA has the philosophy of "raising the bar" so that the now rudimentary behavioral health data will be enhanced in the future.

Give some consideration to becoming the behavioral quality improvement company for third parties. This would be a future step, not an initial step.

You will at times have patients admitted as emergencies to facilities outside your network area. When such services are covered by a health plan, it is described as portability of benefits. As part of your contract with the managed care organization, you may specify that you are not responsible financially for those admissions out of region in a capitated contract. You can agree to return them in plan as soon as possible. You should do the utilization review on these out of plan admissions. You can follow these rules of thumb:

■ Because some requests for service benefit coverage are denied and may be appealed, you will need an appeal process defined if you are not using one stipulated by a managed care organization with which you are contracted.

■ You will cover some emergencies for college students out of the service area, but you will have to cover only the emergency care. If individuals want counseling, colleges usually provide it. If they have to see a psychiatrist very often, this cost will have to be borne by the parents. If this is a serious psychotic disorder, be skeptical that the patient will be kept in school out of your service area and plan to provide that service in plan.

■ Some members will want to continue with former therapists out of plan. You will never be Solomon-like enough in your judgment to decide this. Just say "No." This area has created a great deal of controversy as nonaligned therapists begin to lose patients. No study has been published demonstrating any long-term negative impact. Negotiating at least an evaluation visit can usually break through these objections. In any event, year-after-year therapy is not usual in a managed care contract. Often group therapy is cited as an exception. If this is something that is strongly desired, it will likely have to be self-pay for the member.

Disease management would be a natural addition as a product. At least weekly phone monitoring of at-risk disorders would be easily accomplished. How elaborate you wanted to make this would depend on how much the client was willing to pay.

Claims Paying

You can pay your own claims with a relatively simple customized "off the shelf" database. You will be able to pay claims accurately and have instant access to your "costs incurred but not paid" data for accounting purposes. This gives you your own accounting for utilization purposes and provider profiling so that the cost-effectiveness of providers can be assessed. Data can be analyzed for variations between hospitals in terms of length of stay and day of discharge. Obtaining similar data from a third party is time-consuming, and the data usually have to be "cleaned up."

Member Services

Member services refers to providing members information about available services. You probably cannot market this as a stand-alone service, but it would be, in effect, part of your referral service. Making this point to a third party would be an additional marketing tool. You want your personnel to explain or interpret mental or behavioral health benefits. Member services staff in new organizations should understand the interpretation of medical necessity that will allow you to accurately explain benefits or true medical necessity. If you provide this service, you will need to meet with the insurance plan's member services employees to emphasize that they should not give out any information but should refer all queries.

Combinations of Products

The author worked with one organization in which the preferred provider organization component contracted for utilization review services on a PMPM basis while the HMO component contracted for full capitated services on a PMPM basis. This turned out to be a satisfactory arrangement.

Contract Language

The contract language your organization will have to work with in behavioral health is usually already determined. Interpretation of those services is critical. If, for example, you have 30 inpatient days in a calendar year specified in the contract, it means just that. You may be told that it is a common practice to have a two-for-one tradeoff for partial hospital program for each inpatient day, but if it is not in the contract, it may not be so. Assuming that hospital-based care decisions are made with great specificity by your "hospitalist," this may not be a problem. Partial hospital program is one of the most overrated benefits currently sought after. If the managed care organization insists on this option, or more likely some companies insist, you may comply with strict interpretation of medical necessity.

One service often not specified in a contract is an intensive outpatient program for substance abuse. To provide this service, the outpatient benefit of 20 visits a year can be utilized. Usually, an evening program is the most cost effective and probably mimics the life-style changes that are needed for success. Unless this is done, there are apt to be unwelcome, extensive complaints about lack of service and quality.

Income Sources

Capitation

This will be the preferred method to obtain payment unless legal roadblocks become insurmountable. The plan gives you its membership figures as covered lives, and you are paid a predetermined per member per month fee to provide services. If you provide all services, you will currently need to contract for between $2 PMPM and $2.50 PMPM for an HMO. This is for a standard health maintenance organizations benefit of 30 inpatient days and 20 outpatient visits. Providers cannot be given the option to waive copayments. Some flexibility is helpful in terms of "hours." You can offer essentially unlimited contacts for severe chronic or relapsing illnesses without increasing your costs and probably with decreasing them in the long term. The general principle is that improved quality of care means lower costs. Most of these cases involve medication management and are not inordinately time-consuming. They involve an enhanced tracking process for compliance and follow up.

Case Rates

If you are risk-averse, you may want to structure contracts on the basis of case rates. A contract would have to recognize that the population would be expected to be normally distributed in any particular high-risk area. This may become a future alternative to capitation in the specialty area.

Payments to Providers and Stockholders

Case Rates

As noted above, this could be a basis for continual payments to all providers, including stockholders.

Profits Related to Capitation

If you are successful in reducing costs and have good outcomes, you will have decisions to make regarding the use of "profits." Retaining capital to offset negative years would be one obvious choice. The next choice is whether to pay out anything at all as "bonuses." The author would recommend improving the organization in terms of quality determinations, telecommunications, and provision of more services. If you are capitated, you may be able to avoid being accused of underutilization by investing earnings back into the infrastructure so that, in effect, you do not have any profits. Also, consider that you will need to constantly improve in order to remain competitive. Ultimately, you will have to provide to your stockholders some return that they perceive as equitable. No formula that will satisfy everyone exists, and spelling this out early on probably is the only course you can follow.

Hospital Selection

You will need to negotiate a per diem rate with your hospital. You will probably want a rate separate from that for regular admissions for cases involving 23-hour observation. Generally, charges in behavioral health are frontend-loaded, so that the longer the length of stay, the less the hospital spends on an average daily basis. You do not contract for any services off the behavioral health unit in a general hospital.

If you do not have active support from the hospital, in particular, family interviews in the most timely manner, you may not be able to be cost effective. For example, for an adolescent "overdose," you can frequently discharge the patient after 23 hours' observation if you have a family interview prior to discharge. If the hospital social worker cannot perform the interview, you probably cannot discharge the patient in a timely way. This timeliness could be a contractual issue in negotiations.

In such contracts, you may stipulate a level of performance that penalizes nonperformance or lack of availability of support services on weekends. Psychological services are rarely an acute need, but delay can be costly when services are needed.

Timely determination of serum levels is mandatory, and delays are costly. A master's degree level RN or clinical nurse specialist is an ideal person to have for rounding and/or family interventions, including on-call work. In many ways, the use of these personnel may be preferable to using hospital personnel who may not be trained in crisis intervention. Providing this service yourself can reduce per diem costs.

Asking for "special services" can be helpful. One facility faxed all discharge summaries to the follow-up office as soon as they were dictated. Patients should leave the hospital with a firm appointment. If a weekend discharge is possible, this should be arranged on the preceding Friday so that the patient does not leave the hospital without an appointment. You can always cancel an appointment if the discharge is not possible.

Marketing

You will have to hire a marketing consultant. You will probably want to share a part-time person. For example, if a specialty group is marketing itself, its marketing person is likely calling on much the same clients that you would want to contact. You might see if the specialty group marketing person would be willing to market your group at the same time. If not, the group might be able to suggest an alternative person. The group's consultant will already know the local market in health care. Remember that the marketing person you select will represent your organization to the public and his or her appearance becomes yours. You will have to educate the marketing person who should not be expected to have an intuitive grasp of behavioral health. You will need to expect to spend some time educating a consultant about your network and potential services.

When you have created a network, you need to decide what you must do with it. You will be able to use your network to become a "provider list" for start-up organizations. These organizations may actually require very little of you except to ask your providers to sign contracts. What do you get out of this? Unless the providers are willing to pay a fee for this service, you are simply an uncompensated network development organization for third parties. This may be all you want. In a crowded and competitive market, this might be a way to get started, and your providers may pay a fee to be marketed in this way. You have to consider that the third party might not consider your services worth anything once it has a list and contracts available. Your value added will have to be marketed and your marketing consultant will need to understand this.

You probably have to think in terms of contracting with small HMOs, many of which are being started in order to preserve some market share for relatively small insurance companies. The conventional wisdom is that only very large companies will have the resources to compete and will dominate the health care market. Big companies ordinarily want to do business with other big companies, preferably their own subsidiaries. If you do business with a large company, you should have this expectation. A large company will be working with your organization while it has a small membership in your area, but the relationship is unlikely to last. This does not mean such a relationship is not worth having for even a brief period. The big company will also educate you as to current expectations for a provider group.

If multispecialty provider groups are formed or are being formed, you will want to become their behavioral health contractors. This area holds the most promise for the future, and you are in a position to directly market to them. If you have a regulatory climate in which you can direct contract with self-insured companies, you may consider this option. This arrangement currently is quite difficult to market, but opportunities are improving. Typically, a state organization of self-insured companies has an annual meeting, as it happens in the author's home state of Georgia. This would be a likely place to market your "product." Contacting individual companies can be exhausting and extremely time-consuming. Benefits managers usually are not decision makers in the companies and carving out behavioral health services tends to come as a suggestion from health industry consultants from the large consulting firms. At present, no clear process exists for working directly with large self-insured companies in the behavioral health area. Most likely, large behavioral health companies are already active in this area, and you would find competition quite difficult.

An alternative market now rapidly developing is worker's compensation managed care organizations. There are many start-up managed care companies in this area who want to have arrangements with behavioral health providers. They are the last frontier of managed care and an opportunity for marketing.

What Is Needed to Help Providers Organize?

Prepackaged documents, customized "off the shelf" software for small groups for referrals and claims paying, and quality studies already designed and simple to carry out are some basic requirements. These materials will require some updating as requirements change for the National Committee for Quality Assurance. The American Psychiatric Association (APA) has some services available and has helped one group get started. Objections to these services have been raised in terms of their pitting one group of psychiatrists "against" another. The services will be subject to political pressure as to their appropriateness.

References

1. Handy, C. *The Age of Unreason*. Boston, Mass.: Harvard Business School Press, 1990.

2. Handy, C. *The Age of Paradox*. Boston, Mass.: Harvard Business School Press, 1994.

Charles Haddock Hendry, MD, is President, Positive Resolutions, Atlanta, Georgia.

Chapter 15

Rural Managed Care Behavioral Health Network

by Paulette Gillig, MD, PhD, Kathleen A. Raffo, MSSA,
and Andrew Barr, MA, LPCC

Behavioral Health Generations (BHG) is a collection of Alcohol, Drug Addiction, and Mental Health Services (ADAMHS) Boards that manage community-based, publicly funded services for persons living in 17 rural counties in western Ohio. The 10 boards serve a population in excess of one million people and are political subdivisions within the state of Ohio (Ohio Revised Code, Ch. 340). The boards came together in 1993 to form BHG and to collectively plan and implement managed care in the field of behavioral health for services paid in full or in part by public funds.

Rationale for Managed Care in a Public/Private Rural Behavioral Health System

Even if most mental health services could be reintegrated with physical health services, more intensive services or services for special populations would still likely be the responsibility of state and local governments, either by design or by default. When the for-profit sector has moved into the traditional public mental health market, either as a private for-profit insurer or as a capitated management system of public funds, patients with complex or long-term service needs, such as the chronically mentally ill, often have been deemed ineligible for adequate coverage. Recent trends show that the public system is seeing an increasing proportion of patients with multiple disabilities, patients with dual diagnoses (mental illness plus substance abuse problems or mental retardation), perpetrators or victims of violence, and elderly persons. The population being served is also more diverse ethnically and culturally than has been true in the for-profit private sector. However, in some cases the private sector has been able to provide more flexibility of services, and, in rural locations, various types of nontraditional providers of mental health services (such as churches and schools) are already heavily utilized by patients for reasons of accessibility and cultural values.

History of BHG

In spring 1992, several ADAMHS board executive directors began informally meeting to discuss common issues that were impeding the delivery of mental health and substance abuse treatment in rural western Ohio. Issues such as accessibility, outreach, and marketing of services to residents take on unique challenges for rural boards that have little to no organized transportation services and little to no local information media. The lack of private mental health, drug addiction, and alcohol services (inpatient, residential, psychiatry) in rural Ohio is an issue in that it increases the demand on the public system. In addition, many residents are farmers or belong to working families that have limited insurance coverage. Members of boards believed that members of rural communities placed a premium on collaboration and had a sense of "pride" in being self-reliant when dealing with problems, frequently causing isolation until a "crisis" occurs.

As initial meetings progressed, there was consensus that the formation of a rural alliance of ADAMHS boards could provide four things:

■ A unified platform to identify mutual problems.

■ A forum to advance issues unique to rural delivery systems.

■ An organized vehicle to advocate and address common political and funding issues.

■ An organized entity to prepare the rural service delivery system for managed care.

As a result, a Council of Governments (COG) was formed that ultimately was called Behavioral Health Generations (BHG).

Governing Structure

Each of the 10 boards that participate in BHG is unique and represents unique perspectives on how to address the complicated issues facing rural systems of care. To support this uniqueness, ad hoc committees are formed by board groupings that wish to pursue certain projects. For example, five boards participated in a $1.1 million rehabilitation services project to expand job training opportunities for mentally ill residents, and 10 boards participated on a managed care committee that ultimately became BHG. The committee designed a business plan for the development of a managed care entity that will provide managed care functions and oversight for each board area in a more efficient and cost-effective manner.

Once developed, BHG had to consider its governing structure. Several options were explored, including an association, a corporation, a health care corporation, a health maintenance organization, a partnership, a foundation, and a Council of Governments (table 1, pages 204 and 205). The structure of a regional Council of Governments (COG) was selected because local boards, providers, and state departments had familiarity with COGs. A COG is a formal agreement between the governing bodies of two or more counties, municipal corporations, townships, special districts, school districts, or other political subdivisions (Ohio Revised Code, Section 167). As a COG, BHG has the power to promote cooperative arrangements and coordinate action among its members and to perform planning directly by personnel of the Council or under contracts between the Council and other public or private agencies. A COG allows the merging of funds. As a COG, the Board can merge various state and federal funds that it receives and can seek grants that can be shared by all members.

Each ADAMHS member board appoints one representative to the BHG Board, and the BHG Board elects officers annually. The CEO of BHG reports to the Board and is responsible for management functions, including development and execution of contracts other than provider panel contracts (which are still handled by the local Board), such as contracts for other clinical services and for public information services that include newsletters, brochures, and other informational materials. The CEO is also responsible for development and ongoing monitoring of an operational budget.

Eight separate and distinct functions drive the budget and staffing of BHG: management, contracting, financial payment, panel development, patient care, clinical services, claims processing, and public information. The following paragraphs explain each of the functions.

Function 1: Management

BHG is under the direction of a CEO. Primary management responsibilities include, but are not limited to:

- Reporting on all elements of BHG to the Board of Directors of BHG.

- Oversight of a per member per month (PMPM) enrollment rate for services.

- Development and execution of contracts outside provider panel contracts, such as clinical services, public information, services outside the provider panel, etc.

- Development and ongoing monitoring of an operational budget.

- Development and implementation of policies and procedures related to the personnel and operations of BHG.

- Establishment and monitoring of appropriate contingency fund pools.

- Hiring and ongoing evaluation of BHG staff.

- Ensuring that BHG demonstrates integration of all BHG functions.

- Development of appropriate reporting mechanisms to reflect BHG solvency.

- Monitoring and participation in managed care efforts throughout the state and nation, as appropriate.

- Provision of necessary reports to all state and federal governments.

- Establishment of, monitoring of, and participation in the Quality Improvement Council of BHG.

Clearly, the success of BHG will depend on the leadership capabilities of the administrative staff and Board. It will be necessary for the management of the entity to consistently keep an eye on both the internal functioning of BHG and the managed care industry and to make adjustments accordingly. Full implementation and integration of services will be evolutionary and will require much adaptability by BHG management.

Table 1. Governing Structure Options for Managed Health Care Entity

Name Of Entity	Definition Structure	Organizational Powers/Duties	Limitations
Association	A collection of persons who have joined together for the accomplishment of some purpose, without charter but under the methods and forms used by incorporated bodies.	Because an association is a term of vague and ambiguous nature under law, it has no formal organizational structure, powers or duties.	The Ohio Constitution prohibits any county, city, town or township from becoming a stockholder in any corporation or association (Art VIII, Section 6).
Corporation	An artificial person or legal entity created under the authority of state law that exists as a body separate and apart from its members and is vested with the legal authority to enter into contracts, to sue and be sued, and to conduct other business within the scope of the Articles of Incorporation and state law.	Corporations controlled principally by shareholders (for-profit) corporation or members (nonprofit corporation) that elect a Board of Directors to oversee corporate operations. Directors elect officers, who carry on the day-to-day business of the corporation.	The Ohio Constitution prohibits any county, city, town or township from becoming a stockholders in any corporation or association. (Art. VIII, Section 6.) Only "persons" may form a corporation. A person under corporation law is defined, without limitation, as a corporation, partnership, unincorporated society or association.
Health Care Corporation	An entity created under authority of state law that offers a type or scope of health care services on a group or individual basis.	Health Care Corporation is initiated by the filing of an application for a certificate or license by the Superintendent of Insurance. Once such a certificate or license is approved, organization is similar to a corporation, with a board of directors and officers.	Health Care Corporation may offer services such as dental, vision, nursing, long-term care, outpatient mental health services, but may offer no more than one or two categories of services.	Health Care Corporations are corporations with the permission of and significantly regulated by the department of insurance with regard to financial matters, contracts and rates.

Health Maintenance Organization	A public or private organization that provides to enrolled participants a mandatory array of basic and emergency health care services and is compensated by payments made on a periodic basis without regard to the frequency, extent, or kind or services provided.	An HMO is substantially regulated by state law and requires strict compliance with mandates regarding enrollment, services provided, types of coverages, and financial plans.	An HMO must offer basic health care services, emergency services, outpatient and diagnostic lab services.	Although HMOs are exempt from insurance laws, they are extensively regulated under state law in terms of open enrollment, and provide little flexibility in terms of services that must be offered.
Partnership	An association of two or more persons to carry on as co-owners a business for profit.	A partnership rests on a contractual relationship of the parties and is flexible as to both organization and structure, depending on agreement of the parties.	A partnership may be formed for any lawful enterprise or for-profit business.	Only "persons" may form partnerships. A person under partnership law includes individuals, partnerships, trustees, executors, administrators, other fiduciaries, corporations, and other associations.
Regional Council of Governments	A Regional Council of Government (COG) is an agreement between the governing bodies of two or more counties, municipal corporations.	Membership in the COG shall be pursuant to an agreement establishing the council and its bylaws. The agreement sets forth the manner of determining representation on the council. The state may be an ex officio member of the COG. The COG must adopt bylaws by majority vote designating its officers and their method of selection and providing for the conduct of its business. It may employ staff and contract for the services of consultants and experts and may purchase or lease supplies, materials,, equipment, or facilities under procedures established by the bylaws.	A COG has the power to study area governmental problems: promote cooperative arrangements and coordinate action among its members; make recommendations for review and action; and perform functions and duties as are performed by or capable of performance by the members and necessary or desirable for dealing with problems of mutual concern.	The COG is a viable alternative for a managed care entity. It may accept funds, grants, gifts, and services from the U.S. government and its agencies.

Function 2: Contracting

The contracting function of BHG is broken down into three areas:

- Content of the contract with providers.

- Financial contracting with providers in terms of how BHG will share risk.

- Contracting for the delivery of services through panel development.

Contract Content

In preparation for this plan, multiple managed care contracts were obtained and reviewed. The items that appear consistently in the contracts are identified here. Although the BHG business plan does not contain a specific contract for use with providers, this outline can be used to guide development of a contract.

- Effective date, parties involved, and addresses.

- Definitions of words used, including definitions of the primary persons responsible.

- Verification process—eligibility criteria for providers.

- Maintenance of all utilization review, quality assurance, peer review, and other quality management activities.

- Hold harmless/indemnification provisions. Some contracts specify both parties; some have providers holding BHG harmless.

- Liability, umbrella, and malpractice insurance requirements. Copies of all insurance policies must be provided 30 days prior to contract renewal and notification of all policy changes must be made.

- Requirement to obey all laws and maintain necessary licenses. BHG must be notified of any discrepancies.

- Confidentiality must be maintained, and records must be retained for six years or six years past the "age of majority." BHG has reasonable access to records three years past contract expiration. Anyone legally allowed to review files is given access.

- Dispute resolution. If good faith negotiation is unsuccessful, disputes go to arbitration after 30 days. Costs of arbitration are shared. Arbitrators cannot award damages, and disputes are limited to one year after occurrence.

- Termination clauses, specifying conditions under which either party may sever the contractual relationship.

- Conditions for amendment of contract.

- Conditions under which contract may be assigned.

- Independence of parties to contract.

- Statement of completeness of the contract in describing the parties' relationship.

∎ Waiver of breach. In BHG contracts, waivers are limited to the breach under immediate consideration.

∎ Severability of sections of the contract.

∎ Elimination—special conditions, such as a catastrophe, under which either party may be released from the contract.

∎ Disclosure—All parties to the contract must be disclosed.

∎ Incident reporting—All major unusual incidents must be reported to BHG.

Function 3—Methodology for Financial Payment to Providers

The ultimate goal of BHG is to enter into performance-based (outcomes) capitation contracts with providers. Currently, there are no Boards in the managed care project that fund agencies on a capitation basis, although some funding from State departments is on a per capita basis. Grant and fee-for-service methods are currently used. Under the grant method, an agency is paid for providing a service or task with a fixed amount for a fixed period. There is some form of reconciliation for units either under- or over-produced. Fee for service involves paying a provider an agreed amount after services have been delivered.

During fiscal year 1995, the Boards in the managed care project contracting for mental health services used the fee-for-service method 69 percent of the time and the grant method 31 percent of the time. For drug and alcohol abuse service, fee for service was used 56 percent of the time and the grant method was used 44 percent of the time.

Function 4—Provider Panel Development

As mentioned above, BHG will ultimately be contracting with providers on a performance-based capitation system basis. It will establish a panel of providers using a competency-based approach. All providers, including transfer services, with the exception of pharmacy, will be judged on the basis of the following competencies:

∎ *Administrative soundness.* The provider must demonstrate fiscal and financial soundness and have mechanisms in place for monitoring both. The provider must have information systems in place for billing, tracking costs, and reporting to BHG. Evidence of all insurance policies must be provided. The provider must have a plan for staff training and development and for conducting utilization management.

∎ *Certification/accreditation/licensure.* Providers must document compliance with certification and accreditation standards and with applicable licensure laws. Alternatively, providers must have Medicaid certification and abide with BHG policies and procedures. Procedures for profiling all provider staff members must be in place.

∎ *Customer outcomes.* The provider must have a research-based method for monitoring outcomes and for collecting outcomes data. A mechanism must be in place to link collected data to quality improvement efforts.

■ *Customer satisfaction.* The provider must have a process for measuring customer satisfaction. The process must be linked to quality improvement efforts and must address, at a minimum, customers' perceptions of treatment and of the financial aspects of care.

■ *Quality monitoring.* The provider must have a plan for ongoing quality improvement efforts. Major incident reports must be submitted to BHG.

Function 5—Customer Care Management
Customers may access services from BHG by contacting any member of the provider panel, which is able to complete an immediate referral to an appropriate treatment provider when the customer's problem is best suited to another provider. This gives the customer maximum choice in accessing behavioral health services. Once a diagnostic assessment is completed, a customer may be referred to another provider where appropriate. Customer participation in service delivery, including community support programs, crisis intervention, etc., is highly encouraged by BHG.

All Boards participating in BHG are required to have a singular access point to a comprehensive crisis response system that must be able to provide access to adult and youth mental health and substance abuse services.

Function 6—Clinical Services
Authorization for payment of a treatment plan will be completed through the clinical services function. Appeals of treatment denials will be responded to by BHG in four hours for emergency situations and in eight hours for nonemergency situations. If a response is not forthcoming within these times, approval of the appeal is automatic. Complaints concerning services and processes are reviewed and resolved by BHG and the appropriate Board. BHG is responsible for establishing a Council to oversee quality improvement efforts. The Council has the authority to request participation of members of the provider panel, customers, and experts in the analysis of outcomes, cost, service utilization, customer demographics, and customer satisfaction data.

Function 7—Claims Processing
BHG's information systems must be able to receive standard claim forms electronically. BHG is responsible for adjudicating claims and making payments to providers. BHG is also responsible for meeting all state and federal guidelines for reporting payments for services.

Function 8—Public Information
Because of the nature of business and the highly competitive managed care industry, marketing and education are of primary importance to the BHG Managed Care Project. Issues of access and consumer choice will continue the long-term need for marketing BHG abilities and services in direct competition with other like-minded organizations. As BHG progresses, needs will change and evolve. It is thus imperative to emphasize the need for flexibility in marketing and education strategies. Long-term objectives for education and marketing will reflect ongoing development of the overall organization.

Fiscal Considerations

Each participating ADAMHS board continues to receive its financial allocations directly from the Ohio Department of Mental Health, the Ohio Department of Alcohol and Drug Addiction Services, and its local funding sources(e.g. tax levies). BHG establishes a monthly fee for each ADAMHS board based on the population to be served and the services to be provided by BHG. An example of how one ADAMHS board decided to share service responsibilities with BHG is illustrated in table 2, pages 210-213.

BHG plans to contract with provider agencies in a performance-based capitation system in which the provider is given a set amount of dollars for providing services based on its ability to demonstrate positive outcomes and high-quality care.

Clinical Considerations

In order for ADAMHS boards to be members of BHG, they must have or be able to purchase the following services for their geographic area: psychiatric evaluations and treatment services, case management, crisis intervention services, prehospital services, counseling services, housing, prevention services, psychiatric hospital services, education, vocational/employment services, alcohol and drug addiction detoxification services, therapeutic foster care, residential treatment for youths, residential treatment for adults, home-based therapy, and "wrap-around" (i.e., flexible funding for adults and children). This funding can be used to purchase services or items not available in any other way (e.g., car repairs, summer camp, etc.)

Because of the unique populations that the rural public system serves (i.e., chronically mentally ill, severe substance abusing individuals, and difficult to engage populations—such as farmers with a "take care of our own" attitude and rural minorities), treatment protocols take into account such variables as transportation problems, need for social structure, etc. A traditional managed care approach requires significant amounts of staff time for preauthorization of services. Instead, BHG plans to establish a panel of providers using a competency-based approach. All providers are to be judged in the five competency areas: administrative soundness, certification/accreditation/ licensure, consumer outcomes, consumer satisfaction, and retrospective quality monitoring. Once credentialed in the five areas by BHG, the provider is not required to have preauthorization except for exceedingly high-cost clients, so that BHG does not have to have extensive clinical review staff and time available. Each provider has the opportunity to apply to BHG for an initial evaluation to determine if it meets the competency criteria. Providers are then given a written assessment of their status. Once a provider becomes part of the panel, it will be continuously monitored and evaluated on each of these five competency areas every three years. Thus, providers who meet the competency criteria can be reimbursed by BHG for services provided without prior authorization or approval.

Ethical Considerations for Psychiatrists in Managed Care

The American Psychiatric Association's Council on Psychiatry has proposed the following guidelines with regard to professional responsibilities of psychiatric physicians practicing in managed care entities: responsibility to disclose, responsibility to appeal, responsibility for recommended care, and the necessity to separate the allocation function from the treatment function.

Table 2. The Potential Roles of Public Behavioral Health Authorities

Key

R = Responsibility directly performed by the board and its staff.

R/S = Responsibility carried out by the board and others (probably BHG) sharing responsibility.

A = Role carried out by others (probably BHG) on board's behalf; board approves or disapproves actions/policies proposed to be taken.

I = Role carried out by others; board informed of progress and status. .

? = Board role unclear.

ROLE I. To provide leadership that involved citizens and consumers in planning and public policy, in partnership with other parts of the health care and human services system.

Elements

Ensuring citizen and consumer participation in planning processes.**R/S**

Representing interests of consumers and customers in policy processes, public hearings, and legal proceedings.**R/S**

Involving citizens and consumers in network development.**R/S**

Explicating the role of mental health in all health care, through education, collaboration, and policy development.**R/S**

Organizing public awareness activities.**R**

ROLE 2. To promote access of vulnerable populations to community-based, integrated systems of care.

Elements

Increasing availability of culturally and linguistically accessible services.**A**

Conducting outreach to vulnerable populations.**R/S**

Creating partnerships with other service providers.**R/S**

Ensuring that services reflect reasonable accommodation with individual preferences.**A**

ROLE 3. To collect, manage, and analyze behavioral health and health-related information for the purpose of prospective decision making.

Elements

Ensuring collection of data that enable decisions to be made regarding current and desired behavioral health status of the public.**R/S**

Integrating data from financial, administrative and clinical systems.**R/S**

Collecting and analyzing epidemiological (incidence and prevalence) data.**R/S**

Developing mechanisms for collection and analysis of qualitative information, such as input from consumers, family members, and other system stakeholders. **R/S**

Table 2. The Potential Roles of Public Behavioral Health Authorities *(cont.)*

ROLE 4. To define and evaluate performance, outcome, effectiveness, and costs of behavioral health-related services and systems.

Elements

Establishing effective mechanisms for monitoring, regulating, licensing, certifying, standard setting, and sanctioning for behavioral health service providers.**R/S**

Ensuring consistent implementation of consumer outcome and system performance measures at all levels, and ensuring the use of these measures for provider profiling, system cost-effectiveness monitoring, and continuous quality improvement.**R/S**

Promoting continuity and adequacy of care.**A**

Establishing effective mechanisms for independent monitoring of services and systems by consumers, families, and other citizens.**R/S**

Measuring customer satisfaction and continuously improving quality in response to measurement data.**A**

Working to achieve equity of resources across systems.**R/S**

Preventing cost- and care-shifting.**R/S**

Requiring accountability of service providers.**R/S**

ROLE 5. To ensure that savings are treated as a return on public investment.

Elements

Providing financial incentives to derive savings through management efficiency and clinically appropriate utilization management and to reinvest these savings in new services and essential service system infrastructure.**R/S**

Addressing issues of risk and profitability in service contracts so as to use savings for public purposes.**R/S**

Ensuring that. when decisions are made on the use of these funds, the provision of services to underserved populations is considered.**R/S**

Articulating the mental health needs of communities to elected officials.**R/S**

ROLE 6. To improve the health status of communities, families, and individuals.

Elements

Promoting prevention and early intervention.**A**

Promoting public education.**R/S**

Working with employers.**A**

Promoting availability of community living support in areas such as housing, income and environmental safety.**R**

Working to reduce bias against mental illness.**R/S**

Catalyzing communities and neighborhoods to work in partnership with the mental health authority to achieve progress in these areas.**R/S**

Promoting linkages and partnerships with other human services agendas, such as public health, child welfare, juvenile justice, and criminal justice.**R/S**

. Table 2. The Potential Roles of Public Behavioral Health Authorities *(cont.)*

ROLE 7. To promote safe communities.

Elements

Protecting the rights and welfare of vulnerable clients.**R/S**

Ameliorating violence by intervening in cycle of violence.**R/S**

Providing crisis response in emergency situations.**I**

Promoting early intervention in crises to avoid emergencies.**A≥I**

Making mental health services available in local and state criminal justice facilities.**R/S**

Assuring utilization of appropriate involuntary commitment procedures with due process safeguards.**A≥I**

ROLE 8. To provide a safety net for individuals to access needed services elsewhere.

Elements

Promoting community, county, and state sponsorship of funding for services to individuals who have no other resources.**R/S**

Ensuring provision of services to underserved populations, such as rural residents, minorities and persons with special needs.**R/S**

Identifying the needs of vulnerable groups.**A≥I**

Advocating policies that prevent private insurers from shifting special needs clients to public systems.**R**

Ensuring long-term, 24-hour care for the limited number of individuals in need of such care who cannot be served in any other way.**R**

ROLE 9. To promote innovation and best practices in services and systems.

Elements

Designing and financing research and demonstration projects.**?**

Influencing the design of services research.**?**

Assisting in the development of research topics.**?**

Developing continuous quality improvement systems.**R/S**

Disseminating knowledge and sharing information inside and outside all service system components.**R/S**

Using information about system performance, best practice information, research and evaluation findings, and internally generated continuous quality improvement strategies to develop and revise human resource development activities.**R/S**

Establishing public-academic liaisons.**RIS**

Facilitating relationships among academic centers and communities to ensure a highly trained behavioral health work force.**R/S**

Table 2. The Potential Roles of Public Behavioral Health Authorities *(cont.)*

ROLE 10. To provide disaster-related mental health services at times of local, regional, or statewide emergencies.

Elements

Developing a community or regional response plan.**A**

Ensuring treatment of cases of post-traumatic stress disorder (PTSD).**A**

Facilitating intersystem coordination.**A**

Establishing mutual aid agreements with other human service agencies.**A**

Including a requirement to provide disaster-related services in service contracts with private providers.**A**

* Format adapted from Folcarelli, C., *In the Public Interest: The Role of Public Mental Health Authorities in the Emerging Healthcare System*, Boston, Mass.: Technical Assistance Collaborative, 1995.

"Responsibility to disclose" means that, at the time of evaluation, psychiatrists should inform patients of all treatment options, regardless of insurance coverage. At the outset of treatment, any existing incentive agreements to limit care should be openly discussed with the patient. Patients should be aware of the review and monitoring required by the managed care entity and should know that payment for treatment may be terminated under managed care arrangements.

"Responsibility to appeal" means that a psychiatrist whose patient has been denied payment for care has the responsibility to appeal the managed care entity's decision on the patient's behalf if the treating psychiatrist believes the care is needed by the patient and should fall within the scope of coverage provided by the managed care entity.

"Responsibility for recommended care" means that, in the event a managed care entity denies coverage for recommended care, psychiatrists continue to have obligations to their patients to provide alternative treatment, to provide treatment at a reduced fee, or to arrange for another psychiatrist to care for the patient. If care is terminated, an appropriate manner should be used, such as giving the patient adequate notice (six months is preferred), allowing time for discussion of terminating and working through the relationship, and following the patient in case of a setback after termination is proposed. In emergency situations in which there is a doctor-patient relationship, the psychiatrist has an obligation to provide emergency treatment. Psychiatrists should follow their clinical judgment and ensure that services are provided when failure to do so would fall below recognized standards of care.

"Separating the allocation function from the treatment function" means that, because the treating psychiatrist must serve as guardian of the best interests of patients, the treating psychiatrist should not be the person making important allocation decisions for his or her patients. In rural areas, this separation can be a challenge, because the number of psychiatrists in a given community is usually quite limited. A federation such as BHG can assist in the allocation process by creating a service allocations board with rotating clinician membership. Rotating participation by all clinicians on a centralized allocations board ensures that a range of clinical experience is brought to bear on decisions, helps to ensure fair distribution of resources, and creates an "institutional memory" of case decisions for future reference.

Conclusion

BHG's history is brief, but in this time it has moved steadily forward regardless of state politics. It has succeeded in providing managed care training; has developed a management information system and a costing manual and process; has established a member dues structure; and has set in place a BHG-wide client satisfaction process as part of a national database. It is presently establishing a single quality improvement system, determining practice guidelines, determining cost by diagnosis, and designing job descriptions for BHG management staff who will be hired in 1998.

Failures have been associated primarily with following state directives, only to have them changed or abruptly dropped. This has periodically caused BHG to stop and rethink its position, but it has continued to move forward. To offset some of these barriers, BHG hired its own lobbyist, who has helped keep a path open for BHG through state changes.

Bibliography

Boaz, J. *Delivering Mental Healthcare: A Guide for HMOs.* Chicago, Ill.: Pluribus Press, Inc., 1988.

Feldman, S., Editor. *Managed Mental Health Services.* Springfield, Ill.: Charles C Thomas, Publishers, 1992.

Folcarelli, C. *In the Public Interest: The Role of Public Mental Health Authorities in the Emerging Health Care System.* Boston, Mass.: Technical Assistance Collaborative, 1995.

Garnick, D., and others. "Characteristics of Private-Sector Managed Care for Mental Health and Substance Abuse Treatment." *Hospital and Community Psychiatry* 45(12):1201-5, Dec. 1994.

Kanter, R. "Collaborative Advantage: The Art of Alliances." *Harvard Business Review* 72(4):96-108, July-Aug. 1994.

Lazarus, A. "Managed Care: Lessons from Community Mental Health." *Hospital and Community Psychiatry* 45(4):301, April 1994.

Winegar, N. *The Clinician's Guide to Managed Mental Health Care.* New York, N.Y.: Haworth Press, 1992.

Paulette Gillig, MD, PhD, is Associate Professor, Psychiatry, Department of Psychiatry, School of Medicine, Wright State University, Dayton, Ohio, and Chief Clinical Officer of the Logan and Champaign Counties Alcohol, Drug, and Mental Health Services Board. Kathleen A. Raffo, MSSA, is Executive Director and Andrew Barr, MA, LPCC, is Associate Director of the Board, Logan and Champaign Counties Alcohol, Drug, and Mental Health Services Board.

Chapter 16

The Professional Affiliation Group

by Benjamin Liptzin, MD, Jay M. Pomerantz, MD,
Alfred Carter, MD, and Michael S. Perlman, MD

T he professional affiliation group (PAG), a model for providing mental health services in a managed care framework, has evolved since 1992.[1-4] This chapter will describe why and how the model was developed, how it operates, what its results have been, and how it may further evolve.

History

The PAG approach developed within Health New England (HNE), an independent practice association (IPA) model health maintenance organization (HMO) based in Springfield, Massachusetts. In 1991, Health New England management became alarmed that the cost of providing mental health and substance abuse services to its 40,000 subscribers had increased 126 per cent between 1988 and 1991. In addition to concerns over rapidly rising costs, primary care physicians who functioned as the gatekeepers in the system were frustrated by their inability to determine the need for referrals for patients with mental health or substance abuse problems or to arrange appropriate referrals when the need was determined.

Health New England management responded to the concerns about cost and access by soliciting proposals for a mental health and substance abuse carve-out program from eight national managed mental health care companies. The proposals were reviewed by HNE staff and an outside psychiatric consultant, and two finalists were selected to make presentations. The authors, who were psychiatrist providers in HNE at the time, were constituted as an advisory group to assist in evaluation of the finalists. Following the presentations, we recommended to HNE that they allow us to develop a local alternative to a national managed care carve-out. Within three weeks we developed a proposal that promised to reduce 1992 per capita expenditures by at least 10 per cent below the 1991 level. Although our proposal was 50-60 per cent more expensive to HNE than those of the national managed care companies and contained more financial risk for HNE, HNE management nevertheless agreed to let us develop the program.

The local alternative was chosen for several reasons. First, HNE is owned and controlled by network hospitals and physicians, who wanted to keep local control. The 30 plan psychiatrists (most of whom were also shareholders) unanimously supported the local proposal and convinced the other physicians on the IPA board to support it. Several other HMOs in the state had recently gone through bitter public disagreements between management and physicians. HNE wanted to present a positive image in the community that could help it continue to grow. Second, a national managed care company that had come into the region had generated enormous conflict with patients and providers. HNE wanted to avoid such adverse publicity. Third, HNE psychiatrists indicated their seriousness about controlling costs by agreeing to freeze their fees for one year and to increase their risk sharing by having 18 per cent of their fees withheld in a risk pool to be distributed at the end of the year. Distribution of this withhold was contingent on per-member-per-month (PMPM) expenditures for the year being less than an agreed-upon target figure. Fourth, it was agreed that any administrative management fee would be paid only if there were additional savings below the target figure. If the target figure was not reached, no management fee would be paid. If performance was better than the target, a fee allocated by formula would be paid to providers up to 50 cents PMPM. Finally, nonphysician mental health professionals were willing to join because they were promised a collaborative, clinically driven program with improved access to psychiatric consultation and medication management.

The PAG Model and How It Works

In our system, a professional affiliation group is a group of three to eight fully licensed, independently practicing mental health professionals from different disciplines. There are 15 PAGs with more than 80 outpatient clinicians. Each group has at least one psychiatrist who functions as the PAG leader. Each psychologist, psychiatric social worker, psychiatric nurse, and psychiatrist maintains an office and bills for services independently. Each clinician has full clinical responsibility for his or her patients. The managing psychiatrist who functions as the PAG leader reviews all requests for outpatient treatment beyond the five initial visits that are routinely approved. Additional visits may be approved up to the plan limit of 20 psychotherapy sessions per year. Any disagreement between the managing psychiatrist and an individual clinician is brought to the entire PAG for discussion. A clinician who disagrees with the group consensus can appeal to the HNE medical director, who is the only person who can deny payment.

The managing psychiatrist also provides timely psychopharmacological evaluation and medication management for patients in treatment with the PAG's clinicians. Medication visits do not count against the 20-visit benefit for psychotherapy. Patients who are unstable and at risk of psychiatric hospitalization are also evaluated by the managing psychiatrist. Each PAG meets every two to four weeks, depending on the number of patients in treatment. The discussion focuses on problem cases and the allocation of sessions and provides opportunities for coordination of treatment when a patient is seen by one clinician for psychotherapy and by a psychiatrist for medication. To assist clinicians trained in traditional or long-term psychodynamic psychotherapy models, the discussions often address alternative treatment approaches using focused or intermittent therapy.

The PAG discussions are advisory and educational or consultative and take place in an atmosphere of mutual respect among independently licensed peers. Consultation rather than supervision is provided, and thus the treating clinician maintains clinical and legal responsibility for the patient. For patients who are in treatment with two clinicians, clinical and legal responsibility is shared. In other models, this has raised concerns about possible clinical conflicts and clinician liability, but these concerns are obviated in a PAG model that promotes close collaboration.[5]

How Well Has It Worked?

The PAG model for providing outpatient services is only one element of an overall network that includes three hospital inpatient psychiatric units, two inpatient substance abuse units, five outpatient clinics, three partial hospitalization programs, and two psychiatric emergency services. In addition, a central telephone triage system is staffed by a mental health administrator with extensive clinical experience and two assistants who work closely with providers to see that patients get prompt access to the appropriate treatment program or clinician. The PAGs provide approximately 60 percent of outpatient visits.

Overall enrollment in Health New England has grown from 43,000 members at the end of 1992 to more than 80,000 members at the end of 1997. There are many reasons for the plan's growth, but the smooth, nonadversarial implementation of the managed mental health care program and its ability to reduce costs without draconian reductions has certainly helped. Ironically, the success of the managed mental health program may have led to some adverse selection. Individuals unsatisfied with their treatment elsewhere switch to Health New England so that they can have a wide range of high-quality providers to choose from in a more clinically responsive system.

Overall PMPM costs have been reduced by about 15 percent, despite several fee increases to providers. Before the program began, PMPM costs were more than $7 and in 1997 expenditures were approximately $5.35. The savings have been achieved by almost entirely eliminating referrals to 28-day inpatient substance abuse treatment programs and by reducing inpatient psychiatric days by more than 50 per cent, from more than 100 days/1,000 subscribers to less than 50. The former was achieved by use of detoxification and acute residential programs rather than expensive hospital-based programs. The latter was facilitated by the use of the network inpatient units in general hospitals, where stays average under 10 days; by avoiding some hospitalizations through prompt and expert outpatient evaluations and psychopharmacological interventions; and by the use of partial hospital or intensive outpatient programs as an alternative or step-down from inpatient programs. Annual ambulatory encounter rates are more than 600 visits/1,000 subscribers. Except in emergencies, no patient is admitted to an inpatient unit without an outpatient evaluation, and any admitted patient is immediately connected with the PAG psychiatrist and clinician who will be responsible for ongoing treatment. Outpatient clinicians are then involved with inpatient treatment teams to plan an orderly and prompt transition to outpatient treatment. Prior to the development of the managed care system, the majority of expenditures were for inpatient care. Now, outpatient care accounts for more than two-thirds of expenditures.

Patient satisfaction has been measured in two different years, and both times there was high satisfaction, in the range of 93 to 94 percent. The only complaints were that the benefit was limited to 20 psychotherapy sessions and that there was a restricted panel of providers, both true of many managed care plans. Unlike some other managed care plans, however, as far as we can tell there is little, or no, out-of-plan utilization.[6]

Providers are also quite satisfied. No mental health clinician has ever left because of unhappiness with how the plan is working. In fact, there are now 200 applications from local mental health professionals who want to join the system, which is currently closed to new providers. A study of primary care physicians' (PCPs') satisfaction with the system is currently in process. Anecdotal evidence and PCP support for the program in discussions at IPA board and HNE board meetings suggest that they also have a high degree of satisfaction with the program.

Future Evolution

To date, the PAG model has only been used as part of the network for a single IPA-model HMO. However, we are planning to expand its use to other payers who wish to contract with a recently developed physician hospital organization (PHO) at our principal hospital. The PAG model could theoretically also be used to contract with a carve-out company that wanted to use our network instead of building its own. Various issues would need to be worked out, including credentialing of providers, contracting with providers, data collection and analysis, and quality assurance activities. Even with the basic PAG model in place, providers would still have to deal with different systems of prior authorization, billing, and data collection for quality assurance. In addition, it is unclear how well the model would adapt to plans that had substantially different target figures for expenditures and for related utilization rates and average visits per patient.

Continued attempts will be made to collect outcomes data. Pilot studies in the hospital outpatient department demonstrated that patients are quite impaired on the Role-Emotional and Mental Health scales of the SF-36.[7] Their initial scores improve significantly after treatment, although they are still below norms for the population as a whole. A great deal of thought has been given to what outcome data should be collected from the perspectives of the patient, the family, the employer, and the insurance plan.[8] Even from the patient's perspective, one could look at symptom reductions, psychosocial functioning, or utilization of other medical services. Unanswered are questions about when to measure the impact of a mental health intervention that involves six or fewer psychotherapy sessions and how to get responses from patients who are no longer in treatment. More work also needs to be done on how to adjust for severity of illness and presence of comorbid conditions, such as substance abuse or other medical illnesses. No agreed-upon methodology is currently available.

Summary

The PAG model is a workable way for local privately practicing mental health clinicians to take on financial risk in a managed care plan in a clinically responsible and professionally rewarding way. With a reasonable expenditure target for mental health and substance abuse services, high patient and provider satisfaction can be achieved at a reasonable cost.

References

1. Pomerantz, J., and others. "The Professional Affiliation Group: A New Model for Managed Mental Health Care." *Hospital and Community Psychiatry* 45(4):308-10, April 1994.

2. Pomerantz, J., and others. "Development and Management of a "Virtual" Group Practice." *Psychiatric Annals* 25(8):504-8, Aug. 1995.

3. Pomerantz, J., and others. "Is Private Practice Compatible with Managed Care?" In Lazarus, A., Editor, Controversies in Managed Mental Health. Washington, D.C.: American Psychiatric Press, 1996.

4. Pomerantz, J., and others. "How to Develop a Virtual Group Practice." *Journal of Practical Psychiatry and Behavioral Health* 1(4)232-5, July-Aug. 1995.

5. Busch, F., and Gould, E. "Treatment by a Psychotherapist and a Psychopharmacologist: Transference and Countertransference Issues." *Hospital and Community Psychiatry* 44(8)772-4, Aug. 1993.

6. Simon, G., and others. "Predictors of Outpatient Mental Health Utilization by Primary Care Patients in a Health Maintenance Organization." *American Journal of Psychiatry* 151(6)908-13, June 1994.

7. Ware, J., and Sherbourne, C. "The MOS 36-Item Short-Form Health Survey (SF-36), I: Conceptual Framework and Item Selection." *Medical Care* 30(6):473-83, June 1992.

8. Sederer, L., and Dickey, B. *Outcomes Assessment in Clinical Practice.* Baltimore, Md.: Williams and Wilkins, 1996.

Benjamin Liptzin, MD, is Chairman, Department of Psychiatry, Baystate Health Systems, Springfield, Massachusetts, and Professor and Deputy Chair, Department of Psychiatry, Tufts University School of Medicine, Boston. Jay M. Pomerantz, MD, is in private practice in Longmeadow, Massachusetts; Alfred Carter, MD, is in private practice in Springfield, Massachusetts; and Michael S. Perlman, MD, is in private practice in Northampton, Massachusetts.

Section IV

Integration

Chapter 17

Integrated Group-Model HMO

by Mark F. Leveaux, MD

T his chapter will focus on the integrated staff/group-model HMO delivery system, using the writer's experience in the Kaiser Permanente Health Care System as a point of reference. "Integrated" in this context means that behavioral health services are delivered within the same system that delivers general medical or other health care. "Vertical integration" implies an organization that provides all levels of care and that in some cases, such as the Kaiser Permanente system, may have some role in marketing or developing the actual health care "product" or insurance package sold to groups and individuals. "Horizontal integration" implies that the same organization manages and provides a full range of health services (behavioral, preventive, and medical care) at a given level of care (outpatient or inpatient, for example). A medical group providing a full range of outpatient clinical services is an example. The designation of a "fully vertically integrated health care system" implies a high level of horizontal integration at each level of care.

In contrast to these definitions, the operational reality is that there are few if any completely vertically integrated staff/group-model systems, although some of the Kaiser Permanente regions, with their ownership and management of hospitals, have come the closest. However, in some Kaiser regions, there has been a recent restructuring that has decreased the role of Kaiser-owned and -operated hospitals in the Kaiser delivery system, as well as introduced some role for the use of nonstaff provider networks. At least some aspect of a given level of care may be outside of the organizations. For example, even the most comprehensive staff/group-model HMO behavioral health department will refer out of its internal delivery system for low-volume outpatient services, such as special language needs, just as medical or surgical departments may contract with community resources for such services as dialysis or organ transplantation. Also, many such organizations will contract for hospital and/or professional inpatient psychiatric services, especially for low-volume services, such as child inpatient psychiatry.

For the sake of this discussion, the term "integrated staff/group-model HMO" means that the majority of behavioral health services are provided by staff members who are employees or group shareholders/partners of the same organization that directly provides a full range of health care services to the health plan's enrollees. In group-model programs, professionals are employees of the organizations; in group models, at least a subset of professionals (usually physicians) contract as an independent group to provide services exclusively to the larger organization. In the Kaiser Permanente system, the latter is the structure in which regional "Permanente Medical Groups" contract with the national "Kaiser Foundation Health Plan" to provide professional medical services in their geographical areas.

Current Market Position of Behavioral Health Services in Integrated Staff/Group-Model HMOs

Historically, HMOs have used their own staffs to deliver behavioral health services to a greater degree than is currently the case. This change reflects the entry into the HMO market of many new competitors in the past decade whose service delivery models are based on independent practice associations (IPAs), networks, and/or subcontracting to freestanding ("carve-out") managed behavioral health care organizations (MBHCOs). Hence, integrated staff/group models are seen primarily in older HMOs.

This trend is illustrated by a 1986 InterStudy survey[1] and by more recent information from the Group Health Association of America (GHAA).[2] In the former, it was reported that the number of IPA model HMOs had grown from 37 percent of all HMOs in 1981 to 62 percent in 1988. In the more recent GHAA data, 74 percent of HMOs have an IPA or network structure and have 69 percent of HMO enrollment. Only 20 percent of HMOs classify themselves as staff or group models, and they have 32 percent of HMO enrollment. Even some of these organizations have "unbundled" behavioral health services or contracted for them to be provided by outside organizations.

Despite this clear trend in the past 15 years of newer HMOs' not utilizing a staff- or group-model structure for health care delivery in general, let alone for behavioral health service delivery, there seem to be early signs of countervailing forces coming from two parallel developments. The first is a gradual accumulation of scientific epidemiological literature showing the high prevalence, cost, and morbidity of behavioral health disorders in the primary care setting[3-5] and the accompanying low rate of identification and adequate treatment of the disorders. Second, "carve-out" MBHCOs, after a dramatic period of growth and profit, are now experiencing consolidation and cost reduction. Hence, better collaboration, if not "integration," with primary care medical services has become attractive from a quality, marketing, and potential cost offset viewpoint, and there is greater interest in models in which integration of behavioral health care and primary medical care is possible.[5]

One possible outcome of these countervailing trends already seen in the marketplace is MBHCOs' selectively adapting aspects of integrated and freestanding delivery systems to meet the needs of a particular market or purchaser, while acquiring expertise and experience in what balance will be the optimal in the long run for best cost and outcomes.

Review of Advantages and Disadvantages of Model

It seems prudent to review some of the basic advantages and disadvantages of the integrated staff/group-model HMO before discussing some of the basic "how to" issues. These factors are also worth considering for each level of service provided, because the balance may shift, for example, as one moves from outpatient to inpatient services.

The primary advantages of the integrated staff/group-model include:

- Consistent application of benefits and provision of services to all HMO members.

- Creation of a behavioral staff "culture" that includes population- and service-driven values.

- A stable and loyal provider cadre, especially for a level of service in which there is a shortage of available qualified providers or vendors in the local community.

- Collaboration, if not integration, of services with primary medical care.

- A voice and advocate for behavioral health care services within a larger health care delivery system.

- Optimizing resources of the larger health care organization's support and information systems, especially for population- and disease-focused interventions and for outcomes measurements.

Some of the potential disadvantages of the model are:

- High fixed costs of salary, benefits, and overhead.

- Geographical inflexibility.

- The need to observe regulatory requirements common to any employer-employee relationship, such as due process, equal opportunity, and American with Disabilities Act, to a greater degree than in network models.

- Limited member or group choice of providers compared to network models.

- Need to dedicate management and training resources on an ongoing basis to ensure cultural values are maintained.

- Alienation of community providers previously utilized if moving from another service delivery model.

Although the lists above are by no means comprehensive, they provide a rough guide as to when an integrated staff/group-model is worth considering for at least some levels of care. Put another way, optimal conditions for such a delivery system are:

- A relatively stable membership of enough size and geographical concentration to merit the investment. [6]

- A stable, organized primary care delivery system with which to develop high levels of collaboration/integration in the delivery of behavioral health care services and therefore to maximize cost-sharing and cost-offset potentials.

▌ Availability of supervisory and human resources expertise to support the hiring, management, and supervision of salaried professional staff.

▌ Lack of an already established local source to contract with for behavioral health services that will meet cost, quality, and integration standards as effectively as a staff-model delivery system. (It is of interest to note that this condition almost always existed until the appearance of MBHCOs, which in fact now market their services to HMOs.)

▌ Qualified candidates who can be recruited for staff positions (rarely a problem in urban areas where the impact of managed care has been felt).

Administrative Structure of Behavioral Health Departments

The administrative structure of behavioral health departments in HMOs needs to facilitate efficient delivery of clinical services with competitive levels of quality of service and care. At the same time, the structure needs to provide clear reporting lines to the larger health care organization at a level consistent with the department delivering a major aspect of care. Although no one structure is clearly superior, the common features noted in the literature and from the author's experience are:

▌ **A behavioral health clinical director with oversight over the delivery of both mental health and chemical dependency services.**[7] Within the Kaiser Permanente regions, these directors are usually physicians because of the structure and power of each regions' Permanente Medical Group, while in other HMOs a variety of mental health professionals assume the role. A clinical background is generally a prerequisite to understanding the unique and rapidly changing aspects of behavioral health service delivery and also increases credibility with clinical staff, especially when confronting difficult problems. Oversight of chemical dependency and mental health departments is often divided in Kaiser Permanente regions, reflecting the parallel and often conflicting development of the professionals and the treatment philosophies in these two specialties. However, any division and fragmentation of services between the departments that is visible as part of the "care" experience of members or groups is no longer tolerated in the marketplace. Hence, one clinical director ideally needs to have line authority across both specialties in behavioral health, exerting leadership in such areas as triage and referral standards between the departments and developing dual diagnosis treatment programs and cross-training of staff when needed to serve members.

Operationally, the clinical director needs to be accountable and have authority over all levels of care in behavioral health. This includes budgetary responsibility and authority and the ability to establish revenue and cost centers and allocate resources among different levels of care. Also, within the context of larger organizational budgeting and market forces, the director needs to have input into capitation rates and allocations for behavioral health services. It is particularly important to establish the director's authority and responsibility for those elements of care that are referred out, so as to ensure management and integration of these services. Failure to have such budgetary authority will create barriers to operationalizing the most cost-effective delivery system. In the author's opinion, the lack of such budgetary accountability and authority has been a major handicap to developing competitive and cost-effective behavioral health services in many Kaiser Permanente regions and in other staff/group-model HMOs.

■ **A relatively flat or "horizontal" administrative structure.** Because the core product of the HMO is direct clinical service, the clinical director needs to have those providing these services report to him or her. In most Kaiser Permanente areas, the clinical director also devotes a portion of his or her time to direct clinical service and on-call duties. The second administrative level is usually that of clinic or team leaders who provide direct service and supervision to a multidisciplinary team. Hence, the line clinician is only one level removed from the clinical director.

In larger operations, it may be necessary to have one level of supervision between team supervisors and the clinical director. This role in Kaiser Permanente departments is usually taken by an allied health (nonphysician clinician) clinical director, in part because the majority of clinical staff members are allied health professionals. In such structures, typically there is a separate allied health director for chemical dependency and mental health programs. In the Kaiser Permanente system, physicians report directly to the departments' clinical (physician) director. One caution again, in adding this additional administrative layer, is that it should not isolate team supervisors and line clinicians from the behavioral health clinical director or vice versa.

In the author's experience, an "academic-style" administrative structure does not work well in the staff/group-model HMO setting. For example, in this design psychologists report to a "chief psychologist," regardless of team assignment or geographical location, and so on for each professional discipline. Lines of supervision based on discipline alone that cross team/clinic boundaries often create "guild" and "turf" issues at the expense of service mission and culture of the individual teams. In physician-dominated HMO delivery systems, such as the Permanente Medical Groups, this problem may manifest itself by parallel but separate administrative supervision lines for psychiatric and allied health clinicians. The resultant tendency to reward and recognize physicians to a greater degree than allied health professionals can cause the latter to unionize and/or seek indirect sources of power and recognition. This caution is not meant to prevent professionals from arranging ongoing supervision or training in their areas of special expertise (i.e., psychometrics for psychologist and psychotropics for psychiatrists), as long as it does not interfere with a department's service mission or become a venue for an informal source of power and lobbying based on "guild" issues alone.

■ **Team-based or local autonomy within clear service mandates and cultural norms.** Behavioral health care, like health care in general, is having to assume many of the attributes of a service industry in addition to those of a professional one. While strong administrative leadership is needed in terms of clear service standards, implementation of consistent treatment algorithms and outcomes measures, and observance of policies and procedures stemming from regulatory or customer requirements, the day-to-day experience of members and resolution of their concerns depend on the ability, finesse, and initiative of line clinicians. They, in turn, must have integrated the "cultural" values of the organization and have the flexibility and local support to address the day-to-day challenges of practice.

Teams therefore need to be large enough to have all the necessary professionals to provide most of the services for the level of care that is their responsibility as well as coverage of hours of operation and leave. At the same time, teams must be small enough to allow for frequent interaction, consultation, problem solving, and cultural elements. To create a culture of ownership and flexibility, teams also must have the latitude and authority to resolve day-to-day clinical and operations issues as they come up. Prerequisites for this include local leadership, adequate formal or informal team meeting time, and shared responsibilities. One team-based model in the Kaiser Colorado region created these conditions in part by delegating responsibility for triage, clinical staff evaluation, and scheduling to each clinical team. To create similar team-based values in the Kaiser Northwest region, clinical teams are required to meet daily for case consultation and face-to-face discussion of any case transfers and medication referrals between the clinicians involved.

■ An operations director reporting to or in partnership with the clinical director. Except in smaller operations, supervision of nonclinical support staff and the logistics of claims and authorizations, billings and collections for noncapitated services, management of information systems, handling of nonclinical member concerns, and staff scheduling require a professional business manager. Previous clinical experience is desirable but not necessary in such a manager. In a smaller Kaiser Permanente department, this role may be assumed by the allied health clinical director in addition to his or her clinic supervision duties.

Behavioral Health Staffing: The Basics

Level of Professional Staffing

In the best of all worlds, behavioral health clinical staffing in a staff/group-model HMO is driven by the benefits of the covered population and the overall capitation dedicated to behavioral health services, in the context of a system and process design that delivers services at the least intensive level of care while meeting customer, quality, and service standards. Over time, as benefits are added or changed, experience is gained with utilization patterns, the efficiency of the delivery system is maximized, and adjustments can be made in staffing and capitation with the goal of offering the greatest value in services the market wishes to purchase and a reasonable return to shareholders (for-profit organizations) or capital reserves (not-for-profit organizations).

However, because of the historical "adding on" of behavioral health services driven by the 1973 Federal HMO Act's mandates rather than by their being part of the core of the health coverage of Kaiser Permanente and other older HMOs, there was a rather piecemeal adding of behavioral health staff over relatively brief periods.[8] This occurred around a basic benefit package of 20 outpatient visits per year and 14 to 30 inpatient days per year, with exclusionary coverage language. Each Kaiser Permanente Region and other HMOs developed their own copayment packages, and further variations were driven by requests of large employer groups. Therefore, it becomes difficult to establish a "benchmark" for optimal staffing at the outpatient level (where most of the staff are deployed) in staff/group-model HMOs and to compare behavioral health outpatient staffing levels from one HMO to another.

That said, staff/group-model HMOs tend to describe their behavioral health outpatient staffing levels in terms of the ratio of FTEs (full-time equivalents of professional clinical staff) to membership. This approach is of very limited use, because it is quite uninformative on several critical issues, including:

- The professional mix of the behavioral health staff, which has significant cost and service implications.

- The relative efficiencies or inefficiencies of particular HMOs in delivering behavioral health services and effecting outcomes.

- Cost-shifting to other levels of care that are outside the FTE count.

- Penetration of behavioral health services into the covered population.

- Shifting of behavioral health services into other areas of the health care delivery system.

- Any unique features of the population being served that drive high or low utilization of behavioral health services.

Surveys by The HMO Group[9] and of Kaiser Permanente regions (internal documents) have reported clinician FTE ratios in mental health services in the range of 1:5,000 and chemical dependency staff in the range of slightly under 1:10,000 members. An attempt at upgrading mental health services in Kaiser Permanente of Southern California proposed lowering the ratio to 1:4,700. In response to increasing numbers of large employer groups' requesting enhanced behavioral health services, Kaiser Permanente of Northern California has embarked on a service enhancement project with the goal of decreasing the mental health ratio substantially.

When it becomes possible, it is necessary to move away from this archaic staffing measure to one of dollars per member per month dedicated to behavioral health services and staffing. This measure also focuses on total costs of internal and external services and avoids superficial strategies that merely shift the cost of behavioral health services from one level of care to another. Eventually, this approach, combined with national benefit, outcome, service, and access standards,[10] will establish better benchmark ranges of staffing, at least for outpatient services. Staff/group-model HMOs will continue to have more difficulty in measuring non-staff costs of delivering behavioral health services compared to freestanding MBHCOs, because those costs are frequently absorbed by the larger organization. Finally, if the promise of greater integration of behavioral health services with primary care bear fruit,[5] behavioral health may need to rolled into the capitation of primary care. The message for the time being is to move away from isolated data sets such as staffing ratios and toward total behavioral health service costs and outcomes.

Mix of Professional Staff

Although there are some historical benchmarks on outpatient staffing, professional distribution, or "mix," rapid changes in the behavioral health field necessitate reevaluation of the current staffing mix in any staff/group-model HMO. Such an evaluation needs to be driven by how to maximize the value of care and service delivered to customers in the context of limited resources. For example, in mental health, rapid development of short-term disease- or disorder-based group therapy using cognitive and behavioral techniques is beginning to reduce the need for individual therapy. Although some of the pioneers in this modality were psychologists and psychiatrists, it is now within the scope of practice of many properly trained master's degree-level therapists. Another example is the developing role of psychiatric nurse practitioners in areas of practice once the province of psychiatrists. Finally, an example of a trend in the reverse direction is in chemical dependency, where there is an increasing trend for counselors to be master's degree level trained and licensed, which may eventually be translated into a national standard.[11]

Given the limitations of such data, a recent survey of staff/group-model HMOs revealed an average mix of 18 percent psychiatrists, 26 percent psychologists, 42 percent social workers, and 14 percent psychiatric nurses in mental health departments.[9] This range of professional distribution is similar to that of Kaiser Permanente mental health departments with which the author is familiar. Although a few of them have a much higher percentage of psychiatrists on staff, this may reflect internal bias rather than market-based need.

A few of the current trends in the mental health staffing in staff/group-model HMOs noted above are worth elaborating. First, with the advent of newer and easier to manage antidepressants, primary care is taking a larger role in the prescribing of psychotropics. This accelerates the current trend of psychiatrists' being utilized primarily for management of psychotropic treatment of more difficult patients and syndromes or management of patients' being on psychotropics that require more expertise and experience to use (such as those used to treat bipolars). In addition, adequately trained psychiatric nurse practitioners in states (such as Oregon) where their legal scope of practice is broad enough are beginning to provide services traditionally provided only by psychiatrists. Given that they are the most expensive level of professional to hire, psychiatrists are likely to see no greater and perhaps a smaller representation on the outpatient staffs of staff/group-model HMOs in the future. Therefore, a psychiatrist whose primary interest is not in the medical, psychopharmacological, and consulting aspects of practice will be a poor fit in such HMOs.

A second trend is that PhD psychologists who do not distinguish their scope of practices substantially from master's degree-level clinicians will be under increasing scrutiny as long as PhD salaries remain substantially above those of master's degree clinicians. Psychologists who remain and thrive in HMOs will be those who have differentiated themselves from generic therapists by maintaining their skills and providing services in "value-added" areas of expertise in their profession, such as psychometrics, research, training, and program development. Finally, it appears that the role of the master's degree-level clinician will expand as short-term psychotherapy skills become more specific and standardized and more integrated into their professional training and practice.

In chemical dependency services, the emerging standard is to have an outpatient master's degree-level professional staff that is licensed or certified in addictions counseling. A percentage of "recovered" staff (recovered from a chemical dependency disorder with at least three years of sobriety) is sometimes advocated as optimal. Usually, chemical dependency departments have a physician consultant. Within Kaiser Permanente, they have physician chiefs (psychiatrists or primary care physicians). Outpatient detoxification may be managed by chemical dependency medical staff or in collaboration with primary care, which helps further behavioral health and primary care integration. In residential levels of care, there is usually a staff psychologist and a consulting psychiatrist in addition to master's degree-level counselors. Physicians in the field of chemical dependency are increasingly expected to have training in addictions medicine, and certification by the American Society of Addiction Medicine (ASAM) is desirable.

Recruiting and Hiring

Most staff/group-model HMOs have been around for a while and have the challenge of changing their historical systems and staff culture to more competitive and service-driven ones. Nonetheless, as new staff members are hired in older organizations and as network-model delivery systems consider converting some of their operations to staff ones, it's worth at least describing some important elements in this process and the qualities to look for in a new hire. In no way is this meant to be a personnel or human resources "how to," as that would be beyond the scope of this discussion.

Predating the decision to hire, careful thought must go into the commitment of resources to what will become a fixed cost. This is emphasized because forced staff reductions are just as, if not more, traumatic to the culture of behavioral health departments as they are in other industries. Before permanent hiring, interim steps, such as referrals out to network, locum tenens, or temporary positions that will help confirm if the need for more staff is sustained over time, should be considered.

Decisions as to what category of professional to hire should be driven entirely by service need and not by any professional bias or rigid staffing ratio. Currently, national standards are moving toward a minimum standard of a master's degree-level mental health or chemical dependency professional who is state-licensed or -certified.[10,11] The least costly professional qualified for the clinical duties should be chosen to maximize the use of available resources. Because master's degree-level clinicians are now being trained in the basic repertoire of short-term psychotherapy skills, the extra cost of hiring psychiatrists, psychologists, and/or nurse practitioners will need to be justified by their specific skills in meeting a documented service need.

Active recruitment for purposes of diversity is becoming important as employer groups and memberships increasingly expect the diversity of clinical staff to match that of enrollment. Because older staff/group model systems may have hired a substantial number of their current professional staff members before diversity was an issue both in society at large and for purchasers as well, each new staff opening must be viewed as a potential opportunity to address this issue.

Once the specific professional skills needed for a position are defined, several aspects of the recruitment and hiring process need to be emphasized. First, the presence of in-house training placements or programs are extremely advantageous for recruitment of junior staff members.[12] Participation in professional training creates a network for communicating the availability of a position, identifying strong candidates, and getting the sort of informal recommendations on applicants that is invaluable in the screening process. In addition, one has the advantages of direct observation and experience with candidates who have participated in the on-site training program. Such candidates, if hired, have a realistic view of the working culture and can become maximally productive in a shorter period than can a person not familiar with the organization. Training programs in staff/group-model HMOs must nonetheless be at least cost-neutral by, ideally, offsetting their cost through the services provided.

Second, when time and resources allow it, it is useful to recruit nationally, especially for key positions. Using local, regional, and national professional organizations and publications in the process is important.

Finally, orientation and supervision of new employees in their first few months is critical. If a mismatch is identified, it must be addressed promptly.[13]

Staffing: Core Values to Reinforce

The following sections will attempt to outline structural and management approaches to nurture, reinforce, and maintain professional staff core values and behavior that optimize the quality of mental health services and care delivered to HMO members individually and as a population. As a starting point, it is important to emphasize that a number of routes can be taken to these value endpoints. Also, it is assumed that an individual's values are such that they can accept and be acculturated in these larger organizational values. Put another way, some behavioral health professionals who are highly competent clinicians have personal values and needs that are incompatible with practice in a staff/group-model HMO.

Population-Based Values

The first core value is ownership of the mission to maximize the population's (membership's) health, including maximizing function and reducing illness and impairment within the context of contractual limits and resource limitations. This means the HMO professional has to not only focus on the welfare of the patient he or she is treating at the moment, but also the welfare of the covered population over time.

This value often runs counter to most behavioral health clinical and professional training, which emphasizes the primacy of the relationship to the individual patient and obligations to one's profession. To integrate this relatively "new" value, which has historical roots in public health, often presents ethical and personal challenges to the individual clinician.[14,15] Successful integration of this population-based value into a clinician's other professional values is essential to the professional's success and the success of behavioral health departments within staff/group-model HMOs.

Organization-Based Values

This value involves a provider feeling some responsibility for the member's care experience and perception of the health care organization. When a way to improve either of these member outcomes is found, the provider takes constructive action. This does not mean acquiescing to unreasonable demands or not setting realistic boundaries. It means being as proactive as possible within the context of one's role to improve services and remedy problems. An administrative challenge in staff/group-model HMOs is to support and reward such behavior.

Quality Improvement-Based Values

Once, professionals could learn a set of knowledge, skills, and interpersonal styles that would allow them to be successful throughout their careers. The same might be said of organizations, such as staff/group-model HMOs. Now staff members must learn to value the constant reevaluation, retraining, and delivery system redesign that is necessary for them and their organizations to succeed.

Clinician Skills

The clinical skills best suited for staff/group-model HMOs have been well described by other authors[15,16] and will only be summarized in this chapter. The mental health clinician needs to have a repertoire of brief treatment approaches, including cognitive, behavioral, interpersonal, and solution-focused methodologies, and familiarity and comfort with group, individual, family, and couple approaches. Ability to make rapid assessment and diagnosis consistent with the latest *Diagnosis and Statistical Manual* (DSM) of the American Psychiatric Association also is required. Although clinicians with specialty training and experience in areas such as child and family work need to be hired in proportion to the population's needs, it is important that they have generalist backgrounds and the flexibility to practice outside their specialty areas when necessary.

Chemical dependency clinicians need similar skills, but within the field of chemical dependency and with a greater emphasis on group treatments and 12-step approaches. They also need to be comfortable and skillful with coordination of management of chemical dependency patients and with issues in the context of a larger medical care system. This may include confronting and educating nonbehavioral health clinicians on aspects of their practice that may facilitate or enable addictive behaviors.

Psychiatrists, as alluded to before, need to have current knowledge of psychopharmacology and be able to manage the more difficult and refractory patients referred from primary care and other mental health clinicians. Although supportive psychotherapy is inherently part of medication management, the psychiatrist must be comfortable working within a team where the majority of psychotherapy is provided by other mental health clinicians. Finally, as a consultant within a larger system, the HMO psychiatrist's communications and diplomacy skills need to be well developed.

Staff: Creating and Maintaining the Culture

Staff culture is probably the most critical topic in this chapter for anyone involved in managing a staff/group-model behavioral health delivery system or contemplating developing one. The other sections are necessary to describe the framework of a staff/group model behavioral health service within an HMO, but it is the subtleties of the culture fostered within the service that will determine success or failure in creating value for members, purchasers, and internal customers.

Salary and Incentive Strategies

A key element of the historical culture of staff/group-model HMOs is the structure and security of predictable salary and benefits package, cost-of-living adjustments, duties, and hours. This culture, which isolates providers from market forces, could be maintained because even modest management of care, especially in the inpatient arena, gave HMOs a tremendous cost advantage over relatively "unmanaged care." As all health care is rapidly moving into managed systems, some with very aggressive incentive and utilization management strategies, this historical competitive differential of staff/group-model HMOs has all but disappeared.[17] In Kaiser Foundation Health Plan and Permanente Medical Groups, salary advancement has historically been based primarily on seniority (longevity), and evaluations of performance have had limited impact on salary. This sort of financial compensation systems does not provide incentives for the sort of individual and organizational changes all such HMOs need to make to remain competitive in the next few years.[18] Currently, attempts are under way within the Kaiser Permanente Regions to align financial incentives with organization and individual performance. In a capitated system, ethical incentive systems must be multidimensional and include measures in areas of member satisfaction, productivity, team work, organizational performance, treatment outcomes, and resource utilization in such a way that withholding care at an individual level is not encouraged. Small steps in this direction include the "Team" incentive for nonphysician professional and management staff in the Kaiser Permanente Northwest Region. It appears that financial incentive structures that put at least 25 percent of compensation at risk to performance variables are the most effective, and this represents a radical change for most staff/group-model HMOs.

Team-Based Strategies

In the current absence or very limited presence of performance-based compensation structures, development of other means to support the values in a behavioral health delivery system require management ingenuity and diligence. Indeed, management strategies to support and maintain the culture and values remain important even in the presence of major market-based incentives. A team-based delivery system is one of these strategies. Because this makes a group of behavioral health clinicians (usually divided into chemical dependency and mental health sections) responsible for meeting the behavioral health needs of a subgroup of the HMOs membership (often based on geographic or clinic population), the population-based value is reinforced and the group has an incentive to work together. Usually, this alone is not enough. A further catalyst, such as responsibility to share triaging of all cases (Kaiser Permanente Colorado) or service requirements of access or urgent care availability (Kaiser Permanente Northwest) is necessary to get a group of clinicians to leave their offices and become an interdependent team. In time, functional teams begin to confront tough issues of distributing case loads, dealing with individual staff deficits or self-serving behavior, covering and coordinating leaves, and ensuring that each team member is providing services consistent with the contractual scope of benefits.

Productivity Strategies

An area of much management activity in staff/group-model HMOs is measuring professional staff productivity and attempting to maximize it. This activity is quite rational, given that staff time is a finite resource ultimately purchased to meet members' and the population's health care needs. Unfortunately, rather concrete productivity measurements of available time to see patients and the "fill" rate of that "bookable" time have been exported from the medical care arena to behavioral health and have been fertile ground for tension between staff and management. In the author's experience, this tension has been acted out through numerous guidelines, definitions of what constitutes new referrals, and overt and covert activity by management to increase "bookable" time and fill "open time"; activity with the reverse intent by staff; and a general missing of the point by everyone. This approach seems to come from early industrial management theory, in which each unit of time providing treatment to a member is a unit of "production." Hence, the more units of service generated per FTE, the greater the "production."

A more constructive approach to the productivity issue (in addition to the financial incentives discussed above) is to redefine the "products" of behavioral health services in a staff/group HMO. The underlying assumptions in the redefinition are that the organization is capitated, serves a relatively fixed population, and has the mission of maintaining the health of that population and minimizing the impact of disease and disability while providing high-quality services. The "product" of behavioral health services in this context is outcomes rather than processes, such as filling schedules. The author's list of "outcome" products includes:

- Rapid identification and treatment of mental health disorders, which, in turn, means that behavioral health services are readily accessed and treatment is initiated promptly.

- Treatment focused on minimizing social and occupational impairment and on returning members to levels of function existing prior to disease.

- Accomplishment of the above to create overall satisfaction in members, purchasers, and internal customers with the services they have received.

The focus in "productivity," therefore, needs to be on access, functional and symptom outcomes, and satisfaction. Although routine measurement of functionality and symptom change is only just moving from research into clinical practice, staff/group-model HMOs typically have highly developed information systems to measure access and to determine member satisfaction. A rudimentary translation of this concept of productivity into operations in the Kaiser Permanente Northwest region, among others, has been to set access standards and expect clinical teams to meet them. Clinicians need to adjust the number of new patients ("intakes") seen to meet these service and access standards. This flexibility is important because of seasonal variation in the demand for behavioral health services.[7] Outside certain required functions, such as team meetings, running a minimum number of groups, and seeing the number of intakes necessary to meet initial access standards, clinicians are free to construct their schedules as they see fit, and fill rates are largely ignored. Clinicians who are able to meet access goals and satisfy members are free to use a variety of strategies, such as telephone work, group work, and collaboration with other team members, to manage their case loads.

Paradoxically, despite fears that there would be no time to see return patients, there has been an overall drop in fill rates as clinicians and teams have an incentive to manage case loads creatively and no longer fill their schedules to look "good" or to avoid being given extra patients or duties.

At the same time, member concerns, driven primarily by initial access delays, dropped precipitately. One critical and "negative" element of this system was that teams who failed to meet new patient access standards might have to work extra hours without additional pay (none to this date have had to do this).

Clearly, such approaches are not without their limitations, and the fill rate may be a crude warning sign that staff is overwhelmed or underutilized—as long as the culture does not reinforce its artificial inflation. However, as provider-specific measures of patient satisfaction (e.g., "Art of Medicine Survey" in Kaiser Permanente Northwest and other regions) and functionality and symptom outcome measures come on line, these "outcome" measures of productivity will become more viable, and will ensure that quality is maintained regardless of fill rates.

Implementing Change

Staff members in group-model HMOs have historically been insulated from market forces and are remarkably resistant to change. Like all professionals, behavioral health staff members like to be advised of changes being considered, presented with their rational, given data supporting proposed changes, and allowed to give feedback and feel heard. Even these necessary steps are usually unsuccessful in eliciting acceptance if the change in some way threatens a core value or need. An example is offering more evening hours, which is clearly an increasing need of subscribers and their employer payers. In the Kaiser Permanente Northwest Region, data based on member and employer surveys, current available evening hours, and their utilization were presented to mental health staff. (Chemical dependency staff had long ago created evening treatment programs to meet member needs). Mental health staff had perceived "working hours" as an entitlement benefit and argued with the data and the need. It was agreed to incrementally increase evening hours and monitor their use, as well as to empower teams to develop their own strategies to meet the standard for evening hours. In this process, management emphasized and honored population and service values, reinforced the team structure, and offered compromise in terms of speed of implementation.

Evaluation of Staff

Although the management literature abounds with strategies for staff evaluation and feedback, the standard "annual evaluation" is hopelessly inadequate in reinforcing the values described above and in addressing performance problems. Current national Kaiser Permanente efforts to provide provider-specific quarterly membership satisfaction information ("Art of Medicine" survey) will provide more frequent feedback on this "outcome" measure. In Kaiser Permanente of Colorado, team-based evaluations provide direct peer feedback. Future evaluations will need to include data on the outcome domains of symptoms change and functionality and be linked to compensation.

Creating a Learning Environment

It is important to create a value and expectation for continuous learning and modification of clinical technique and approaches in HMO behavioral health departments. Because staff may remain with the organization for extended periods, they need to continue to keep up with advancements in the field and respond to changing customer needs. Organizational support via educational leave and CME support within the Kaiser Permanente systems are incentives for this, especially if approval is based on the training being related to the needs of the HMO's membership. Shifts in the population served as well as media or public interest in certain conditions or treatment may necessitate development of skills and expertise. Department-based and team-initiated in-service education should be encouraged as long as the focus is membership-driven and clinical service needs are met. This aspect of HMO culture may be uncomfortable for clinicians who wish to focus on only one technique or problem area and are confronted by a wide array of problems and members to manage.

Benefit Design Issues

In vertically integrated HMOs, behavioral health leadership needs to take an extremely active and vocal role in the design, marketing, and sale of behavioral health benefits. Although the foundation of HMO benefits was created by the 1973 Federal HMO Act, benefit designs are increasingly driven by state mandates, state Medicaid agencies, the Health Care Financing Administration (HCFA), and large employer groups. The result is an increasingly complex patchwork of behavioral health benefit packages that is difficult to translate into operations. Although it may be impossible to modify many of the mandates of a large purchaser, at least feedback can be given and staff and systems can be prepared to proactively manage subpopulatons with new behavioral health benefits packages. Also, if the goal of large commercial purchasers for changing behavioral health benefits can be clarified, behavioral health managers can often offer alternative and operationally easier modifications to reach the same goal.

Increasingly, staff/group-model HMO behavioral health staff must take a greater role in being aware of these benefit changes, and this is one more change that will need to be supported by management. The days in which HMOs offered a limited number of chemical dependency and mental health benefit options has passed, and an awareness of a member's coverage is increasingly critical in treatment planning.

Medical Necessity and Exclusions

Two areas in contractual benefit implementation are especially critical. The first is familiarity with contractual medical necessity language and consistent interpretation and operational application of it across all levels of care.[8,9] This holds special significance in mental health and chemical dependency services because of the tendency within the popular culture to apply diagnostic and illness labels to an increasing array of human experience and behavior. In addition, "fad" treatments of real conditions, with no scientific support of efficacy or value for the treatments, come and go with alarming frequency.

The second critical area is the operational definition and implementation of exclusionary contract language.[19] This may become less important over time as states mandate coverage of chronic mental illness and as larger purchasers seek more comprehensive behavioral health benefits. However, because many market competitors, both managed care and indemnity, continue to apply exclusionary language to limit risk, staff/group-model HMOs cannot avoid the issue and remain competitive in most markets.

Levels of Care: Mental Health

This discussion of the service delivery design at each level of care will attempt to emphasize the elements that are critical or unique to the operation of a staff/group-model HMO. It will also attempt to provide guidelines for when contracting out for services is preferable to using HMO staff and facilities.

Outpatient

Outpatient services are the linchpin of behavioral health services for several reasons. First, it is the level of care at which the preponderance of behavioral health services can be delivered to members and to external and internal customers (such as employee assistance programs and primary care physicians). It is also the level of care with the highest potential for addressing and stabilizing problems before a higher level of care is needed and, therefore, for reducing cost, morbidity, and impairment. Key features for this level of care should include:

- An immediately accessible telephone triage function staffed by master's degree-level clinicians who can provide a consistent first contact experience, application of the benefit and assessment of medical necessity, evaluation for acuity, and referral to an appropriate level of care. Recently, The HMO Group has recommended hours of service and telephone access standards for such triage services in HMOs.[11]

- Mental health and chemical dependency outpatient clinicians at locations convenient to members.[11] Currently, placement of behavioral health clinicians in primary care settings is being piloted at several HMOs.

- Ability to provide same- or next-day urgent care chemical dependency and mental health appointments at convenient sites in order to address the needs of members in crisis. In the Kaiser Permanente Northwest Region, this level of care has been successfully integrated in all the outpatient mental health teams. Appointments link an allied health clinician with a psychiatrist so that crisis intervention and medication evaluation can occur in the same contact.

- A limited outside referral network to handle members with dual relationships; low-volume special needs, such as signing for the deaf; and overflow during periods of peak demand.

Emergency Services

In vertically integrated HMOs, which often own and manage their own hospitals, the ability to provide mental health consultation and assessment services to emergency department patients is a critical service to the larger system and also ensures that patients are stabilized and routed to the appropriate level of care. Because the emergency department is a major entry point to inpatient psychiatry, assessment and intervention are especially important there. These services are sometimes provided by outpatient staff during the day and by on-call staff (often a psychiatrist) at night. In the Kaiser Permanente Northwest Region, a team of allied mental health clinicians staff the emergency departments of the two Kaiser Permanente hospitals, with a back-up psychiatrist available to them. In Kaiser Permanente of Colorado, a staff clinician covers the emergency department of the primary contract hospital during the day and a contracted community vendor provides crisis services after hours. Any inpatient psychiatry admissions must be approved by a staff psychiatrist.

Typically, because of limited resources, chemical dependency departments cannot have on-site staff available to emergency departments, but provide phone and on call consultation. Frequently, mental health staff will need to assist with addiction problems involving members who are threatening harm to themselves or others.

Inpatient Services
The delivery model for mental health or psychiatric inpatient services should be driven by the facility and professional resources of the local HMO market. In Kaiser Permanente of Southern California, the high cost of community beds and contract physicians drove the development of a Kaiser Permanente-owned and -staffed freestanding psychiatric hospital. In Kaiser Permanente of Colorado, psychiatric beds and nursing services are contracted for at a community hospital, and a Kaiser Permanente "inpatient team" of a psychiatrist, social worker, and psychologist provide professional services. In Kaiser Permanente Northwest, psychiatric hospital and professional services are both contracted out to a local not-for-profit hospital and its staff. A long-standing relationship with the hospital's behavioral health director, who is committed to meeting Kaiser Permanente's customer needs, and a case rate reimbursement strategy with the hospital's professional staff has driven "staff-like" behavior and values. To continue a Kaiser Permanente presence and involvement, a full-time Kaiser Permanente psychiatric hospital liaison nurse comes to the hospital daily to coordinate care and disposition of cases.

The overall goal, no matter the design of inpatient psychiatry services, is to provide rapid assessment, stabilization, and disposition services with extremely good linkage, communication, and coordination to all other levels of care in chemical dependency and mental health services, as well as medical care. Management of inpatient psychiatry utilization is critical to containing behavioral health costs and, in the context of capitation, to ensuring that adequate funding is available for other levels of care. Benchmarking both internal to the Kaiser system, as well as by national actuarial consultants, have set the target for psychiatric inpatient utilization in highly managed systems at 13 days per thousand members per year. However, adjustments to this figure must be made for state mandates, for benefit structures, and for higher risk populations.

In chemical dependency services, some residential and detoxification services may be hospital-based, but the direction currently is toward community-based residential programs with variable lengths of stay. Also, a substantial portion of admissions to inpatient psychiatry (20 percent) have a primary chemical dependency diagnosis or a combined chemical dependency and mental health diagnosis. Therefore, availability of chemical dependency assessment and treatment services to inpatient psychiatry is critical, as is coordination of the management of "dual diagnosis" patients and their discharge planning.

Finally, a "23-hour" or "holding" bed to assess and stabilize patients who are likely to have their acute symptoms resolved in less than a day is a useful level of care to have in a system. These beds can be emergency department-based or based on inpatient medical or psychiatric units. Emergency department- and medical unit-based holding beds require ongoing training and support of medical and nursing staff members who are often very anxious about caring for such patients. Inpatient psychiatry unit holding beds need to be segregated from the general unit and milieu and linked with rapid and frequent reassessment. The Kaiser Colorado region has found the most effective strategy for having holding beds on a psychiatric inpatient unit is to have them in rooms in a separate area of the unit and to not have holding bed patients participate in milieu or therapy activities on the unit itself.

Residential and Day Treatment Services

In mental health, "day hospital" services are an important level of care to which to divert potential inpatient admissions and to step down inpatients to reduce length of stay. These programs are usually based on or near inpatient units to "piggy back" on inpatient programs, to allow smoother "step downs" for inpatients, and to provide back-up support for higher acuity "diversion" patients. Problems for members using this level of care include the need for safe daily transportation, family support and involvement because the patient will be home at night, and physician incentives that support its use, because professional services need to be of an intensity comparable to those for inpatients.

Mental health "day treatment" services usually tend to be longer term and targeted for the chronically mentally ill. Because this population is often subject to contract exclusion, utilization of such services tends to be limited in most staff/group-model HMOs. Hence, when needed, these services are provided by contracted community vendors.

Chemical dependency residential treatment is an important level of care, usually for those who have failed in an outpatient intensive treatment program. Such programs are much less costly if they are community- rather than hospital-based, and the chemical dependency field has moved from a "fixed" to a "variable" length of stay. The decision to develop and staff one's own residential chemical dependency program versus contract for it is market-driven, but contracting is the predominant approach. In the Kaiser Permanente Northwest Region, the lack of residential programs for adolescents led to the development of an adolescent residential chemical dependency program that is also utilized by other managed care organizations.

The line between chemical dependency intensive outpatient programs and "day programs" is sometimes hard to distinguish, because the former requires a minimum treatment of several hours per day several days per week. Northern California Kaiser Permanente has developed several more intense chemical dependency "day " programs at regional sites.

Consultation and Liaison Services

Mental health or psychiatric consultation services to medical and surgical services play a critical role in assessment, management, and disposition of complex patients, and it is important that HMO mental health departments make provision of such services a priority. In larger HMO medical centers, such as Kaiser Sunset Medical Center in Southern California, there may be sufficient volume to justify devoting a full-time individual or multidisciplinary teams to this service. This certainly facilitates continuity of follow up and establishment of working relationships with key inpatient staff. In other Kaiser Permanente settings, consultation services and other on-call duties are usually rotated among psychiatric physician staff. This often results in lack of time for adequate follow-up and continuity, especially if outpatient facilities are distant from inpatient medical beds. In Kaiser Permanente Northwest Region, a joint funding pilot of a consultation psychiatrist aligned with several community hospitals is being proposed in order to have an adequate volume to support the position.

As greater collaboration with primary care is becoming important, more formal outpatient linkages between HMO behavioral health and primary care services will become critical. Models for this include placement of chemical dependency and mental health professionals in primary care offices,[5] and a consultation telephone line in the Kaiser Permanente Northwest Region staffed by a psychiatrist who provides consultation to primary care in "real time" as they are seeing the patient on whom they need help.

Chemical dependency services need to be able to provide assessments to medical and surgical inpatients on request. As with mental health consultations, the episodic nature of such requests makes staffing for them difficult. Collaboration between mental health and chemical dependency consultation services can be useful in this area.

Innovations in Service Delivery

Clearly, one of the opportunities yet to be fully exploited by integrated staff/group-model HMO behavioral health services is greater collaboration and integration with primary care services. This represents one of the competitive advantages of the model. Currently, Group Health Cooperative of Puget Sound is piloting primary care integration and primary care mental health models.[5] Kaiser Permanente Northwest has piloted a mental health consultation line and placed behavioral health providers in primary care modules in 1997. The long-term potential of such initiatives is in addressing the large amount of behavioral health illness that is not adequately identified or treated in primary care and that drives a great deal of primary care utilization[3] in a manner that will affect outcomes for member symptoms, function, and satisfaction. There is also some promise of eventual reduction in heath care costs, although the jury is still out on this achievement. The short-term challenge is to develop outpatient systems and processes that optimize collaboration between primary care and behavioral health providers. Most of the current successful pilots rely on the personality strengths of individual "pioneers" and may be difficult to generalize. Finally, if such collaborations and integration prove effective, the issue of who funds and manages which staff members will need to be resolved between the historically separated services of primary care and behavioral health.

Currently, one of the critical building blocks of this innovation is the flow of clinical information between primary care and behavioral health services. Although certain regulatory and ethical concerns present barriers to full integration of medical and behavioral health records, a greater flow of information with appropriate safeguards can be established. In the Kaiser Permanente Northwest Region, the availability of limited mental health information in the electronic chart has been welcomed by primary care providers and has not created member concerns.

Quality Management

A comprehensive review of how to develop and maintain a quality management infrastructure[20] and of current regulatory quality management requirements is beyond the scope of this chapter. The author will focus on current trends and opportunities within staff/group-model HMOs.

Quality management is now moving from utilization management, access measurements, and documentation standards to more sophisticated outcome measures.[11] Because of their greater integration with health care delivery systems, staff/group-model HMO behavioral health services have a greater opportunity to develop critical pathways for detection, treatment, and management of behavioral health disorders across all levels of care than have freestanding managed behavioral health care organizations. These pathways will need to incorporate outcome measures in the domains discussed earlier in the chapter.

The current industry standards include those of the American Managed Behavioral Healthcare Association (AMBHA), and the National Committee for Quality Assurance (NCQA) HEDIS standards. In 1997, NCQA issued behavioral health-specific standards for accreditation. Although the standards were developed primarily for freestanding MBHCOs, HMOs that have their own behavioral health departments will need to meet the standards for general NCQA accreditation starting in 1999. It is hoped by many that meeting these standards will address the concerns of most purchasers and become an industry standard. Familiarity with these standards is critical for HMO behavioral health leadership, as is their integration into quality management and operational planning.

Conclusion

This chapter has attempted to provide an overview of the critical structural and management issues in a behavioral health delivery system in the context of a group- or staff-model health maintenance organization with significant vertical integration. Recently, this older delivery system model has been challenged in the marketplace by the flexibility and "agility" of newer models, such as network-based freestanding managed behavioral health care organizations. These organizations have had the ability to seek out higher and segregated capitation rates from sophisticated purchasers; create, manage, and provide incentives to contracted provider networks with greater flexibility than staff models; and produce group purchaser-specific outcomes and utilization information. Hence, the staff/group-model HMO behavioral health service delivery system has begun to look like a dinosaur as employer groups request HMOs to "carve out" behavioral health benefits so they can purchase them elsewhere.

With current restructuring of health care in general and increasing information that supports the need to integrate behavioral health services with primary medical care, the integrated staff/group-model HMO now has the opportunity to exploit certain aspects of its structure for competitive advantage. However, this will only be achieved by changing certain aspects of the "old dinosaur," including its culture's incentives, values, and ability to change in response to market forces. Strategies to facilitate this cultural shift have been reviewed along with examples of recent successful changes. It is hoped this information will assist physician executives and other managers in trying to change the old managed care dinosaur into one that can prosper in the new managed care era, or at least to be aware of its competitive potential.

References

1. Shadle, M., and Christianson, J. "The Organization of Mental Health Care Delivery in HMOs." *Administration in Mental Health* 15(4):201-25, Summer 1988).

2. *National Directory of HMOs.* Washington, D.C.: Group Health Association of America, 1994.

3. Simon, G., and others. "Health Care Costs of Primary Care Patients with Recognized Depression." *Archives of General Psychiatry* 52(10):850-6, Oct. 1995.

4. Slay, J., and Glazer, W. "'Carving In,' and Keeping In, Mental Health Care in the Managed Care Setting." *Psychiatric Services* 46(11):1119-25, Nov. 1995.

5. Quirk, M. "Primary Care Mental Health Integration at Group Health Cooperative of Puget Sound." Presentation at Behavioral Healthcare Tomorrow Conference, Dallas, Tex., 1995.

6. Dorwart, R., and Epstein, S. "Economics and Managed Mental Health Case: The HMO as a Crucible for Cost-Effective Care." In *Managed Mental Health Care*, Feldman, J., and Fitzpatrick, R., Editors. Washington, DC: American Psychiatric Press, Inc., 1992, pp. 11-27.

7. Schneider-Braus, K. "Managing a Mental Health Department in a Staff Model HMO." In *Managed Mental Health Care,* Feldman, J., and Fitzpatrick, R., Editors. Washington, DC: American Psychiatric Press, Inc., 1992, pp. 125-41.

8. Levin, B., and Glasser, J. "Comparing Mental Health Benefits, Utilization Patterns, and Costs." In *Managed Mental Health Care,* Feldman, J., and Fitzpatrick, R., Editors. Washington, DC: American Psychiatric Press, Inc., 1992, pp. 29-51.

9. Levin, B. "Mental Health Services within the HMO Group." *HMO Practice* 6(3):16-21, Sept. 1992.

10. "NCQA Issues First National Accreditation Standards for Managed Behavioral Health Organizations." News Release. Washington, DC: NCQA, Apr. 10, 1996.

11. Towers Perrin. *Mental Health and Substance Abuse Capabilities Assessment, Report Findings.* Buffalo, N.Y.: HMO Group, March 1996.

12. Sabin, J., and Borus, J. "Mental Health Teaching and Research in Managed Care." In *Managed Mental Health Care,* Feldman, J., and Fitzpatrick, R., Editors. Washington, DC: American Psychiatric Press, Inc., 1992, pp. 185-201.

13. Kiley, M. "An Orientation Program for Mental Health Providers." *HMO Practice* 6(3):41-42, March 1994.

14. Feldman, J. "The Managed Care Setting and the Patient-Therapist Relationship." In *Managed Mental Health Care,* Feldman, J., and Fitzpatrick, R., Editors. Washington, DC: American Psychiatric Press, Inc., 1992, pp. 219-29.

15. Hoyt, M., and Austad, C. "Psychotherapy in a Staff Model Health Maintenance Organization: Providing and Assuring Quality Care in the Future." *Psychotherapy* 29(1):119-29, Spring 1992.

16. Bennett, M. "The Managed Care Setting as a Framework for Clinical Practice." In *Managed Mental Health Care*, Feldman, J., and Fitzpatrick, R., Editors. Washington, DC: American Psychiatric Press, Inc., 1992, pp. 203-17.

17. Governance Committee. *Rewarding Cost-Effective Medicine: Aligning Physician Incentives Under Managed Care.* Washington, DC: Advisory Board Company, 1995.

18. Governance Committee. *State of the Union: Briefing for Board Members, Physicians and Senior Administration.* Washington, DC: Advisory Board Company, 1995.

19. Bonstedt, T. "Managing Psychiatric Exclusions." In *Managed Mental Health Care,* Feldman, J., and Fitzpatrick, R., Editors. Washington, DC: American Psychiatric Press, Inc., 1992, pp. 69-81.

20. Savitz, S. "Measuring Quality of Care and Quality Maintenance." In *Managed Mental Health Care,* Feldman, J., and Fitzpatrick, R., Editors. Washington, DC: American Psychiatric Press, Inc., 1992, pp. 143-57.

Additional Reading

Abrams, H. "Harvard Community Health Plan's Mental Health Redesign Project: A Managerial and Clinical Partnership." *Psychiatric Quarterly* 64(1):13-31, Spring 1993.

AMBHA Quality Improvement and Clinical Services Committee. *Performance Measures for Managed Behavioral Healthcare Programs.* Washington, D.C.: AMBHA, Aug. 1995.

Babigian, H., and Reed, S. "Capitation and Management of Mental Health in the Public Sector." In *Managed Mental Health Care,* Feldman, J., and Fitzpatrick, R., Editors. Washington, DC: American Psychiatric Press, Inc., 1992, pp. 111-23.

Chaplain, R. "Treatment of Drug Abuse in the Managed Care Setting." In *Managed Mental Health Care,* Feldman, J., and Fitzpatrick, R., Editors. Washington, DC: American Psychiatric Press, Inc., 1992, pp. 305-19.

Durham, M. "Can HMOs Manage the Mental Health Benefit?" *Health Affairs* 14(3):116-23, Fall 1995.

Freeborn, D., and Hooker, R. "Satisfaction of Physician Assistants and Other Nonphysician Providers in a Managed Case Setting." *Public Health Reports* 111(6):714-9, Nov./Dec. 1995.

Jones, W., and others. "Why Employers and Physicians Select HMOs: An Analysis with Management Implications." *Journal of Managerial Issues,* 6(1):88-100, Spring 1994.

Lange, M., and others. "Providers' Views of HMO Mental Health Services." *Psychotherapy* 25(3):455-62, Fall 1998.

Muller, D. "The External Provision of Health Maintenance Organization Mental Health Services." *American Journal of Psychiatry* 135(6):735-8, June 1978.

Nash, D., and others. "A Study of HMO Physicians' Receptivity to Special Programs for Sociomedical and Behavioral Problems." *Journal of Community Health* 7(4):239-49, Summer 1982.

Reidy, W. "Staff-Model HMOs and Managed Mental Health Care: One Plan's Experience." *Psychiatric Quarterly* 64(1):33-44, Spring 1993.

Schneider-Braus, K. "A Practical Guide to HMO Psychiatry." *Hospital and Community Psychiatry* 38(8):876-9, Aug. 1987.

Senge, P. *The Fifth Discipline: The Art and Practice of the Learning Organization.* New York, N.Y.: Doubleday/Currency, 1990.

Weitekamp, M., and Ziegenfuss, J. "Academic Health Centers and HMOs: A Systems Perspective on Calibration in Training Generalists Physicians and Advancing Mutual Interests." *Academic Medicine* 70(1 Suppl):S47-53, Jan. 1995.

Zwick, W., and Bermon, M. "Spectrum of Services for the Alcohol Abusing Patient." In *Managed Mental Health Care,* Feldman, J., and Fitzpatrick, R., Editors. Washington, DC: American Psychiatric Press, Inc., 1992, pp. 273-303.

Mark F. Leveaux, MD, is Chief, Mental Health, Kaiser Permanente Northwest, Portland, Oregon.

Chapter 18

Issues in the Integration of Primary Care with Managed Behavioral Health Care

by Raymond Fabius, MD, FACPE, and Lawrence W. Osborn, MD, MPH

Primary Care Physician Model and Mental Health Services

The purpose of the primary care physician (PCP) model is to create a single "medical home" for patients that is responsible and accountable for orchestrating the total care of the panel of members who selected that office to provide primary health services, which include primary behavioral health care.

Patients seek primary care for four reasons or for combinations of these four reasons:

■ To receive screening tests and wellness check-ups.

■ To be treated for acute illness.

■ To be monitored for chronic illness.

■ To obtain therapy and guidance for psychosocial problems.

Some studies[1-4] have suggested that the majority of primary care physician office visits are generated to respond to psychological or sociological concerns that may manifest themselves as physical or somatic complaints. Stress at home or at work may cause headaches, or school problems may cause abdominal pains. It is therefore imperative for the primary care physician to be an active part of the mental health delivery team.

Effective delivery of mental health services depends on appropriate referral of patients from multiple sources, including PCPs. The mental health delivery system must rely on primary care providers to diagnose and treat common conditions, such as depression, anxiety, somatic complaints, attention disorders, and substance abuse. Therefore, because they are in the mental health delivery system's as well as the patient's best interests, efforts should be made to enhance the primary doctor's involvement and basic knowledge of at least these conditions: recognition of the problems, their initial treatment, and criteria for specialty referral.

Through this primary care approach, only more complex psychological and psychiatric care would require referral, "freeing up" specialty consultation level of care resources for patients whose conditions justify the attention of mental health specialists, e.g., patients with serious personality disorders, severe depression, psychotic disorders, and disabling addiction. In future models, psychiatrists who have been trained in internal medicine may also serve as primary physicians for some subsets of these patients.

Until the emergence of managed care's interest in the functional integration of health care delivery, mental health and medical services were often disconnected, causing mismanagement of care and patient dissatisfaction. As a consequence, the common man has been more likely to share life's crises with bartenders, taxicab drivers, hairdressers, clergy, neighbors, and teachers. To the fullest extent possible, primary care physicians should reach out to their patients, and to all involved parties and resources in the community, to improve access to mental health services.

Because of the continuing stigma attached to mental health treatment, the mental health provider must rely on primary physicians and community resources to support appropriate early recognition, initial treatment and understanding, and referral. It can be assumed that most patients want, and need, their PCPs to understand their psychic pains. Whether or not PCPs can take effective psychotherapeutic action or make proper psychotropic medication interventions, communication of understanding is crucial to members' optimal care and their satisfaction with care. The imparting of empathy is therapeutic, but it may occur more as the exception than the rule in busy PCP offices. Consumers of health care have long complained that some such offices have left them feeling as if they were on an assembly line. Those with practices that demonstrate an interest in patients' emotional well-being will inherit the marketplace.

In addition, mental health providers should be a resource to refer patients to available community resources. For example, a child with special needs whose parents are having problems with the school district may need referral to the local educational law center. A family burdened by the care of an infirm and senile grandparent may need a list of long-term care facilities rather than time-consuming counseling.

Some patients want to go to a mental health clinician without their primary doctor knowing it. This wish should be respected. Managed care organizations (MCOs), large employers, physicians, unions, and behavioral health professionals have recognized that requiring members to go to primary doctors first may interfere with this necessary (also, convenient or easy) access to behavioral health services.

However, it is still necessary to strike a balance between the patient's understandable right to direct access and the collaboration among caregivers required to ensure safe, efficient, and effective treatment. The referred mental health provider should encourage the inclusion of the primary doctor, particularly when medication is necessary. Drug-to-drug interactions can be prevented, and all treatments, medical and mental, can be evaluated for safety.

While medical records at the primary doctor's office and the mental health provider's center should be comprehensive, they must also provide confidentiality. The charts, whether in files or electronic format, must have very limited access.

Primary care physicians not only can and should be included in the care of patients with mental health support needs but also should be the front line resource for primary and secondary prevention programs in mental health. Training patient populations about stress management, conflict resolution, the ills of addiction, dealing with attention or motivational problems, and much more must be at least started at the primary practice level. PCPs have early intervention opportunities that psychiatrists and other mental/behavioral health specialists will never enjoy.

All stakeholders must recognize that the presence of direct access "carved-out" mental health programs can potentially present the primary care physician with a "message of exclusion." The primary physician is told to refer any patients with mental health issues through a contact point or central phone number. In fact, some behavioral health vendors' phone numbers may appear on the member's card and appointments may be scheduled only if the member calls directly. This arrangement may result in less involvement by the PCP. In addition, carved out programs may not encourage their providers to contact the PCP, citing confidentiality concerns to excuse this failure, even when the patient has no problem with the PCP's being involved. Carved out mental health services will need to improve their integration with the medical delivery system, using PCPs as the primary vehicles to achieve this.

Primary care physicians, in a functionally integrated care model, will assist the mental health delivery system with even more focused prevention approaches. They will identify high-risk populations for intensive preventive care. They will reassure the "worried well," treating most of these patients themselves through less formal counseling. They will direct chronically medically ill patients in their practice to mental health services. At present, this is a highly underutilized service. Psychologists, social workers, psychiatrists, and others can contribute greatly to the successful care of a poorly compliant asthmatic or a depressed diabetic. Maximizing the functional status of the chronically ill population realizes not only cost savings but also societal gains. Finally, the PCP will refer seriously and chronically mentally ill patients for intensive psychiatric care.

When discussing mental health services, we need to keep in mind who the stakeholders are. When someone is met with a crisis, they will first approach family and friends. If the crisis is not resolved, they may seek counsel from friends and other nonprofessionals. Only after all of these avenues are exhausted do people access the health care system for help. This tendency on the part of many people to take care of distress themselves, without the assistance of medical, psychiatric, or other mental health professionals, may be based in part on understandable denial and in part on fears of stigma. In some cases, it may be based on untreated pathology, e.g., significant paranoia. It may also, however, in part be based on factors of pride and self-reliance that can represent personal strengths and what could be called latent mental health. Some psychiatrists may see such reluctance to contact a behavioral health professional as only a sign of untreated mental illness rather than as also a possible sign of strength to be capitalized on in treatment, especially by the willing, able, and available primary care physician.

All of us in health care need to understand the social stigma related to seeking mental health services. For this reason, all potential stakeholders—providers such as physicians, pharmacists, social workers, and psychologists and delivery systems such as independent practice associations, integrated delivery systems, mental health consortiums, and health maintenance organizations—should be incorporated into the delivery system.

Purchaser-stakeholders, such as large employers, government agencies, unions, and business groups, should also be incorporated into the delivery system. Only through a process of inclusion will we be able to reduce the stigma related to receiving mental health services and focus efforts on populations of patients who can best benefit from treatment. Until stigma is dealt with more effectively within the provider community, which arguably ought to know better, such fears within member populations will be formidable barriers to the integration of care.

Large employers are realizing that they are de facto providers, in the sense that they have both minds and bodies onsite for often more than 40 hours a week. People become ill or have illnesses aggravated at work, e.g. accidents, chemical toxins, and job stress. Their health care may also be maintained or enhanced at the workplace, e.g. early education about alcoholism, depression, and marital stress or blood pressure or blood sugar checks that are very convenient and cost-effective for member, employer, and PCP.

Occupational cost-offsets await further definition by health plans. How a health plan and employer, in partnership, address the needs of an employed population and the families involved can potentially influence many costs of doing business. Among these costs are absenteeism days lost from work, workers' compensation, disability insurance, employee turnover and training, and productivity.

Using well-established disease management concepts, we need to identify populations at risk that represent opportunities for targeted interventions. We then need to measure the impact of integrated care efforts that are focused by these clearly defined opportunities. We need to identify the right patients and get them to the right service at the right time for the right cost. By doing this, we will reduce economic and societal burdens while improving the productivity and functional status of the American workforce. Early identification of depression by well-trained PCPs using reliable screening tools is the first step in helping this targeted population. Referring them to appropriate behavioral health resources is the next step. Finally, we must measure the impact of such interventions, testing for effectiveness. Did the interventions improve quality of life and productiveness of the depressed patients treated?

Confidentiality: Reason for Special Precautions, But Not an Excuse for Not Communicating

Because of the stigma still attached to mental illness and addiction disorders, confidentiality issues relating to behavioral health care services will always require special attention and extra precautions. Historically, special attention has taken the form of specific releases of information by patients to designated parties and physical security precautions for medical records. In the age of electronic utilization management and medical records systems, it is important to build in special security systems that prevent access to behavioral health records by unauthorized and inappropriate personnel, including those responsible for medical (nonbehavioral) information and records. While nonbehavioral, e.g., primary care physician, records can conceivably contain information (HIV status) as sensitive and as confidential as any to be found in records maintained by an outpatient psychiatrist, extra precautions are required by the fact that service is provided by a designated "mental health" or "chemical dependency" provider.

The capacity to take such extra security precautions is abundantly present in our current electronic technologies. Paper information systems may be less inherently secure than electronic systems on an individual case basis, but they may be more secure with respect to the potential for loss of security on a large-scale, high-volume, systems basis.

While extra and special precautions are required with behavioral information, there is an equal and opposite danger that clinicians and utilization managers will use the need for special precautions as a rationale for not effecting the communication required to ensure high-quality and safe care. It is imperative that primary care physicians know that their patients are being evaluated and/or treated for mental or addiction disorders. It is not medically safe for antidepressants to be prescribed by an outpatient psychiatrist for a patient with a history of hypertension who may be on medication for that disorder. The primary care physician does not need to know the details of the patient's history relevant to a depressive disorder, but he or she does need to know if antidepressant medication is being considered.

On the other hand, the outpatient psychiatrist or another clinician may benefit from the PCP's understanding of the patient's medical and personal history. A primary care physician who has known and treated a whole family for a decade or more will have special knowledge of the family's medical history, relationships, strengths, and dysfunctions.

When the teenage daughter makes a suicide gesture after losing a boyfriend on the heels of her parents' deciding to separate, the primary care physician can be a critical evaluation and treatment resource. Failure on the part of mental health professionals treating the patient and the family at any level of care to utilize this primary care resource produces a significant reduction in the efficiency of care and often also leads to poor quality of care outcomes. Any confidentiality concerns on the part of the patient or family with respect to the primary care physician's learning personal details not already known to the PCP can be discussed with the treating psychiatrist, who must negotiate what must be shared for reasons of medical safety and what can be kept confidential from the primary physician.

Details of a person's life relevant to one caregiver relationship, e.g., with a PCP or a psychiatrist, may be negotiated with one party before release of information is granted to the other party. The first party must therapeutically negotiate with the patient the issue of the need for negotiated communication with all other relevant treatment partners.

For instance, it is conceivable that an outpatient psychiatrist who thinks antidepressant medication is medically necessary to treat a major depressive disorder would have to consider advising a patient that the psychiatrist would be unable to assume responsibility for care if the patient was known to be in treatment with medication by the PCP for hypertension and refused to permit the psychiatrist to discuss the specifics of medication interaction possibilities with the PCP.

It is not clinically safe for outpatient mental health professionals to use a generalized worry about confidentiality to avoid having to call a PCP or to negotiate with a patient about which information should or could be shared. Individualized attention to special, patient-specific, and disorder-specific confidentiality issues is a necessary part of treatment for behavioral disorders. Important confidentiality considerations in fact deepen the need for relevant communication between PCPs and outpatient behavioral health care providers rather than obviate the need for such communication and teamwork on the patient's behalf. Mental health providers must not use general fears about confidentiality to avoid oversight by appropriate parties of the medical necessity and quality of the services that they are rendering.

As managed care plans and purchasers push toward systems of integrated care, creating new incentives for providers who share responsibilities for the mind-body health status of populations, the confidentiality of information about behavioral disorders will continue to require special attention and extra precautions. It will become increasingly untenable financially, however, for providers and purchasers alike to solve the problem by not communicating much at all and blaming other providers or patients for the inefficiencies and suspect quality of care that will often ensue.

Behavioral Interfaces beyond Primary Care: Prevention Challenges

Behavioral health care organizations, providers and purchasers alike, enjoy the opportunities and the burdens of the middleman position when seeking to define and improve working relationships with physical health care organizations on the one side and social, community, and self-help organizations on the other. Managed care's goal is to establish an accountable system of population-, community-, and geography-based network providers for the health and behavioral health status of member populations. This goal creates a serious focus on prevention services and dramatizes the need to coordinate all services, including physical health, mental health, and social services. There is no illness, symptom, or complaint that cannot benefit from such a coordinated effort.

The primary care physician's office represents the first place where all three dimensions to an illness may be addressed, to the degree necessary and practical. The well-informed, well-networked PCP sits in the middle.

While the primary care interface with behavioral health is the central focus of this chapter, emergency departments, hospitals, medical specialists, schools, employers, and community sites and resources, represent other important interfaces for both PCPs and mental health providers with social services resources. Behavioral health specialists and primary care physicians can realize many opportunities for health education (primary prevention), early intervention (secondary prevention), and cost-effective care (tertiary prevention) far more easily if they

Behavioral Health Interfaces

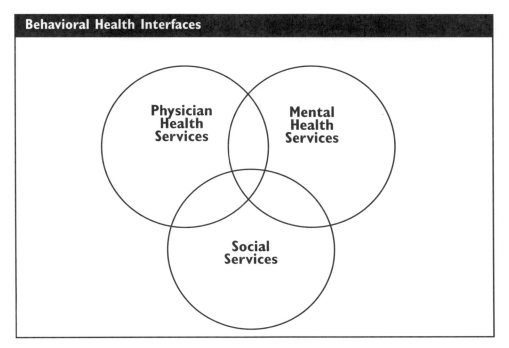

work in close collaboration for the populations they share than if they remain alien to each other on separate provider "islands."

Because it is at the level of the health status of populations that the thoughts of clinicians and businessmen may meet, the several interfaces for mental health—including the critical interface of primary care—can be explored through the lens of prevention. Prevention is viewed here as encompassing a full range of activities from health promotion and primary prevention (e.g., educational efforts directed at high-risk families) through tertiary prevention strategies (e.g., screening heart attack victims for comorbid depression.

Just as physical health conditions may serve as factors of cause, concurrence, or consequence for mental and addiction disorders, and vice versa, so may social and environmental factors of job or marital stress, transportation, housing, income, community resources, etc. serve as important variables in development and severity of and recovery from both physical and behavioral health conditions.

The U.S. Preventive Services Task Force offers many practical suggestions and specific targets for prevention services in critical areas for improving the physical and behavioral health care status of populations, e.g., depression, suicide risk, family violence, problem drinking, dementia, chronic medical illness.[5] Most of the Task Force recommendations in the behavioral health care area are designated as "C" level, indicating that evidence does not support the efficacy of screening activities directed at general populations. However, the risk factors identified for each condition give very concrete guidance for targeted screening and assessment of special populations (e.g., screening for depression in members with chronic medical illness) and for targeted educational efforts (e.g., improving the skills of primary care physicians and families in dealing with traumatic losses resulting from death, divorce, or serious medical illness).

Health care provider groups wishing to function as integrated delivery systems responsible for whole individuals, whole families, and whole populations, both at any point in time and over time, will need to learn how to use databases to preselect subpopulations and members for whom risk factors suggest that screening, assessment, and treatment will be clinically and financially successful. Health plans and purchasers will need to identify the incentives and the data capacities required to assist network providers with this set of opportunities. The simultaneous realization of the twin goals of clinical and financial impact for "prevention" efforts targeted at populations defined by formal risk assessment will become a necessity for survival, rather than just the clinically right thing to do, as delivery systems assume greater degrees of risk for both physical health and behavioral health status.

The National Committee for Quality Assurance (NCQA) requires managed care organizations (MCOs) to document population-based prevention activities directed toward populations targeted by defined risk criteria. NCQA has recently established *Standards for Accreditation of Managed Behavioral Healthcare Organizations* that include strikingly similar requirements that are specific for mental and addiction disorders.[6] This supports the notion that delivery of physical and behavioral health care should be functionally integrated and that MCOs and MBHOs alike must work at documenting their efforts and the results of those efforts for future NCQA accreditations, regardless of administrative or financial arrangements in terms of carved-out or carved-in structures and incentives. In fact, NCQA accreditation standards now require documentation of this functional integration. MCOs are required to demonstrate at least one quality improvement effort within mental health and MBHOs are required to document collaboration with physical health care delivery systems, especially at the level of the PCP.

It is time to cease arguments and academic debates about primary prevention efforts versus secondary prevention/early intervention efforts. It is time to expand our knowledge base by implementing programs and measuring impacts. Integrating behavioral health care services within the medical delivery system will improve both clinical impact and "profitability," not to mention enhanced member satisfaction.

Improved awareness of the hidden burden of undetected and undertreated mental and addictive disorders offers great opportunities to improve the functional status of a population and has great potential cost offsets. Examples include the alcohol abuse often associated with trauma resulting from motor vehicle accidents, the increased risk that heart attack patients have of developing a major depressive disorder, and the high prevalence of behavioral disorders associated with many patient presentations in primary care, e.g., somatoform disorder, irritable bowel syndrome, and back pain. To pay attention to the comorbid depression that may be associated with low back pain may reduce the need or medical necessity for multiple orthopedic interventions.

Seizing such opportunities through interventions that include targeted screening of patients at risk, and communication among caregivers sooner rather than later in the course of an illness of condition, will help realize both clinical and financial improvements. Such collaboration among caregivers, with a PCP taking a leadership and integrating role, is key to successful integration of care.

There is enough evidence[7-11] of unmet need and sufficient evidence of the possible impact of both educational and early intervention efforts to make it reasonable that MCOs engage in and/or help finance well-defined, targeted, and risk-based prevention activities in the behavioral health care area for specific member populations. Such efforts could help the PCP to direct more appropriate physical and behavioral health care to his or her panel of members.

The growth of audiovisual, computerized, electronic, telecommunication capacities and products, e.g., Internet, leading toward interactive TV, has created vehicles for prevention efforts barely imaginable 10 years ago. The content only needs to be packaged for us to engage in specific prevention activities and measure the results. An initial point of contact for these efforts could be in the PCP's office. Studies have demonstrated that PCP involvement and recommendation leads to greater compliance (smoking cessation programs as an example).

If the specific goals of an MCO's or managed behavioral health care organization's prevention efforts are to define at-risk populations that can be targeted for prevention services, PCPs and their mental health/chemical dependency (MH/CD) provider colleagues need to ask where these populations live, how they can be accessed and engaged, and how the impact of collaborative activities can be measured.

One process for identifying, defining, and targeting specific at-risk populations for which prevention resources may be efficiently and cost-effectively allocated is to envision a series of questions:

■ What populations can be identified and helped by medical and behavioral health interventions?

■ Where can the assessments and interventions be delivered effectively?

■ Is there a time sensitivity to the assessment and treatment?

■ How will we measure the effectiveness of our efforts?

Answering such questions will help us explore collaboration at the several kinds of interfaces that offer opportunities for improved allocation of health and behavioral health resources, including the PCP-MH/CD provider interface. If PCPs and outpatient MH/CD providers can work collaboratively, many opportunities that are hard to realize when approached by one party will present themselves. Opportunities at work, school, media and community sites come easily to mind, sites at which at-risk populations may be approached and engaged with resulting impacts on member satisfaction, member retention, and optimal utilization of health care resources.

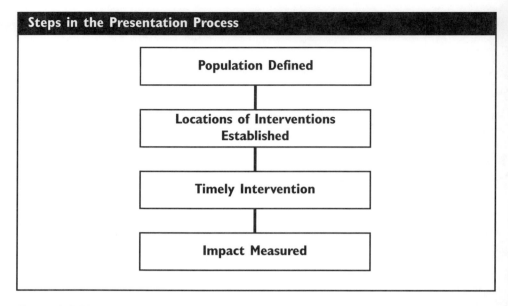

Steps in the Presentation Process

- Population Defined
- Locations of Interventions Established
- Timely Intervention
- Impact Measured

Financial Models and Incentive Structures

In trying to understand what helps and what hinders development of integrated working relationships between primary care offices and behavioral health care providers, it is important to understand the nature of the economic incentives that operate for stakeholders who are responsible for the health status of the population, e.g., premium payer (employer, health plan, behavioral health care vendor—if there is one), primary care physician, MH/CD providers, other medical specialists, and health plan members themselves.

While the structure of the operative system and the economic incentives and risk accountabilities that are implied or declared by the system are not the only factors governing stakeholder behavior, they cannot be ignored. Allocations of risk and reward among stakeholders in any system will always be a major determinant of behavior, but they may also hold the key to motivating change in the future.

Among noneconomic factors that operate to frustrate the development of integrated delivery systems in real world situations is the specialty training received by most health care professionals, including those "specializing" in primary care. Because of their training, some psychiatrists may not feel the need to communicate with anyone but the patient in order to understand the problem and to effect treatment. They may obtain the relevant history without talking to the primary care physician, despite the fact that this potential colleague may have known the patient and the family for years. They may justify this lack of communication with vague references to confidentiality (see earlier discussion). Because of their training, some primary care physicians may believe that mental illnesses are not "real" and that it would be a poor use of their time to understand or treat them or to communicate with anyone who claims competence in this mysterious domain.

Allocations of economic risk/reward in any system of care moving toward functional integration will vary tremendously. On the one extreme is the carved-out model, in which a behavioral health vendor is contracted with directly by an employer or employer group that also contracts with one or more physical health care vendors, purchasers, or providers who have no organizational or economic relationship to the behavioral health care vendor. Technically, and perhaps legally, the only level within this system from which integration efforts may emanate is the employer organization itself. Such a model normally provides little or no incentive for physical and behavioral health care providers to work together.

Employers have chosen carved-out models in part because of a perception that HMOs have not been sufficiently responsive to the behavioral health needs of their members. Formalizing this boundary problem can aggravate the issue.

Structural variations on the carved-out model include HMOs that contract with behavioral health care vendors or brokers that arrange for services via direct contact from members seeking care. In this model, the primary care physician is often left out of the picture and is certainly not encouraged to be the gatekeeper for behavioral services or even expected to be the overall coordinator of care. The HMO/MCO has been expected to provide oversight of carved-out services, according to NCQA standards, but such oversight may not have been robust.

The purely economic forces operating in carved-out models, especially when primary care and behavioral health care providers are separately and independently capitated, may encourage PCPs to over-refer to behavioral health care providers and encourage behavioral health care providers to underserve their assigned populations. PCPs who are told that their panels' mental health is prepaid may refer without much involvement, On the other hand, they have no financial disincentives to make that referral. Mental health/chemical dependency providers who receive capitation may not encourage use of their services despite the knowledge that social stigma, high copayments, and difficult systems of access interfere with their ability to reach patients in need.

It is estimated that more than 50 percent of persons with diagnosable mental conditions, and a greater percentage of persons with addiction disorders, are not recognized as having these disorders.[12-13] Further, a majority of these persons may have contact with primary care without referral and/or without proper and timely treatment. As we move into the future, it is important to create rewards for the mental health/chemical dependency provider and the PCP to work collaboratively.

On the other extreme is the "carved-in" staff- or group-model HMO that does not contract for its behavioral health care services, but employs psychiatrists and other licensed mental health clinicians to provide services at locations that are owned by the HMO and at which the HMO's primary care is also delivered. Many staff-model HMOs, however, do not include behavioral health professionals, carving out this specialty function. Some staff-model HMOs have mixtures of carved-in and carved-out arrangements. When mental health professionals are part of the "owned" HMO staff, they may not work at the same location with primary care providers, partially defeating the clinical purpose of being carved-in. When a staff-model HMO runs out of space at a service site, it may be the mental health staff that is first to go. The stigma issue is also disturbingly alive and well in the health care provider community.

Conversely, when a staff- or IPA-model HMO administratively and financially carves out its behavioral health care services, it may still chose to locate behavioral health care specialists in primary care settings, although this is still the exception rather than the rule. Whether a behavioral health component is administratively carved-in or carved-out is itself no absolute barrier or absolute guarantee to fully integrated care. However, being able to deliver physical and mental health services at the same location dramatically increases the likely integration of care.

The carved-in versus carved-out dilemma should be resolved through rational balance. Patients who need specialized mental health care that can only be properly delivered in specialized settings or who will only engage such services in specialized settings should have easy access to medically necessary behavioral health care. Patients who would only engage services or who would be served earlier and more effectively by having access to behavioral health care in non-specialized sites, e.g., primary care, should also have access to prompt and competent care.

To complicate matters further, a given HMO may have several different types of arrangements with the same or different managed behavioral health care vendors for different subpopulations of its members. Also, a given MBHO may have several different types of risk and carved-in versus carved-out arrangements with HMOs.

To comprehend the economic forces at play in facilitating or hindering development of functionally carved-in or integrated service delivery, there is no substitute for assessing the risk arrangements at work among those who share responsibility for the health status of a given population of plan members. HMOs, MBHOs, PCPs, behavioral health care providers, and members themselves may have different plan types with copayments and deductible and benefit limits and access rules that affect utilization of behavioral services in ways that may be different from the use of traditionally unlimited medical/surgical benefits.

Such an assessment, or diagnosis of operative risk and economic incentives, is always done against the background of stigma, denial, mind-body splitting, and under-recognition realities that are endemic to the behavioral health care area and to all efforts to effect more functionally integrated care.

So-called "Cartesian Dualism," from the French philosopher Rene Decartes, views mental and/or emotional phenomena as belonging to a sphere of reality completely separate from physical, somatic, anatomical, or neurological reality. This view of the human mind and body has deep roots in western culture, originally serving to excuse the so-called sane from responsibility for the mentally ill because the latter could be viewed as morally flawed or possessed by spirits beyond the control of their supposedly saner fellow man. Evidence amassed by Damasio[14] demonstrates, however, that rational thought is impossible without the presence of feeling and emotion, even though the latter may also contribute to illogical thought and irrational behavior.

It would also seem to be indisputable that there is no mental process that exists without a coexisting brain process. It is not adequate to declare all etiologies of illness either physical/organic/biological or mental/functional/psychogenic, when they are probably almost always combinations in often indeterminate proportions. There is no psychogenic reality that does not have a biological and brain-based representation.

The issue of etiology or cause of any given disorder cannot be settled with a simple separation of physical factors versus mental factors, for the latter are as body- and brain-based as the former. True cause is usually multifactorial or overdetermined. Because all mental and behavioral phenomena are brain-based, interventions such as medications and psychotherapy may produce effective treatment and symptom relief even when the true cause may lie in genetic factors that are early developmental or environmental in character. It is almost never nature or nurture but rather the interplay of nature and nurture that produces the set of causative factors responsible for a given mental or physical disorder in a given individual.

Although the forces to continue the artificial separation of mind from body, and rational thought from any and all emotion, are deeply rooted in our culture, it is nonetheless imperative for the difficult work toward greater integration of care to proceed, as difficult as the task may be, for reasons of improved quality of care and cost containment/justification. An ultimate model is the health care delivery system at "total risk" (via member-based reimbursement) for all medical expenditures, both physical and mental, within the same premium dollar. In this total-risk situation, the cardiologist and the psychiatrist will be obliged, for reasons of financial survival as well as the best clinical outcomes, to collaborate on the patient with noncardiac chest pain due to unrecognized panic disorder.

Even when economic forces are rationally aligned for the realization of integrated care, the forces of stigma, Cartesian Dualism, and specialty parochialism make success, simultaneously from patient, provider, and payer viewpoints, far from automatic. Health plans will have to continue to help their provider partners and member populations be successful in such "total-risk" situations.

Efforts of Integration: What's Working? What Doesn't?

Many of the larger health plans are practicing integration of care, specifically with a focus on improving working relationships between primary care and mental health/chemical dependency providers. These efforts reflect the structure of the specific medical delivery system, e.g., staff model versus IPA, and the risk and administrative relationships with behavioral health providers, e.g., degrees and balance of carved-in versus carved-out arrangements.

Some of these efforts include "psychiatric hot lines" for primary care physicians; location of mental health professionals in PCP offices; behavioral health continuing medical education offerings for PCPs; introduction of systematic screening protocols for targeted primary care populations; and various efforts to personalize the face of behavioral health care to the PCP community, to improve communications between these two provider groups, and to create incentives for both parties to improve the effectiveness of their partnership for enhanced member health status and utilization outcomes. In addition, several projects are under way that explore the effectiveness of telecommunications as a vehicle for bringing psychiatrists and other behavioral health clinicians into the primary care setting.

One dilemma inherent in all these efforts, more pronounced perhaps in IPA and carved-out models than in staff- or group-model HMOs, is that all PCPs and PCP offices are not equal in their degree of interest in new forms of collaboration, in their capacity to respond to such out-reach efforts, and in their skill at using new resources wisely or efficiently. Equally true, all psychiatrists and behavioral health providers are not equally interested, capable, or skilled in relating to primary care physicians and their offices in ways that are accepted, mutually comfortable, and successful from patients' points of view. An IPA with thousands of PCPs will find a wide variety of provider responsiveness and capacity. An MBHO with thousands of contracted MH/CD providers will likewise find tremendous variation in ability to respond to the needs of PCPs, both their stated and their felt needs, in improving recognition and treatment of mental and addiction disorders.

PCP survey data from thousands of primary care physicians in one health plan's IPA-model HMOs revealed that, while 70 percent of PCPs view their role in behavioral health as diagnosis and referral, only 30 percent view their role as including treatment. This discrepancy is most pronounced for addiction disorders, but is also significant for mental illness.

This finding stands juxtaposed to the fact that the vast majority of psychotropic medications for an HMO population are prescribed by PCPs, not by network psychiatrists. PCPs, in fact, provide a significant amount of treatment for behavioral disorders. The literature indicates that the majority of PCP prescriptions for antidepressant medication are suboptimal with respect to drug choice, dose and/or duration.[15] In an integrated delivery system, this "problem" is not owned exclusively by primary care physicians, but is equally the responsibility of mental health providers.

What will further motivate primary care physicians to accept, even demand, more behavioral health help and resources in their daily practices? What will motivate mental health and chemical dependency providers to view the shared population of members as their responsibility, even and especially before a member has been referred to them?

PCP compensation strategies that do not reward excessive medical specialty referrals and that do reward high member satisfaction and low out-of-practice transfers will encourage PCP offices to selectively use behavioral health interventions that maximize financial return.

Behavioral health care provider compensation strategies that reward lower inpatient utilization if it can be documented to result from improved outpatient care, including outreach to PCP offices, will encourage these providers to find and work with PCP offices that are receptive.

One large pilot program conducted in an IPA-model HMO placed licensed mental health professionals in 30 PCP offices covering more than 60,000 plan members. The pilot demonstrated several positive findings in terms of PCP satisfaction, member satisfaction, increased penetration of service delivery—especially for medically ill patients with hidden behavioral comorbidities—improved prescribing of antidepressant medication, and significantly improved clinical outcomes that were documented by standardized clinical and functional scales.

Even some carefully selected PCP offices in the pilot program, however, had difficulty using the new resource wisely. The presence of a behavioral health specialist in a PCP office may be seen as obviating the need for any relationship with a network MH/CD provider, rather than an opportunity for improving those working relationships. From this large pilot program experience, it was estimated that a third of PCP offices will use such resources wisely, a third will profess interest in integrated care but not respond, and a final third will have trouble working with mental health professionals at all. Future study will need to be done to discover more effective strategies for improving PCP responsiveness.

It was not easy, however, to demonstrate medical cost offset in the short term for the population served in this large pilot program. While many academic studies over several decades document potential cost offsets and improved clinical outcomes from integrated "primary behavioral healthcare" with specific patient groups, they are not entirely trusted by HMO executives, precisely because they were academic studies whose design may have included strong self-fulfilling prophecy factors that cannot be replicated cost-effectively in real-world, real-time medical delivery systems.[9,16-18]

Cost Offsets: Whose Costs? Whose Values?

Most physician executives in mature HMOs believe that medical/surgical cost offsets already exist, just waiting to be defined and realized as a result of integrated care models in which behavioral health care resources are carefully targeted on specific member populations with defined risk factors and on specific provider locations (e.g., primary care) where unrecognized, untreated, and undertreated behavioral disorders (e.g., depression, anxiety, and addictions) result in avoidable medical costs. Systematic demonstration of integration strategies that may prove to be cost effective in the short term such that up-front costs can be justified, however, remains problematic on a large-scale systems basis.

Some MCOs have compensation systems in place that offer real economic incentives for PCPs and behavioral health providers to improve their working relationships, but improvements are still far from easy or automatic. This leads us to the conclusion that economic incentives and additional resources are not the only or the most crucial factor in engendering changes in the direction of integrated medical delivery. Attitude and "state of mind" may be more important, suggesting that significant provider education and re-education may be as necessary as identification and development of reasonable economic incentives.

For instance, in systems in which a behavioral health provider is at risk for both inpatient and outpatient care (full-risk arrangements), it would seem economically rational for the provider to reach out to receptive primary care offices to ensure that PCPs were appropriately and aggressively screening for hidden major depression and serious addiction, properly prescribing antidepressant medication, and referring patients early for outpatient evaluation and treatment before the first behavioral intervention required becomes an acute inpatient stay.

On the other hand, in systems in which a PCP is economically rewarded for high member satisfaction, low out-of-practice transfer rates, lower medical specialty referrals, and lower rates of nonemergency emergency department utilization, it would seem that PCP offices would welcome, if not demand, behavioral health assistance.

For the many reasons discussed throughout this chapter, economic incentives do not automatically translate into new and more integrated behaviors on the part of either PCPs or behavioral health providers. An integrated game plan requires willingness and competence on the part of both players, simultaneously. Purchasers, employers, and health plans and provider organizations will have to work hard to develop and reward the requisite competence and skills among all types of caregivers sharing responsibility for member populations.

A cost-offset potential far greater than the medical/surgical one is the occupational or employer-based cost offset from the delivery of both physical and behavioral health care. The costs to employers from untreated and undertreated depression and addiction disorders, in terms of days lost, employee turnover and training, reduced productivity, and workers' compensation and disability premiums are estimated to be in the billions of dollars nationally on an annualized basis.

Apparent underutilization of a comprehensive occupational health and mental health set of strategies at the employment site in this country is striking in comparison to that of most other industrialized nations. Our relative failure to capitalize on the healthy and nonstigmatized motivations deriving from the weekly or monthly paycheck for improved consumer behavior in the health care arena is remarkable. This failure takes the form of "missed opportunities" for wellness screenings and for heath care monitoring of chronic illnesses at employment sites, as well as missed opportunities for counseling, screening, and educational interventions for alcoholism and depression prevention. While some large employers have excellent programs, many still do not, and a closer collaboration with health plans for employers of all sizes would seem to present great opportunities for all parties.

While a lengthy discussion of occupational and educational cost offsets is beyond the scope of this chapter, it would be a great day for an HMO when a given employer or community agreed to pay a higher health care premium because the manner in which the HMO delivered physical and behavioral health services achieved documented cost savings, e.g., heightened productivity, for the employer. Costs of heath care coverage would be regarded as an investment in the workforce with a quantifiable return. Similar cost offsets for society at large may be envisioned in the educational area. The data are now in from longitudinal studies of substance abuse prevention efforts in school systems and demonstrate the cost effectiveness of carefully controlled, school-based interventions.

Finding the right balance between short-term and longer term goals, where both clinical and financial success may be achieved, is a central and creative challenge for all managed care organizations. Physician executives and business leaders must work together to make the issues clear to the public and to make the return on investment provable to the investors on a case-specific and program-specific basis. Managed care has created the structure and opportunity for a new set of partnerships between the business/employer and the medical/clinician communities, partnerships that are in the interests of both the public and investors. A new set of partnerships between primary care and behavioral health care will be a cornerstone in demonstrating the effectiveness of the first set.

Conclusion

Functional integration of care, in terms of improved working relationships between primary care and behavioral health resources, still may be more dream than reality in most medical delivery systems, including most mature and otherwise sophisticated managed care organizations. Although the number of efforts to improve this situation across the country is impressive, equally impressive are the difficulties and barriers that stand in the way of our easily or quickly realizing the clinical and financial opportunities and "payoffs" from successfully integrated care. Mind-body splitting and specialty parochialism phenomena, with their stigma baggage, are deeply embedded in our ways of thinking and reacting, on both the customer-patient side and the provider-purchaser side of the managed health care equation.

Such barriers notwithstanding, the clinical and financial potentials are so enormous that the work toward integrated care will proceed despite the fact that success will not come easily. Never before have customer, provider, and purchaser needs been so well aligned for integration efforts to be successful. It will be a long but rewarding process, with few instant successes that achieve the gold standard of proving both clinical and financial impact on a short-term basis. Physician executive and administrative leadership need to provide us the guidance to get us there. Each successful and measured step should provide the courage necessary for us to take additional steps. There is no more natural or more potentially rewarding laboratory than the relationship between primary care and behavioral health care in which we can work together to improve efficiency in medical delivery and the health status of member populations.

References

1. Barrett, J., and others. "The Prevalence of Psychiatric Disorders in Primary Care Practice." *Archives of General Psychiatry* 45(12):1100-6, Dec. 1988.

2. Regier, D., and others. "The De Facto U.S. Mental Health Services System: A Public Health Perspective." *Archives of General Psychiatry* 35(6):685-93, June 1978.

3. Schurman, R., and others. "The Hidden Mental Health Network: Treatment of Mental Illness by Nonpsychiatrist Physicians." *Archives of General Psychiatry* 45(12):1117-9, Dec. 1995

4. Stuart, M., and Lieberman, J. "Finding Time for Counseling in Primary Care." *Patient Care Canada* 6:42-54, 1995.

5. U.S. Preventive Services Task Force. *Guide to Clinical Preventive Services.* Washington, D.C.: Superintendent of Documents, U.S. Government Printing Office, 1997.

6. *Standards for the Accreditation of Managed Behavioral Healthcare Organizations.* Annapolis Junction, Md.: National Committee for Quality Assurance, 1997.

7. U.S. Preventive Services Task Force. *Guide to Clinical Preventive Services.* Washington, D.C.: Superintendent of Documents, U.S. Printing Office, 1997.

8. Eisenberg, L. "Treating Depression and Anxiety in Primary Care: Closing the Gap between Knowledge and Practice." *New England Journal of Medicine* 326(16):1080-4, April 16, 1992.

9. Cummings, N., and others. *The Impact of Psychological Intervention on Healthcare Utilization and Costs: The Hawaii Medicaid Project.* San Francisco, Calif.: American Biodyne, 1990.

10. Zung, W. "Prevalence of Depressive Symptoms in Primary Care." *Journal of Family Practice* 37(4):337-44, Oct. 1993.

11. Katon, W., and Schulberg, H. "Epidemiology of Depression in Primary Care." *General Hospital Psychiatry* 14(4):237-47, July 1992.

12. Williams, J., and others. "Depressive Disorders in Primary Care: Prevalence, Functional Disability, and Identification." *Journal of General Internal Medicine* 10(1):7-12, Jan. 1995.

13. Schulberg, H., and others. "The 'Usual Care' of Major Depression in Primary Care Practice." *Archives of Family Medicine* 6(4):334-9, July-Aug. 1997.

14. Damasio, A. *Descartes' Error: Emotion, Reason, and the Human Brain.* New York, N.Y.: G.P. Putnam, 1994.

15. Coulehan, J., and others. "Treating Depressed Primary Care Patients Improves Their Physical, Mental, and Social Functioning." *Archives of Internal Medicine* 157(10):1113-20, May 26, 1997.

16. Mumford, E., and others. "A New Look at Evidence about Reduced Cost of Medical Utilization Following Mental Health Treatment." *American Journal of Psychiatry* 141(10):1145-58, Oct. 1984.

17. Von Korff, M., and others. "Disability and Depression among High Utilizers of Health Care: A Longitudinal Analysis." *Archives of General Psychiatry* 49(2):91-100, Feb. 1992.

18. Mintz, J., and others. "Treatments of Depression and the Functional Capacity to Work." *Archives of General Psychiatry* 49(10):761-8, Oct. 1992.

Raymond Fabius, MD, FACPE, is Medical Director and Lawrence W. Osborn, MD, MPH, is Medical Director, Mental Health/Substance Abuse, Aetna U.S. Healthcare, Blue Bell, Pennsylvania.

Section V

Location-Based

Chapter 19

Nursing Home Psychiatric Care

by Martin Macklin, MD, PhD

There are two simultaneous but related trends that drive the need for ongoing psychiatric care for nursing home patients. First, an increasing number of elderly individuals in this country have become residents of nursing homes. There is a substantial life-time risk of entering a nursing home and spending a long time there. Of those who died in 1986 at 65 years of age or older, 29 percent had at some time been residents in nursing homes and almost half of those who entered nursing homes spent a cumulative total of at least one year there. The probability of nursing home use increased sharply with age: 17 percent for age 65 to 74, 36 percent for age 75 to 84, and 60 percent for age 85 to 94. Of the approximately 2.2 million people who turned 65 in 1990, more than 900,000, or 43 percent, were expected to enter a nursing home at least once before they died. Thus, a large percentage of our elderly population is increasingly relying on nursing home care for the latter parts of life.[1]

The second factor leading to increased psychiatric care in nursing homes is federal regulations mandating quality standards in nursing homes. In particular, the Omnibus Budget Reconciliation Act (OBRA) of 1987 significantly increased regulations that relate to psychiatric care. The long-term care regulations of the Act contain a number of items specifically relating to psychiatric medications. They state, in part, that "each resident's drug regimen must be free from unnecessary drugs." An unnecessary drug is any drug when used in excessive dose or excessive duration or without adequate monitoring or without adequate indications for its use. Adverse consequences might also indicate that the dose should be reduced or discontinued. For any nursing home resident who receives antipsychotic, antianxiety, or antidepressant medications, there must be a specific documented indication for their use. There are also rules specifying maximum doses of certain medications, depending on diagnoses contained within the Health Care Financing Administration (HCFA) interpretive guidelines for the Long Term Survey, Section 483.25. The medication categories include long-acting benzodiazepines, short-acting benzodiazepines, hypnotic/ sedative drugs, and antipsychotic drugs.[2]

Therefore, careful psychiatric assessment and medication monitoring are needed for successful long-term care facility certification. The facility must ensure that residents who have not used antipsychotic drugs are not given these drugs unless antipsychotic drug therapy is necessary to treat a specific diagnosed condition. In addition, residents who use antipsychotic drugs must receive gradual dose reductions and behavioral interventions, unless clinically contraindicated, in an effort to discontinue these drugs. Side-effects, including tardive dyskinesia, must also be monitored. OBRA regulations also mandate that restraints should be used as infrequently as possible. This includes both physical and chemical restraints. Nursing facilities must make an effort to use methods other than restraints to help redirect the behavior of residents.

HCFA regulations outline the need to provide psychotherapy in nursing home settings.[2] "Each resident must receive and the facility must provide the necessary care and services to attain or maintain the highest practicable physical, mental, and psychosocial well-being, in accordance with the comprehensive assessment and plan of care." This requirement combines with another regulation that states that, based on comprehensive assessment of a resident, the facility must ensure that a resident who displays mental or psychosocial adjustment difficulty receives appropriate treatment and services to correct the assessed problem and ensure that a resident whose assessment did not reveal a mental or psychosocial adjustment difficulty does not display a pattern of decreased social interaction and/or increased withdrawn, angry, or depressive behaviors, unless a resident's clinical condition demonstrates that such a pattern was unavoidable. The guidance for surveyors on these two sections of the law clearly points out that, when problems appear, the nursing facility must provide treatment for them. The provision of psychotherapy is clearly delineated as one of the treatment approaches for these difficulties. In addition, residents with schizophrenia or other major psychiatric problems must be provided ongoing care for their disorders, even though they are not the primary causes for their being in nursing home settings.

Thus, there are many interrelated pressures on the nursing facility that make it imperative for it to have psychiatric care available for its residents. For the psychiatrist, this provides an opportunity to facilitate the care of residents in a nursing home setting and to provide an organized approach for their care. We have found that, when a psychiatrist provides an organized approach to psychiatric care for nursing home residents, the residents' overall care and well-being is much improved. The psychiatrist also finds that there is less interruption to his or her normal work schedule than if only intermittent services are provided. Of course, it is possible to always respond to nursing home requests for psychiatric care on an ad hoc basis, but we believe this is a disruptive and expensive way to provide care. The approach we feel is most helpful in providing continuity of care and high-quality care for nursing home residents is outlined below.

Organization of Psychiatric Team

A variety of team arrangements are possible for providing psychiatric care to nursing home residents. The description that follows is the one that we have found to be advantageous to us in working with nursing home residents. The system that we have developed over time has worked for us in that we are able to provide appropriate levels of care for the residents of nursing homes and to provide consultation to the staff of the nursing homes during the same visit. Also, we are able to use different staff members to provide services appropriate to their level of training.

The head of the team must be a physician who is a trained psychiatrist. We would recommend that the psychiatrist have additional training in geriatric psychiatry, although it is not required by any regulations. This additional training will certainly facilitate the psychiatrist in his or her understanding of the problems seen in nursing homes and of the complications of physical illnesses and how they affect the emotional well-being of their patients. The other team members should either be employees of the psychiatrist or employed by the entity that employs the psychiatrist. This is important, because many of the services rendered will be those that are considered "incident to services" under Medicare rules. Reimbursement for supervised or "incident to services" activity is the same as for services provided by the physician. However, the physician must be on the premises where the service is being provided. A second alternative would be to have a licensed clinical psychologist, as defined by Medicare, employ the nonpsychiatric staff. The most efficient program for providing care is for the psychiatrist and nonmedical staff to go to the nursing home at the same time. This satisfies the Medicare "incident to services" rules as well as the rules of any insurance companies that have similar standards for supervision of nonphysicians. The psychiatrist will also be on the premises to facilitate medication prescribing and medication side-effect monitoring.

It is preferable for the psychiatrist to perform a psychiatric evaluation for all patients that are to be followed. A psychiatric evaluation may also be appropriate for patients who are to be seen only as a single visit evaluation. Psychotherapy should be provided by a nonpsychiatrist to most of the patients who are appropriate for psychotherapy. This latter statement is a judgment of the author's and of many of those working in nursing home settings. It is certainly not similar to some office-based psychiatric practices and may be uncomfortable for psychiatrists who are not familiar with working with nonpsychiatrists. Most of the psychotherapy that is going to be delivered in a nursing home setting will be supportive, although some will be insight-based psychotherapy. In our experience, supportive psychotherapy and brief psychotherapy can be performed by well-trained social workers or counselors. In Ohio and many other states, there is licensure for licensed independent social workers and licensed clinical counselors. These master's degree-level trained and licensed individuals are usually capable of providing a high level of psychotherapeutic service. The psychiatrist is available during the time psychotherapy is being provided and immediately after the session for feedback and assistance with difficult issues.

Frequently, the psychotherapist will have questions surrounding the medical condition of patients and/or the level of their psychiatric illness, and it may be necessary for the psychiatrist to provide a brief evaluation on the same day as the psychotherapy. In our experience, however, this need is infrequent. There is also a need for monitoring of psychiatric medications.

Generally, residents with significant dementia or severe mental retardation are not appropriate for psychotherapy. However, evaluation and management of medication by the psychiatrist may still be required for these residents. One must be careful that medication decisions are always made by the psychiatrist. Also, the psychiatrist must be familiar with all the medication rules in the nursing home standards and must constantly evaluate the medication regimens of residents with this in mind. Medications must also be monitored for the control of psychiatric and behavioral symptoms.

In terms of testing, it is desirable to administer the mini-mental state exam[3] to most residents in a nursing home during the initial assessment. This is a commonly used test of cognitive functioning and a good method of documenting the onset and progression of dementia. This should be repeated periodically to document any changes in cognitive function. This is an efficient and easily administered test that does not require special training to administer. Also, any residents receiving antipsychotic medications should be administered the Abnormal Involuntary Movement Scale (AIMS).[4] This is the commonly used evaluation for tardive dyskinesia. As patients age, the risk of tardive dyskinesia increases.[5] Also, HCFA guidelines[2] require monitoring antipsychotic drug side-effects. Psychiatrists are better trained and more experienced in evaluating these side-effects then are other physicians. Testing every six months is needed to document any changes in the patient's condition. Both the mini-mental state exam and the AIMS test can be administered by nonpsychiatrists who have had some training from the psychiatrist.[6]

During nursing home visits, the psychiatrist should spend most of his or her time evaluating medication effects for residents and providing supervision for nonpsychiatric staff. The psychiatrist should also anticipate spending time consulting with nursing home staff members, especially the head nurse and the social worker. This will facilitate their dealing with problems that may occur in the nursing home, particularly behavioral and/or emotional issues. This latter recommendation is important, because nursing home patients frequently manifest behavioral symptoms more than they manifest emotional or intrapsychic symptoms. This is particularly true for patients with dementia. Consultations with the nursing home staff will help them to understand how to deal with these behavioral problems. As an example, the psychiatrist may find him- or herself in a position to recommend behavioral interventions, including diversionary tactics or comforting measures, to help orient or calm patients with advanced dementia. At times, it has been helpful to make nursing home staff more comfortable with friendship relations that develop between patients and help them sort out the staff's feelings about sexual or interpersonal behavior and how they are imposing their own moral standards on the patients, which may or may not be appropriate.

Another intervention that has been found to be helpful in nursing homes is really an indirect intervention. Patients are frequently evaluated with either the head nurse or social worker present, particularly when the issues involved are not intrapsychic issues. This helps to educate the staff about the mental condition of the patient and also provides ongoing teaching and education for the nursing home staff in interviewing techniques.

In terms of numbers of staff, for a nursing home of approximately 100 residents, I would recommend that the psychiatrist have two to four nonpsychiatric staff. This provides staff for engaging in psychotherapy with residents and frees the psychiatrist to evaluate new problems and do medication evaluations. Seeing patients in a 100-bed nursing home may consume three or four hours of the team's time. If there are many new residents to evaluate, longer periods may be necessary. It's true that this is a broad range for the number of staff. In attempting to more readily describe the staffing pattern, I have a couple of recommendations. When you first begin to see patients in nursing homes, the amount of psychiatric time is much greater than after the same home has been visited for six months or longer. This is because of the large number of medications to review and the large number of patients to evaluate. After the patients have become more familiar to the psychiatrist and his or her staff, the amount of psychiatric time, per patient, will decrease. In a nursing home, up to one fourth of the residents will be appropriate for psychotherapy and will respond to psychotherapeutic intervention. With four therapists, eight patients can be seen in an hour. It therefore will take three hours to provide therapy for 25 patients in a nursing home. During this time, the psychiatrist will be doing medication evaluations, consulting with the staff, and providing psychotherapy for additional patients.

With fewer staff members, the time will be extended at the nursing home, and the psychiatrist will see more patients for psychotherapy. The decision about the number of staff is based on the number of nonmedical staff available to the psychiatrist that he or she has confidence in and the frequency with which the psychiatrist visits nursing homes.

In terms of frequency for nursing homes visits, the intervals for medication follow-ups should be monthly. The interval for reevaluating patients with major disorders should be monthly or quarterly. It is necessary to evaluate any interactions with or anticipated changes in their physical condition that may affect their psychiatric condition. For psychotherapeutic or counseling interventions, biweekly sessions are usually satisfactory for most long-term nursing home patients. Some psychiatrists make weekly visits to nursing homes to engage in psychotherapy. Although this is a frequent pattern for office practice, it is not commonly done in nursing home practice.

It is imperative that the head nurse and/or the social worker be available during the time that the nursing home is being visited. This is important for two reasons: First, the social worker and the head nurse are usually the individuals at the nursing home who have full knowledge of the behavior and emotional status of the patients that you will be visiting and their input is going to be very useful. Also, it is desirable to provide feedback to these individuals so that they can provide recommended interventions that may be needed between visits.

It is also important to schedule visits to make certain that residents are going to be at the home when you arrive. Many nursing homes have regularly scheduled trips, and it is very frustrating to arrive at a nursing home and discover that all the patients you planned to see that day have gone to a ball game or movie. Staff members should be available to bring patients to the psychiatrist. Otherwise, much time is spent in looking for residents in their rooms or in activity areas. The best situation is one in which there is good cooperation between the psychiatric team and the nursing home staff.

Some nursing homes have physician offices available for seeing patients, and it is important to schedule a time so as not to be in conflict with a physician doing physical exams or providing physical care. This is usually a relatively easy scheduling problem to sort out, but one that must be thought of in advance.

Although it is certainly appropriate to dictate notes, unless the nursing home has a transcription service, progress notes and evaluations should be written by hand and left in the patient charts.

In some settings, physicians write brief notes and indicate that a progress note is being dictated. If the transcription is going to be done in the psychiatrist's office or another location, there must be a system in place to get the notes back to the nursing home and placed on the patient's chart in a timely fashion. Although in principle this is a good idea, in our experience it does not always work as planned. Snafus occur and progress notes end up not getting placed on the charts. Also, transcribing 25 progress notes for a morning's work is a hefty amount of work for a transcriptionist. It significantly adds to the psychiatrist's office expenses, and this is something that most psychiatrists are not willing to incur. Therefore, my recommendation is to either fully write the note at the nursing home or have a nursing home transcription service provide a typed progress note. It is important for the psychiatrist to document all the psychiatric medicines that the patient is receiving and to document the reason for each of these psychiatric medications. Also, because of the need to comply with HCFA regulations for decreasing psychiatric medications to the minimal dose, the psychiatrist must document all attempts to decrease dosage and any reasoning behind not decreasing the medication dose.

When the nursing home is visited on a biweekly basis, most behavioral changes can be anticipated and treatment regimens can be adjusted in an appropriate fashion. The more the psychiatrist and his or her team become familiar with the residents of the nursing home, and the more the residents and the staff become comfortable with the psychiatrist and his or her team, the better the relationship is going to be. It will also be easier to anticipate problems, and the social worker and head nurse can frequently be assisted in learning to deal with these problems in anticipation of the next psychiatric team visit.

Nursing home residents will generally be followed over long periods. The psychiatrist will develop an insight into the dynamics of the facility and how it affects the mental health and behavior of the patients. For example, a nursing home undergoing change in management or change in administration will usually cause the staff to be in a state of anxiety about the new administration. The staff's anxiety will usually be felt by the patients, and patients with fragile emotional states will begin to act out. Some of them will decompensate, especially if they suffer from schizophrenia or major affective disorders. As the anxiety level of the staff returns to normal, patients will gradually also return to normal. However, psychiatric intervention will generally be required during this high-anxiety period, and medication doses may have to increased. On the other hand, a nursing home with a high level of staff satisfaction, a very pleasant environment, and well-planned activities will generally have residents who are more comfortable with their environment and will have lower levels of emotional distress. The psychiatrist will frequently find himself in a position of pointing out these issues to nursing home management in helping them to deal with staff anxiety and understanding its impact on patients.

In areas of the country in which population density is high and nursing homes are heavily concentrated, nursing home psychiatry could potentially become a full-time practice. The choice is up to the psychiatrist and the ease with which contact can be made with various nursing homes.

Treating a geriatric population,[7] particularly residents in nursing homes, provides a different insight into humanity then we frequently find in an office-based or hospital practice. We hear many fond tales of childhood, learn many of the details of life from 80 years ago, and are fascinated by the changes in society. We learn about the dynamics of families, the pain that comes with the decision to place a loved one in a nursing home, and the stress on the patient who has had to give up the independence of his or her home. Psychiatrists are accustomed to dealing with these issues, but we find them in much greater concentration in a nursing home setting then we do in the usual office setting. If the psychiatrist is comfortable working with trained nonpsychiatrists and with the problems of aging patients, a nursing home practice can be very rewarding both professionally and financially.

References

1. Kemper, P., and Murtaugh, C. "Lifetime Use of Nursing Home Care." *New England Journal of Medicine* 324(9):595-600, Feb. 28, 1991.

2. *The Long-Term Care Survey.* Washington, D.C.: American Health Care Association, 1995. Contains Regulations, *Federal Register,* pages 48867-48800 of Sept. 1991 and pages 43922-43925 of Sept. 23, 1992., and Medicare Survey Process and Survey Protocol of the Health Care Financing Administration.

3. Folstein, M., and others. "Mini-Mental State: A Practical Method for Grading the Cognitive State of Patients for the Clinician." *Journal of Psychiatric Research* 12(3):189-98, Nov. 1975.

4. Tracy, K., and others. "Interrater Reliability Issues in Multicenter Trials. Part 1: Theoretical Concepts and Operational Procedures Used in Department of Veteran Affairs Comparative Study #394." *Psychopharmacology Bulletin* 33(1):53-7, 1997.

5. Jeste, D., and Wyatt, R. "Aging and Tardive Dyskinesia." In *Schizophrenia and Aging,* Mitler, N., and Cohen, G., Editors. New York, N.Y.: Guilford, 1987.

6. Lair, T., and Lefkowitz, D. "Mental Health and Functional Status of Residents of Nursing and Personal Care Homes." DHHS Publication 903470. Rockville, Md.: Agency for Health Care Policy and Research, 1990.

7. Curlik, S., and others. "Psychiatric Aspects of Long-Term Care." In *Comprehensive Review of Geriatric Psychiatry,* Sadavoy, J., and others, Editors. Washington, D.C.: American Psychiatric Press, 1991, pp. 547-64.

Martin Macklin, MD, PhD, is Vice President, Medical Affairs, UHHS Geauga Regional Hospital, Chardon, Ohio.

Chapter 20

In-Home Behavioral Health Care Model

by Nina M. Smith, RNC, MEd, and Nina Klebanoff, PhD, RN, CS, LPC

I n-home behavioral health care is cost effective in several ways. Fewer emergency department visits and decreased hospitalizations may occur because of the attention and intervention of the in-home team. If rehospitalization is needed, the process may be more effective and may be conducted in a more expedient manner because of home care assessment and intervention. Crisis stabilization and discharges are facilitated by immediate follow-up by the in-home team. Healing is promoted by the sense of security and independence afforded the client who remains at home. As changes within the health care delivery system affect lengths of stay, home care services will expand to meet the needs that traditional services no longer satisfy. Managed care companies are looking for cost-effective alternatives to traditional inpatient services, and home care delivers what they are seeking.

Recent studies have reported on the benefit and effectiveness of behavioral in-home care:

- In a Connecticut study of an in-home crisis intervention program, 80 percent of clients referred to hospital care could have been treated at home.[1]

- The Visiting Nurses Association (VNA) of Louisville showed that psychiatric home care can reduce the incidence of rehospitalization of patients with serious mental illness by 70 percent.[2,3]

- Although more than 50 percent of patients discharged from psychiatric facilities may need psychiatric home care, few are willing to seek help. A study in England found that, of 120 recently discharged clients who were diagnosed with schizophrenia, more than 50 percent had a need for continuing care but were reluctant to seek help.[4]

- The VNA of Cleveland found that psychiatric home care can increase medication compliance by more than 60 percent. It found that six months after discharge from inpatient hospitalization, patients who received home care were more compliant about taking medications than were those in the control group—64 percent versus 43 percent.[4]

Benefits of In-Home Care

In-home behavioral health care provides clients with mental health services in the least restrictive environment. It provides support, education, and assistance to the family/caregiver. There is improvement and integration in community support networks that were initiated during the intensive treatment process. In-home care can prevent unnecessary hospitalizations and may allow earlier discharge from more intensive settings by providing services in the home milieu. The patient experiences improved quality of life and is assisted in coping with adjunctive stress-related and medical problems. Regular home visits assist the client in maintaining a therapeutic alliance and increases medication compliance. Clients are involved in their own care and can take responsibility for their treatment.

Scope of Services Provided

Services provided can include:

Assessment

- Psychiatric nurse evaluation
- Physical, behavioral, mental status
- Social service assessment and intervention
- Evaluation of home environment for safety
- Suicide assessment, intervention, and prevention
- Emergency department evaluation
- Ongoing assessment and monitoring of physical illness or disability that may affect patient's ability to cope with mental illness

Intervention

- Crisis intervention and prevention
- Administration of intramuscular (IM) long-acting psychiatric medications
- Obtaining laboratory values and medication monitoring
- Follow-up care after electroconvulsive therapy (ECT)
- Bathing and personal grooming
- Activities of daily living, training, and safety management
- Energy conservation and management
- Mobility and gait evaluation and management
- Speech and communication evaluation and management
- Counseling on death and dying

■ Behavior modification

■ Reality testing and orientation

■ Individual psychotherapy

■ Family therapy

Education

■ Medication management and education

■ Patient and family/caregiver teaching

■ Community resource education and reintegration

■ Nutritional education and management

■ Stress management and coping/relaxation education

Interdisciplinary Services

In-home services can be provided by caregivers from the entire continuum of health care professionals: psychiatrists, primary care physicians, skilled psychiatric and medical nurses, occupational therapists, licensed social workers, psychologists, licensed professional counselors, physical therapists, speech therapists, rehabilitation counselors, substance abuse counselors, home health aides, and others. Although each caregiver provides a different service, when all services are coordinated and communicated synergistically among caregivers, the patient's ability to benefit and improve is enhanced.

Medicare Requirements for Home Care

Medicare has recognized psychiatric home care as a reimbursable service since 1979. However, very little is addressed in the *Medicare Home Health Agency Manual* (HIM 11). Section 205.1, #15 of HIM 11 (April 1996) states:

A Psychiatric Evaluation and Therapy. The evaluation and psychotherapy needed by a patient suffering from a diagnosed psychiatric disorder that necessitated active treatment in an institution requires the skills of a psychiatrically trained nurse and the costs of the psychiatric nurse's services may be covered as skilled nursing care. Psychiatrically trained nurses are nurses who have special training and/or experience beyond the standard curriculum required for an RN. The services of the psychiatric nurses are to be provided under a plan of care established and reviewed by a physician. A psychiatrist may also prescribe services of nonpsychiatric nursing, such as intramuscular injections of behavior-modifying medications.

"It is not necessary for the patient to require active treatment in an institution to be eligible. A psychiatric nurse must furnish care under a plan established, reviewed, and signed by a physician."[5]

Because the law precludes agencies that provide care and treatment primarily of mental diseases from participating as home health agencies, psychiatric nursing must be furnished by agencies that do not primarily provide care and treatment of mental diseases.

Medicare home health rules require that certain conditions be met before a patient is admitted to this level of care:

■ Care must be ordered by a physician.

■ Care must be reasonable and medically necessary for the treatment of illness.

■ A primary skilled service—a skilled nurse, a social worker, a physical therapist, etc.—must be needed.

■ Skilled nursing and aide service must be needed on an intermittent and part-time basis.

■ The patient must be homebound.

Homebound criteria are met when:

■ There is not a normal ability to leave home.

■ It takes considerable and taxing effort to leave home.

■ Absences from home are infrequent, of short duration or to receive medical care.

Homebound criteria are not met when:

■ There are frequent absences from the home for social reasons or for shopping or business purposes.

■ The patient drives a car.

■ The patient attends a day care center for nonmedical purposes, e.g., socialization.

As applied to the psychiatric patient, the criteria for Medicare coverage are:

■ Illness is manifested by a refusal to leave home (e.g., because of severe depression, paranoia, agoraphobia, etc.).

■ Because of illness, it would be unsafe for patient to leave home (e.g., hallucinations, violent outbursts, or confusion).

■ These patients may have no physical limitations

■ The psychiatric symptoms that make the patient homebound must be clearly and specifically documented on an ongoing basis in the medical record.

The Role of Managed Care in In-Home Behavioral Health Care Services

As health care evolves, managed care programs will increasingly look for integrated systems of care and for providers who are able to provide services in the ambulatory behavioral health continuum. In-home behavioral health care can present a clinically efficacious, cost-effective, efficient, and high-quality service. Creating standards of care and providing practice guidelines will assist programs utilizing in-home services to structure their care. Both payers and providers will be challenged to demonstrate why their programs are successful and valid and what parameters they follow for quality.

High-Quality In-Home Behavioral Health Care Programs

Quality in in-home behavioral health care programs is determined by a number of factors:

■ Includes professional services that are not custodial in nature and that do not add unnecessary cost to an episode of illness.

■ Improves the efficiency and consistency of interdisciplinary care and case management and maximizes cost effectiveness.

■ Provides comprehensive services that utilize recognized and traditional psychiatric and substance abuse modalities of treatment, including ongoing monitoring and assessment, medical management, psychoeducation, and counseling therapies.

■ Has staff specifically trained in in-home behavioral health care.

■ Has interdisciplinary team that consists of licensed psychiatric nurses, social workers, counselors, occupational therapists, speech therapists, physical therapists, psychologists, and others.

■ Provides services under order and direction of a physician (or psychologist, depending on state statute).

■ Provides visits, when necessary, on a crisis basis.

■ Provides 24-hour telephone triage and onsite emergency response.

■ Provides or contracts for psychiatric emergency response team.

■ Expects fewer emergency department visits and decreased hospitalizations as outcomes of programs, due to clinical attention and intervention of the interdisciplinary team working with the patient/family/caregiver.

■ Safely facilitates crisis stabilization and discharges from other more structured programs because of scheduled and immediate follow-up in the patient's home.

■ Encourages patients to maintain maximum level of independence.

■ Provides quality improvement programs and outcome measurement systems that measure clinical effectiveness, outcomes, and patient satisfaction; provide effective levels of services; assess patients' levels of functioning within their natural environments; and review medical resources utilized.[6]

The possibilities for the use of in-home behavioral health care services are endless. Different payer sources and providers are creating programs that utilize the concept of in-home care to deliver care in the home milieu. Integrated delivery systems are increasingly beginning to realize the importance of this level of care in a medical cost-offset program. Findings show that in medical cost-offset studies, for every dollar spent on behavioral health care issues, at least three dollars can be saved in overall health costs because of additional (and often vague) medical symptoms that are recognized, acknowledged, and treated.[7]

In-home services should be provided only if the patient can be safely maintained in this milieu and when the patient's family, caregiver, and/or support network are invested in the patient to the degree that they work cooperatively with the therapeutic team.

A person of any age may be treated in a home setting. Children and adolescents and dual-diagnosed patients may have attending complications that require in-home behavioral health care services until they are capable of moving to alternative types of care outside the home. Older adults, as well as seriously and persistently mentally ill individuals, may benefit from in-home behavioral health care programs because of the resulting active participation in their own milieu and of their taking responsibility for their own treatment.

The implications and uses of this unique type of care are illustrated in the following examples:

Case 1

Anna, 8 years old, lives at home with her mother and father. The mother and father are in their early 20s, are unmarried, and have many friends who spend time at their apartment. Anna was admitted to a psychiatric inpatient child unit for two weeks, followed by one month of partial hospitalization and then follow-up outpatient care. Her diagnosis is depression and an adjustment reaction. She made one suicide attempt in the past three months, the most recent precipitating a hospitalization. During inpatient and partial hospitalization, Anna made remarkable gains. She did well in the structured environment.

In outpatient therapy and living with her mother and father, her progress stalled. She presented well in outpatient therapy, but her school grades were falling, she was acting out and had continued symptoms of depression. During family therapy, the parents could not identify what she might be reacting to. In-home behavioral health care intervention was initiated to identify the family system dynamics, to assess the home milieu, and to assist in problem solving at this level. Visits were made in the home at various times of the day. Family therapy and individual sessions were held. During one late night visit, it was noted that friends stayed until late hours. Anna had no bedroom and slept on the couch. When friends were over late, Anna could not go to "bed" until everyone left.

The parents did not see this as a problem, because it had always been a way of life. Through an immediate intervention, a small room was made in a closet. Anna now had a space to call her own, a sense of belonging, somewhere to get away from the noise and adults and a chance to get to bed early. Her grades picked up in school. She was not tired and paid attention. Anna finished individual outpatient therapy, and her parents were enrolled in a parenting course. In-home intervention sped progress in therapy and helped the patient attain independence quickly, efficiently, and cost effectively.

Case 2

Mary, a 21-year-old diagnosed with bipolar disorder, posttraumatic stress disorder (PTSD), and borderline personality disorder, was first seen in home care during one of her outpatient trials. Mary lived with her mother and father until she was 14; then she was raised by her grandmother. From the time she was eight until she was 14, Mary's father sexually abused her. Her grandmother was demanding and overprotective, making their relationship difficult. At 18, Mary moved four states away to go to college. In her freshman year, the pressures of school, little structure, drugs, alcohol, and sexual encounters contributed to a major depression, followed by a manic episode. She attempted suicide and was hospitalized. On discharge, she returned to school, only to repeat old patterns.

Mary was hospitalized six more times in the next three years. After this period, her treatments changed. She started seeing a psychiatric clinical nurse specialist (CNS) on an outpatient basis. The CNS had prescriptive abilities, took the time to note medication effectiveness, and make changes as necessary. The CNS worked with the insurance case manager to devise a plan to keep Mary from further hospitalizations. She integrated Mary into community services and support groups. Mary was improving and working on issues. Home care was sought by the CNS to assist Mary in avoiding hospitalizations during peak crisis times. Mary was able to identify the critical periods. In-home care provided a registered psychiatric nurse to stay with Mary during these times.

In the beginning, the RN was in the home from 8 p.m. to 8 a.m. to provide support, safety, and one-to-one counseling during the night. Mary was able to process her "ghosts" in a safe environment, work through her issues, and avoid hospitalization. The case was managed through home care for about 18 months. The safety interventions were so successful that the managed care company allowed Mary to determine the crisis times and schedule her own home care assistance.

On Mary's 22nd birthday, she was discharged from home care and moved back to her grandmother's town to continue outpatient therapy and attend another school. By receiving home care at critical periods, Mary stopped her cycle of hospitalizations and gained a maximum therapeutic impact from the integrated therapy systems.

Case 3

Jackie, a 45-year-old diagnosed with bipolar disorder and borderline personality disorder, was first seen through in-home care after using her maximum mental health lifetime benefits. She had been hospitalized on and off for the past 20 years. During treatment, she received medication; ECT; and group, individual, and family therapy. Jackie was married this entire time to the same husband and had a 20-year-old son. The patient alienated most of her therapists, changed psychiatrists many times, and was not welcome in any of the hospitals in her area. She was a difficult patient, and the case manager was out of traditional resources.

The case manager had recently learned about psychiatric home care and found an agency that provided this service. The managed care company contracted with the patient, family, agency, and psychiatrist to provide in-home care, including home health aide services 12 hours a day. A psychiatric nurse visited two times a week, coordinated care services with the case manager, and provided individual and solution-oriented therapy. The home health aide was in the home from 6 a.m. to 6 p.m., Monday through Friday, to assist Jackie with safety, structure, and redirection. Jackie continued to see the psychiatrist once a week for individual and medication therapy. The nurse, aide and physician conferred at least one time a week.

The regimen was successful. The patient avoided hospitalization for more than six months. The longest she had previously gone between hospitalizations was six weeks. During the first six months, her son was in an automobile accident that left him paraplegic in a rehabilitation facility with little promise for improvement. Despite this, the patient did not regress. After six months, supervised and structured hours were decreased to eight hours a day.

Jackie had many ups and downs in the 18 months of service, but only one hospitalization for a major medication change and titration. Her husband and son were supportive of her efforts, the psychiatrist was committed to providing this level of care, and the in-home agency was able to provide the staff and training to maintain her at this level of functioning. The cost savings to the managed care company was significant. She went into case management, where a separate pool of money was used to pay for this service. The patient was able to gain a sense of accomplishment for the work she did and was able to make significant life-style changes to maintain the therapeutic gains.

Case 4

John, a 27-year-old construction worker, received a traumatic brain injury after falling 50 feet off a building scaffold. After hospitalization and rehabilitation, John was diagnosed as being medically disabled and became eligible for worker's compensation benefits for life. The managed care company disability case manager had been working with John's case for over a year. John was able to live at home in a supervised situation, but he had violent outbursts, periods of depression, speech problems, and difficulty ambulating.

The case manager, the agency, the physician, and John's family collaborated on an individualized care plan to assist John in gaining a level of functional independence, allowing his mother to go back to work. A home health aide was with John 24 hours a day at first, assisting him with personal care, activities of daily living (ADLs), and behavior redirection. The psychiatric nurse worked on a behavior management plan and dealt with the anger and the violent outbursts. A speech therapist was utilized for the first two months, and a physical therapist assisted in range of motion and strengthening exercises.

Progress was slow, but, within three months, John's care was decreased to one RN visit a week and a home health aide 18 hours a day. A social worker was included at this time to provide social services and community assistance. John has now been on service for three years. The home health aide is still provided four hours a day for ADLs, structure, and community integration. His mother is the primary support for the family.

John is beginning to function independently and maintains appropriate behavior, which allows him into social integration programs. John has not been hospitalized for psychiatric services and is maintained on antipsychotics for behavior management control.

Case 5

Bertha, a 78-year-old widow diagnosed with depression, diabetes, and congestive heart failure, was admitted to in-home care after inpatient hospitalization for depression. Her family noticed that the patient was having trouble coping with independent living and showed increasing symptoms of depression after the death of her husband. Bertha was married for 59 years and had three children. Her two older boys lived at opposite ends of the United States, and her youngest daughter lived nearby. Susie, her daughter, had sole responsibility for taking care of Bertha. Susie's family had its own problems, and taking care of her mother in the daughter's home was not an option.

"Mom" was too well to go into a nursing home or into an assisted living situation. The hospital had a psychiatric partial hospital program (PHP) that Bertha could attend after in-patient hospitalization, but she would need assistance to attend the PHP. Home care was requested by the discharge planner. Bertha was able to attend PHP two days a week. A home health aide assisted Bertha in personal care and medication compliance five days a week for four weeks. Her daughter, Susie, helped on the weekends. The psychiatric nurse visited the patient two days a week for four weeks to provide skilled psychiatric nursing interventions.

Bertha benefited from the group processes in PHP, and the in-home psychiatric nurse helped her translate the information learned in group into practical considerations at home. In-home care provided Bertha with education, medication administration, and observation of her psychiatric symptoms. It also helped Bertha achieve a level of functional independence in which she could live on her own and manage her depressive symptoms with medication management and coping skills.

Bertha was discharged from the PHP after two months and from in-home care after four months. Her primary care physician continued to manage her medical and psychiatric needs. Coordinated, interdisciplinary psychiatric and medical care worked conjointly to provide this patient with a level of service that independently would not have helped Bertha progress as rapidly to recovery.

These scenarios are just a few examples of the many uses for behavioral in-home care. Behavioral in-home care is an integral piece of the ambulatory behavioral health continuum. It is not a linear position but the heart of a matrix of interconnecting and intersecting services that can be accessed at any time.

References

1. Bedgio, H. "Home Behavioral Health Management a Cost-Effective Alternative." *Home HealthCare Today* 2(1):28-9, 1996.

2. Hobbs, B. "Visiting Nurse care and Hospitalization Rates among the Seriously Mentally Ill." *Report for the VNA of Louisville, Ky.*, May 28, 1993.

3. Special Report. Psychiatric Home Care. *Home Health Business Report* 1(6):10-1, July 1994.

4. "Psychiatric Home Care. Niche Market Focus: Opportunities in Psychiatric Home Care." *Eli's Home Care Management Advisor* 2(5):3915-22, May 1995.

5. U.S. Department of Health and Human Services. Health Care Financing Administration Publication 11, Section 205.1.15, April 1996.

6. Smith, N. "Behavioral Health In-Home Care Standards and Guidelines: Implications and Impact." *Continuum: Developments in Ambulatory Mental Health Care* 3(3):199-204, July 1996

7. Friedman, R., and others. "Behavioral Medicine, Clinical Health Psychology, and Cost Offset." In *Medical Cost Offset.* Portola Valley, Calif.: Partnership for Behavioral Healthcare, Fall 1996, pp. 24-45.

Other Reading

Carson, V. "Bay Area Health Care Psychiatric Home Care Model." *Home Healthcare Nurse* 13(4):26-32, July 1995.

Grant, S. "Psychiatric Home Care and Managed Behavioral Health: Finding Common Ground." *Continuum: Developments in Ambulatory Mental Health Care* 3(3):193-7, Fall 1996.

Quinlan, J., and Ohlund, G. "Psychiatric Home Care: An Introduction." *Home Healthcare Nurse* 13(4):20-4, July 1995.

Nina M. Smith, RNC, MEd, is President, Integrated Behavioral Health Consultants, and Nina Klebanoff, PhD, RN, CS, LPC, is a Behavioral Health Consultant.

Chapter 21

Modular Model for the Operation of a Managed Behavioral Health Care Organization

by Stephen B. Connor, MD

There has been a rapid evolution of the managed behavioral health care movement over the past decade. Managed behavioral health care organizations (MBHCOs) that did not even exist in 1986 are now nationwide entities that cover millions of members. These rapidly growing companies must constantly reorganize and evolve to become ever more efficient and effective as they apply their respective visions of behavioral health care to newly covered populations. For example, much progress has occurred in the area of utilization review, where costly, intrusive, individual case management of large fee-for-service networks is gradually being replaced by more selective oversight of groups of practitioners in shared financial risk arrangements. However, operational and financial systems that are more easily measured have often noticeably improved without documented measurement of corresponding increases in the quality of clinical care that a member can expect to receive from a network practitioner.

The quality of the individual behavioral health practitioner is the foundation of any clinical system and should be the "touchstone" by which all visions and new models of behavioral health care are assessed.[1] While this may be the most difficult system component of all to measure, because it includes ethical and personal behavior as well as professional acumen, it may also be the most important. If a member walking into a network practitioner's office cannot be reasonably assured that he or she is dealing with someone who is significantly more likely to give high-quality treatment than if he or she had randomly selected a name from the telephone book, the managed behavioral health care movement will have failed—regardless of how much cost savings are achieved. If this vision of practitioner merit is to be attained, it must be pragmatically inculcated into very complex systems.

Many clinical models postulated for MBHCOs show excellent vision and provide a map for these systems to deliver ever higher quality of care. Operational difficulties often arise in the attempt to bring a vision to reality, however. The difficulties occur so often and to such an extent that the final model is likely to be much simpler and more pragmatic and perhaps serve the original vision in name only.[2] The power of a truly visionary model is paramount in improving complex systems. It is in the service of validating these models in a full and fair way that I believe attention should be given to the details through which they either become a functional advance in clinical care or may be compromised to the extent that they are of little added value for the patient.

If a vision is truly a goal to be aspired to, but rarely fully attained,[3] its implementation may be embarked upon in the service of true, continuous quality improvement. Whenever a new model is conceptualized, it is only a vision until it is translated into active practice. The operational compromises inherent in the translation from vision to working model determine whether value is ultimately derived for the patient. These compromises are by nature pragmatic and often fall short of the vision, sometimes to the point of undermining the model itself. They still may be chosen because they are expedient and allow the system to function under the auspices of the model. All too often, an MBHCO presents its system as a complete, functional model when close scrutiny of day-to-day operations would reveal many variances from the vision. While this practice may be commonly accepted in marketing an MBHCO to a customer, astute clinical observers cannot allow it to divert attention from the real issue of the quality of patient care delivered under the final working model.

On the other hand, the dilemma for the MBHCO is that it must be self-sustaining and therefore profitable if it is to survive. Even not-for-profit organizations must generate enough revenue to offset financial risk and grow. A model that is too operationally difficult or too costly to implement, no matter how clinically advanced it may be, is likely to be adopted only as a shell polished for outsiders to view.

The multimillion dollar sums of money involved in capitalizing and operating an MBHCO dictate that any vision for the optimum delivery of behavioral health care be supported by a reasonably pragmatic operating model or the company will be left at risk for significant financial consequences. It is axiomatic that the clinical community does not have the managerial background or interest to successfully operate a capital-intensive business; therefore any clinical model utilized must make sense to someone with business training or it will be constantly subject to modification according to the dictates of standard business practices.

In today's fast-changing behavioral health care climate, few companies believe they can see as much as five years into the future, and most business plans are really structured for three years or less. Because constructing a new model of behavioral health care for a large system could easily require 5 to 10 years to complete, the risks of change tend to limit the process. It would seem wise to consider possible operational difficulties before adopting a new clinical model. Some examples of questions that might be asked:

▌ Does the model require new information systems? A new computer system can be expected to take one to three years to design and up to several million dollars to develop, with no assurance that it will work as planned.

■ Does the model require changing and/or recontracting the provider network and therefore hiring additional provider operations staff?

■ Are there sufficient controls on excess utilization to safeguard the MBHCO's financial risk?

Not considering at length the answers to these and many other questions beforehand is likely to jeopardize the final working model's being reasonably close to the original vision.

This chapter will develop a clinical model in which many elements have already been tested and proved to be of value. The model will be separated into discrete modules that can be selected as needed to assist an MBHCO attempting partial reorganization that may ultimately be in the service of a greater vision but that initially needs smaller building blocks to reach that goal.

Structuring the Vision

The guiding vision for change within a complex clinical system is born of a recognizable philosophy; is translated into a mission statement; and finally becomes operationally effective only if all stakeholders in the system fully understand and agree with the philosophy. Hence, it is important to build a clinical system on a clearly enunciated treatment philosophy.

As an exercise in maintaining close adherence of an operational system to its theoretical model, the Modular Model will be introduced as if it were being operationalized through a standard business plan:

■ *Statement of the clinical philosophy.* For the majority of the membership of most MBHCOs, high-quality care can be attained cost-effectively by first selecting short-term treatment interventions when they are administered by a skilled practitioner (as a precondition to utilizing longer term treatment techniques).

■ *A business vision for an MBHCO advocating this philosophy.* The goal should be to be a positive force in the improvement of the mental health of the community by providing the highest quality behavioral health care in a cost-effective manner by utilizing accomplished providers trained in shorter term treatment techniques.

■ *The resulting mission statement.* Value is brought to customers[4] by building an administratively efficient, cost-effective organization through partnership with selected providers who focus on providing high-quality care with demonstrated outcomes to members.

■ *An implementation guide for day to day operations.* The best possible providers should be obtained and assisted in delivering high-quality care by providing them with a simple operating structure, minimal clinical intrusion, and all relevant treatment outcomes data.

■ A motto for all the MBHCO's staff: "Find and assist the best practitioners."

It is now possible to design a series of operating modules consistent with these guidelines. Six core modules constitute the clinical nexus to which additional system components, such as member services, practitioner credentialing, account management, etc., may be added:

▌ The System Description and Documentation

▌ The First Contact with the Member

—Intake Assessment

—Referral Triage

▌ Utilization Review

▌ Relationship with the Provider

—Network

—Financial Arrangements

▌ Integration with the Primary Care Physician/Medical Group

▌ Quality Improvement

—Treatment Outcome

—Patient Satisfaction

System Description and Documentation

The working description of the system should be a brief, clearly worded explanation of how the philosophy of treatment is operationalized. It should be readily available to all participants (members and providers) and stakeholders (customers and shareholders). It should be carefully thought through and described in sufficient detail so that all who read it can understand how it functions and see value in it. This documentation stands as both a template and a precedent, thereby setting up a condition of accountability for any future deviation from it by a provider or by the MBHCO itself. This discourages piecemeal changes that might temporarily serve the interests of the MBHCO, but disrupt the provider and thereby undermine trust in the partnership.

In a tightly constructed system one interrelated component relies on another. To repeat, it is important to build the system on a clearly enunciated clinical philosophy and document that the rules of the system are consistent with the philosophy. If the expressed clinical philosophy is for early, rapid evaluation and stabilization of the patient, followed by assessment for the most appropriate and effective treatment, with emphasis on short-term interventions, rules such as the following will operationalize the philosophy: "When a member is referred for treatment, the first priority will be crisis intervention to stabilize him or her, followed by a full historical evaluation and assessment for the appropriateness of brief, focused therapy. Consideration of authorization of longer term or maintenance treatments will only occur if the member is not thought to be suitable for short-term treatment."

Additional rules for long-term, maintenance, or medication treatment would be listed. To keep the system's construction logical, therapists who would function best within it would have demonstrated expertise in crisis intervention techniques and brief treatment strategies and would have strong knowledge of differential diagnosis. Also, treatment authorization schedules should be constructed according to recommendations from the literature on each treatment technique.

First Contact with the Member

In an MBHCO in which a primary care physician is not the gatekeeper for mental health benefits, first contact may occur through a published directory listing of contracted providers given to the member at enrollment. Most commonly, however, first contact occurs when the member calls the MBHCO and an eligibility check, a clinical assessment, and triage/referral may be completed. The importance of the first contact with the member should not be underestimated, because that first impression may linger in the member's mind. If it is a negative experience, it may have a chilling effect on not only patient satisfaction with the MBHCO, but also the success of the treatment intervention. Long hold times, confusing automated voices, or curt staff representatives can undermine even the best designed clinical system.

The advantages of the first call's going to the practitioner rather than to the MBHCO are thought to be both fiscal and in patient satisfaction. Redundant administrative procedures and staffing are minimized, with resulting cost savings for the provider. Also, a member typically prefers to tell his or her story only once and if possible directly to the treating practitioner. (This is not likely, however, if the designated provider is a group of practitioners.) For the MBHCO, the expense of obtaining utilization review, quality improvement, and treatment outcomes data may increase because of time lag and collection difficulties.

A major disadvantage of the first call's going to the practitioner/provider group is that checks and balances that should exist throughout the system are loosened at the very outset of treatment. Specific, immediate knowledge of both the individual member and the overall patient population is central not only to ensuring referral to the most appropriate level and intensity of care, but also to meaningful follow up. This immediacy is best achieved by the MBHCO's receiving the first call from the member. The checking of eligibility and benefits can thus be combined with a quick collection of demographic information and a brief assessment of presenting symptoms. Clinical trials have demonstrated that in a five to eight minute call, well-trained staff can elicit basic demographics, description of the chief complaint, and severity of presenting symptoms. With this information, triage may be made into a carefully reasoned referral schematic designed by the MBHCO.

MBHCO first contact with the member thus provides immediate awareness of eligibility problems or employer account issues as well as close oversight of the patient's care if deemed necessary. The provider, in turn, is relieved of the risk of treating ineligible patients, of hiring additional staff for intakes, of expensive telephone performance monitoring systems, and of sole responsibility for providing intake data for utilization review, quality improvement, and treatment outcome studies.

Improving the Intake Assessment

The intake assessment can be made significantly more succinct and objective by using straightforward numerical rating scales that can be administered effectively over the telephone. When the results are computerized and joined to a numeral triage schematic, a very efficient process results that can also greatly facilitate follow-up studies. An example of one such initial assessment that has been clinically tested would be recorded as: 32-2-5-4-0-0-1-1-(44). This would be read out as: A 32-year-old female (2) with onset of panic attacks within the past 30 days (5), mild depression (4), no evidence of mania (0) or thought disorder (0), minimal suicidal ideation or hostile intention (1), and experiencing moderate impairment of functioning in her daily life (1). This assessment series included six scales that measure the severity of the member's anxiety, depression, mania, thought disorder, suicidality, and anger/homocidality, each on a ten-point scale. The degree of any resulting behavioral dysfunction (44) was measured on a 100-point scale that incorporated work and social functioning as well as activities of daily living (figures 1-7, pages 290-295).

Figure 1. Chief Complaint—Anxiety

Interviewer: "Let me be sure that I understand you and how you would like us to help you...(paraphrase chief complaint back to patient).

"Now I'm going to ask you some questions that we ask everyone who calls us.

"On a scale of zero to 10, with zero being none at all and 10 being the worst that you have ever experienced in your life, how anxious have you been feeling over the past two weeks?"

0 1 2 3 4 5 6 7 8 9 10

If self-rated 4 or higher, review the anxiety symptoms checklist:

1   Excessive anxiety or worry (4 or above)
2   Feeling restless, "shaky"
3   Difficulty with shortness of breath, sweating, or lightheadedness
4   Feeling on edge, trouble sleeping, or difficulty concentrating
5   Sudden onset of severe anxiety attacks in past 30 days
6   Four or more panic attacks in past 30 days
7   Eight or more panic attacks in past 30 days
8   Fear of being in a crowd, standing in line, being on a bridge, going outside
     of house or neighborhood, driving on a freeway, being
     alone, or unable to get help in an emergency
9   Unusually strong obsessive thoughts or compulsive rituals
10   Continuing intense distress after an unusual traumatic event

ADD THE TOTAL NUMBER OF SYMPTOMS CHECKED ON ANSWER SHEET

Figure 2. Chief Complaint—Depression

Interviewer: "Next, I'm going to ask you about any feelings of depression that you have had for the past two weeks or longer.

"On a scale of zero to 10, with 10 being the worst depressive feelings that you have experienced in your life, where would you rate yourself over the past two weeks?"

0 1 2 3 4 5 6 7 8 9 10

If self-rated 4 or higher, review the depressive symptoms checklist:

1   Depressed mood (4 or above)
2   Irritable; inability to concentrate
3   Obsessive ruminations; brooding
4   Appetite loss or gain
5   No energy, fatigued every day, don't feel well
6   Insomnia or hypersomnia
7   Marked decrease in interest in daily life, experiences little pleasure in life
8   Extreme slowdown in all movements or constant restless movement, as in wringing hands while pacing back and forth
9   Sense of hopelessness and helplessness
10   Paranoia—delusions/hallucinations of death, disease, punishment, guilt, nihilism, etc.

ADD TOTAL NUMBER OF SYMPTOMS CHECKED

Figure 3. Chief Complaint—Mania

Interviewer: "Have you been feeling unusually "high" during the past few weeks?"

Yes _____   No _____

1   Elevated, expansive mood
2   Excessive irritability
3   Extra high energy
4   Major decreased need for sleep
5   Grandiosity
6   Pressured speech
7   Flight of ideas/racing thoughts
8   Increased activity socially, at work, in school, etc.
9   Poor judgment (spending sprees, risky business deals, gambling, etc.)
10   Paranoid delusions

ADD THE TOTAL NUMBER OF CHECKS

Figure 4. Chief Complaint—Thought Disorder

Interviewer: "Have you had unusual or strange thoughts or experiences in the past month?"

        Yes _____   No _____

If answered yes, complete the following checklist.

1   Auditory hallucinations
2   Delusions
3   Loose associations
4   Inappropriate mood/affect
5   Confused/disorganized
6   Bizarre presentation
7   Paranoia
8   Repeated long pauses before answering even simple questions
9   Inability to abstract concepts; literal, concrete understanding of simple questions
10   Jealousy

ADD THE TOTAL NUMBER OF CHECKS

Figure 5. Chief Complaint—Suicidal Index

Interviewer: "Have you had any thoughts of harming yourself?"

        Yes _____   No _____

Suicidal Index (for psychiatric not medical treatment)

0   Never thinks about suicide
1   Has wondered what it would be like a few times in his or her life, but would "never do it"
2   Occasional thoughts but would not do it because of family, friends, etc.
3   Recurrent thoughts but no plan or history of attempts
4   White, male, over 65, and lives alone
      Family history of suicide or knew someone well who committed suicide
5   Uncontrolled panic attacks, mixed manic state with irritable mood and depressive thoughts, or strong paranoid delusions of persecution
6   Feels hopeless, helpless, and just wants to "end the pain"
7   Suicide index and a history of self-harm or minor self-mutilation
8   Suicide index and a history of previous suicide attempts
9   Has a plan, the means to accomplish it, and a history of previous serious attempts
10   Sequence is already in motion (has already begun to ingest pills, has loaded gun, has written suicide note, etc.)

THIS SCALE IS SCORED ON THE HIGHEST NUMBER THAT FITS WHAT THE PATIENT SAYS—THIS IS NOT AN ADDICTION SCALE.

Figure 6. Chief Complaint—Anger/Homicidal Index

Interviewer: Have you been unusually angry or felt like harming someone?"

Yes _____   No _____

Anger Index (Homicide Index)

0   Appropriately assertive when angry and no history of significant violence

1   Hostile thoughts but no history of acting on them

2   Victim of childhood abuse—physical or sexual

3   Temper tantrums with angry words or throwing objects

4   History of self-harm—cutting or scratching wrists and arms, burning oneself, banging head against wall

5   Male—victim of violence or childhood history of firesetting, torturing animals, etc.

     Female—chemically dependent with history of violence against children or property

6   Has history of violence (fist fights, wife battering, beats children, injures animals, etc.)

7   Is paranoid and has previous training in weaponry, such as police officer, military, etc.

8   Is very angry and owns gun or other lethal weapons

     Is intoxicated on alcohol or other drugs

     Has a history of assault and battery, robbery, or possession of firearms

9   Makes a clear threat to kill or seriously harm someone

10   Intends to kill a specific person and has the weapons to do so

     Has a history of murder or attempted murder

THIS SCALE IS SCORED ON THE HIGHEST NUMBER THAT FITS WHAT THE PATIENT SAYS—THIS IS NOT AN ADDICTION SCALE.

Figure 7. Index of Dysfunction Scale

0 (low dysfunction, high functioning)   100 (high dysfunction, low functioning)

Have your symptoms affected your performance at work, school, or taking care of your home?

Yes _____ No _____ (If yes, complete sections A, B, and C)

How many total absentee or sick days have you had in the past 30 days? _____
Six months _____

A. Work or Job Performance

Please identify work or other duties:

Example_____   Example_____   Example_____

Please choose a percentage that most closely matches the degree of change in your overall job performance.

          0%   10%   20%   30%   40%   50%   60%   70%   80%   90%   100%

Explain please (match to list below)

0   Fully productive and able to do your best
1   Slight decrease in productivity
2   Mild decrease (difficulty concentrating etc.)
3   Moderate (difficulty completing assignments)
4   Significant loss of interest in duties
5   Feelings of shame about difficulties/nonperformance
6   Feeling very distressed about work
7   Interpersonal conflicts with supervisor or co-workers
8   Clearly inadequate productivity; job may be at risk
9   Intermittent absenteeism (1 to 3 days at a time repeated 2 or more times in previous 30 days
10 Unable to work/not going to school at all

B. Leisure and social activities or hobbies

Please give examples of 2 or 3 of your main interests.

Example_____   Example_____   Example_____

Figure 7. Index of Dysfunction Scale *(continued)*

Again, please choose a percentage that reflects any change in interest or time devoted to these interests because of your symptoms.

0%   10%   20%   30%   40%   50%   60%   70%   80%   90%   100%

Explain please (match to list below)

0   Enjoy them just as much as I ever have
1   Slight decrease in interest/time spent
2   Slight decrease in social activity
3   Mild decrease (occasionally skips activities)
4   Mild decrease (affecting relationships)
5   Moderate (regularly skips activities)
6   Moderate (social withdrawal—friends/family)
7   Great decrease (rarely does things anymore)
8   Major withdrawal (just wants to be alone)
9   Does very little except go to work
10 Has lost all interest in hobbies and doesn't want to be with people

C. Activities of Daily Living

Once again, please give a percentage matching any change in your performance of day-to-day chores, errands, and other nonwork, nonpleasure activities.

0%   10%   20%   30%   40%   50%   60%   70%   80%   90%   100%

0   Doing well, taking care of everything satisfactorily
1   Slight decrease
2   Mild decrease
3   Moderate
4   Major decrease
5   Not fully taking care of pets
6   Not properly caring for children
7   Not wearing clean or pressed clothes in public
8   Not eating well
9   Poor grooming or not bathing
10 Staying indoors or in bed all day

Scoring*

A _____ x 5 = _____
B _____ x 3 = _____
C _____ x 2 = _____

Example:

$5 \times 5 = 25$
$4 \times 3 = 12$
$3 \times 2 = \underline{6}$
43 (JDS Score)

* In this example, scoring is weighted toward job/work performance.

A further illustration uses an eight-point scale/spectrum. If a member were to complain of depression the following sequence would occur:

1. The Depressed Mood Checklist is quickly reviewed with the patient and marked off after a brief introduction as to the purpose of the questions.

   "Do you have: X Difficulty concentrating or obsessive brooding thoughts

                _ Significant loss or gain in appetite

               X Can't sleep through the night or sleep too much

               X Don't feel well; irritable or restless much of the time

               X No energy, always tired, have slowed down a lot

               X Don't enjoy "fun" things anymore

               X Feeling hopeless and helpless

               X Feel very guilty; think a lot about being punished, disease, or death.

   This member's score of 7 out of a possible 8 points would suggest a moderate to severe depression and indicate a need for further questioning before a referral is made in order to ascertain if there is any suicide risk, need for an immediate medication evaluation, or potential for hospitalization.

2. In the next illustration, a seven-point Suicidality Checklist is chosen:

   (1)____ Occasional thoughts but would never do it

   (2)____ Recurrent thoughts but no plan or history of attempts

   (3)____ Suicidal thoughts and a family history of suicide or knew a friend who committed suicide

   (4)____ Just wants to "end the pain" and has history of minor self mutilation

   (5)____ Severe panic attacks, apparent manic state with depressive thoughts, paranoia with persecution fears.

   (6) XXX Has a plan and is able and willing to carry it out within a short time frame and/or a history of previous suicide attempts.

   (7)____ Has begun the attempt—written a suicide note, loaded a gun, taken a pill, etc.

   With this scale, the number of the most severe response is the patient's rating, so that the patient in the example is rated as a 6 out of a possible 7 points.

3. The profile of all the member's intake scores would then be matched against the triage schematic in order to make an initial referral to the most appropriate level and intensity of care (figure 8, page 297).

Figure 8. Triage Grid—Mental Health

	Anxiety	Depression	Mania	Thought Disorder	Suicide Index	Anger
Emergency Services (hospital)	8	8	8	7	6	6
Urgent Care System (with 18 hours)	7	7	7	6	5	5
Medication Evaluation	6	6	6	5	4	4
Diagnostic Evaluation	5	5	5	4	3	3
Crisis Intervention/ Stabilization	4	4	3	3	2	2

These examples of rating scales are meant to be illustrative not definitive. The MBHCO's clinicians may elect longer or shorter ones or may tailor the wording to best accommodate their members and clinical emphasis. As long as the scales are numerical, brief, and to the point, they will be of significant value. Also, the scales are *not* meant to be diagnostic—diagnosis should occur only in the office of a practitioner—but they are very suggestive, and experience has demonstrated that a great deal of valuable clinical information can be learned within a few minutes at the first contact with the member. As older medical textbooks often stated, if you just take a minute to listen to the patient he or she will tell you what the diagnosis is.

Versions of scales for adults, adolescents, children, and other groups can be formulated in such a way that, once the age or other demographics are entered, the computer will automatically call up the appropriate scales. Criteria can be based on the Diagnostic and Statistical Manual of Mental Disorders (DSM-IV)[5] or on other basic texts and can be modified through clinical experience to more closely fit special characteristics of any member group. For example, the results of a chemical dependency intake scale might be summarized as 28-1-21-4-7-2-3. This is a 28-year-old male using heroin intravenously seven days a week, twice a day, for 3 years. Almost a hundred different drugs and medications were covered in this chemical dependency version, and it was periodically updated for changing "street" names for drugs and for new designer drugs (figure 9, pages 298 and 299).

Triage/Referral

All providers, be they practitioners or treatment facilities, can be coded for as many variables as desired, such as licensure, specialty training, level of care, location, unit cost of treatment, etc. A schematic may then be constructed that not only tracks the entire referral process, but also sets the criteria by which the intake staff will make a referral.

Figure 9. Chemical Dependency Rating Scale

I. Drug of Choice

#10   Alcohol*
     #11   liquor (whiskey, reinforced wine ETOH>20%)
     #12   beer, ale, malt liquor, etc.
     #13   wine (table wine ETOH<20%)
     #14   mixed usage

#20   Opiod*
     #21   heroin
     #22   methadone
     #23   morphine

#30   Cocaine
     #31   crack

#40   Amphetamine
     #41   methamphetamine
     #42   "ice"

#50   Cannabis (marijuana, THC)
     #52   hash, hashish

#60   Hallucinogen
     #61   LSD
     #62   mescaline (peyote)
     #63   mushrooms

#70   Phencyclidine (PCP)

Prescription Medications (unauthorized use/dosage)

#80   Analgesics (pain killers)*
     #81   codeine
     #82   demerol
     #83   dilaudid
     #84   Vicodan
     #85   Darvon
     #86   Fiorinal
     #89   Other _____

#90   Sedative, hypnotic, or anxiolytic*
     #91   benzodiazepine (Valium, Xanax, Ativan, Halcion, Serax, Tranxene, Librium, etc.)
     #92   barbiturate ("downers," "barbs," etc.)
     #93   meprobamate
     #94   methylquinone (Quualude—illegal in United States)

Figure 9. Chemical Dependency Rating Scale *(continued)*

II. Route of Administration

#1   inhaled into lungs/smoking

#2   under skin/intradermal/"chipping"

#3   by mouth (p.o.) or by nose/nasal

#4   intravenous/I.V.

III. Frequency

#1   2   3   4*   5*   6*   7*   days per week

IV. Severity

#1   one episode/administration/dosage per 24 hours

#2   two episodes per 24 hours

#3   three episodes per 24 hours*

#4   four or more episodes per 24 hours/continuously*

V. Number of years of usage (0, 1, 2, 3, 10, 20, etc.)

THE SCHEDULE OF THE PATIENT'S ACTUAL USAGE IS PROBABLY MORE RELIABLE THAN REPORTED DOSAGE FOR DETERMINING TRIAGE TO DETOXIFICATION OR OTHER LEVELS OF CARE.

* May require acute inpatient medical detoxification.

The use of rating scales allows for standardization of clinical intake profiles throughout the system. If triage options are also numbered, they become readily identifiable "tracks" of treatment that, when used in conjunction with provider numbers, create a straightforward yet highly detailed historical map. The map greatly facilitates study of the "flow" of the member's care and the effectiveness of the treatment system, whether from the perspective of an individual case or a much larger grouping. A partial triage schematic constructed for the clinical treatment philosophy previously presented and using only three of the symptom rating scales (8 point scales this time) is illustrative:

Anxiety	Depression	Suicidality	Treatment Track
1-4	1-4	1-2	#1, Crisis intervention/stabilization (Authorize five 50-minute sessions at 1 to 2 per week)
5	5	3-4	#2, Diagnostic consultation (One 90-minute session)
6	6	5	#3, Medication consultation with a psychiatrist (One 90-minute session)
7	7	6	#4, Urgent Care outpatient stabilization program (Eight 50-minute sessions daily, as needed)
8	8	7-8	#5, Emergency inpatient evaluation

In this illustration, a 54-year-old severely depressed man with a history of previous suicide attempts would be coded as: 54-1-3-8-7. This triage grid would direct the patient into hospitalization. The grid is not absolute and can always be overridden by designated clinicians, but full documentation of their rationale would first be required. When the process and results are computerized, this can be made into a foolproof system in which no authorization can be made without proper documentation. Two of the most elusive components of intake/triage—documentation and accountability—would then be fully controlled.

By further enumerating the providers and elements of treatment in sequence, this depressed man's ongoing treatment course could be coded as: #5-157-109-5X2-4X3-3X7::358-90844X8/109-90024X4. This would read out as: Admitted to hospital #157 under psychiatrist #109, on a locked unit for 2 days, stepped down to a general open unit for 3 days, then day treatment for 7 days, and discharged to outpatient status for 8 psychotherapy sessions with psychologist #358 and 4 concurrent medication checks with psychiatrist #109. This simple code could be rewritten hundreds of ways to fit the needs of any system large or small and to achieve improved standardization and outcome monitoring.

Utilization Review (UR)

Case management UR is certainly the most distasteful aspect of managed care for most practitioners, but less known is that it is just as onerous for the clinical staff of the MBHCO. Other than financial issues, nothing has more potential to improve the MBHCO/practitioner partnership than progress at this interface. Several components useful to improving UR have already been alluded to, for instance a system has been described so that the practitioner signifies agreement with it during the contracting process. This description would include guidelines for all utilization review, especially a clear legal/contractual definition of medical/psychological necessity. UR guidelines, if drawn directly from the clinical philosophy, should dictate a framework for a logical and consistent treatment authorization schedule.

For example, the clinical literature suggests that five sessions is a reasonable number for which to complete a typical crisis intervention. It follows that, on a standard case, which is commonly 80 percent or more of new referrals, the initial authorization should be for five sessions even if fewer are needed. Members with diagnostic dilemmas, medication issues, and other high-risk conditions identified at the intake assessment can be authorized for one 90- to 120-minute initial consultation followed by discussion with the case manager to formulate a full treatment plan within the member's benefit structure. This approach improves the partnership by informing the practitioner from the outset of what to expect of all referrals.

The first written documentation from the provider would serve as either completion of treatment report within the first five sessions or evaluation of the appropriateness of the patient for authorization of brief, focused psychotherapy. Rather than a complete case history, it would be a one- to two-page document addressing salient questions for brief therapy. Most major illness or chronic conditions would have been identified at intake and referred accordingly. The case manager would make authorizations on the basis of the brief treatment report and would only contact the practitioner if the report was unclear. Some period (4 to 8 months) or total number of sessions (10 to 25) should be established as a point beyond which further treatment is defined as being long-term.

In order to cross over into long-term treatment, it is appropriate to require a more comprehensive case history. If a practitioner has been treating a patient for up to six months and believes significant additional time is necessary, he or she should be able to present a well-grounded patient history, case formulation, and treatment plan to justify the request. In reviewing such requests, one is able to get a very strong sense of the quality of the practitioner and whether there is a reasonable chance the treatment will succeed. Good practitioners come through very clearly and tend to inspire confidence in the reviewer that the patient is in good hands.

This leads to an important question: should the system's better practitioners have to keep proving themselves over and over and face an endless series of written or oral reports? In a true partnership, the answer is no. Instead they should be able to rise to a point where minimal reporting is necessary, primarily for treatment outcome purposes. These high-quality practitioners should be rewarded further with an increased volume of referrals and possibly with higher fee schedules. This can all be accomplished through a ranking system that will be covered in the following section.

Relationship with the Provider

The Network

Achieving significant control over the provider network is the only way that a MBHCO can be sure to reach a goal of high-quality, cost-effective health care.[6] This degree of control need not always be onerous. It can also be the result of a joint effort on the part of providers and the MBHCO to establish a mutually enhancing partnership. If the MBHCO's system description and documentation are sufficiently clear, agreement with it can be made a precondition for contracting to join the network. A lack of agreement on both the necessity and the functions of managed care is certain to lead to adverse consequences for both the organization and the provider. To enhance the partnership, the MBHCO should be open to provider input and constructive criticism and also should include provider representatives on all essential clinical committees.

An effective working relationship with a provider must include not only clinical and administrative but also new financial interfaces. Sharing the work load in these areas of mutual interest facilitates development of rapport and ultimately of genuine trust. Eliciting provider input when developing clinical protocols and using practitioners as part-time case reviewers and as members of important committees such as peer review and quality improvement gives them an increased voice in the evolution of the system. Administratively, matching the MBHCO's operations as closely as possible to providers' needs reduces the costs of doing business. This can be as elementary as reducing time-consuming case management oversight through a provider ranking system or as futuristic as establishing full electronic connectivity that allows many things to occur via computer, including scheduling of referrals by the MBHCO, transmission of patient data, and even payment of provider billings.

Mechanism for Ranking Practitioners

Some practitioners are cooperative with managed care, and others are consistently in opposition. Some are more knowledgeable clinically or have particularly useful therapeutic skills, such as crisis intervention/brief treatment. Most managed care companies have lists of preferred providers who are chosen whenever possible. Usually there are only two subgroups and rarely more than three. This usually leaves a practitioner in an "in" or "out" status and often not knowing what can be done to change his or her status. As a result, there can be no true partnership of the MBHCO with the full network and special connection to only a small number of practitioners. Also, it is well known to MBHCOs that only 30 to 40 percent of a typical network is needed to adequately treat up to 80 to 85 percent of its membership. Few companies believe that they need the extensive networks that state regulators require and that marketing departments insist are necessary to be competitive. The costly process of credentialing and recredentialing is a detriment, as is the expense of doing utilization review/case management on thousands of practitioners, many of whom receive only a few patients a year and are therefore unfamiliar with the MBHCO's policies and procedures. This volume unnecessarily burdens quality improvement departments, which must investigate the many minor issues generated by these rarely used practitioners.

If the ultimate goal is to provide the best clinical care by employing the most knowledgeable and effective practitioners, it becomes necessary to develop some kind of rating or ranking system for practitioners. An MBHCO owes it to its members and customers to take an strong stand for recognition of quality by attempting to recruit outstanding practitioners and striving to terminate ones whose knowledge and effectiveness are inadequate. Doing the latter will overcome what has been perhaps the greatest failing of certification agencies, professional associations, and training programs in America to date and is perhaps the reason why a need arose for managed care.

If taken as a whole for all licensure, in all geographic areas, in all treatment settings, the task of developing a ranking system would be so daunting as to be beyond the resources of any one MBHCO. For any given system, however, a limited number of criteria can be clearly stated and practitioners who chose to join the system can be rated against the criteria. In an MBHCO, of necessity, the criteria must include utilization statistics and patient satisfaction as well as academic knowledge and treatment outcomes, but, as long as the criteria are published and applied fairly, an equitable system can arise that balances the interests of members, practitioners, and the MBHCO.

The two to three subgroups of practitioners usually found in MBHCOs' rankings are not sufficient to differentiate the many variables. Not only are there the preferred and the nonpreferred practitioners, but also entry level practitioners, those under quality improvement investigation, those awaiting legal clearance for termination, and those who are the most highly regarded of all. Some practitioners are known to be outstanding and to have performed repeatedly to all expectations. They have excellent technical knowledge and clinical performance, exemplary ethics, excellent reputations, and the ability to work effectively in a managed care system. It is a waste of time and valuable resources to use customary management techniques for such practitioners. Worse, it violates the creed of cost-effectiveness. These practitioners should be honored with top ratings and rewarded with increased referrals and decreased paperwork. They become the standard, the "touchstone," by which other practitioners are measured. While they may initially make up only 5 to15 percent of a typical network, that percentage can grow if nurtured sufficiently by the MBHCO, which should keep in mind that only 30-40 percent of high-quality network practitioners are needed to treat the majority of the membership.

Experience suggests that covering all possibilities from termination to top ranking requires five to eight levels. This is well within the limits of what practitioners and staff can relate to, particularly if a numbering system is used. Their positions on the practitioner ranking spectrum and how they can raise them is of greatest interest to practitioners and a strong reinforcer of knowing the quality tenets of the system.

The above considerations are most applicable to either working with an already established network or to shifting later through a large, new network rapidly constructed to meet an imminent demand, be it driven by regulations or sales. Occasionally the question arises: Is it more advantageous to plan and build a network from the ground up, if the opportunity exists, or to use the more commonly sought mail order networks (developed through mail or telephone solicitation)? Again, experience strongly suggests the former. Intensive early efforts and start-up costs are more than made up for over time by decreased case management costs, provider maintenance issues, and utilization expense, as well as patient satisfaction and treatment outcomes. An MBHCO must understand this longer term payback in order to fund the extra costs of beginning with a higher quality network.

To construct the inner core of a superior network, personal interviews are still the best way to identify special people. The only way to really experience and know a "touchstone" is to touch it! In two recent successful developments of new regions, a simple strategy was successful. Provider relations personnel contacted local hospitals, university clinics, and a sample of well-established area practitioners and asked for the names of the most highly regarded behavioral health practitioners. These lists were matched against board certification and other indicators of achievement. If a name was on three or more lists, an invitation to an interview was extended. MBHCO staff members with equivalent licensure conducted the interviews. The subject matter covered dealt with understanding of managed care and demonstration of clinical expertise. Approximately 70 percent of the interviewees were invited to join the network. The selected practitioners were asked who they referred to or who took care of their patients when they were on vacation, etc., and a secondary list was constructed for additional interviews to fill out the network. This approach obviously works best in encapsulated areas with high population density. Even in rural areas, however, there are always small centers of relative population density and the rule of 40 percent of practitioners treating up to 85 percent of the population still usually holds true.

Whenever mail-order type networks are unavoidable because of time limitations or cost controls, their quality can be enhanced by selective interviewing as well as by improvements in the application form. In addition to asking about managed care experience and requesting documentation of training in specialty interests, it is critically important to inquire as to the practitioner's clinical philosophy of treatment: How would the practitioner manage certain types of clinical problems? What is his or her attitude on working with managed care? Not much space is needed; one or two pages are usually more than enough. If the effort is too much trouble for the practitioner and only two lines or even a blank space is returned, the analysis is apparent. It is just a question of how much more evidence the MBHCO needs of the likely unsuitability of the practitioner for its network.

Groups as Providers

There is a strong movement toward networks of practitioner groups in managed behavioral health care because of the possible administrative cost savings. There is much less improvement possible in reduction of clinical utilization. Groups are easier to contract with and make capitation possible. There are also good clinical reasons to lean toward groups, one of the biggest being availability during off hours. It is easy to insert a clause in a contract with a group requiring 24-hour, 7-day coverage.

Smaller groups orchestrated by only two or three owners/partners seem to be especially good in managed care. The less owners are invested in day-to-day operations, the more likely it is the group will be a problem.

Hospitals as Providers

The role of psychiatric hospitals has changed markedly over the past decade as a direct result of the managed care movement. Inpatient stays have been sharply reduced, and crisis stabilization on a brief stay unit is now the norm. Day treatment and intensive outpatient treatment programs contribute an increasing proportion of a psychiatric hospital's revenues, and there are fewer specialized inpatient units. It may be appropriate to look to the next stage of evolution.

Acute stabilization units should now be the core around which all general psychiatric hospitals are constructed. This should also include adolescent and geropsychiatric treatment. Referral to a more specialized unit should be available for the subgroup of patients who are diagnostic dilemmas or who cannot be stabilized in 7 to 14 days. To borrow from the medical/surgical concept, centers of excellence need to be developed in order to efficiently diagnose and initiate treatment for these patients before returning them to the referring practitioner for continuing treatment. A center of psychiatric excellence would have a staff of accomplished specialists who, by virtue of the volume of patients assessed, would be more efficient in working through a full differential diagnosis and either instituting optimum treatment themselves or making consulting recommendations. This approach is perhaps most easily seen to be of value in the areas of eating disorders, dementias, and the use of electroconvulsive shock treatment. Obviously, high volume is conducive not only to having more experienced practitioners of specialty care, but also to contracting arrangements that are more cost-effective in treating difficult disorders. Centers of excellence can be located so that they serve a designated geographic area, which would allow for building rapport with referring practitioners and reasonable travel time for family members.

The Information System
The need for extensive systemwide information with which to rate all types of providers as well as to enhance the partnership by instant communication helps to define important design components of the information system:

■ As simple and inexpensive for the provider as possible in order to advance toward full electronic connectivity.

■ To have a central data bank where all pertinent information on providers from throughout the system is gathered to facilitate evaluations for the rating process. Ideally, anyone in the system could feed into the data bank, but only a limited number of authorized clinical personnel could access and analyze the information.

Financial Arrangements
Jointly sharing the financial risk of negative consequences can be very effective in developing a partnership. Early MBHCOs acquired large networks of individual practitioners contracted with on a fee-for-service basis. This arrangement left all of the financial risk for adverse utilization, controlling operations costs, and the uncertainties of sales and marketing on the MBHCO. Hedging against these risks necessitated that the MBHCO not only accrue large cash reserves, but also develop a complex infrastructure of forecasting analysts and clinical case managers replete with burdensome UR protocols. In an attempt to trim administrative expenses, many MBHCOs are beginning to shift to capitation contracts that reduce the need for reinsurance and other operational expenses and replace extensive case management oversight with a greater emphasis on quality improvement and utilization review.

A major danger to quality of clinical care under capitation, however, lies in the possibility of transferring too much of the risk for excess utilization to the provider. Increased utilization is due most often to a greater than expected number of members accessing benefits and/or an increase in the average intensity of treatment provided per patient. In a capitated contract, this degree of risk dictates that a provider must be a large, financially sophisticated multispecialty group or hospital-financed IPA, thereby excluding not only individual providers but also small groups without significant financial reserves. The MBHCO is then further limited by becoming dependent on one-sided, exclusive contracts with these groups, which often cover a wide catchment area. Alternative referrals are therefore not available in the area, and, if quality or other contractual obligations are not met by the provider, locating a new group of sufficient size, redirecting patient flow, and changing member materials is an expensive and time-consuming process. As a result the MBHCO/provider "wedding" tends to be insufficiently affected by quality improvement protocols, which are frequently too spread out over time to provide for a satisfactory response to recent patient care issues. An additional consideration for any MBHCO considering shifting from fee for service to capitation is that the many operational systems changes required are extensive and expensive and may take two to three years or longer to complete.

Consideration, therefore, should be given to case rate contracting, an effective alternative midway between the risks of fee for service and capitation. A case rate is payment of a predetermined fee for a behavioral health episode of treatment as defined by either a set period or a set number of sessions. A case rate splits utilization risk by keeping the risk of increased member access with the MBHCO while transferring the risk of increased frequency or length of treatment to the provider.

Case rates might be especially useful to a small- to mid-sized MBHCO which may not have the critical mass to capitate effectively. They may also have value for a larger company in the process of changing from a fee-for-service system to capitation, but wanting to spread the expense over several years and still see some results in each fiscal year. Even for companies that are ready and willing to fully capitate, there may be advantages in case rates worth considering:

- *Shares the financial risk.* The MBHCO is better able to predict the risk of higher than expected access by a member group and reserve funds to cover it. This relieves small provider groups of their worst fear—large numbers of acutely disturbed patients materializing all at once. They are paid a full case rate for each patient referred. On the other hand, it is the provider with first-hand knowledge of the patient who is best suited to determine the course and response to treatment. The MBHCO no longer has to intrude on the patient-practitioner relationship to closely monitor every aspect of treatment. Instead, it can step back and gather utilization information in the service of quality improvement.

- *Allows smaller, more personalized groups.* Practitioners know each other by first name and are aware of each other's clinical strengths and weaknesses. A smaller group can meet on a frequent basis to present and discuss treatment plans, with an MBHCO clinical liaison representative in regular attendance. A rule of thumb is that a group can function in this manner if it has between 8 and 20 practitioners.

- *Avoids exclusivity.* Using smaller groups allows for reasonable competition within sufficiently populated catchment areas. If a group fails to meet quality of care standards or patient satisfaction goals, effective shaping of future performance can occur by referring subsequent patients to a nearby group without violating contractual agreements or losing capitation monies. This avoids the all or none contract cancellation necessary with capitation and is effected more rapidly than quality improvement studies, which may take months to determine if improvement has occurred.

- *Is simple.* The rule of simplicity should be the guide in determining the fee schedule for and administration of a case rate. Done appropriately, the case rate method may have significant advantages over both fee for service and capitation. "Simplicity wins" both in lower costs and ease of operation each of which further enhances the relationship between the provider and the MBHCO.[7] A case rate can be made complicated by multiple exclusions, withholds, divided payment schedules, and additional sessions requiring new authorizations, or it may be simplified by large sample cost averaging, early fee payment to improve provider cash flow, and a set treatment episode period, usually 6 to 18 months.

- *Reduces recidivism.* Recidivism is perhaps the most troublesome variable in all three types of payment systems. In fee for service, recidivism is conducive to provider gain, while in capitation it reduces provider profit. In either case, it remains a significant quality concern for the MBHCO. In a case rate, the longer the period of treatment agreed upon, the more the onus falls on the provider to minimize recidivism through sufficient and adequate treatment. One of the few instances in which it may be appropriate for the MBHCO to add a rider to a case rate is when a chronic, relapsing patient who would otherwise accrue multiple hospitalizations is stabilized by frequent regular outpatient visits and the group receives additional fees to provide those services.

Psychiatric Hospitalization

Case rates are also applied to inpatient stays, usually for stays of 30 days or less with riders for prolonged stays or recidivism. While in theory this reduces the cost to the MBHCO for the most expensive type of intensive case management, in practice it still requires frequent contract interpretations and case discussions, particularly regarding premature discharges. As a result, a next stage has evolved—the refund per diem contract. This is usually offered by hospital chains, as it is based on volume. If a "trigger" number of referrals is met and the average length of stay (ALOS) of all the MBHCO's referrals exceeds an agreed upon target (usually in the range of 7 to 10 days), the hospital will refund all monies previously paid for any inpatient days over the target. For example, the targets may be 100 referrals per quarter with a target LOS of 8.0 days at $550.00 per diem. If there are 101 referrals and the LOS is 8.5, 101 X 0.5 X $550 = $27,775.00 is returned to the MBHCO. As a sign of intense competitive pressures among psychiatric hospitals, volume triggers are now often dropped, even as the per diems are lowered. For the MBHCO, the maximum cost of the average episode of inpatient treatment is set and UR labor costs are greatly reduced, leaving only the number of inpatient accesses as the MBHCO's financial risk. Concerns about early discharge, recidivism, quick transition to outpatient treatment, and the hospital's refusal of highly problematic patients often persist beyond what quality improvement programs alone can address, thus still requiring more utilization management than originally predicted.

Chemical Dependency Treatment

Case rates are well suited to chemical dependency (CD) treatment, in that an effective CD program should have not only multiple levels of inpatient, residential, and outpatient care, but also an extended support period to minimize relapse. A case rate allows the CD program to finance alternative treatment measures, such as support groups, self-help networks, and sober living houses, that are not usually authorized by third-party payers. The contracted episode of case rate treatment should be a minimum of at least one year.

Integration with the Primary Care Physician

Much continuing discussion is occurring among MBHCOs, HMOs, purchasers (employers), and members as to which of two models is the best for overall quality of care within the medical/psychiatric interface. The first, known as the carve-in or fully integrated model, has the primary care physician (PCP) as the gatekeeper for all mental health referrals. Behavioral health providers are part of the same HMO staff, sometimes even located in house. In the second model, the carve-out, access to benefits is through an 800 number and completely independent of the primary care gatekeeper. Referral is to a network practitioner who is unaffiliated with the primary medical group. If there is to be communication between the PCP and the network practitioner, it usually occurs on their own initiative. The arguments around each model center on whether there is sufficient communication between all providers of care to allow for full integration of all treatment modalities.

Although it is hard to dispute that full integration is most likely to result in effective patient care, the real driver in the issue appears most often to be economic, as determined by which way the payment monies will flow. Certainly there are outstanding examples of fully integrated treatment programs, but it is not hard to see that they are the exception rather than the rule. Much effort by knowledgeable, dedicated people is required to instigate and maintain fully integrated programs. It often seems as if the law of entropy weighs in after a few months or years, when the founders move on and the program gradually returns to baseline, where some medical/surgical caregivers are very busy and not particularly interested in the vagaries of behavioral health care. Even with financial incentives and improved education, there will always be some medical/surgical physicians and staff who are unable or unwilling to recognize and respond appropriately to behavioral health issues. It would not seem to be fair to subject emotionally troubled patients to the luck of the draw as to the type of training and the level of interest in psychology that they experience when they present for treatment.

A reasonable solution could be to provide useful elements from both models in the delivery system. Patients who have psychophysiolgical illness and those who have good rapport with their PCPs could initiate behavioral health treatment upon the PCP's referral, while patients who hardly know their PCPs or who have symptoms that they do not feel comfortable discussing with their PCPs could chose to access their benefits through the MBHCO 800 number. For this latter group of patients, the established policy should be for only medically necessary levels of feedback to PCPs—i.e., all medications prescribed, any significant diagnoses, and the projected lengths of treatment. The patient should be made fully aware of and understand the need for this policy. If the patient objects to any communication with the PCP, the behavioral health provider must carefully consider his or her explanation but should have the option of terminating treatment if the request is not thought to be in the patient's best interests. An example might be a chemically dependent patient with concurrent medical illness who does not want the PCP to know about his or her drug use.

This dual entry approach would improve total access to behavioral health care by allowing the patient to chose a comfortable entry point for the full spectrum of his or her possible needs, from adjustment disorders and couples therapy to chemical dependency and major psychosis. It is likely mental health will always be the less favored stepchild of U.S. medicine. In recognition of this, a delivery system must allow caregivers who give high priority to mental health to be reasonably available to members, without needing clearance by a nonmental health physician.

An additional advantage of a dual access model could be establishing standardized treatment protocols across the entire system. At the present time, if a child with a hyperactivity syndrome presents to a PCP, he or she is most likely to be referred to a pediatrician if one is on staff, or to be medicated by the PCP if a pediatrician is not available. However, if the child's mother were to access care through the MBHCO 800 number, the child would probably be evaluated by a psychologist with child training and, if medication is indicated, it would be prescribed after further referral to a child psychiatrist. This degree of variability in evaluation and treatment approach does not seem justified and would seem to preclude effective quality assurance/quality improvement with traceable treatment outcomes. A mutually agreed upon treatment protocol could be of great value to all interested parties and a prelude to more cost-effective care in this and other areas where parallel tracks of treatment occur (dementias, psychophysiological illness, anxiety and depressive disorders, etc.).

Quality Improvement

The quality improvement modular component is critical to the MBHCO for both clinical and financial reasons. By continually asking what is really going on in the clinical system, careful scrutiny can occur without the coloring of what the staff thinks is supposed to be happening or what the marketing arm of the MBHCO claims is happening. Assessing what is really going on in the system is different from what the individual provider or case manager is aware of or from what is seen through solely business/management approaches. It should be the starting point for a quality improvement process. An individual provider typically believes that he or she is providing effective treatment and always has anecdotal evidence to prove it, while unsuccessful interventions are usually explained in terms of circumstances outside of treatment. Rarely does a provider have any idea as to whether his or her average treatment is longer or shorter than the norm or how his or her success rate compares to those of peers. The MBHCO, on the other hand, may have normative statistics developed for management or underwriting needs but little understanding of what the data mean in terms of clinical practices.

By asking straightforward questions (What happens to an anxious 35-year-old female who comes into our system? Who treats her and with what licensure? How long does her treatment take and to what degree is it successful? What about recidivism?), we can begin to discover what is really happening. Without answers to these kinds of questions, the more simplistic business data may rule the day, which lends itself to focusing on known costs over unknown quality. For instance, if all that is known about anxiety disorders in a particular MBHCO is that they constitute 23 percent of the intake diagnoses; that the average length of treatment is 8.4 outpatient visits, with providers of all licensure lumped into the same pool; and that most patients sampled in telephonic follow up were satisfied to very satisfied with their treatment, internal pressures would always have the MBHCO leaning toward using the lowest cost licensure and using providers within that licensure whose average length of treatment is below the sample's norm. Questions of severity of illness and valid outcome notwithstanding, such a decision could have a significant impact on improving the margin of profit for a company.

Without quality data, there will be a tendency for fiscal issues to rule. If up to 85 percent of an MBHCO's patient population completes treatment in 12 visits or less, with a constant 20 percent recidivism rate within one year and 86 percent patient satisfaction on follow up, why not shift the financial factors as much as possible to achieve maximal cost control. Business systems are routinely analyzed internally as if they are unique. While a profitable system can tolerate many internal cost variations, an unprofitable system is analyzed and usually benchmarked against the unit costs of competitor companies. Regardless of what is known about the outside world, management of a business system will lean toward maximum conservatism on costs unless good quality indicators are available as a counterbalance.

On the other side, there is perhaps too great a tendency among clinicians to devalue data collected for financial management purposes as being too general and nonclinical. The data may have great value in understanding treatment outcomes within the system if they are interpreted properly. When utilization data confirm a null hypothesis (i.e., for this individual business, all patient, provider and treatment tracks are essentially the same in statistical outcome[8]), it is reasonable for the MBHCO to ask clinical managers to explain the results; if they cannot, change directed at financial variables is likely to occur irrespective of the effect on quality of care.

Treatment Outcome

Although knowledge obtained from published scientific research should always be the standard for decision making, that knowledge must be integrated thoughtfully into any complex, dynamic system in order for it to be used effectively. For example, in a research study of treatment of anxiety disorders, only those patients who complete the prescribed course of treatment are included in the outcome. While the reason for this may be self-evident, it is easy to forget that the majority of persons who present with anxiety, depression, stress, etc. do not complete a research-validated course of treatment. Clinicians charged with maintaining the mental health of a large member population and with minimizing recidivism must look beyond research to locate factors that influence their outcomes.

To illustrate, suppose that up to 50 percent of one sample of over 20,000 patients terminated their treatment within the first five visits. Clearly, these were not completed treatments unless the patients were in no more than mild crises. And if the patient satisfaction group sampled in follow up listed themselves as largely satisfied with the treatment given, how is this to be interpreted? Perhaps practitioners failed to establish sufficient rapport early in treatment? Was 5 to 10 miles too far to drive? Was the copayment too high? Are most crises resolved within a few weeks even without treatment? Does the satisfaction survey reflect what it is supposed to?[9] This type of questioning may be the starting point for effective quality improvement studies. Without sufficient answers derived from the specific system, management will most likely fall back on a null hypothesis in which cost is the only clearly quantifiable variable.

Outcome studies for an MBHCO may include small, discretely chosen cohorts of patients or larger general surveys of hundreds to thousands of patients. The value of detailed study of a selected group of patients with limited variables is its clarity and closeness to published research. In a managed care setting, this usually involves having a practitioner fill out pre- and post-treatment rating scales that are then correlated by the research department of the MBHCO. A difficulty with this approach in a large nonacademic system is the great number of variables, which can often compromise the results, especially when the attempt is to compare one provider or group to another. For instance, among the variables for a patient who receives a diagnosis of major depression are patient demographics, symptom profile, and case history; provider demographics, such as licensure, theoretical orientation, experience, and specialty training; use of medication; type of therapy (individual, couples, group, etc.); accuracy of the diagnosis; any concurrent diagnoses, socioeconomic factors, etc.

There is also the daunting problem of collecting all of the data and analyzing them in a manner timely enough to influence patient care. This is especially difficult when employer, hospital, and provider contracts are renewed every one to three years and when, once a year during open enrollment, members have the option of changing their managed care companies. Even though all of these factors greatly increase the difficulty in determining treatment outcomes, the business functions of the MBHCO (budgetary management, financial planning, risk management, etc.) are still completed and analyzed, not only because they are given priority, but also because they are not held to a research standard of accuracy. (Witness the often-heard business cliché: In business, decisions are made on the basis of 80 percent of the information necessary to make the decision).

Given this situation, if the clinical outcomes information is tied as closely as possible to financial and management indicators that are reliably gathered on the entire membership, a constant stream of data will be also be available for clinical analysis.[10] For instance, when the member first makes contact with the MBHCO, demographic information is requested in order to determine benefit eligibility. That information can also be coded as part of a treatment outcome profile. Next, the basic clinical information, the severity of the presenting symptoms, and the degree of resulting behavioral dysfunction, all of which are necessary for effective triage, can also be coded as the initial statistical profile of the patient. By quantifying these factors and numbering the various treatment tracks available (including level of care, classification of practitioner, etc.), a large number of data points are possible with which to begin outcome studies. Follow up of a selected patient sample can be accomplished over the telephone at a later date by the same intake personnel, using the same format. Any additional information supplied by the provider and the case management/utilization review process can be numerically coded and readily added to the study.

Patient Satisfaction

To complete the illustration of the numerical standardization approach, at a 12-month follow up from the point of initial intake, the record of the 34-year-old female with anxiety presented earlier would now include—in addition to her demographics, intake assessment, triage, and treatment data—the scores of the follow-up severity of symptom and dysfunction index scales. These would be cross-sectional snapshots taken at any time intervals required by the MBHCO and totally independently of any information provided by her treating practitioners. Her follow up might read 2-1-0-0-0-1-(12), demonstrating significant improvement in her presenting symptoms of anxiety (80 percent) and depression (75 percent) and a 73 percent improvement in her sense of her own functioning and well-being. Her entire treatment course might be summarized in this manner:

Presentation at Intake: 32-2-5-4-0-0-1-1-(44)
          at one year: 33-2-5-1-0-0-0-1-(12)

Treatment Track #1: Practitioner #358/90844X5
           #3: Physician #109/90864X8 (may also include any case manager ratings, diagnosis codes, medications, dosages, etc.)

By choosing variables thought to be most applicable to the MBHCO's specific membership and the design of its clinical system, standardizing those variables in ways easily understood by all participants in the system, and by tying the variables to business functions, the stage can be set for a first generation of relevant outcome studies that can evolve into ever more cogent quality improvement successors.

In summary, the increasing size and scope of behavioral health managed care organizations has resulted in a tendency to treat delivery of mental health care as more of a commodity to be priced by the "lot" rather than the valued "piece work" of trained craftsmen. This chapter advocates an ongoing process of selecting the most qualified practitioners and compensating them on the basis of shared risk for individual episodes of care.

In support of this model, numerical rating scales, triage schematics, and practitioner ranking systems have been presented, along with concepts of treatment outcomes and utilization management. All are closely tied to business and financial indicators to ensure that the final operational model continues to adhere closely to the original vision. This vision can be stated simply as: Putting the best possible practitioner in front of the member is the single most important thing that an MBHCO can do to ensure cost-effective, high-quality behavioral health care.

References and Footnotes

1. Matthew Arnold, *Poems,* 1853 Edition. The great English critic and poet writes on how to discern objective quality amid the literary output of the ages.

2. For a common example of such a shortfall, consider the MBHCO goal of making an optimum match of the member's needs with the best and most appropriate practitioner. This matching is usually considered to be a major advantage over unmanaged delivery of care systems. Up to several hundred practitioners may be maintained in a geographic area to ensure that a member will be within 10-15 miles or a 20-minute drive of his or her practitioner. The practitioners selected would include a mix of gender, race, licensure, and specialty interests so that a full spectrum of behavioral health providers and services is available to the membership. In the service of this goal, practitioners are asked to fill out questionnaires documenting their areas of interest and expertise. Intake procedures are then developed to match members' clinical needs and special requests to the clinical profiles of the practitioners. The MBHCO's marketing arm invariably touts this "best fit" process as a major selling point that enhances the value of the product to members.

Although the concept is laudable, in the dozen or so MBHCOs that I have had the opportunity to examine, none have come close to effectively operationalizing it. I have seen questionnaires listing as many as 50 areas of interest/expertise, but I have not seen any that require documentation of training or specialty experience. In fact, seldom is there ever verification of a practitioner's background beyond degree and licensure. The information collected from the questionnaires also undergoes compromise in the intake process. Computer screen fields are usually set up to list only 3 to 5 areas of practitioner specialty. A data entry person has to chose 3 to 5 interests from the questionnaire. Defenders of this process within an MBHCO often counter that intake personnel choose the best match available at the time, but too often the determining factors are whoever is closest and has available time.

3. Groves, M. "Today a Company Needs More than a Mission; It Needs Some Vision, Too." *Los Angeles Times*, Business Section, Dec. 26, 1995.

4. It may be useful to include in either system documentation or the mission statement the MBHCO's position on the employer versus employee issue. It is common for most case managers, intake personnel, and other clinical line staff to consider the employee-member as the customer, while management, sales and marketing, and stockholders may see the employer as the customer. This dichotomy is seldom satisfactorily dealt with, leaving split loyalties between the clinical and operations divisions of the company. Rather than submerge the issue by glibly stating that both are equally important, perhaps it would be better to let clinicians advocate for employee-members while account managers and salespeople lobby for the employer purchaser—and delegate final decisions to senior management as long as strong clinical representation is always included.

5. *Diagnostic and Statistical Manual of Mental Disorders,* Fourth Edition. Washington, D.C.: American Psychiatric Association, 1994.

6. Richard Chung, R., MD, Senior Vice President and Chief Medical Officer, Medco Behavioral Healthcare, Inc., St. Louis, Mo., personal communication, Feb. 1996.

7. Rommel, G., and others. *Simplicity Wins, How Germany's Mid-Sized Industrial Companies Succeed.* Boston, Mass.: Harvard Business School Press, 1995.

8. Hassad, T. *Understanding Biostatistics.* St. Louis, Mo.: Mosby-Yearbook, Inc., 1991, p. 61.

9. Nguyen, T., and others. "Assessment of Patient Satisfaction: Development and Refinement of a Service Evaluation Questionnaire." *Evaluation and Program Planning* 6(3-4):299-313, 1983.

10. The cohort may be as small as the smallest employer/customer or as large as the entire United States, but whether it is 50, 500,000 or 5 million, business systems will always collect data adequate to keep financial accounts accurate.

Stephen B. Connor, MD, is Director of Behavioral Medicine, St. Luke's Medical Center, San Francisco, California, and a management consultant in managed behavioral health care.

Section VI

Quality and Outcomes

Chapter 22

Total Quality Management and Related Techniques in the Delivery of Behavioral Health Care Services

by Sarath Gunatilake, MD, DrPH, and F. Theodore Helmer, PhD

TQM Terminology and Related Concepts

The field of quality assessment and improvement(QA&I) has undergone so many twists and turns over the past couple of years that it has become difficult for even the most experienced health care managers to fully understand the relationships among various concepts and issues related to it. Concepts such as total quality management, quality management at the systems level, quality assessment, quality assurance, continuous quality improvement, performance assessment, benchmarking, clinical practice guidelines, critical paths, decision analysis, and patient care outcomes have become buzz words. However, few understand the exact meaning of and the relationships among these concepts and how they can be used to enhance patient care while reducing costs. Application of these techniques and concepts is abundant in the area of physical health; their application in mental and behavioral health is still in a relatively rudimentary state.

The purpose of this chapter is to provide a framework for understanding some of the concepts mentioned above and to discuss the application of total quality management(TQM) and continuous quality improvement (CQI) in health care settings, with examples from behavioral health situations wherever they are available.

Process versus Outcome

The objective of health care is to achieve good or improved outcomes for patients. However, other qualifiers may be added to this objective, depending on the nature of the health care organization and the nature of the services. For example, conforming to specified standards, containing costs, and achieving a reasonable profit margin may all be legitimate pursuits, depending on the situation and the organization involved. Health care processes are a series of linked steps, often (but not necessarily) sequential and designed to cause good or improved outcomes for patients. Quality measurement, in whatever form, is intended to assess the degree to which the processes of care provided to a single patient or a patient population achieved good outcomes (outcome measurement) or are regarded as best practice and are known to be associated with good outcomes (process measurement).

Dozens of models have been put forward to depict the ways in which health care organizations measure patient care outcomes. Each of these models has its advantages and disadvantages; some emphasize certain elements of the organization over others and even provide a rationale for doing so. The common denominator of most of these organizational models is that they take into account certain inputs that are transformed through a process of care to produce the desired outcomes for a single patient or a group of patients. This basic organizational system can be broken down further to its component subsystems (information, medical records, laboratory, etc.). The main organizational system and its subsystems have their own structures, functional processes, and outputs. The outputs of one subsystem may serve as inputs to another subsystem and its functional processes. All these functional processes, when integrated and coordinated in a efficient manner, are expected to result in integrative patient care outcomes. For example, the outputs of the laboratory subsystem serve as important inputs to the patient care subsystem, which, in turn, depend on inputs from a number of other subsystems, such as dietary, educational, etc. Figure 1, below, illustrates these interrelations among inputs, organization processes, and patient care outcomes. This model represents a synthesis of the structure-process-outcome model of Donabedian[1] and the people-structure-process-outcome model of Beer.[2] It also takes into account the functional processes that the Joint Commission on Accreditation of Healthcare Organizations (JCAHO) uses in assessing the performance of health care organizations. The processes and the outcomes specified in this model have been used repeatedly by the authors in conducting performance assessments in psychiatric hospitals.

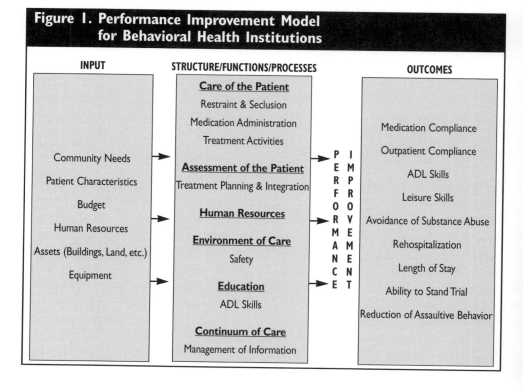

Figure 1. Performance Improvement Model for Behavioral Health Institutions

Table 1. Mental Health Outcome Measures	
■ Living situation	■ Involvement with legal system
■ Financial status	■ Substance abuse status
■ Daily activities	■ Social support network
■ Client and family involvement in the service plan	■ Unique needs satisfied

As Donabedian describes,[1] in assessing health care quality we make assumptions or inferences about the interrelations of all the elements in the model and make measurements to evaluate each element's contributions to patient care outcomes. This model also illustrates some of the problems associated with quality assessment and measurement of outcomes. First, we are faced with the issue of selecting appropriate outcome measures. Even in measuring physical health, we are far from designing a single outcome measure that reflects the results of all the inputs and processes involved. In behavioral health the problem is even more complicated. Table 1, above, illustrates some of the outcomes used by California's Metropolitan State Hospital.[3]

None of the above measures are comprehensive in nature. In addition, causal relationships among these outcomes and the processes that take place in behavioral health institutions is weak at best. Sometimes it is possible to achieve a high level of outcomes in spite of what we practice and perform in our behavioral health care institutions. The reverse is also true. Sometimes we get bad outcomes in spite of the fact that we do everything right. This is particularly so when the outcomes in question are affected by a multitude of factors that operate outside of the behavioral health institution—normal biological variations, the presence of comorbidities, and other factors related to the patients environment, family, community, etc. Therefore, if we measure only outcomes, we cannot with reasonable certainty infer that the mental health processes associated with the institution that produced the favorable outcomes is of high quality. However, if we measure both outcomes and mental health care processes for a sufficiently large number of patients and both are of high quality, we can say that it is more likely that the high-quality processes contributed to the high-quality outcomes.[4]

Practice Guidelines

As defined by the Institute of Medicine (IOM), Practice Guidelines are "systematically developed statements to assist practitioner and patient decisions about appropriate health care for specific clinical circumstances."[5] That is, practice guidelines are explicit descriptions of preferred clinical processes. The Agency for Health Care Policy and Research (AHCPR) was mandated by the Congress in the Health Care Quality Improvement Act of 1986 to develop practice guidelines in the untested belief that practice guidelines would result in good patient care outcomes, eliminate inappropriate medical interventions, and reduce health care costs. Over a period of approximately three years, AHCPR released practice guidelines for 15 clinical conditions and diagnoses. The list included only one behavioral health condition—major depression—developed by a panel of experts in the field. The guideline contains a discussion of major depression along with the panel's findings and recommendations. Supporting evidence and references from a review of more than 3,500 articles are also included.[6] Many professional groups, health care purchasers, and commercial enterprises are also working to generate practice guidelines—often, however, with different objectives, different definitions, different levels of sophistication, and unequal quality in their final products.

It is difficult to generate good guidelines, particularly in the field of behavioral health, because of the rigor of the process involved and of the inconsistency of research-based evidence to support definitive recommendations on treatment for many psychiatric conditions. Conceptually, the steps in the process of moving from outcomes to guidelines are straightforward. We first use large databases to establish monitoring systems; we identify variations in outcome in different areas and differences in procedures or interventions (the health care processes) that are associated with the differences in outcome; we use nonrandomized trials, meta analysis, decision analysis, or randomized controlled trials to assess the results of different interventions; and we incorporate the results of data analysis into appropriate guidelines.[7] The process of developing guidelines is expensive and time-consuming, Therefore, at present, development and application of clinical practice guidelines is limited to common procedures that have substantial volumes of use, high costs, and stable therapeutic options, with adequate scientific evidence about their effectiveness, along with unexplained variations in the use of these options for the prevention, diagnosis, and treatment of a particular condition.[8]

Critical Care Pathways

A critical path is optimal sequencing and timing of interventions by physicians, nurses, and other staff for a particular diagnosis or procedure, with the intent of better utilizing resources, maximizing the quality of care, and minimizing delays. Unlike practice guidelines, critical paths deal not only with physician and practitioner decision making but also with the entire process of care, involving other services and interactions among all providers of care. Critical paths also deal with timeliness of services and collaboration by multiple health care professionals and often involve a case manager or a case coordinator, usually a nurse.

Performance Measurement and Medical Review Criteria

By following critical paths, case management, and practice guidelines, we can limit variation in clinical processes and expect to achieve good patient care outcomes. The process of performance review is intended to check whether health professional behavior conforms to expected patterns of behavior as specified in the practice guidelines and the critical paths. In order to conduct a performance review, we need to apply performance or medical review criteria for each patient. For example, a medical review criterion that applies to all admissions to a behavioral care institution is completion of the admission assessment within 24 hours. Performance measures calculate the proportion of assessments that conform to the guideline by satisfying the specified medical review criterion. Table 2, page 321, provides some examples of commonly used performance measures in a psychiatric unit.

With a performance measure, we are in a position to set a standard of quality or an acceptable standard of performance. For example, depending on how rigorously we wish to pursue quality, we can specify whether 90 or 95 percent of the patients should have their admission assessments completed within 24 hours.

Table 2. Performance Measures in a Psychiatric Unit

- Percentage of patients on suicide precautions
- Percentage of patients on suicide precautions checked by staff every "x" minutes
- Proportion of medication errors
- Evidence of patient falls and other injuries
- Client and family involvement in the service plan
- Percentage of medical records showing adequate justification for restraint/seclusion
- Number of scheduled group sessions not conducted as planned

Benchmarking

Benchmarking is another key ingredient in the organization's continuous quality improvement efforts. Benchmarking involves selecting and trying to emulate a demonstrated standard of performance for systems that are very similar to yours. The goal is to develop a target at which to shoot and to develop a standard or benchmark against which to compare your performance. A good example might be to benchmark medication errors, using statistics of other major providers in an environment similar to yours. The first major decision is to determine what to benchmark and then to collect and analyze benchmark information. Finally, decisions must be made on actions to meet or exceed the benchmark. The latter task is ordinarily undertaken by a team formed to recommend and develop quality improvement initiatives. In the ideal situation, you would find one or two organizations with operations similar to yours who are demonstrably leaders in the areas you want to study and compare. The organizations you look to need not be in the health care industry For example, a materials management department may want to use a benchmark for order handling and delivery from Federal Express or L.L. Bean.

Benchmarks must be measurable and should be established in numerous departments within any health care setting. The real strength of benchmarking is that it saves time and energy that might be spent in reinventing the wheel. Many quality improvement teams start reevaluation of work practices by brainstorming improvements based solely on an analysis of problems inherent in the existing process and can end up making minor changes to a weak system. Today, only a few health care organizations use benchmarking to free quality improvement teams from thinking only in terms of current practices.

Quality Assessment and Improvement

Outcome analysis, practice guidelines, critical pathways, case management, and benchmarking, when considered individually, are necessary but not sufficient elements in the quality assessment and improvement process. Success depends to a large extent on including as many as possible of the above techniques in a single quality assessment and improvement process. However, the state of the art of the quality assessment process is such that it often is not possible to do this. In fact, 80-90 percent of common medical practices may not have a firm scientific basis in published literature.[9] This does not mean that 80-90 percent of medical practices are wrong. It only means that they are based on a long history of tradition and experience and only about 10 percent of them have firmly established guidelines based on scientific research. James suggests a number of reasons for this situation. First, much of the research that does exist is not available to medical practitioners; second, even such limited scientific information as is available may overwhelm the capacity of the human mind; third, humans are inherently fallible information processors.[10]

Therefore, any mechanisms, such as the use of computers and large databases, that facilitate the acquisition and assimilation of information, leading to generation and implementation of consensus practices and procedures and measurement of patient care outcomes, will definitely enhance health care quality. Total quality management (TQM) provides a proven vehicle, a sound philosophy, and a set of small group techniques for achieving this end and can be used effectively for generation of practice guide lines, critical care pathways, case management protocols, medical review criteria, performance measures, and outcome measures.[11] Donabedian describes the process of generating practice guidelines as technology assessment[1]; i.e., we are not exactly sure of the right thing to do, so we make use of TQM techniques to generate as much consensus as possible to create guidelines and agreement on how we should go about treating the condition.

In contrast, when there are agreed-upon practice guidelines, critical pathways, etc., we can use TQM techniques to assess practitioner performance in accordance with what is known as the right thing to do (or the right way to practice). This is what Donabedian calls performance assessment or quality assessment.[1] Traditionally, TQM techniques were used mainly for this purpose, but, if managed properly TQM techniques are equally effective in both kinds of assessments.

What are the inherent features of TQM that makes it eminently suitable for both technology assessment and performance assessment? We have devoted the rest of this chapter to answer this question and to spell out practical details for using TQM to achieve both ends.

Total Quality Management as a Philosophy

TQM is a quality philosophy that encompasses the entire health care organization—a major change in health care thinking—which strives for excellent services and better patient care outcomes at all times to all customers. The complex definition of the customer varies from organization to organization, and includes patients, patients' families, physicians, licensing and accrediting agencies, the community, and any other group affected by or affecting the organization. The term continuous quality improvement (CQI) embodies the concepts of TQM in its implementation. CQI is an approach to quality management that builds on traditional quality assurance methods by emphasizing the organization and its systems; it focuses on process rather than on the individual and promotes the need for objective data to analyze and improve processes in an attempt to satisfy the needs of all customers. Total involvement is important; everyone from the chief executive officer and the medical staff on down must be involved and committed.

The TQM philosophy can be described as follows:

■ The various "customers" of the organization define quality, and the customer's needs are paramount. Patient surveys, physician surveys, focus groups, interviews, the requirements of licensing and accrediting agencies, or any other technique may be used to integrate customers' inputs into the organization's decision-making process. Each health care organization needs to define its customers for itself; no generic definition is useful.

■ With top management leadership, the organization must be designed to meet and exceed what the identified customers define as value and what the medical staff defines as desirable patient care outcomes.

■ Systems must be designed to continuously monitor results, which must be statistically evaluated to guide constant improvement of the system.

Total quality management is a management philosophy that focuses on quality improvement as the major driving force for the entire organization. The guiding principles of TQM can be summarized as follows:

■ Top management must provide leadership for quality improvement.

■ Quality is a major strategic issue of the organization and the primary focus of strategic planning.

■ Quality is the responsibility of everyone in the organization.

■ All functions of the health care organization must focus on continuous quality improvement to achieve strategic goals.

■ Problems are solved through team efforts involving empowered interdisciplinary teams and management.

■ Problem solving and continuous quality improvement are based on the use of statistical quality control methods.

■ Training and education of all employees is essential for continuous quality improvement.

Successful TQM programs are built through the dedication and combined efforts of everyone in the organization. The most essential ingredient is commitment and involvement of top management and physicians. If this ingredient is missing, TQM becomes another fad that quickly dies and fades away, with accompanying loss of management credibility.

The preceding description provides a good overview of the TQM philosophy, but it does not tell the whole story. A number of elements of TQM are especially important:

■ **Continuous Improvement.** TQM requires a never-ending process that we call continuous quality improvement, where perfection is never achieved but always sought.

■ **Employee Empowerment.** Giving employees responsibility for improvements and the authority to make changes to accomplish them suggests a management style of employee empowerment. Techniques for building employee empowerment include strong communications networks for all employees; open, supportive supervisors; movement of responsibilities to staff employees; focus on organizational morale; and formal approaches, such as team building and quality circles. Team building is the process of identifying, training, and empowering teams of employees to address common problems. A similar technique is quality circles—a formal system of volunteer staff who meet regularly on paid time to address and make recommendations on process or quality improvements. The techniques are similar in that they involve empowered groups, but teams are typically put together for a one-time problem, while quality circles are institutionalized for long periods of involvement

■ **Benchmarking.** Identification of other health care organizations that are the best at something and modeling your own organization after them. The organization being modeled need not be in the health care business, just one that is the best.

■ **Team Approach.** Use of interdisciplinary teams for problem solving and to achieve consensus. Takes advantage of involvement, group thinking, and brainstorming, and promotes a spirit of cooperation and shared values among staff.

■ **Knowledge of TQM Tools.** Everyone in the organization must be trained in the techniques of TQM that are helpful in the quest for continuous quality improvement. These techniques include flow charts, Pareto charts, check sheets, statistical quality control, cause-and-effect diagrams, and brainstorming, all of which are defined later in the chapter.

TQM and Process Variation

All processes that provide a service exhibit a certain amount of "natural" variation in their output. Variation is created by the combined influences of countless minor factors (people, training, equipment, humidity, changes in temperature, electrical fluctuations, reaction to medications, interpreting of lab results, etc.), each one so unimportant that, even if it could be identified and eliminated, the decrease in process variability would be negligible. In effect, this variability is inherent in the process, is referred to as chance or random variation, and cannot be traced to specific causes. The amount of inherent variability differs from process to process, from unit to unit, and from physician to physician. For example, an older piece of laboratory equipment will probably generate a higher degree of natural variation than newer equipment because of worn parts and because newer machines may incorporate design improvements that lessen output variability. Eliminating natural variation is almost impossible; it exists in every process.

A second kind of variability in processes is called assignable variation, or special variation. Unlike with natural variation, the main sources of assignable variation can be identified (assigned a specific cause) and eliminated. Equipment that needs calibration, defective laboratory samples, human factors (carelessness, fatigue, failure to follow correct procedures, and so on) are typical sources of assignable variation. Elimination of assignable variation typically requires management intervention with inputs from the staff. This might involve capital expenditures for better equipment, more training, a change of protocol, different materials, job redesign, and a host of other options. The TQM philosophy tells us that everyone on the health care team has the responsibility to be a part of attempts to eliminate these variations.

Evolution of Total Quality Management

The term quality assurance was first used at Bell Telephone Laboratories during the 1920s and included control charts and sampling techniques for statistical quality control. While these techniques formed the foundation for quality assurance, about 25 years ago the focus of quality changed from these technical aspects to a managerial philosophy. Today, quality assurance refers to a commitment to quality throughout the entire organization. A primary precept of total quality control is strong leadership from top management to improve quality and make it a continual process. Furthermore, quality improvement is a continual process, giving rise to the term continuous improvement or performance improvement. Performance improvement has received a major emphasis from the Joint Commission on Accreditation of Healthcare Organizations (JCAHO).

W. Edwards Deming first applied his theories of quality management in Japan, where he went after World War II to assist that nation in improving quality and productivity. The Japanese learned well and came to revere Dr. Deming, establishing the Deming Prize, which is awarded annually to firms that distinguish themselves with quality management programs. Dr. Deming worked with the Japanese for almost 30 years before he gained recognition in his own country. Only in the past decade have U.S. companies turned their attention to Deming, embraced his philosophy, and requested his assistance in establishing quality programs.

Deming compiled a list of 14 points he believed were needed to achieve quality in an organization (table 3, page 326).[12] His message is that the cause of poor quality and inefficiency is the system, not employees. Management's responsibility is to change the system to achieve the desired results. Dr. Deming's impact on the quality movement in health care today cannot be overstated. Other quality experts, such as Joseph Juran, Philip Crosby and Kaoru Ishikawa, have similar philosophies on quality issues and support the work of Deming.[13-15]

Joseph Juran, like Deming, went to Japan to teach manufacturers how to improve quality. He also believes that roughly 80 percent of quality defects are management controllable; thus, management has the responsibility to correct the deficiency. According to Juran, quality planning is necessary to develop systems that are capable of meeting quality objectives; that quality control is necessary in order to know when corrective action is required; and that quality improvement will help to continuously find better ways of doing things. A key element of Juran's philosophy is management commitment to continual improvement.[13]

The "Customer" Emphasis in Health Care

As has been mentioned, experts suggest that quality be defined as a continuous effort by all members of the organization to meet the needs and expectations of the customer. In health care, this definition needs to be modified to carefully think through who the customer is and what the customer expects. In most cases, the answers are multidimensional and include patients, patients' families, physicians, the community, and employees. Many departments can define their customers in terms of other departments.

Table 3. Deming's 14 Points[12]

1. Create constancy of purpose toward improvement of health care services with a plan to become even better. Decide to whom top management is responsible, and what "customers" expect. Develop a mission statement addressing patients, providers, and staff.

2. Adopt a philosophy of continuous improvement instead of accepting common levels of delay, mistakes, defective supplies, and inefficiency.

3. Eliminate the need for inspection to achieve quality by relying instead on statistical quality control to improve system outcomes.

4. Select a few suppliers and vendors based on their quality commitment rather than on competitive prices.

5. Find problems. It is management's job to work continually on the system of health care delivery.

6. Develop better staff training that focuses on prevention of quality problems and use of statistical quality control and TQM problem-solving techniques.

7. Develop leadership among supervisors to help staff perform better.

8. Drive out fear. Many staff members are afraid to ask questions, even when they don't fully understand the planned way to do a job. When people feel secure about asking, quality and productivity improve.

9. Break down barriers between departments, and promote cooperation and teamwork.

10. Eliminate slogans and numerical productivity targets that urge staff to higher performance levels that sacrifice quality without providing training on better methods to achieve higher performance.

11. Eliminate numerical quotas that staff members attempt to meet at any cost, without regard to quality.

12. Enhance staff pride, motivation, and self-esteem by improving supervision and the health delivery process so that staff can perform to their capabilities.

13. Institute vigorous education and training programs in methods of quality improvement throughout the organization, from top management down, so that continuous improvement can occur. .

14. Develop a commitment from top management and a plan of action to implement the previous 13 points.

Each organization that embarks on the quality pursuit should answer the following question: "Who are our current customers, what are their expectations, and when are we meeting and when are we not meeting their expectations?" Every health care organization has a customer/supplier relationship with everyone for which it provides care or services. Services may include receiving information, providing information, soliciting feedback, following through on requests, identifying and solving problems, watching or observing, organizing, and many other activities. For example, at each step in the medication delivery process, there is a customer/supplier relationship—physician to nurse, nurse to pharmacy, etc. To analyze current customer relationships, each person in the organization should list customers in the categories of external customers, internal customers, and co-workers and then develop a comprehensive department list together.

Next, the department, meeting with customers or customer groups, needs to clarify expectations for each key customer relationship:

∎ What are you providing to your customers?

∎ What do you think your customers' expectations are?

∎ What expectations do your customers express?

∎ How well do you think you are meeting your customers' expectations?

∎ How well do your customers think you are meeting their expectations?

Meeting one on one with customers is one of the best methods for learning more about their expectations. However, many other methods may also work, depending on the size of the customer group and other customer characteristics:

∎ Involving representatives of the customer group in a cross-functional team meeting in which you work together to analyze expectations and make improvements.

∎ Organizing focus groups of representatives of customer groups.

∎ Handing out written surveys or questionnaires for customers to complete.

∎ Calling representatives of customer groups to conduct a telephone survey.

∎ Talking to customers before they leave your facility to ask them informally how well you met their expectations.

With this information, each health care organization can design a mission statement to define its customers and their needs, a set of quality objectives and a way to measure progress against these objectives, and a quality plan that lists the projects to be accomplished in order to meet and exceed customer expectations. Although this exercise seems time-consuming, it is the best way to start the quality improvement process in any health care organization in which the customer definition is complex.

Top Management's Role in TQM

Top management has the responsibility for setting organizational goals, including those for quality. Health care organizational goals typically focus on long-term issues, such as patient care outcomes, profitability, competition, market share, and growth. The strategic plan addresses these issues. The major change in health care today is the impact of quality on market share, profitability, and growth.

It is natural that quality and quality management are important issues in the strategic planning process and should be an integral part of the process. Through establishment of goals and development of strategic plans to achieve the goals, top management ultimately determines the level of quality that is required in service design and the degree of commitment to quality management necessary to achieve it.

It will ultimately be up to middle management and staff to translate goals and plans developed by top management into operation. Top management must make the initial and strong commitment to quality management and ensure that all departments and functions within the organization share a common commitment to the quality goals developed.

Middle Management's Role in TQM

A key role of middle management in any health care organization is to implement strategic plans developed by top management, although an astute top management team will involve all managers in the planning process to enhance their commitment to the plans that are developed. Middle management has the responsibility to design and control health delivery systems to meet the goals and objectives of the strategic plan. Middle managers must make sure that the quality management program is implemented organizationwide. They must design and implement a quality appraisal system for every phase of the health care delivery system. Typically they will design customer surveys to obtain feedback from various customer groups. A key survey that needs to be designed and implemented is the patient satisfaction survey, along with a system of evaluation and reporting.

In large health care systems, a quality council reporting directly to top management will be entrusted with the responsibility of managing the quality improvement program. This group will design systems for formal quality team reporting, and a system of reporting quality progress to top management. Typically, the middle management group will develop a quality council charter, along with referral forms, performance improvement team status forms, and annual quality improvement reports, all of which provide the framework for the quality management system. The importance of this group cannot be overestimated, for it takes the quality direction from top management and makes it happen. Although middle management never loses its responsibility for TQM oversight and leadership, it is the quality council that becomes the medium for directing the quality improvement process and reporting. Representatives of middle management typically make up the quality council.

Supervisory Management's Role in TQM

Supervisors are the first line of management. Much of the supervisor's time is spent managing staff who actually do the nursing, fill the prescriptions, do the tests, interview patients, make and deliver the meals, do the maintenance, and answer telephones. Supervisors manage the people who can identify problems and who can be involved in seeking solutions.

When quality problems are identified, supervisory management works with involved employees to correct and improve processes. This usually involves selecting people to work on quality teams, helping them, empowering them, freeing them up to attend meetings, scheduling them to be available for team meetings, etc. Often, supervisors have to either train employees themselves or ensure training of their employees by others so that they can be effective quality team members. Supervisors must constantly reinforce the quality emphasis at staff meetings and encourage everyone to become part of the process. In our experience, the most effective quality management programs are found in organizations in which first-line supervisors are continuously making their employees aware of quality.

It is human nature for middle and supervisory managers to be threatened by the concept of empowering employees to propose changes rather than to take orders. Supervisors may fear that their positions will be eliminated, that they will lose control over decisions; that TQM will distract employees from their "real" jobs, and that employees will become rebellious and difficult to handle. Another threat is the requirement that these managers change their styles to allow greater employee involvement. There is often a feeling that they will be unable to deal with new terminology and acquire skills for listening, facilitating, making decisions based on statistical data, and seeking ways to ease employees' jobs instead of protecting the budget. The solution to this problem is to understand middle and supervisory management's fears and to launch an all-out effort to combat them. If careful consideration is given to these steps, health care organizations can design programs that transform middle and supervisory managers into leaders of change.

There are three steps for developing managers who lead rather than impede progress:

1. Communicate the imperative of learning new TQM management techniques and setting specific expectations for managerial behavior.

2. Assist managers in developing and perfecting new skills. Some organizations offer peer analysis and skip level reviews to help managers assess their management styles. In skip level reviews, an executive two levels above a manager provides counsel and advice on management styles. This is typically less threatening for a manager than seeking advice and input from his or her immediate supervisor, suggesting a depth of wisdom and experience at that higher level.

3. Emphasize the vital importance of middle managers' participation by giving them the lead roles in implementation. Some of the best hospitals train their middle managers first, giving them supplementary coaching in team leadership, having the managers train their employees, and giving them opportunities to assume team leader positions.

The Role of the Physician in TQM

Health care organizations that practice TQM best realize that few meaningful changes can be made without MD involvement. These hospitals are getting the physicians engaged from the start. Most hospitals hesitate to involve their physicians primarily from fear of failure. Many hospitals state a preference for waiting until they are up the curve on TQM before they introduce it to physicians. They are concerned that the hospital will be unable to respond to physician demands adequately. Also, hospitals fear upsetting physicians if they perceive TQM as yet another unwanted intrusion into clinical practice. Finally, many hospitals rationalize not bringing physicians aboard sooner by assuring themselves that physicians would not have the time to devote to TQM or would not be willing to devote any time for such activities.

There are many reasons why noninvolvement of physicians can hurt the TQM effort. Hospitals avoiding physician involvement end up selecting less important projects for quality improvement, where physician participation does not matter. Also, hospitals that select important projects without MD input can arrive at suboptimal solutions. Finally, hospitals that do complete important projects without physicians may encounter roadblocks during implementation unless physicians have bought into the change.

The sooner physicians buy into the TQM process, the more likely the hospital can focus its TQM efforts on key clinical processes that can result in major service improvements. Arousing widespread physician interest is a time-consuming process, but hospitals that wish to guarantee their success should involve physicians as early as possible. There are several steps to facilitate involvement of physicians. First, hospitals must enlist the advice and support of physician leadership to introduce TQM concepts to the medical staff. Second, the hospital must arrange convenient physician education sessions, ideally taught by a physician in concise, convenient, scheduled sessions. Finally, physicians can be invited to join quality improvement teams on topics directly related to their practice, with the object of getting the physicians involved in improving patient care and hospital systems. Physicians can be consultants to the teams and only attend sessions when decisions are being made. They can assume leadership roles on topics of immediate interest to them. Some hospitals are offering physicians who participate in hospital TQM projects free training for their office staffs, thereby giving them some immediate, personal benefits from the TQM process.

The Role of Employees

In order for any health care organization to achieve results in a continuous quality improvement program, it is necessary for management and staff to cooperate and for each to have a strong commitment to quality and patient care outcomes. This essential cooperation and commitment is not possible when management dictates quality programs to staff. Quality management programs in which employees participate in both identifying and solving problems have been shown to be very effective, not only in improving quality but also in increasing employee morale and satisfaction, reducing staff turnover and absenteeism, improving technical skills, and increasing productivity.

Some of the keys to success for quality improvement teams include a formal mechanism, such as a quality council, to focus teams right from their start; definite time limits for project completion; and reductions in the time teams spend on data gathering and analysis. Successful teams have project charters that define the problem, the expected team outcomes, anticipated measures of success, and the expected support from other departments and "consultants" to the team. In addition, teams provide progress reports to the quality council and typically have a team sponsor appointed by the quality council who sits in on meetings to assess process and acts as a team champion to solve any organizational constraints or roadblocks. This sponsor is typically an upper-level executive who can help the team solve interdivisional issues and assist in getting the necessary resources and decisions to aid in team progress. The authors have found that the services of a sponsor are an important factor in the success of most TQM groups and projects in which they have been personally involved. Management of hospitals that report success also have developed means to recognize and reward team members for quality improvement solutions and for on-time delivery of results. These teams also have the aid of management engineers or outside consultants to help in data gathering and analysis, thus preventing team burn-out if data collection is a major burden. The danger of using outside members is the risk of reducing staff ownership of the project and the additional costs involved.

Tools of Total Quality Management

Some frequently used techniques for identifying causes of quality problems include customer surveys, benchmarking, Pareto analysis, flowcharts, histograms and check sheets, cause-and-effect diagrams, and process control charts. These techniques are time-proven and relatively simple to grasp.

Customer surveys are an essential way to get feedback from the various customers of any health care organization. They were discussed above and are included here to emphasize their critical importance as a source of information for quality improvement teams. The most typical survey is the patient survey. Often, the patient survey does not contain crucial information necessary for quality improvement and must be redesigned to collect meaningful data. Our experience is that many quality improvement teams begin by reviewing the patient survey and then modify the form as necessary to ensure that it contains the proper information. In addition, it is essential that patient surveys be returned directly to the team for analysis and not first flow through some time-consuming bureaucratic system. The amount of information that can come from these surveys can be of crucial importance in defining quality projects for team analysis and solution.

A hospital must define its physicians as customers and then survey them on a routine basis. Functional departments, such as housekeeping or engineering, have multiple customers who must be surveyed to gain this essential insight about how well the organization is doing in the eyes of the customer. The nursing department can survey patients, physicians, the pharmacy, laboratories, housekeeping, dietary, the business office, and anyone else who can provide them with data on customer satisfaction.

Patient care outcomes are an essential part of the informational needs of quality teams and could be argued to be even more crucial than patient surveys. Because data on outcomes can show trends, systems problems, training problems, equipment problems, medication problems, etc., they must be tracked and evaluated by quality improvement teams with heavy physician input.

Check Sheets and Histograms are used to collect and display data on quality problems. A typical check sheet of quality problems tallies the number of occurrences for a variety of previously identified categories. When the check sheet is completed after the agreed-on interval, the total tally of problems for each category can be used to create a histogram. The challenge here is for the quality improvement team to design simple check sheets that can be readily checked by any person in the system as the problem category occurs.

Pareto analysis is a method of identifying the causes of poor quality in any system. It was developed about 40 years ago by Joseph Juran, who named the method after the Italian economist Vilfredo Pareto, who determined that about 20 percent of Milan's citizens had more than 80 percent of the wealth. Pareto speculated that this was true for other economies as well, and the 80:20 rule was born. Juran's findings follow Pareto's, in that he found that most quality problems come from only a few causes. For example, he discovered that almost 75 percent of defective cloths in a textile mill was caused by only a few weavers and that, in a paper mill, more than 60 percent of the cost of poor quality was caused by a single category of defects. In other words, he discovered that quality problems are not uniform across all causes. Thus, correcting the relatively few major causes of most quality problems will yield the greatest improvements.

Pareto analysis can be applied by determining the number of possible causes of poor quality in a system and collecting data in each category over some appropriate time interval. A frequency distribution is drawn, rank ordering the categories from the largest to the smallest on a category percentage. This "Pareto Chart" can then be analyzed for improvements. An example regarding delays in treating patients in the emergency department is shown in table 4, page 333.

The Pareto diagram shown in figure 2, page 334, clearly identifies the major cause of the problem as delays in obtaining laboratory results. This delay must be evaluated by the team to determine if expediting laboratory results is cost effective. If not, other causes must be examined in the order of their importance. The Pareto diagram simply identifies the quality problem causes that need to be examined first. It does not take away any decision-making responsibilities of the group; it merely points the way for analysis. Obviously, the secret of success lies in categorization of the causes and subsequent data collection, leading to further analysis and their elimination.

Flowcharts are designed to help the quality improvement team understand the sequence of events in a job, an operation, or a process. It enables the team to have a clear picture of how a specific operation works and gives it a common frame of reference. It helps the team determine where problems might occur in the system and whether the system needs modification. Development of the flowchart alone can help identify problems and is in itself a useful exercise. Typically, the team drawing the flowchart will see inefficiencies and attempt to correct them in the conceptual phase. The final, modified flowchart can be a useful document in training and indoctrinating new staff to the process. Many symbols are used in the flowchart, usually an oval to indicate the beginning and the end of a process; a rectangle to indicate an action step; a diamond to indicate a decision point, expressed as a question that can be answered "yes" or "no," with branches from each answer; and a half oval (looking like the letter "D") to indicate a delay.

A typical flowchart analysis can help identify the best data collection points, isolate and discover the origin of problems, identify the best checkpoints in the system, and identify opportunities for improvement. An example of a flowchart of the x-ray process is shown in figure 3, page 335.

Table 4. Delays in Emergency Department

Check Sheet for Data Collection

Reason for Delay	Frequency of Delay
Delay in housekeeping service	10
Lack of nursing staff	21
Waiting for physician	30
CAT scanner unavailable	5
Admissions computer down	2
Delay in receiving laboratory results	50
No bed available	2
Total	120

Work Sheet for Data Analysis

Reason for Delay	Frequency	% of Total
Delay in receiving laboratory results	50	42%
Waiting for physician	30	25
Lack of nursing staff	21	17
Delay in housekeeping service	10	8
CAT scanner unavailable	5	4
No bed available	2	2
Admissions computer down	2	2

Statistical Process Control (SPC) is concerned with monitoring standards, collecting information, and taking corrective action when warranted. A control chart is a graph with a horizontal line through the middle representing the process mean or average, a line below the mean representing the lower control limit and a line above it for the upper control limit. Observations of the system are taken over time and measurements are taken for some process attribute. If a measurement is within the control limits, the process is said to be in control and the variability represents no quality problem, but if the measurement is outside the limits, a problem probably exists and must be investigated.

To best understand control charts, we must first understand that every system has some variation in its outcomes. This variation can be normal, which is present in every process and is due to the combination of existing staff, procedures, equipment, and supplies. It is also predictable

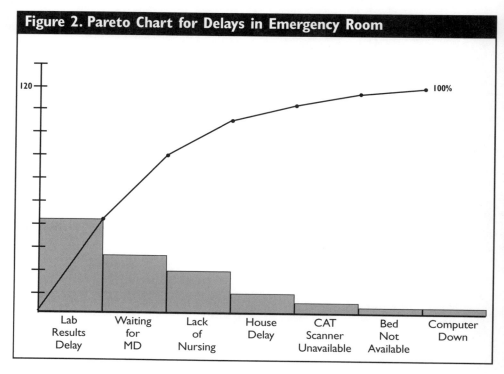

Figure 2. Pareto Chart for Delays in Emergency Room

and requires management intervention for a major change in the system. The other type of variation is usually abnormal and is due to extraordinary occurrences in the system, such as poor supplies, uncalibrated equipment, unqualified technicians, part-time help, poor procedures, etc. This type of variation is unpredictable and requires investigation. Abnormal variation will show up on the control chart as a point above the upper control limit or as a point below the lower control limit. This variation would be highly unlikely to have occurred by chance and must be investigated.

The control chart, then, is a picture of the system over time. The rules for control chart analysis are simple. First, every observation out of the control limits must be investigated. Second, a run of 8 points above or below the mean is another out-of-control signal indicating a trend.

In general, statistical process control charts are extremely important tools for quality improvement. By training staff in these methods, we enable them to identify quality problems and their causes and to make suggestions for improvement. Control charts can be drawn for any number of items:

■ Total costs per discharge

■ Average waiting time of patients

■ Delays due to equipment

■ Clinical patient care outcomes by diagnosis

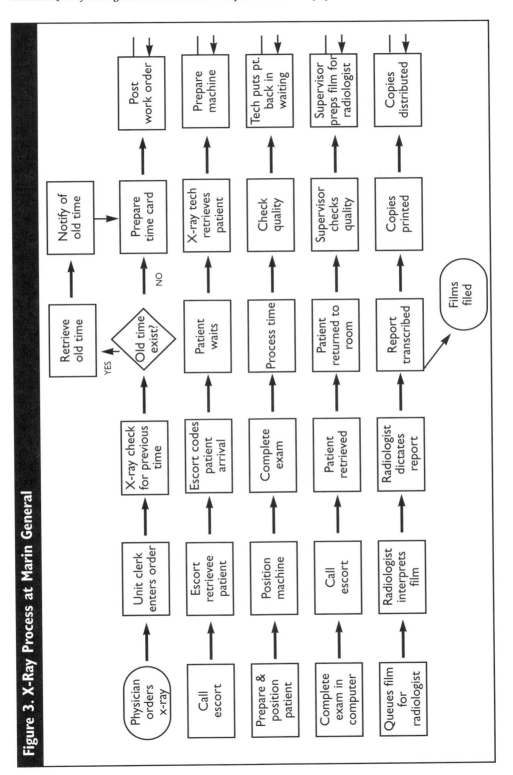

Figure 3. X-Ray Process at Marin General

■ Patient complaints

■ Number of repeat exams

■ Number of failures to have reports on charts within 24 hours

■ Number of infections

Control charts must be used for only those indicators worth tracking and must have a foolproof system for identifying troubling trends. Keeping score should not be the goal; the goal is always quality improvement. People do not like to measure after changes in a system have been implemented, but there is always room for improvement. With trained personnel and control charts on only those indicators worthy of tracking, quality improvement will occur. There is a big risk of having too many things tracked at once at high levels, thereby overburdening already scarce management resources. The best control chart tracking is done at the department level.

Cause and effect diagrams, also called "fishbone" diagrams, are a graphical description of the elements of a specific quality problem and of the relationship between those elements. It is used to identify the potential causes of a quality problem so that the team can correct it. Cause-and-effect diagrams are usually developed by the continuous quality improvement team to help members identify causes. This tool is a normal part of the team's problem-solving resources and is popular, as are all of the tools discussed above, with quality circles.

Figure 4, page 337, shows the general structure of a cause-and-effect diagram. A center line connects the effect box to the major categories of possible problem causes, displayed as branches, or "bones," off the center line. The box at the end of the line describes the major problem. The diagram starts out in this form, with only major categories on each branch or bone. Individual causes associated with each category are attached as separate lines along the length of the branch during the brainstorming process.

The cause-and-effect diagram is essentially a means for thinking through a problem and recording possible causes in an organized and easily seen manner. The causes listed along the branches under each category are typically equipment, policies, procedures, people, measurements, supplies, and the environment, but every diagram is tailored to its specific problem. This very useful and simple technique gets a lot of use by quality improvement teams and, once learned, is invaluable in uncovering quality problems.

Typical processes that can be studied using cause-and-effect diagrams are:

■ Laboratory test turnaround times

■ Errors on patient diet orders

■ Transcription errors

■ Equipment calibration errors

■ Nursing procedure errors

Figure 4. Cause and Effect Analysis

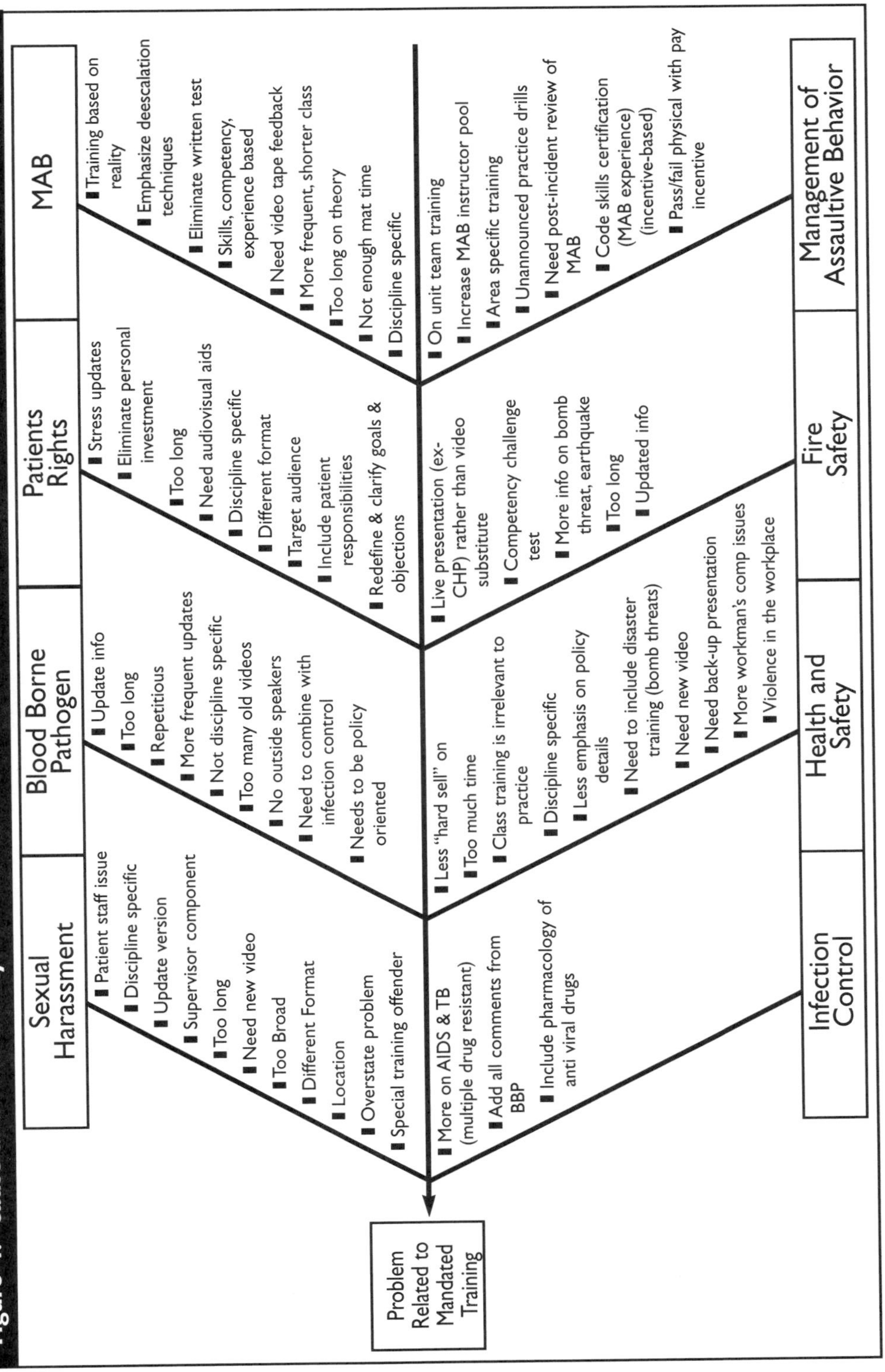

Sexual Harassment
- Patient staff issue
- Discipline specific
- Update version
- Supervisor component
- Too long
- Need new video
- Too Broad
- Different Format
- Location
- Overstate problem
- Special training offender

Blood Borne Pathogen
- Update info
- Too long
- Repetitious
- More frequent updates
- Not discipline specific
- Too many old videos
- No outside speakers
- Need to combine with infection control
- Needs to be policy oriented

Patients Rights
- Stress updates
- Eliminate personal investment
- Too long
- Need audiovisual aids
- Discipline specific
- Different format
- Target audience
- Include patient responsibilities
- Redefine & clarify goals & objections

MAB
- Training based on reality
- Emphasize deescalation techniques
- Eliminate written test
- Skills, competency, experience based
- Need video tape feedback
- More frequent, shorter class
- Too long on theory
- Not enough mat time
- Discipline specific
- On unit team training
- Increase MAB instructor pool
- Area specific training
- Unannounced practice drills
- Need post-incident review of MAB
- Code skills certification (MAB experience) (incentive-based)
- Pass/fail physical with pay incentive

Infection Control
- More on AIDS & TB (multiple drug resistant)
- Add all comments from BBP
- Include pharmacology of anti viral drugs

Health and Safety
- Less "hard sell"
- Too much time
- Class training is irrelevant to practice
- Discipline specific
- Less emphasis on policy details
- Need to include disaster training (bomb threats)
- Need new video
- Need back-up presentation
- More workman's comp issues
- Violence in the workplace

Fire Safety
- Live presentation (ex-CHP) rather than video substitute
- Competency challenge test
- More info on bomb threat, earthquake
- Too long
- Updated info

Management of Assaultive Behavior

Problem Related to Mandated Training

337

■ Operating room turnover times

■ Emergency department delays

■ Medication errors

■ X-rays repeated

■ Patient care outcome problems

Figure 4 provides an example of how a psychiatric hospital brainstormed the causative factors that contributed to ineffective and costly mandated training in areas such as sexual harassment, bloodborne pathogens, management of assaultive behavior, fire safety, and infection control.

Total Quality Management in Health Care

Based on a 1992 Health Care Advisory Board study of TQM practices,[15] much has been learned about the application of TQM in health care. Some of the observations in the study are:

"1. Despite its growing popularity, TQM is likely to be a multimillion dollar mistake for many hospitals.

2. The vast majority of hospitals are seeing small or no results; even the most celebrated TQM hospitals cannot attribute business success to quality improvement.

3. The biggest surprise is that, despite the lack of results, most hospital executives are pleased with TQM progress, certain that big results are just a few months or years away.

4. The Advisory Board View: Hoped for results are likely to materialize; TQM at many hospitals is more about appearance than substance.

5. The failure to generate results is not an inherent weakness of TQM but is due to both a basic misunderstanding of what TQM can achieve and faulty implementation.

6. Many hospitals believe that TQM, a means of improvement, is an end in itself; expectation that simply unleashing the process (training and forming teams) will inevitably bring success.

7. The most effective efforts are those that strategically direct TQM, tightly focusing the improvement process on core business problems (i.e., 15 percent cost reduction, 10 percent increase in MD retention, etc.).

8. Properly directed, TQM can be a powerful tool; the true value of TQM is that it can be an effective vehicle for changing organizational culture."

It is our strong belief that TQM can and will work in health care. It provides a means for making proactive and continuous improvement rather than accepting the current state of affairs. It charges those closest to an operation with responsibility for improvement. TQM provides a structure for data collection and analysis for better decision making. It forces every organization to set aggressive goals and time-lines for quality improvement teams and then provides the teams with focus, support, recognition, and implementation leadership. There must be complete support from physicians and the entire management team, and training in TQM and leadership

338

must be provided to every manager in the organization. With these stipulations in place, TQM will work well and provide the framework for meeting and exceeding the expectations of JCAHO, patients, and all other customers.

References

1. Graham, N., Editor. *Quality in Health Care*. Gaithersburg, Md.: Aspen Publishers, 1995, pp. 198-209.

2. Beer, M. *Organizational Change and Development*. Akron, Ohio: Goodyear Publishing Co., 1980, p. 19.

3. QA and I Plan, Metropolitan State Hospital, Norwalk, Calif., 1996.

4. Donabedian, A. "Quality Assessment and Assurance: Unity of Purpose , Diversity of Means." *Inquiry* 25(1):177-90, Spring 1988.

5. Institute of Medicine (IOM). *Clinical Practice Guidelines: Directions for a New Program*. Washington, D.C.: National Academy Press, 1990, p. 8.

6. Agency for Health Care Policy and Research. "Depression in Primary Care Clinical Practice Guidelines." Vol. 1: Detection and Diagnosis. Vol. 2: Treatment of Major Depression. Washington, D.C.: AHCPR, 1993, No. 5.

7. Ellwood, P. "Outcomes Management: A Technology of Patient Experience." *New England Journal of Medicine* 318(23):1549-56, June 9, 1988.

8. Agency for Health Care Policy and Research. "Using Clinical Practice Guidelines to Evaluate Quality of Care." AHCPR Publication No. 95-0045, March 1995, p. 4.

9. Graham, N., *op. cit.,* p. 173.

10. *Ibid.,* pp. 173-4.

11. *Ibid.,* Chapters 9 and 10.

12. Deming, W. "Philosophy Continues to Flourish." *APICS-The Performance Advantage* 1(4):20, Oct. 1991.

13. Juran, J. "Made in the U.S.A.: A Renaissance in Quality." *Harvard Business Review* 14(4):35-8, July-Aug. 1993.

14. Crosby, P. *Let's Talk Quality*. New York, N.Y.: McGraw-Hill, 1989.

15. Health Care Advisory Board. *Total Quality Management*, Volume II: "TQM, 14 Tactics for Improving the Quality Process," 1992.

Bibliography

Carey, R., and Lloyd, R. "Measuring the Success of CQI." *Health Care Executive* 9(2):9-11, March-April 1994.

Corrigan, P., and others. "User-Friendly CQI for the Mental Health Care Team." *Medical Interface* 7(12): 89-92, Dec. 1994.

Laffel, G., and Blumenthal, D. "The Case for Using Industrial Quality Management Science in Health Care Organizations." *JAMA* 262(20):2869-73, Nov. 24, 1989.

McConnell, C. "Total Quality and the Shifting Management Paradigm." *Health Care Supervisor* 13(3):71-9, March 1995.

Motwani, J., and others. "The Need for Implementing TQM in the Health Care Industry: An Empirical Investigation." *Journal of Hospital Marketing* 9(2):45-62, Sept. 1995.

Ross, R. "What Makes for Successful TQM?" *International Journal of Health Care Quality Assurance* 7(7):4-9, July 1994.

Shortell, S., and others. "Assessing the Impact of Continuous Quality Improvement." *Health Services Research* 30(2):377-401, June 1995.

Smith, G.B. and Hukill, E., "Quality Work Improvement Groups: From Paper to Reality." *Journal of Nursing Care Quarterly* 8(4):1-12, July 1994.

Smith, J., and others. "Using Patient Focus Groups for New Patient Services." *Joint Commission Journal of Quality Improvement* 21(1):22-31, Jan. 1995.

U.S. Department of Health and Human Services, Agency for Health Care Policy and Research. "Using Clinical Practice Guidelines to Evaluate Quality of Care." AHCPR Publication No.95-0045, 1995.

Sarath Gunatilake, MD, DrPH, is Professor, California State University, Long Beach, California.
F. Theodore Helmer, PhD, is Professor of Management, Northern Arizona University, Flagstaff.

Chapter 23

Public Issues Related to Measuring the Quality and Effectiveness of Behavioral Health Services

by Sandra Raynes Weiss

How should behavioral health be defined in the era of managed care? Should it be defined narrowly as behavior requiring psychiatric and chemical dependency services?[1] Should it be defined more broadly to include the behavioral component of physical health, such as proper diet and exercise, use of seat belts in motor vehicles, adherence by diabetics to diet, and general adherence to drug regimens?[2-5] Semantics aside, should managed care firms concern themselves with one or both kinds of behavior in the same or different organizations?

However perceived, behavioral health has massive consequences for society, its economy, the physical health and functioning of its citizenry, its children, and its justice system. The direct costs of mental health and substance abuse services in 1990 were estimated to be $54 billion[6]; indirect costs, such as lost or inefficient work time and repair of defective work, $108 billion[7]; costs of crime, criminal justice, and property loss due to illegal drug use, $46 billion[7]; economic costs of alcohol-related motor vehicle accidents, $46 billion[8]; and lifetime excess medical expenditures due to current or previous tobacco use, $500 billion.[9] These estimated costs do not take into account any of the emotional, behavioral, and financial burdens on relatives, friends, and others affected by people with mental illness or substance abuse disorders, nor do they reflect the life-long impact on abused and neglected children and subsequent long-term costs to society.

In a democratic society adhering to the rule of law, government has, among other roles, a protective function. This function may be performed by direct acts, such as police investigations and health and safety inspections, and indirectly via education and transmission of information to the general public and those charged with formulating policy. A democratic government needs accurate information on which to base its legislative and regulatory decisions and a well-informed citizenry that can both inform and judge those decisions as well as use the information for other more parochial purposes. The federal government collects data, supports research that provides the underpinnings for knowledge, and brings diverse groups together to address unmet needs and develop consensus about ways to meet them.

In the case of behavioral health care services, the federal government plays multiple roles. It collects and disseminates information and encourages the private sector to do the same. The goal is to provide information needed for objective and beneficial decision making. The remainder of this chapter is devoted to an overview of some of the issues surrounding data collection in the more narrowly defined behavioral health field and brief descriptions of public and private databases that can be used to measure some aspects of the quality and effectiveness of behavioral health services.

Measuring the Quality and Effectiveness of Behavioral Health Systems

Process and Outcome Measures

Traditionally, private and public accreditation agencies set standards of quality by prescribing specific functions that hospitals and other service-providing facilities should follow.[10] Implicit in these process-oriented mandates is a link between specific processes and structures of care and the outcomes of that care. For instance, dispensing the proper amounts of penicillin at the proper times over the proper intervals to people with bacterial infections will lead to cures. Requiring documentation of the time a medication is administered, the amount dispensed, the name of the person dispensing the medication, and the condition of the patient at the time the medication was given means greater accountability on the part of service providers and is likely to lead to better patient care with fewer complications and faster recovery.

Outcomes, on the other hand, are indicators of performance, i.e., measurable results of health care processes. Outcomes are intrinsic to the definition of quality of care and may be free of rules prescribing how care should be provided.[11] Increasingly, the federal government is becoming more results-oriented and less prescriptive in terms of how and what services and treatments will be provided.[12,13] The federal government is ever more willing to trust market and other forces to maintain services that are expected to lead to desirable outcomes.

Limitations to outcomes-directed quality improvement, however, have been inadequately recognized. Hammermeister *et al.* have enumerated some of these limitations[11]:

- Mortality, the most commonly used outcome measure, is usually sufficiently rare that it results in inadequate statistical power.

- Nonfatal outcomes are much more difficult to measure reliably than mortality.

- Outcomes may not be measurable for long periods after the care has been provided, making linkage to quality improvement inefficient.

- Patients usually desire good process of care as well as favorable outcomes.

Information Needs

Everyone using and delivering behavioral health services requires accurate, valid, reliable information. To get appropriate, timely, affordable health care, patients need information about access to appropriate services and the quality and costs of those services. To ascertain that they are purchasing services that ensure that employees and citizens can work productively, employers, governments, and other payers need information about the overall costs and effectiveness of services. To determine whether the level of services and capitation rates will be attractive to payers and patients, administrators of managed behavioral health care organizations need information about the number of potential patients, their general health and risk status, and the number and costs of providers needed for different patient populations. To plan effective use of their time and fair payment schedules, providers need information about the number and requirements of their clients. To ensure that their taxes are not being wasted, the public needs to know that behavioral health care organizations receiving public funds benefit the people they serve and that society at large is better off because of the services provided.

Definitions of Outcomes

Public sector mental health outcomes typically include measures of hospitalization, incarceration, community tenure, housing status, vocational status, educational achievements, consumer satisfaction, and quality of life.[14]

Groups define outcome success differently, and sometimes definitions of success conflict. Successful outcomes for patients are represented by the ability to function normally in all spheres of their lives; for payers by cost containment, productive workers, and increased payer/employer profits; for private managed care firms by profits and healthy clients; for providers by healthy clients and good financial remuneration; for the public by lower taxes and a better quality of life.

To further complicate the issue of the meaning of "successful outcomes," ideas about what constitutes "health" in the mental health field are often viewed differently by patients, families, and providers. For example, some mental health care consumers perceive that mental health professionals form negative judgments of patients who express anger, refuse medication, or maintain distance from their families; these consumers, however, view these very same acts as possibly promoting the potential for growth, independence, and recovery.[15]

Health-related quality of life is increasingly used as an outcome in clinical trials, effectiveness research, and research on quality of care.[16] Measures of health outcomes are divided into five levels[16]:

1. Biological and physiological

2. Symptoms

3. Functioning

4. General health perception

5. Overall quality of life.

Each level affects the others, each can be modified, and each can be measured.

The most complex and difficult-to-measure outcomes are those needed for public policy purposes. Taxpayers pay not only for health care but also for services related to education, welfare, justice, police, and other purposes. The need for these services is frequently predicated on human behavior. The public interest is not limited to discrete, short-term outcomes in one or another of these areas, but rather to broad, interrelated long-term outcomes that necessitate continual monitoring of public health and related fields.

Questions Govern Data that Are Collected

The needs of data collectors determine the kinds of data they collect. For instance, public payers should be interested in cost offsets of general health care and other kinds of services that potentially exceed the costs of mental health interventions. Thus, in the interest of reducing overall costs in the long term, data should be collected that compare the physical health care costs of people with mental illness who do and do not receive behavioral health care services. In the same spirit, data should be tracked that compare justice system costs of people with substance abuse disorders who do and do not receive behavioral health care services.

Managed care firms are concerned with outcomes in their own companies and are motivated to keep costs low. If managed care firms do not have long-term commitments from clients to stay with the firms, they have little motivation to provide preventive care and even less to collect data about anything that does not concern short-term costs and data related to the current and near-term needs of their clients.

Data Collection Issues

As the mental health care system focuses on social as well as therapeutic outcomes provided in managed care organizations, large-scale, quantitative data will be collected and linked in many computer data banks. The potential for unauthorized access to these huge pools of data and for linking specific data to identifiable persons raises great concern about the confidentiality of mental health treatment. Mental health law faces the challenge of accommodating legitimate interests for data with the protection of patients' privacy and of arranging for patients to retain some degree of control over personal medical information.[17]

During the past decade, public and private institutions have increased their use of electronic data storage technology, primarily for administrative purposes such as processing and paying claims for services, developing and evaluating provider networks, designing benefit packages and cost containment methods, and assessing patient clinical needs.[18]

Policy analysts and other researchers confront a number of problems when attempting to use large composite databases to understand the effects of changes in the health delivery system and to plan for the future. Some of the data needed to answer analyst questions were not collected. The large size of the data sets tends to make them unwieldy and expensive to analyze. Analysts not involved in the creation of the data sets may not be familiar with all their idiosyncrasies, limitations, and meanings. Further, when composite results are reported, the heterogeneity of the different databases limits their usefulness for program evaluation and administration.[19]

Interpreting Outcome Measures

In the lexicon of behavioral health care, outcomes are the demonstrable differences that services make on the behavior and functioning of clients. However, linking cause and effect is no simple matter, because many variables affect behavior in numerous ways, and correlations are often confused with causality.

It is necessary to have studies and demonstrations with suitable comparison groups or comparison sites to determine what constitutes ever more effective services. To understand the consequences that changing behavioral health systems of care are having on society, at a minimum, public measures such as mortality and birth statistics and data related to education, employment, housing, and the justice system must be tracked at local and national levels.

Current Efforts at Determining Quality and Effectiveness

The managed care industry and local and federal governments have been attempting to determine the quality and effectiveness of managed care services for some time. The National Committee on Quality Assurance (NCQA) developed the Health Plan Employer Data and Information Set (HEDIS) to assist employers wanting to compare managed health care plans for their employees. It has modified HEDIS to help state Medicaid agencies assess the managed care plans with which they contract.[20] The American Managed Behavioral Healthcare Association (AMBHA) has developed a standardized "report card" assessing the overall performance of managed behavioral health care delivery systems.[1] The Health Care Financing Administration, the federal agency responsible for administering and overseeing the Medicare and Medicaid programs, has developed a number of databases to track its programs, one of the latest being the State Medicaid Research Files (SMRF). Within the Substance Abuse and Mental Health Services Administration (SAMHSA), the Center for Mental Health Services, another federal public health agency, is developing a report card under its Mental Health Statistics Improvement Program that is designed to help consumers compare alternative behavioral health plan services and to promote managed care accountability. The National Association of State Mental Health Program Directors Research Institute administers a State Mental Health Profiling System.

In the interest of advancing a wide array of policy objectives supported by objective research and demonstrations, Section 1115 of the Social Security Act allows states to waive certain requirements of the Medicaid program.[21] Virtually all the waivers that have been proposed or implemented to date have expanded managed care services for Medicaid recipients. Approval by the federal government mandates that, among other requirements, states plan evaluations of the quality and effectiveness of new managed care services.

The remainder of this section of the chapter provides brief descriptions of some of the databases that are being developed and used to track behavioral health processes and outcomes.

Medicaid HEDIS

NCQA is an independent, not-for-profit organization that accredits health maintenance organizations. It developed the HEDIS instrument to help employers compare managed health care plans for their employees. Medicaid HEDIS is an adaptation for use in Medicaid managed care programs. It addresses overall health care performance, with a very small subset of measures devoted to behavioral health care services. Its primary focus is on service access and quality for women and children, who make up the majority of Medicaid managed care enrollees, and as yet contains no formal outcome measures.[22]

Medicaid HEDIS is based on administrative data and medical records. Data are collected in six major areas: beneficiary traits, finance, utilization, quality of care, access to services, and health plan management. Two of the six areas, utilization and quality of care, specifically address behavioral health care services. Utilization and quality of care are categorized by a variety of services that include mental health and chemical dependency, but the range of services and diagnoses assessed are limited. Two other measurement categories, access to services and health plan management, specify mental health and substance abuse as part of larger measures; beneficiary traits and finance do not separate behavioral health from other services.[22,23]

AMBHA's Report Card

AMBHA, an association of private managed behavioral health care organizations, has developed a standardized report card to assess the overall performance of managed behavioral health care delivery systems.[1] The report card uses client surveys in addition to administrative data and medical records.

AMBHA's Performance-Based Measures for Managed Behavioral Healthcare Programs (PERMS 1.0) are classified into three domains: access to care, consumer satisfaction, and quality of care. Access to care is measured by variables such as the percentage of the enrolled population receiving services categorized by age, diagnosis, treatment setting, and clinician type; alternatives to inpatient utilization; cost data; and issues related to length of time consumers wait on the phone before speaking to someone. Consumer satisfaction is measured by variables that include the length of time to a first appointment, satisfaction with intake workers and therapists, and assessment of outcomes. Some of the quality of care performance indicators are ambulatory follow up after hospitalization for major affective disorders, treatment failure for substance abuse, continuity of care, medication management for schizophrenia, and family visits for children under 12.[1]

State Medicaid Research Files (SMRF)

The State Medicaid Research Files are the fourth national data system HCFA developed to track the Medicaid program. Its primary purpose is to create a national uniform research database. SMRF is based on person-level state administrative data on enrollment, claims utilization, and expenditures. It is organized by state, type of service, and calendar year of services. Six file types have been created: person summary, outpatient, drug, inpatient, long-term care, and provider. SMRF personal summary files contain indicators for eight specific conditions, among them mental health and substance abuse diagnoses.[18,24]

Twenty-two states currently have SMRF files, and more will be added in the future. The files, available from 1992 on, are in a research format and documentation is available online.[24]

MHSIP Mental Health Report Card

The broad purpose of the Mental Health Statistics Improvement Program (MHSIP), a program component of SAMHSA's Center for Mental Health Services, is to improve mental health services by fostering and enhancing the quality and the scope of information used to make decisions concerning mental health care and by promulgating uniform standards for data collection. The MHSIP report card was developed with the help of consumers and families and emphasizes the needs of persons with severe mental illness.[23,25]

MHSIP initiated the development of a report card when health care reform proposals were being formulated in 1994.[25] The measures are based on research and values that are founded on consumer choice, empowerment, and involvement and that take account of data collection costs and burdens. Although its primary purpose is to help consumers evaluate health plans, the report card will also help payers, providers, and state mental health agencies monitor the quality and the effectiveness of managed care and other provider systems.[25,26] The report card, which focuses on performance accountability, contains both process and outcome measures acquired from administrative data, clinician reports, and consumer self-reports. Service issues include access, appropriateness, outcomes, illness prevention, and consumer satisfaction. Outcome measures concern physical and psychological health, independence and functional measures, social relationships, environment, provider costs, and service utilization.[26]

State Mental Health Agency Profiling System

The National Association of State Mental Health Program Directors, under the sponsorship of SAMHSA's Center for Mental Health Services, maintains a database that provides descriptive and quantitative data about the organization, funding, operation, services, policies, statutes, and clientele of state mental health agencies. The system includes both quantitative data, such as state mental health agency revenues, expenditures, and mental health services, and nonquantitative data, such as policies and administrative practices.[27]

Conclusion

Tracking outcome and other kinds of data is imperative in these times of rapid transition to managed health care in the health care delivery system. Particular attention should be given to systems that deliver mental health and substance abuse services, because they affect physical health and every other area of economic and social life.

In the past, health maintenance organizations have provided limited behavioral health care services to their enrollees. As managed care becomes the mechanism by which Americans receive health care services, it is incumbent upon governments at all levels to monitor the services being provided, how they are administered, to and by whom they are furnished, the events leading to their provision, and the short- and long-term effects of the care.

The federal government should be the leader in data collection efforts and should furnish guidelines that help both the public and the private sectors set standards and understand the consequences of their activities. National data sets allow localities and businesses to compare themselves with similar entities. Knowing how processes affect outcomes assists decision makers in their difficult task of providing good, affordable behavioral and physical health care that will benefit everyone.

References

1. "Performance Measures For Managed Behavioral Healthcare Programs." American Managed Behavioral Healthcare Association Quality Improvement and Clinical Services Committee, Washington, D.C., Aug. 1995.

2. Pace, T., and others. "Psychological Consultation with Primary Care Physicians: Obstacles and Opportunities in the Medical Setting." *Professional Psychology Research and Practice* 26(2):123-131, April 1995.

3. Clifford, P., and others. "Efficacy of a Self-Directed Behavior Health Change Program: Weight, Body Composition, Cardiovascular Fitness, Blood Pressure, Health Risk, and Psychosocial Mediating Variables." *Journal of Behavioral Medicine* 14(3):303-23, June 1991.

4. Rogers, R. "Preventive Health Psychology: An Interface of Social and Clinical Psychology." *Journal of Social and Clinical Psychology* 1(2):120-7, 1983.

5. Matarazzo, J. "Behavioral Health's Challenge to Academic, Scientific, and Professional Psychology." *American Psychologist* 37(1):1-14, Jan. 1982.

6. Frank, R., and others. "Paying for Mental Health and Substance Abuse Care." *Health Affairs* 13(1):337-42, Spring 1994.

7. Rouse, B., Editor. *Substance Abuse and Mental Health Statistics Sourcebook*, DHHS Publication No. (SMA) 95-3064. Washington, D.C.: Superintendent of Documents, U.S. Government Printing Office, 1995.

8. Blincoe, L., and Faigin, B. *The Economic Costs of Motor Vehicle Crashes*, 1990. Washington, D.C.: National Highway Traffic Safety Administration, Department of Transportation, DOT HS 807 876, 1992.

9. Hodgson, T. "Cigarette Smoking and Lifetime Medical Expenditures." *Millbank Quarterly* 70(1) 81-125, 1992.

10. *1995 Accreditation Manual for Hospitals.* Oak Brook, Ill.: Joint Commission on Accreditation of Healthcare Organizations, 1995.

11. Hammermeister, K., and others. "Why It Is Important to Demonstrate Linkages between Outcomes of Care and Processes and Structures of Care." *Medical Care* 33(10 Suppl):OS5-OS16, 1995.

12. Health Care Financing Administration's Draft Revision of Conditions of Participation, 1996.

13. *HHS News*, Office of the Secretary, March 18, 1996.

14. Adams, N. "Outcome Evaluation Based on Life Domain Function," Abstracts of Concurrent Sessions, Sixth Annual National Conference on State Mental Health Agency Services Research and Program Evaluation, Feb. 11-13, 1996, Arlington, Va.

15. Campbell, J. "Values and the Generation of Outcome Measurements." In *Outcome Issues in a Managed Care Environment*, Report of the Ninth Annual WICHE Decision Support Conference, Jan. 6-8, 1994, San Francisco, Calif., McGuirck, F., and others, Editors.

16. Wilson, I., and Cleary, P. "Linking Clinical Variables with Health-Related Quality of Life: A Conceptual Model of Patient Outcomes." *JAMA* 273(1):59-65, Jan. 4, 1995.

17. Applebaum, P. "Managed Care: The Next Generation of Mental Health Law." *Psychiatric Services* 47(1):27-8,34, Jan. 1996.

18. Harrington, M., and others. *Mental Health and Substance Abuse Data Assessment*. Washington, D.C.: Mathematica Policy Research, Inc., June 1995.

19. Pandiani, J., and others. "A Methodology for Using the Longitudinal Database of Inpatient Episodes in State Psychiatric Hospitals With Demonstrations Predicting Hospital Length of Stay and Community Tenure." Alexandria, Va.: National Association of State Mental Health Program Directors Research Institute, Inc., March 1995.

20. Page, A. Presentation at Medicaid HEDIS meeting, July 25, 1995, Rockville, Md.

21. *Federal Register* 59(186):49249, Sept. 27, 1994.

22. Draft of Medicaid HEDIS (Health Plan Employee Data and Information Set), National Committee for Quality Assurance, Washington D.C., July 1995.

23. Robinson, G. Medicaid HEDIS (draft), Mental Health Policy Resource Center, Washington, D.C., 1996.

24. State Medicaid Research Files Workshop Notebook, Feb. 27-29, 1996, Baltimore, Md.

25. Mental Health Statistics Improvement Program Mental Health Report Card Phase II Task Force, Progress Report, Presentation at National Conference on Mental Health Statistics, Center for Mental Health Services, Washington, D.C., June 1995.

26. The MHSIP Consumer-Oriented Mental Health Report Card, April 1996.

27. Project Status Reports, State Mental Health Agency Profiling System, National Association of State Mental Health Program Directors Research Institute, Inc., Alexandria, Va., Feb. 1996.

Sandra Raynes Weiss is Special Assistant to the Administrator, Substance Abuse and Mental Health Services Administration, Public Health Service, Department of Health and Human Services, Washington, D.C. The opinions expressed in this paper are those of the author and do not necessarily reflect the policies of the Center for Mental Health Services, Substance Abuse and Mental Health Services Administration.

Chapter 24

Outcomes Management Model

by Diehl M. Snyder, MD

Introduction

Philhaven is a behavioral health care system in south central Pennsylvania that has been operating for 50 years and serves a region that includes about 1.7 million people. The organization is not-for-profit and is owned and operated by the Lancaster Mennonite Conference. It offers a full range of behavioral health care services to all ages. Philhaven works closely with many other mental health providers in its six-county area and has close working relationships with several large general hospital systems. Managed care payers provide approximately one-third of the system's revenues, with another one-third reimbursed through the Medicaid system. Medicare covers 10-15 percent of our services, and the remainder of our clients are either self-pay or have commercial insurance. Philhaven provides inpatient, day hospital, residential, intensive outpatient services, as well as a variety of outpatient services and educational programs.

Philhaven Outcomes Management Program

Because of today's push for administrative and clinical efficiencies, Philhaven attempted to integrate several management functions—quality assurance, performance (quality) improvement, utilization management, risk management, outcome measurements, and cost data—into a single Outcomes Management Program.

Philhaven's working definition of quality is "the degree to which health care services for individuals and populations increases the likelihood of desired health outcomes consistent with current professional knowledge."[1] An operational strategy to achieve quality is to "do the right thing, the right way, the first time, on time." The Outcomes Management Program is designed to address overuse, underuse, and misuse problems in behavioral health care quality. Recognizing the current limitations of management information systems, the Philhaven Outcomes Management Program was designed to take the organization from the acquisition of data to wisdom. The process begins with raw observations (data), continues by organizing that data into information, organizes the information into knowledge, and finishes when knowledge is integrated into wisdom.[2]

Key participants in behavioral health care have different perspectives and outcomes interests. Clinicians are interested in the clinical status of their clients. Clients tend to measure outcomes by their ability to function in everyday life. Families' primary outcome interest is impact on family life. Purchasers are interested in the cost of care, and society is interested in allocation of scarce resources. Other participants include researchers, who are interested in what is truly measurable and by what means.[3] To address these different perspectives and outcomes interests, the Outcomes Management Program measures multiple domains: intake/triage data, expectations (patient, family, referral source, staff), functional abilities, symptom distress levels, satisfaction (patient, family, referral source, aftercare provider, staff), medications (preadmission, current regimen, discharge regimen), and critical incidents (sentinel events and PHICO Event Reporting and Trending Systems (PERTS) forms).

Philhaven Outcomes Management Domains

Intake/Triage Data

Standardized intake information is required on every new patient in the Philhaven system. Finding the balance between enough information to make appropriate level of care and program assignment decisions and not adding to our clients' mental distress by too many or repeated questions has been a challenge to our system. None of the commercially available intake instruments met our needs. We interface with multiple managed care organizations, some of whom have their own level of care and/or triage questionnaires. We attempted to design our intake database as a standardized set of questions that satisfied all of our payers. Feedback from some of the managed care organizations reported that our clients complained if the intake process took longer than one hour and included more than one self-report instrument. Demographic, clinical, and basic financial information are included in the intake data set. Figure 1, page 353, is a schematic of the clinical variables collected for each adult client in the Philhaven Initial Evaluation (PIE) instrument. We currently have approximately 5,000 patients with this data set in our outcomes management files. We are still looking for a brief, fully computerized questionnaire that will assist us in making the appropriate level of care and program assignment for each client as soon as possible. Several intake/triage instruments show promise, but none has met all our system needs.[3-6]

Expectations

The expectation domain, which is a key determinant of satisfaction, has been difficult to quantify. We began with focus groups, querying patients, their families, referral sources, payers, and staff. The common expectations emerging from these focus groups centered on understanding the process of treatment prior to engaging in it. Families and referral sources were quite helpful in suggesting there are three critical points at which behavioral health problems emerge and need to be addressed: at the client's home, at the client's primary care center, and at a behavioral health specialty care center. The focus groups pleaded that these three locations needed better coordination and needed to work more in concert with the client and family while treating the behavioral problem.

Figure I. Philhaven Initial Evaluation (PIE) Instrument Variables

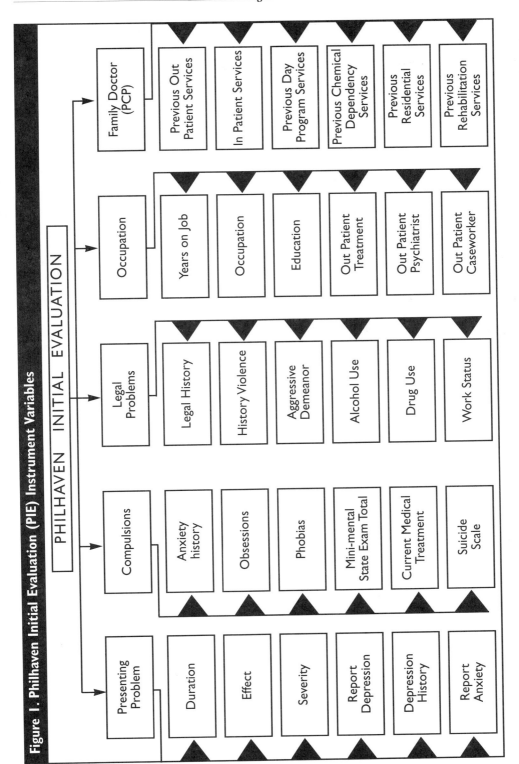

PHILHAVEN INITIAL EVALUATION

Figure 2, page 355, is a schematic of the interface of home, primary care and specialty care services for a patient with a serious and persistent behavioral problem. It highlights the need for each area that interacts with the client to understand what other areas are capable of doing to treat the behavioral problem. The core expectation is understanding the process of treatment prior to beginning it. Viewing this model as an encouragement to inform clients, their families, and primary care physicians of what constitutes behavioral specialty care, Philhaven attempted to write clinical pathways for the processes of care we use in treating common mental disorders.

The intake/triage data were used to outline which mental disorders we were treating most frequently on the adult service. Table 1, page 356, shows the discharge diagnoses for more than 1,300 patients admitted to our inpatient service and suggests that our clients' expectations could be well served by formulating five pathways that could be given to clients and their families during intake to help meet their expectation of knowing the treatment process.

Clinical pathways were developed for major depression, schizophrenia, bipolar disorder, dissociative identity disorder, and impulse control/intermittent explosive disorder. The task forces that developed these pathways had as their task production of easy-to-read pathways that outlined the daily tasks of each staff member and the outcomes expected of the client for each day of treatment on the Inpatient Service. The task forces used data from the Outcomes Management Program to help them select reasonable length-of-stay targets. As they worked at completing the diagnosis-driven pathways, they also developed 14 alternate pathways that were problem-driven to guide their interactions and to help inform clients and their families on how their specific problems would be addressed in our specialty treatment setting. A list of these alternate pathway problems is given in table 2, page 356.

An example of the printed clinical pathway for day 1 for major depression is shown in figure 3, page 357. Client outcome expectations, as well as "evidence that patient is not responding," are listed on the pathway. However, these detailed pathways became too extensive and laborious for the shortened lengths of stay experienced by most adult inpatients today. Clients expect something more understandable and less detailed to inform them about the process of treatment. Therefore, in recent months the five diagnosis-driven and 14 problem-driven inpatient adult pathways have been condensed into four and then three pathways, which facilitated meeting the expectations of our inpatients. Table 3, page 358, shows the results of surveys done on our inpatient service to determine the percentage of clients on each of the four and then three pathways. Clinical pathways for our day hospital, intensive outpatient, residential, and outpatient programs are still being formulated.

Functions

This domain is of primary interest to clients and attempts to measure how they function in their homes and vocational and social settings. Most of us in behavioral health care wish we had a uniform data set similar to the Functional Improvement Measure (FIM) to measure functions.[7] This instrument, developed by providers of medical rehabilitation services, enables clinicians and facilities to document the severity of patient disability and to measure outcomes of medical rehabilitation in a uniform way. It establishes a common language that can be used to discuss

Figure 2. Clinical Pathways for Behavioral Problems

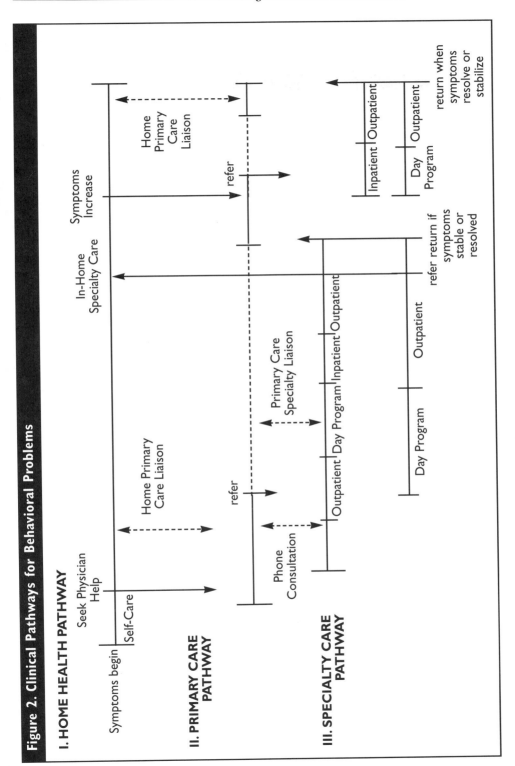

I. HOME HEALTH PATHWAY

Symptoms begin
Self-Care
Seek Physician Help
Home Primary Care Liaison
In-Home Specialty Care
Symptoms Increase
Home Primary Care Liaison

II. PRIMARY CARE PATHWAY

Phone Consultation
refer
Primary Care Specialty Liaison
refer

III. SPECIALTY CARE PATHWAY

Outpatient | Day Program | Inpatient | Outpatient
Day Program
Outpatient
refer return if symptoms stable or resolved
Inpatient | Outpatient
Day | Outpatient Program
return when symptoms resolve or stabilize

Table 1. Adult Services, Discharge Diagnoses, 1/1/93-6/1/94 (N=1,321)

Diagnosis	No. of Cases	% of Total	Cumulative %

Major Depression
    Single episode, 116
    Recurrent, 389
    Depressive, NOS, 60
	565	43%	43%

Schizophrenia
    Schizoaffective, 156
    Schizophrenia, 127
    Psychotic, NOS, 43
	339	25	68

Bipolar	104	8	76
Dissociative Identity Disorder	87	7	83
Impulse Control Disorder (Intermittent Explosive Disorder)	58	4	87
Adjustment Disorder	104	8	95
Dysthymic Disorder	37	3	98
Panic Disorder	15	1	99
Organic Personality Disorder	12	1	100

Table 2. Inpatient Adult Critical Pathways

Problem-Driven Alternate Pathways

I. Noncooperation with assessments
II. Noncompliance with treatments ordered
III. Organic mental disorder
IV. Contraindications to preferred treatments
V. Comorbid disorders
VI. Denial of illness
VII. Predominant personality pathology
VIII. Imminent danger to self or others
IX. Lack of appropriate aftercare supports
X. Regression secondary to acute stressor
XI. Reemergence of admission symptoms
XII. Sustained medication-seeking or drug craving
XIII. Refusal of aftercare plan
XIV. Mental retardation

Figure 3. Clinical Pathway for Major Depression

		Remarks
Estimated L.O.S. – 7 Days Date_____Day 2		
PSYCHIATRY ▮ Assessment ▮ Teaching ▮ Review of Pt. Work ▮ Team Communication ▮ Order RX's	▮ Lab rev., EKG, clearance for Rx. ▮ Rx. options/role of meds. & interpret lab results ▮ Review completion of psych. test. ▮ Set D/C criteria ▮ Begin antidepressant	
PSYCHOSOCIAL INTERVENTIONS (To be done by Social Worker, Psychologist, Allied Mental Health Worker, or Certified Addictions Counselor)	▮ Contact previous provider ▮ Contact family ▮ Coordination of multidisc. treatment plan ▮ Assessment of coping skills & clarification of treatment goals	

SOCIAL WORK	▮ Social History completed
	  Axis IV Dx.
	  Axis V Dx.
	▮ D/C goals written	

PSYCHOLOGY REGULAR DIAGNOSTICS NEUROPSYCHOLOGICAL EVALUATION	▮ Cmpl't computerized testing ▮ Report on projectives entered on chart	
OUTCOMES Patient will:	▮ Begin self-awareness of problems ▮ Movement toward hopefulness or exercises option to decline spiritual involvement	
EVIDENCE THAT PATIENT IS NOT RESPONDING:	▮ Contradictions to preferred medication ▮ Alternate dx. or mixed dx. ▮ Pt. refuses meds. ▮ Testing identifies predominate Axis II ▮ No family or social supports	
Multidisciplinary Progress Notes PH 07-06 (Rev. 7/93)		Patient Name:_____ Patient No:_____

Table 3. Problem-Driven Pathways

Implemented August 25, 1995

#1 Danger to self or others
#2 Acute psychotic episode
#3 Noncompliance with treatment/aftercare problems
#4 Organic disorder/mental retardation—unable to care for self

Census = 61

Problem #1	43 clients	70%
Problem #2	18 clients	30%
Problem #3	14 clients	23%
Problem #4	12 clients	20%

Two clients did not fit into any of the above categories:
—Chronic depression, receiving ECT treatments
—Extreme anxiety, needs medication adjustment

Twenty-six clients (43%) fit into more than one category.

Implemented September 15, 1995

#1 Danger to self or others
#2 Acute psychotic episode
#3 Organic disorder/mental retardation—unable to care for self

Census = 79

Problem #1	60 clients	76%
Problem #2	19 clients	24%
Problem #3	9 clients	11%

All children (11) and adolescents (11) in the census were listed under problem #1.
Eight clients (10%) fit into more than one category.

Table 4. Functional Improvement Measure (FIM) Levels

Level	Description
No Helper	
7	Complete independence
6	Modified independence
Helper	
5	Supervision
4	Minimal assistance
3	Moderate assistance
2	Maximal assistance
1	Total assistance

disability across disciplines and to provide a basis for comparison of rehabilitation outcomes. The specificity of functional measurement in FIM and the uniformity with which it is used in nearly all medical rehabilitation settings allow for real comparisons in functional outcomes between programs and different types of pathology.[8] Seven FIM levels are outlined in table 4, page 358, ranging from "no helper" to "total assistance" needed. Seventeen functional tasks, listed in figure 4, below, are evaluated for each patient, and a polar graph representation characterizes a patient's functional ability at a given time. Sequential measurements of these functional levels at different times can be shown on the same polar graph and indicate improvement or deterioration.

Philhaven has used the Global Assessment of Functioning (GAF) scale. This is a modified version of the Global Assessment Scale developed by Spitzer *et al.* from the Health Sickness Rating Scale.[9] The GAF instrument is a scale of 1 to 100 that attempts to rate the psychosocial functional abilities of patients. It is used as Axis V of the DSM IV's multiaxial diagnostic system. The GAF score is reported on Axis V for the current evaluation, and a second rating for other periods, such

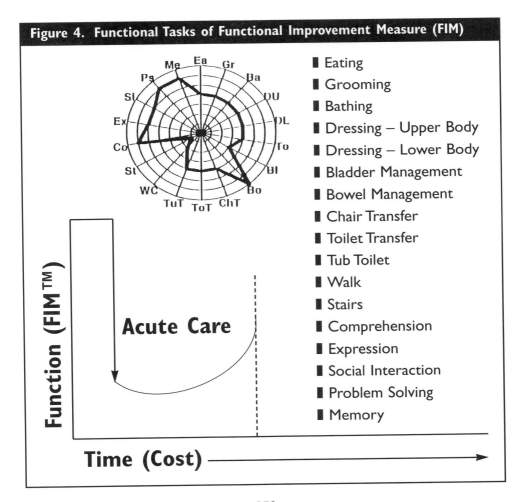

Figure 4. Functional Tasks of Functional Improvement Measure (FIM)

- Eating
- Grooming
- Bathing
- Dressing – Upper Body
- Dressing – Lower Body
- Bladder Management
- Bowel Management
- Chair Transfer
- Toilet Transfer
- Tub Toilet
- Walk
- Stairs
- Comprehension
- Expression
- Social Interaction
- Problem Solving
- Memory

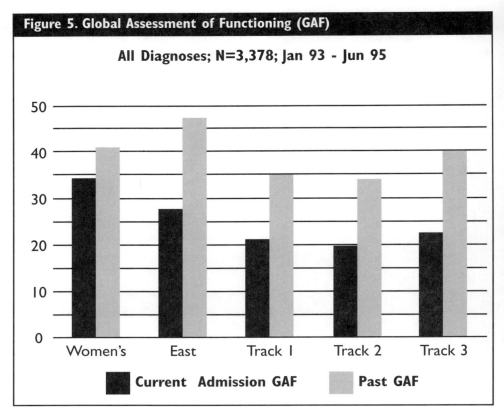

Figure 5. Global Assessment of Functioning (GAF)

All Diagnoses; N=3,378; Jan 93 - Jun 95

Current Admission GAF   Past GAF

as time of admission to or discharge from care, and/or based on the highest level in the past year can be reported. The GAF scale is to be rated with respect only to psychological, social, and occupational functioning. The instructions specify not to include impairment in functioning due to physical or environmental limitations. The GAF scale we hoped would be useful in tracking the functional progress of our clients in global terms, using a single measure.

Figure 5, above, shows GAF scores for clients admitted to Philhaven's inpatient service for all diagnoses over a two-year period. Current and past GAF are plotted for each of the adult units. It was comforting to note that, on all adult services, we appeared to be admitting patients whose functions had been compromised by their illness.

Figure 6, page 361, shows GAF scores between January 1993 and June 1995, plotted by quarter, for three of our adult units. Philhaven staff believed the patients being admitted were less functional, but their GAF ratings, reviewed by quarter, did not support staffs' feelings. When these data were shared with staff, it was concluded that the decreasing length of stay, which meant that patients' functioning did not improve as much during the hospitalization, caused staff to develop the impression that patients' overall level of functioning had been decreasing.

The domain of functioning is so important to clients that it warrants further attention by all behavioral health care systems. The MOS 36-item Short Form Health Survey (SF-36)[10] and the

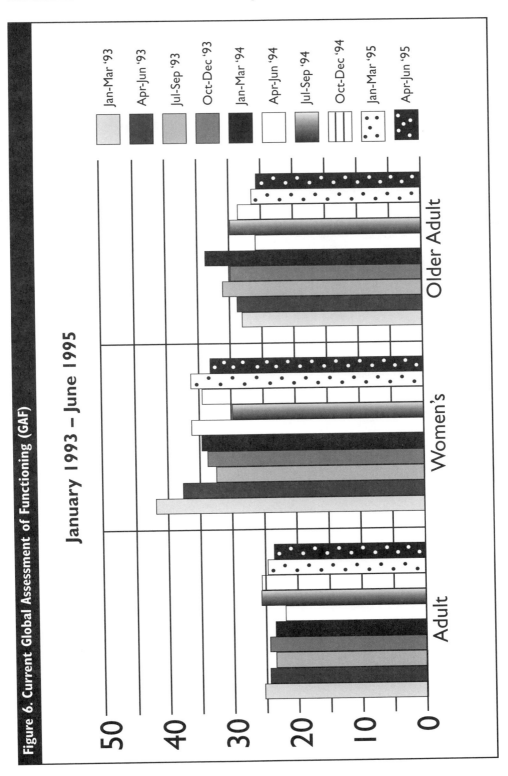

Figure 6. Current Global Assessment of Functioning (GAF)

January 1993 – June 1995

Legend:
- Jan-Mar '93
- Apr-Jun '93
- Jul-Sep '93
- Oct-Dec '93
- Jan-Mar '94
- Apr-Jun '94
- Jul-Sep '94
- Oct-Dec '94
- Jan-Mar '95
- Apr-Jun '95

Categories: Adult, Women's, Older Adult

BASIS-32 instrument,[11] both of which are in the public domain, attempt to measure some functional capacities. However, there is nothing in behavioral health comparable to the Functional Improvement Measure (FIM) of the medical rehabilitation field.

Symptoms

The domain of patient symptoms, because it is very clinically focused, has been of immense help to patients and clinicians in appreciating the "real time" clinical relevance of outcome measurements. Most adult patients can use one of many self-report symptom distress instruments available in the public domain and from commercial vendors. Many are specific for diagnostic categories and/or specific age groups. The self-reporting format often does not work well for cognitively impaired older adults, children, or adolescents. Clinician-scored symptom instruments have proved more helpful for these groups. Philhaven, in an attempt to encourage clinicians to use symptom measurements as an aid in their clinical work, selected two general adult instruments to begin its study in late 1992. We chose BASIS-32,[11] which is in the public domain, and Brief Symptom Inventory (BSI),[12] a commercially available instrument, with computer generated reports that gave our clinicians immediate graphic feedback on symptom distress that they could share with patients. These two instruments were given on admission and at discharge to all our inpatients. We now also administer the BSI to day hospital and outpatient clients. Both of these symptom distress instruments were normed, and we were able to quickly compute for individual patients and aggregate groups the amount of change in symptom distress experienced by our clients.

Philhaven clinicians favored the BSI as an easy-to-use, quick-glance measure of clients' symptomatology. The BASIS-32 measured many of the same areas, but it was not available to us with a computer-based graphic report at the time the study began in 1992. We are not in a position to say that either of these instruments is better than the other or as good as any of a number of other instruments that are available. We will report on our findings using the BSI because it became the most accepted in our system. By being available on the patient's chart within five minutes of admission, this measurement of patient self-reported symptomatology did more to develop and encourage a "culture of measurement" at Philhaven than any other outcome instrument. In other settings, perhaps other instruments, if used consistently and made available in real time to clinicians, could accomplish a similar goal.

Philhaven's adult inpatient services consist of four discrete units that all treat general adult clients. In addition, each unit has a specialty focus: Impact—mentally ill, substance-abusing patients; Womens'—gender-specific illness; East—dissociative disorders; and Structured—mentally retarded, mentally ill patients. All adult patients are asked to complete the Brief Symptom Inventory (BSI) on admission and at time of discharge from the inpatient service. The Global Severity Index (GSI) is the single best overall measure of symptom distress reported by the BSI.[12] BSI change is, thus, the GSI T-score on admission minus the GSI T-score at discharge. Philhaven uses the BSI change score as a way to follow overall effectiveness in reducing the symptom distress of patients on the inpatient service.

Figure 7, page 363, shows BSI change results for the four quarters of 1993. With the exception of the Impact unit for mentally ill, substance abuse patients, the second quarter BSI change was

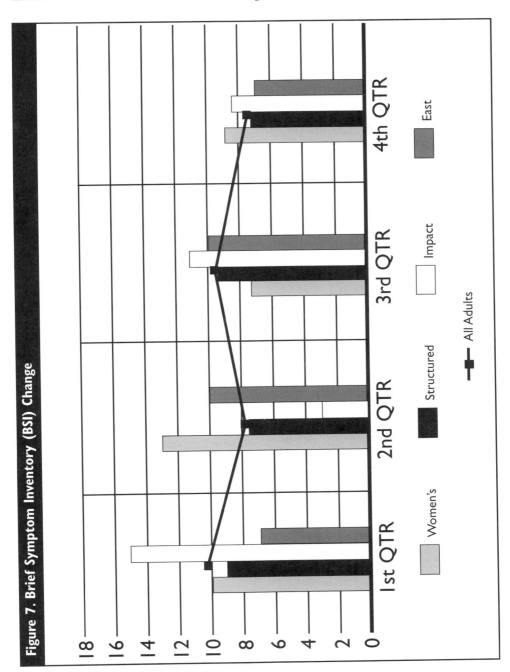

Figure 7. Brief Symptom Inventory (BSI) Change

relatively stable for all groups. We have found that most adults experience at least a seven point T-score change on BSI from admission to discharge. Therefore, the Impact unit's average of less than three T-score points of BSI change during the second quarter warranted exploration. In conference with unit staff and after reviewing patient records for the second quarter, it became apparent that during that period two locum tenens psychiatrists, who each worked four weeks, had relational skills that did not match well with staff or patients. Unit staff were not surprised that patients did not report as much symptom improvement during this period as when they were attended by our regular staff psychiatrists. We concluded that following BSI change by unit over time was helpful in monitoring whether treatment outcomes were maintained at acceptable levels. As Philhaven explores alternate models of delivering care, we believe that monitoring BSI change will alert us if we make changes that do not maintain patient outcomes.

Clinicians, program managers, and the administration at Philhaven are increasingly using these symptom measures to make important decisions regarding program development, staff management and patient care. As a way of validating efficacy of care, we hope to have every adult patient complete a symptom distress self-report when admitted and discharged.

Shifting to outpatients, figure 8, page 365, shows that each client completes a BSI on admission, at the fourth session, and every six sessions thereafter. Scanable answer sheets are scored and automated reports are sent back to each clinician to monitor improvement. Again, most clients average an improvement by session four of about seven T-score points on the BSI. Average improvement in symptom reduction continues at each succeeding administration, although to an ever-diminishing extent. Our data corroborate the results of the Kopta *et al.* study relating treatment dosage of psychotherapy to symptom reduction.[13] This pattern, curiously, does not hold for eating disorders or drug and alcohol problems. We theorized that this population showed increased symptomatology early in the therapy process as the patient comes out of denial and begins to directly face the pain and symptoms of the disorder.

Average BSI T-scores on admission to the outpatient service are quite similar to the discharge T-scores from the inpatient service. Patients are entering the inpatient service with average BSI T-scores in the 72 to 74 range (greater than two standard deviations above the general population norm) with a reduction during inpatient care to the 62 to 64 range. Outpatients continued to see symptom reduction of six to 10 T-score points and showed symptom distress T-score levels in the 50s after four sessions. These T-scores were generated from a large community norm and, therefore, represent the population on which most managed care behavioral health firms wish to base their comparisons.[11]

We continue to search for effective symptom measures for use in providing care to our child and adolescent patients. However, patients whose primary diagnosis is conduct disorder and/or impulse control disorder are not reliable on self-report instruments. For this group, we have found reporting by parents and/or teachers to be more effective. For our eight-week Child and Adolescent Summer Day Program in 1994, we asked parents to complete a Connors' Parent Rating Scale[14] on admission and at discharge. Figure 9, page 366, shows the results of these ratings and highlights the importance of understanding the mission of a program when evaluating its symptom change outcome data. At first glance the outcomes appear to be rather lackluster, showing little to no symptom improvement. However, we had been approached by county agencies to design a program that would help socially and emotionally disturbed children in the school system to maintain, over the summer, the gains they had made during the school year. In the past, most parents and teachers felt that if the student made three steps forward during the

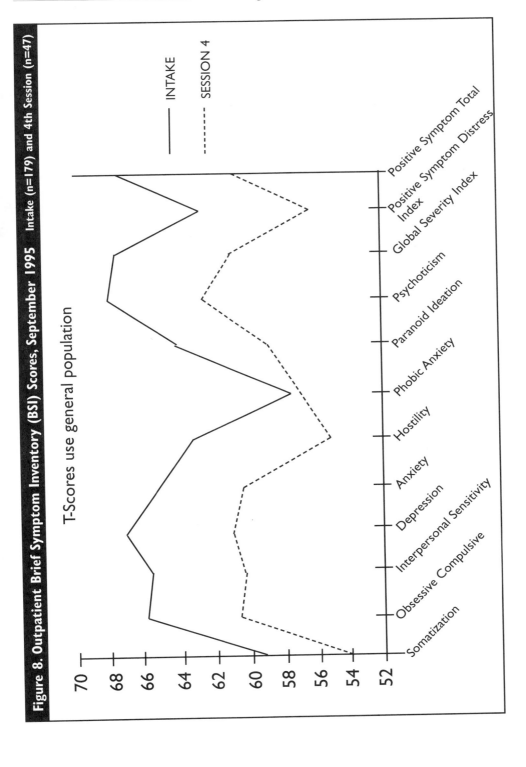

Figure 8. Outpatient Brief Symptom Inventory (BSI) Scores, September 1995   Intake (n=179) and 4th Session (n=47)

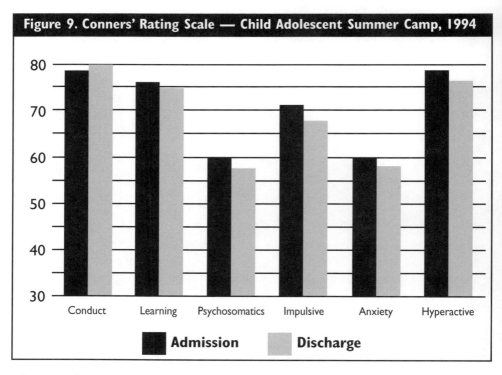

Figure 9. Conners' Rating Scale — Child Adolescent Summer Camp, 1994

school year they often took one or two steps backward over the summer vacation. Our goal was to maintain the symptoms at their June levels without having the distress level rise by the end of the summer. Figure 9 shows that the summer day program was able to accomplish that goal in all five dimensions measured by the Connors' Parent Rating Scale.

The challenge of measuring symptom distress levels in the cognitively impaired elderly has not yet been well addressed by our system. We have used clinician-scored instruments and are looking forward to better measures becoming available and to gathering enough data to organize into some helpful information regarding this population group.

Satisfaction

The outcomes management domain for satisfaction has several key groups who need to be surveyed. At Philhaven, we have worked hardest at measuring patient satisfaction, but our experience tells us that measuring family, referral source, and staff satisfaction is equally important to performance improvement efforts. To date, we have used focus groups to assess family satisfaction and to obtain referral source feedback. Because of the many transitions necessitated by multiple changes in programming, staff members have been quite verbal in their feedback, but no standardized instrument for measuring their job satisfaction has been given. An additional group whose satisfaction must be measured is payers. We have been assessed by a managed care firm that sent surveys directly to patients, with analysis of questionnaires by the managed care firm.

Philhaven's primary instrument to measure patient satisfaction has been the Client Satisfaction Questionnaire (CSQ).[15] CSQ uses a four-point rating scale. Additional satisfaction questions regarding specific services at Philhaven were added to the questionnaire, which is in the public domain.

Figure 10, page 368, shows client satisfaction as reported on the CSQ by quarter from January 1993 to June 1995. All average scores are above three on a four-point scale. We use these satisfaction ratings to compare different units and different periods to help guide performance improvement efforts. Unfortunately, the scores have been relatively positive and stable and have not pointed out discrete problem areas. For this reason, we have moved toward a new satisfaction questionnaire that uses "yes-no" questions to better focus on the problems that we need to address.

Client satisfaction as reported on the CSQ by diagnosis by quarter is shown in figure 11, page 369. Philhaven staff looked at these data when compiling clinical pathways in order to see if any of our treatment plans for specific diagnoses were better received than others by patient groups. In Figure 11, the CSQ score shows very little variation in satisfaction either by diagnosis or over time. We concluded we were getting satisfaction reports in the same range as other facilities, but the CSQ instrument did not discriminate which diagnoses we treated most effectively or which services needed performance improvement strategies. We hope the "yes-no" format of our new satisfaction questionnaire will better discriminate and help focus our performance improvement efforts.

Table 5, page 370, shows combined data for use of the new Philhaven Parent Satisfaction Questionnaire in all child and adolescent service programs. Specific "yes-no" response percentages, as well as the overall quality rating by parents, are tabulated. By analyzing the dissatisfaction expressed for each question in light of parents' overall quality rating, we are able to focus our improvement efforts on specific issues that caused parents to give us poorer overall quality grades. For example, although 16 percent of parents said yes to "treatment in this program ended before my child was ready," parents still gave a very positive (B+ or better) overall rating. Because further analysis of questions 3 and 4 regarding "opportunities to ask questions" and "aftercare planning processes" indicated that these parts of our treatment process affected the overall quality rating, we are focusing our performance improvement efforts in these areas.

Table 6, page 370, compares the results of satisfaction questionnaires sent by a managed care organization to its enrollees who had received inpatient services at Philhaven. The ratings are tabulated on a five-point scale, where five is "very satisfied" and one is "very dissatisfied." Many patients complained that the length of our questionnaires and the number of forms that they needed to complete during the admission process was stressful and taxing. They did not wish to take more than 10 or 15 minutes to fill out our self-report symptom and/or functioning instruments. Also, they did not feel it was appropriate to have the same questions asked of them by multiple Philhaven staff. These satisfaction reports have helped our efforts to standardize the admission process using the shortest effective intake questionnaire and limiting the patient self-report survey to one that can be completed within 10 to 15 minutes. Philhaven would be pleased if all managed care organizations conducted patient satisfaction surveys and gave us periodic feedback. In this day of shrinking resources, it is very helpful to have as much feedback as possible to help focus our performance improvement efforts.

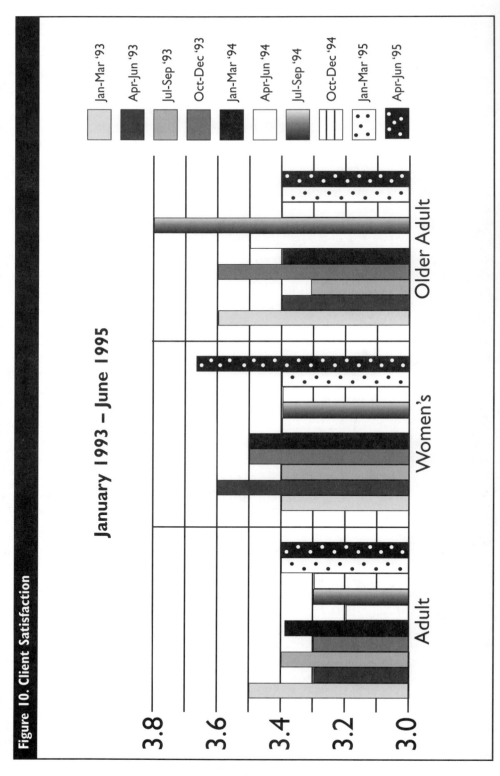

Figure 10. Client Satisfaction

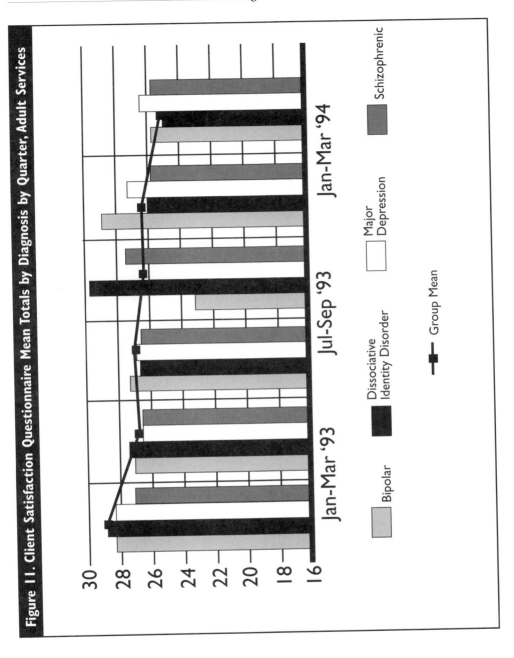

Figure 11. Client Satisfaction Questionnaire Mean Totals by Diagnosis by Quarter, Adult Services

Table 5. Philhaven Parent Satisfaction Questionnaire

Question	Responses to Date	
	Yes	No
The plan for treatment addressed my child's problems.	95.5% (85)	4.5% (4)
Treatment in this program ended before my child was ready.	16.3% (14)	83.7% (72)
I had enough opportunities to ask questions about my child's treatment.	88.2% (82)	11.8% (11)
I was informed about the time and plans for ending treatment and arranging follow-up care.	92.1% (82)	7.9% (7)
Philhaven staff showed a caring attitude toward my child.	98.9% (92)	1.1% (1)
I felt my child was emotionally and physically safe while under Philhaven's care.	98.9% (92)	1.1% (1)
I felt my cultural and ethnic identity was respected during the course of treatment.	100% (89)	
Someone explained the treatment plan so I could understand it.	93.5% (86)	6.5% (6)

Overall Ratings

Excellent:	A	45.7% (37)
Good:	A-	22.2% (18)
	B+	13.6% (11)
	B	4.9% (4)
Fair:	B-	3.7% (3)
	C+	4.9% (4)
	C	3.7% (3)
Unacceptable:	F	1.2% (1)

Table 6. Philhaven Hospital Inpatient Satisfaction Survey Comparison Chart*

Rated Item	February 1995	September 1995
Admission process	3.9	4.0
Appearance of facility	4.6	4.5
Professionalism of staff	4.5	4.6
Care delivered	4.3	4.2
Condition at discharge	3.9	4.2
Overall facility rating	4.3	4.3

* 5 = very satisfied; 1 = very dissatisfied

Medication

The medication domain of our Outcomes Management Program looks at clients' previous medication regimens, current regimens, and discharge regimens. We became interested in this domain because managed care organizations were very concerned with the use and cost of medications in their primary care practices. We were aware that selective formularies were being proposed for most managed care systems, and we received outcome and utilization reports for specific practitioners regarding their use of medications.

In anticipation that, in the near future, clinician-specific utilization and outcome data regarding medications would be expected, we began organizing some of the medication data that we had in our outcomes data base. We focused on discharge medication regimens of our inpatients because we had the most data in this area. More recently, we have begun to analyze medication regimens prescribed in our home care program to assess how well patients are complying with them. Unfortunately, our analysis is not yet rigorous enough to imply that any substantial information is currently available. Our primary goal in looking at this outcome domain is to be prepared for the future, when health care systems require outcome information regarding medications.

Because our outcomes database recorded discharge medications ordered for each of our inpatients, we decided to compare utilization and cost of different regimens. We grouped patients according to attending psychiatrist and, using the average wholesale price (AWP) of psychotropic medications, we computed an AWP of the total discharge medication per day per patient for each clinician. Table 7, below, shows, for each of the 12 psychiatrists who attend inpatients at Philhaven, the number of patients discharged during the six-month period and the number of different medications ordered at discharge per inpatient. The table also shows the cost per day to a patient for a discharge psychotropic medication regimen. The number of patients discharged varies from 3 to 153 per physician, and the average number of prescriptions per inpatient varies between 1.1 and 2.3. The average daily cost of these discharge medication regimens varied between $0.67 and $2.97.

Table 7. Psychotropic Utilization Data

Physician Code	Number of Patients Discharged	Number of Discharge Medications per Inpatient	Average Wholesale Price of Discharge Medications per Day per Inpatient
14963	75	1.2	0.67
15301	70	1.1	0.83
16811	48	1.4	1.04
16108	3	1.7	1.31
10781	149	2.0	1.63
16229	153	1.7	1.64
15798	75	2.3	1.98
7638	150	2.1	2.01
16156	73	2.2	2.12
16105	128	2.1	2.65
13193	58	1.9	2.75
15435	55	2.3	2.97

The first three psychiatrists in the table work on the child and adolescent unit and perhaps prescribe more conservatively for this age group. The variations in cost among the other nine adult psychiatrists, however, are more difficult to explain. Our medical staff is still pondering the differences and has asked to see more data regarding how the ratios were computed. The medical staff, through its pharmacy and therapeutics committee, began the process of developing a selective formulary by discussing what the indications should be for using new psychotropic medications in our system. No conclusions have been reached, and freedom of choice in prescribing has only been limited to filling out a formulary exception request form. We feel, however, that this opportunity to look at comparative costs of discharge regimens raises the awareness of our psychiatric staff. We are planning to compute this ratio every six months and look at patterns, over time, for individual practitioners and the group.

In the process of trying to explain variations for specific medications, the medical staff questioned how often patients followed through on their discharge medication regimens. We asked our Psychiatric Home Care Program to conduct an "Adherence to Medication Regimen Study." The study instrument is shown in figure 12, page 373. The form is completed every 60 days for all patients, who are primarily older adults with very extensive medication regimens. Our medical staff wanted to know who keeps the medications, how many different physicians are prescribing, what medications have been prescribed, and which medicines are taken when. To date, the reasons for not adhering to prescribed medication regimens have been rather evenly divided between availability problems, side-effects, and lack of understanding. Medical staff members were quite surprised to learn, as the individual case reports came in, that their carefully ordered medication regimens were not always followed at home. They have discussed how less complex medication regimens are, obviously, more easily followed after discharge. Again, this "culture of measurement" and the extent to which medication regimens were adhered to led our staff to question and over time improve the quality of our psychotropic discharge regimens. These improvements were accomplished by group discussions to develop consensus regarding medications of choice for common symtoms.

The data available for this outcome domain is almost limitless. Likewise, the analyses possible are almost infinite. We look forward to the time when standardized formats for recording medication usage and efficacy are established and to comparing our use with that of similar programs and facilities. Until such standardized formats are available, however, our pharmacy and therapeutics committee plans to continue organizing our data to attempt to uncover some information that will be helpful in caring for our patients in our specific programs.

Critical Incidents

The outcome domain for critical incidents is Philhaven's attempt to incorporate into the Outcomes Management Program most of the data formerly reviewed by the risk manager and the safety committee. The data come from the PHICO Event Reporting and Trending System (PERTS) form; "Green Staff Reports" that record behavioral emergencies on the different units; and grievances that are voiced by patients, their families, or referral sources.

Figure 12. Adherence to Medication Regimen

Completion with each admission to Psychiatric Home Care and every 60 days in conjunction with recertification.

Client Name: _____

Age:_____ Setting: n Home   n Personal Care

Marital Status: ❏ Married   ❏ Divorced   ❏ Separated   ❏ Single

1. Who manages the medications?

   ❏ Self   ❏ Spouse   ❏ Other Family Member

2. Number of physicians involved in the care of this client? _____

3. What medications have been prescribed?

4. What is being taken?

5. Reason for the difference?

   ❏ Availability: _____ Cost _____Logistics

   ❏ Side Affects

   ❏ Lack of Understanding

   ❏ Other:

Nurse: _____ Date:_____

These data can best be visualized by looking at figure 13, page 375, which shows in broad strokes the file structure for the Outcomes Management Program. A breakdown of the type of incidents reported during 1995 and 1996 is shown in figure 14, page 376, including medication errors, self-inflicted injuries, treatment processes omitted, and injuries from recreational activities.

To help the risk manager and the safety and performance (quality) improvement committees focus their efforts, Philhaven is beginning to organize data by computing a ratio of critical incidents to patient days. The denominator is the number of patient days or contacts in a specific program during a three-month period and the numerator is the number of critical incidents per quarter. Likewise, a clinician-specific ratio of the number of patient contacts divided into the number of complaints and/or critical incidents can be computed. Philhaven hopes to include such ratios in its outcomes management report cards and follow them over time.

Report Cards

Combining outcome management domains into user-friendly reports is an ongoing challenge. Report cards, defined as a mechanism for continually collecting, analyzing, and distributing comparative performance data, are of at least three types.[3] Internal report cards compare performance of various staff members within a single organization. External reports cards compare performance of various organizations, and public report cards compare organizational performance to standards or benchmarks.[5] Philhaven's report cards have matured with our Outcomes Management Program but are admittedly still quite primitive. We began with internal report cards to help our staff develop a "culture of measurement." Philhaven then shared some external report cards with payers. Staff members are becoming interested in going public with our data to compare it to regional and national standards.

Our first report card was requested by service line directors and was most beneficial on adult services. Figure 15, page 376, shows this report card for adult inpatient services and covers the two-year period 1993-94. Four outcomes are portrayed on this crude report card. First, the bars above each quarter show the average length of stay for patients treated during that quarter. Service line directors were pleased that the average length of stay decreased an average of five days over the two-year period. The top line on the report card shows the average score on the Client Satisfaction Questionnaire (CSQ). Again, the service unit directors were pleased that satisfaction ratings, with a maximum possible score of 32, were in the high 20s and were very stable over the two years. A third factor attempted to measure severity of illness or patient acuity using the Modified Scale for Suicide Ideation (MSSI)[16] that was administered to each inpatient on admission. For the more than 1,200 patients viewed in aggregate on this report card, this measure of acuity showed relative stability, as represented by the second line from the top, during the eight quarters. The fourth outcome graphed on this report card, the bottom line, summarizes the BSI symptom distress change reported in T-score differences between admission and discharge. As previously discussed, the service line directors noticed a change during the second quarter of 1993.

The service line directors concluded from the report card that the organization was successfully shortening its length of stay, maintaining client satisfaction, perhaps treating slightly more

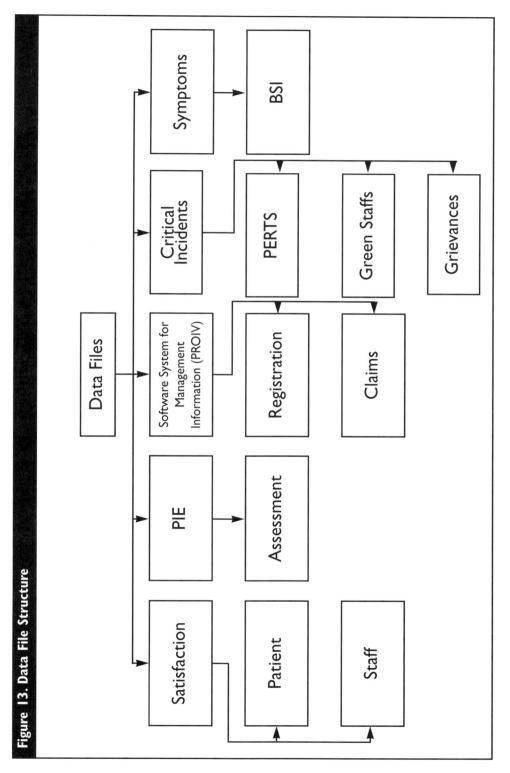

Figure 13. Data File Structure

Figure 14. Incident Reporting, January through December 1994

INCIDENT CATEGORIES	# of Incidents 1995 (957)	# of Incidents 1996 (699)	% of All Incidents 1995	% of All Incidents 1996	% of Change	Incident Per Patient Day 1995	Incident Per Patient Day 1996
Medication Errors	256	241	27%	34%	+7%	Adult .006 C/A .002 CR .019	.006 .003 .025
Falls	170	135	18%	19%	+1%	Adult .008	.009
Self-Inflicted Intentional	95	43	10%	6%	-4%	Adult .004 C/A .002	.001 .002
Treatment Process-Omitted	85	8	9%	1%	-8%	Adult .0006 C/A .009	
Injury from Recreational Activity	73	64	8%	9%	+1%	Adult .0008 C/A .005	.001 .004
Self-Inflicted Unintentional	72	33	8%	5%	-3%	Adult .002 C/A .002	.001 .001
Threat/Aggression from Another	--	21	--	3%	--	Adult -- C/A --	.001 .0006

ADULT - Inpatient Service
C/A - Child and Adolescent Inpatient Service
CR - Crossroads Residential Program

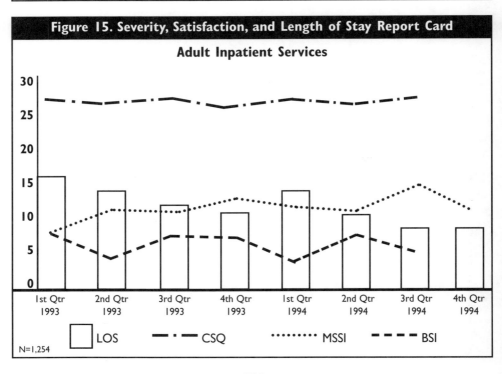

Figure 15. Severity, Satisfaction, and Length of Stay Report Card

Adult Inpatient Services

N=1,254

LOS — · — CSQ ·········· MSSI — — — BSI

acute patients, and seeing relative stability in symptom distress change in adult services. They felt some comfort in the stability of the data and looked forward to the next quarter's results. Our "culture of measurement" was enhanced by quarterly review of outcome measures.

By late 1995, organizational restructuring and incorporation of additional outcome domains matured the internal Philhaven report card to the format shown in table 8, page 378. Patient days are shown over a three-year period, with critical incidents listed for the period as well. As previously mentioned, future report cards could well include a ratio generated by having the patient days as the denominator and the critical incidents as a numerator for each quarter. The CSQ mean score was amazingly stable over the 10-quarter reporting period. The BSI, GSI change showed some variation by quarter and by unit, and our performance improvement committees at the unit, service line, and organizational levels are investigating the possible causes of these variations. "Total charge" is added to the internal report card to highlight the importance of cost to all staff reviewing the outcomes data. Our staff would like to have this line replaced by "total cost" so this more relevant fiscal measure could be incorporated with the other outcome domains. Listing of past and admission GAF scores is Philhaven's attempt to include a function domain measure that can be followed over time.

We hope that, in the future, computing ratios that show the total cost of care divided by either symptom distress change or some other functional measure of improvement will be beneficial in giving feedback to specific programs and clinicians regarding the value of their services. Figure 16, page 379, shows a program score (report) card format that Philhaven hopes to use. This score card will report resources used as a total cost for different customer groups, specific by gender, age, diagnosis, clinician, therapy type, and specific medications. The average amount of symptom change seen by these different groups will be computed and a "cost of care" ratio will be generated by dividing total costs by this average change in BSI T-scores.[5] The satisfaction ratings of these different groups will also be shown. Ideally, the "cost of care" ratio multiplied by the satisfaction mean scores should give a helpful statistic to compare different customer groups within a program to see to whom the most cost-effective and customer-appreciated services can be offered or to identify where types of care might be altered in an attempt to improve outcomes.

A future Philhaven clinician score card, shown in figure 17, page 379, is specific for patients cared for by one clinician, and, again, customer groups can be divided by gender, program, diagnosis, therapy, or medications. Total costs and symptom change give rise to a "cost of care" ratio. Satisfaction scores are also reported. By reviewing these score cards, clinicians can determine which patients they treat most effectively. Clinicians, of course, enjoy helping patients with all types of disorders, but it is probable that they give the most value to certain specific disorders, and behavioral health care systems of the future need to be able to match patients' needs with clinicians' strengths. Philhaven hopes to provide the best value to its customers by sharing our outcomes management data through report cards to clinicians and program managers.

Figure 18, page 379, shows a future potential score card for a problematic or refractory patient X. The report card shows the costs of care or the resources used for patient X in inpatient, day treatment, and outpatient services for a given year. Adding these figures gives the total one year's

Table 8. Outcomes Variables

	1993				1994				1995	
	Q1	Q2	Q3	Q4	Q1	Q2	Q3	Q4	Q1	Q2
Patient Days										
Adult	4,108	3,889	3,911	3,727	3,769	3,730	3,647	3,442	3,358	2,584
Women's	1,181	1,017	889	923	914	808	928	835	730	765
Older Adult	1,360	1,374	1,384	1,277	1,208	1,234	1,246	1,341	1,051	1,098
Critical Incidents										
Adult								29	131	163
Women's								4	20	25
Older Adult								12	26	28
CSQ Mean Score										
Adult	3.5	3.3	3.4	3.3	3.4	3.2	3.3	3.3	3.4	3.4
Women's	3.4	3.6	3.4	3.5	3.5	3.4	3.4	3.4	3.4	3.3
Older Adult	3.6	3.4	3.3	3.6	3.4	3.5	3.8	3.4	3.4	
BSI GSI Change										
Adult	9.8	6.7	10.2	6.8	8.3	7.8	15.1	8.4	12.7	10.4
Women's	7.5	10.5	9.5	9.0	7.3	9.5	7.4	7.8	8.0	8.2
Older Adult	2.9	9.4	4.5	12.4	10.1	9.7				12.7
Total Charge ($)										
Adult			7,098	9,529	9,489	9,621	9,094	8,758	8,506	8,325
Women's			5,132	6,854	7,287	7,182	6,757	6,957	5,420	5,825
Older Adult			9,520	13,467	10,877	11,513	12,258	12,650	11,646	11,142
Past GAF										
Adult	44.3	40.3	38.0	43.3	39.0	36.1	44.9	46.5	45.2	44.0
Women's	55.6	53.9	35.6	40.2	41.2	46.4	38.1	43.1	42.0	26.2
Older Adult	41.7	41.5	42.7	38.9	29.4	32.3	38.2	39.2	37.5	37.7
Current Admission GAF										
Adult	27.2	25.0	24.4	25.0	23.7	22.8	27.1	27.0	25.5	24.9
Women's	41.9	38.1	32.6	33.7	34.6	35.7	30.4	34.9	36.5	33.8
Older Adult	28.4	29.4	31.4	29.5	33.4	27.8	30.1	29.6	27.7	26.9

Figure 16. Program Score Card

Customer Group	Costs (Resources Used)	Symptom Change (BSI T-Score)	Cost of Care Ratio Costs/BSI^	Satisfaction (CSQ-Mean Score)	
All					
Females					
Males					
Age Specific					
Diagnosis Specific					
Clinician Specific					
Therapy Specific					
Med. Specific					

Figure 17. Clinician "A" Score Card

Customer Group	Costs (Resources Used)	Symptom Change (BSI T-Score)	Cost of Care Ratio Costs/BSI^	Satisfaction (CSQ-Mean Score)	
All					
Females					
Males					
Prog. Specific Inpatient Day Patient Outpatient					
Diagnosis Specific					
Clinician Specific					
Therapy Specific					
Med. Specific					

Figure 18. Patient "X" Score Card

Customer Group	Costs (Resources Used)	Symptom Change (BSI T-Score)	Cost of Care Ratio Costs/BSI^	Satisfaction (CSQ-Mean Score)	
Inpatient 1995 1994					
Day patient 1995 1994					
Outpatient 1995 1994					
Total Year's Episode of Illness 1995 1994					

cost for patient X's episode of illness. Likewise, the symptom change experienced by patient X over the year could be determined using a symptom distress instrument, and a "cost of care" ratio could be generated for each year for each program. Also, satisfaction scores could be listed for the different programs and, by looking at the "cost of care" ratio and satisfaction ratings, one should be able to determine which programs for patient X were most cost-effective and satisfying. Philhaven hopes that, by generating patient score cards for refractory patients, we can better determine where and how to best care for these patients within our system.

Additional future developments include generation of external and public report cards using our outcomes management data. To further this goal, we are meeting every six months with four other not-for-profit behavioral health systems to begin standardizing our outcomes management methodologies and report card formats. Once our measuring and reporting formats are similar, establishing benchmarks and standards of care should follow.

Summary

Philhaven initiated its behavioral health Outcomes Management Program in late 1992. We attempted to integrate multiple administrative and clinical functions to build a system that supports quality assurance, performance improvement, utilization management, outcome measurement, risk management, and fiscal performance of the organization. Outcomes from the domains of intake/triage, expectations, functions, symptoms, satisfaction, medications, and critical incidents were shared. Combining these outcomes into useful report/score cards is an evolutionary process. Sharing these data with our staff and other facilities helps to create and nurture a "culture of measurement" within our organization. The primary goal of the Philhaven Outcomes Management Program is to guide our behavioral health care system in providing high-quality, cost-effective treatment to all our clients.

References

1. Chassin, M. Keynote Address at the Pennsylvania Health Care Cost Containment Council National Symposium on Outcomes and Quality Assessment: State of the Art and Future Directions; Harrisburg, Pa., May 31-June 2, 1995.

2. Ruffin, M. Presentation at American College of Physician Executive's Perspectives in Medical Management Meeting, Chicago, Ill., May 3-6, 1995.

3. Sederer, L., and Dickey, B., Editors. *Outcomes Assessment in Clinical Practice.* Baltimore, Md.: Williams and Wilkins, 1996.

4. Docherty, J., and others. *Outcomes Assessment Monograph.* Washington, D.C.: National Association of Psychiatric Health Services 1995.

5. Migdal, K., Editor. *The 1995 Behavioral Outcomes and Guidelines Sourcebook.* New York, N.Y.: Faulkner & Gray, Inc., 1995.

6. Vibbert, S., Editor. *The 1996 Behavioral Outcomes and Guidelines Sourcebook.* New York, N.Y.: Faulkner & Gray, Inc., 1996.

7. Phillips, J. Presentation at the Pennsylvania Health Care Cost Containment Council National Symposium on Outcomes and Quality Assessment: State of the Art and Future Directions, Harrisburg, Pa., May 31-June 2, 1995.

8. Uniform Data System for Medical Rehabilitation, Center for Functional Assessment Research, Department of Rehabilitation Medicine, School of Medicine and Biomedical Sciences, State University of New York, Bufffalo, N.Y.

9. *Diagnostic and Statistical Manual of Mental Disorders,* 4th Edition. Washington, D.C.: American Psychiatric Association Press, 1994.

10. Ware, J., and others. *SF-36 Health Survey Manual and Interpretation Guide.* Boston, Mass.: New England Medical Center, The Health Institute, 1993.

11. Eisen, S., and others. "Reliability and Validity of a Brief Patient-Report Instrument for Psychiatric Outcome Evaluation." *Hospital and Community Psychiatry* 45(3):242-7, March 1994.

12. Deragotis, L. "Symptom Checklist-90-R (SCL-90-R)," *Administration Scoring and Procedures Manual,* 3rd Edition. Minneapolis, Minn.: National Computer Systems, 1994.

13. Kopta, S., and others. "Patterns of Symptomatic Recovery in Psychotherapy." *Journal of Consulting and Clinical Psychology* 62(5):1009-16, May 1994.

14. Connors, C. *Manual for Connors' Rating Scales: Connors' Teacher Rating Scales and Connors' Parent Rating Scales.* North Tonawanda, N.Y.: Multi-Health Systems, 1990.

15. Attkisson, C., and others. "The Client Satisfaction Questionnaire-8" and "The Service Satisfaction Questionnaire-30." In Maruish, M., Editor, *Treatment Planning and Outcome Assessment,* New York, N.Y.: Lawrence Earlbaum Associates, 1994.

16. Miller, I., and others. "The Modified Scale for Suicidal Ideation: Reliability and Validity." *Journal of Consulting and Clinical Psychology* 54(5):724-5, May 1986.

Diehl M. Snyder, MD, is Medical Director, Philhaven Behavioral Healthcare Services, Mt. Gretna, Pennsylvania.

Chapter 25

Clinical Guidelines in Mental Health Care

by William H. Reid, MD, MPH

First, a personal note. If our patients are to be well served, I believe the entire health care field must address *mental illness,* not *behavioral health,* and recognize that such illness and our patients are far more serious topics. Terms such as "behavioral health" promulgate a mental image that separates psychiatric patients from those with "real" illness and that allows payers and administrators to treat mental illness and mental patients differently, with less attention to their clinical, medical, and resource needs. The point is not a semantic one. It is far easier for a legislature, a corporation, or a union negotiator to cut "behavioral health" benefits than "medical" benefits. So, throughout this chapter, I refer to clinical guidelines for the treatment of mental illness.

What's a "Guideline"?

A guideline is a suggested goal, designed to spur thought and action in a logical direction as one performs a task. It is not a rigid template, nor is it designed to be followed in all cases of the task that is contemplated. Individual cases of deviation from a guideline need not always be justified. If it is a good guideline, the practitioner may be expected to follow it, to some measurable extent, in a large portion of routine cases. On the other hand, several conditions may dictate acceptable deviation from the guideline, including nonstandard patients or settings and improvements in clinical knowledge or opportunity.

A guideline is not a "standard." A standard is something that one strives to meet completely in all but the most unusual cases (e.g., a speed limit). Deviation from a standard is usually cause either to criticize or to expect justification. A standard very often creates a legal duty (e.g., in tort law). Thus, careless use of the term or concept of "standard" can, because of its rigidity, easily lead to unintended consequences.

Some guidelines are "recommendations," but most have more expectation that they will, on balance or average, be followed. One is generally free to accept or reject recommendations out of hand. For example, a cake recipe may recommend two cups of sugar, but there is little peril in changing the amount. Our concept of clinical guidelines suggests that they carry some weight of general "rightness" and approval by some influential source (e.g., peers, supervisors, organizations).

Some guidelines are protocols, but the expectation that one will follow a protocol is more rigid than in many guidelines. Further, protocols are usually quite specific and prescriptive; guidelines leave room for flexibility and assume both that the practitioner is qualified to choose the best avenue for the case at hand and that allowing that opportunity for choice is a good idea in the long run.

Of Guidelines, Standards, Recommendations, and Protocols, Why Choose "Guideline"?

Clinicians, whether physicians or other independently licensed professionals, need flexibility. They know they must make independent medical decisions, and they know the ethical and legal responsibilities that ensue. In addition, most health care professionals operate within the upper rungs of the "hierarchy of needs."[1] They are rewarded by their altruism and by feelings of a job well done. They work better and enjoy work more when they have respect and flexibility.

The health care organization should also be aware that keeping clinical decisions independent of administrative ones limits the organization's risk of liability. The extent to which the clinician can deviate from an organizational rule (not necessarily one generated by the medical/professional staff) and the extent to which he or she can act outside, or in spite of, lay or organizational interference when clinically necessary, is the extent to which clinicians assume their own risk. This is usually a good thing for both parties in the employment or contractual relationship.

Finally, words such as "standard" or "protocol" often establish a legal expectation called the "standard of care," which is directly related to malpractice liability (and often woefully misunderstood by physicians, who generally have a less formal concept of "standard"). Standard of care is a legal duty that must be met by the doctor and the organization in every case; if it is not met, there is a *prima facie* breach of duty to the patient and an important element of the plaintiff's lawsuit has been proved. In the past, standard of care has referred largely to the community standard for diagnosis and treatment. Today, however, many lawsuits have been able to establish that a hospital's or health care organization's internal policies, procedures, protocols, or standards establish enough of a duty that failure to follow them to the letter creates liability for the facility.

Do Guidelines Increase Quality of, and Access to, Medical Care?

Among guidelines developed for cost containment or system efficiency, the answer is usually "no," although scientific evidence for either good or bad clinical effects is limited. This form of practice guideline—i.e., one defined by fiscal, administrative, or political interests—rarely defines optimal care, because many (but not all) of its sponsors use inadequate science and imperfect analytic processes, do not have "excellent" patient care as a high priority, and/or do not allow sufficiently for individual differences among patients. Clarity and specificity often come at the expense of scientific validity. Rigid enforcement of such guidelines can harm patients, decrease individualized care, and promote unfair criticism of clinicians who deviate from them for good reasons,[2] all without necessarily decreasing costs.

What Is the Source of Most Clinical Guidelines?

Most physicians assume that clinical knowledge is the foundation for clinical guidelines. Many others, however, know this is a naive supposition. In order to develop clinical guidelines that are appropriate for patient care, it is important to understand and address the nonmedical forces influencing that care.

First, and more practically than cynically, "follow the money." This means examining those who pay for patient care, those who stand to benefit from the payments, and those for whom patient health and recovery are important. In some cases, these entities overlap greatly. In most, they represent separate, often competing, interests.

Those who pay and/or stand to benefit from payment. Mental health systems that provide only a portion of the patient's medical care and that may enjoy the "safety net" of a financial stop-loss or an opportunity to refer very expensive care to another provider (e.g., a state mental health system), have little financial incentive to develop guidelines that meet comprehensive clinical and long-term patient needs. In private specialty-limited programs where acute care and symptom control rise to greatest importance, primary prevention, relapse prevention, long-term improvement, and chronic care are lower priorities. This is especially true of systems or provider organizations that contract for only one to three years of care at a time, but the effects can be mitigated by carefully written service contracts.

All other things being equal, public or private systems that have long-term responsibility for all of the patient's health or mental health care, over many years or a lifetime, are motivated to decrease chronic need *and* to develop a community reputation for quality, particularly if their compensation is linked in some way to quality and consumer satisfaction. Note, however, that "consumer satisfaction" may refer to patients, families of patients, government officials, or the general population. Guidelines that satisfy one set of consumers may or may not be appropriate for the others.

The most comprehensive, if somewhat socialistic, solution to payer satisfaction is found when the same payer is directly responsible for mental health, other medical, social, law enforcement, and judicial costs. It is only in this setting that one is able to treat psychiatric patients definitively in order to decrease the numbers of mentally ill persons who end up in emergency departments, state hospitals, jails, or prisons, or on the street. In the practical world of business and politics, the entity that contracts to provide psychiatric care alone has no real incentive to control other family, community, or state costs, in spite of their demonstrable relationship to inadequate mental health care, if the latter costs come out of someone else's budget. If satisfying the payer means addressing other organizations' or departments' needs as well, a broader view will be taken by the provider entity.

Thus, the management of different kinds of mental health care organizations will support widely differing clinical guidelines. The organizations' business objectives may not be in what psychiatrists and other mental health professionals believe is the patient's best interests, but they will often prevail unless vigorously challenged.

Recipients of care and their advocates. This concept refers to several groups, some of which have considerable influence over clinical guidelines.

First, in spite of occasional popular cynicism, one should not forget that the helping professions, such as medicine, have a great interest in the proper treatment, outcome, and health of patients. This is evident in hundreds, sometimes thousands, of years of professional tradition; in the character of those who choose the professions; and in the culture imparted in their training. It is enforced by very strict ethical canons, peer pressure, licensure laws, practice regulations, credentialing requirements, and vulnerability to malpractice litigation.

Next, patients and their families frequently can tell us what works and what does not. Small, vocal groups of "psychiatric survivors" are often influential, but their knowledge and understanding of medical care are limited, and their attitudes may be skewed by idiosyncratic views or experiences.

Organizations such as the National Alliance for the Mentally Ill (NAMI), local alliances for the mentally ill, and the Depressive and Manic-Depressive Association (DMDA) are well informed; provide carefully considered recommendations; and, because of their size and frequent political sophistication, are sometimes quite influential with payers. The national Mental Health Association (MHA) and local mental health associations are also strong voices for high-quality care. The advantage of such patient- and family-connected advocacy is at least twofold: its participants reap no financial benefit from clinical or payer outcome, and it includes (but is not limited to) recovered patients and family members who have closely observed severe mental illness but whose understanding, communication, or credibility are not impaired by continuing symptoms.

Finally, the community and society have an interest in maintaining a population that is content and productive. The ability to participate in family and community affairs has value beyond simple reduction of direct treatment costs, and even beyond social costs such as those associated with housing or law enforcement. Children develop better when mentally ill parents have appropriate clinical care. Neighborhoods that have experience with appropriately treated mentally ill persons develop, in turn, more constructive attitudes toward both the people and their illnesses. Patients treated with newer antipsychotic and antidepressant medications are far more likely to be able to return to work or school—and to continue their productivity—than those given older, "traditional" drugs.

What Should the Clinical Guideline Be and Do?

First, it must encourage patient diagnosis and treatment that, to the extent scientifically possible, meets patients' clinical needs. This implies that the relevant standard of medical care is met as well, and that liability risk is minimized.

Second, both physicians and patients should be enthusiastic about the level of care provided. This implies not only clinical appropriateness but also reasonable patient cost, physician flexibility and rewards, and adequate access to care.

Third, the guideline must be within the ethical bounds of psychiatrists and other mental health professionals. Of course, it must meet statutory requirements as well.

Fourth, the guideline should be realistic, and not promise care that cannot reasonably be delivered. We should be honest about whom we can and cannot treat, no matter what the reason.

Fifth, it must be compatible with the fiscal integrity of the system, although fiscal integrity should not have to compete with clinical or ethical integrity.

What Must the Guideline Avoid?

As already discussed, wording and policies related to the guideline should be created in such a way that the guideline does not create a legal duty; it is separate from the standard of care and should not define it. In particular, developers of guidelines in large provider systems should be cautious about creating broad regional expectations that do not apply to all parts of the demographic area. Similarly, guidelines should not be based on "average" patient demographics or on limited samples unless physicians are free to be flexible in their exercise of clinical procedures. It is generally a mistake to create guidelines that purport to cover every eventuality or are "all things to all patients."

Those who develop the guidelines should both involve field clinicians and enjoy their respect. Clinical guidelines or procedures created by lay or administrative staff (often including quality assurance or quality improvement staff) tend to be narrow and either inflexible or so vague that they are not very useful. In addition, the morale of clinicians who see patients every day is seriously undermined when guidelines are developed by people who do not have to use them often (or ever). Patients, families, and advocates may be part of the process, but clinicians should be in the majority. Merely including a few doctors on a committee or task force charged with developing clinical guidelines is not sufficient.

Many health care systems take the position that all patients must have the same quality or level of care, regardless of plan or resources. This often places an unreasonable burden on the system and brings down the level of care for patients who may, for some reason, be in a position to benefit more than others. In some states, for example, patients eligible for Medicaid are sometimes deprived of access to covered treatments (e.g., expensive atypical neuroleptic medication) because it is felt to be somehow "unfair" to provide them with treatment that non-Medicaid-eligible patients cannot afford.

Similarly, some full-coverage systems (e.g., state mental health systems) take the position that all financially eligible patients will be seen and treated, even if such a policy draws the level of quality or completeness of care down to a "lowest common denominator." When resources must be rationed, guidelines should specify clinical priorities, not financial ones, for "triage" criteria. In this way, those who are accepted will receive at least adequate care. To do otherwise threatens the adequacy of care for all.

Models for Care

A number of practice guidelines, regulations, and standards already exist in the form of health care organization protocols and utilization review requirements, isolated government regulations, comprehensive government (e.g., Medicare) certification requirements, professional consensus documents, local medical staff protocols, local or broad treatment algorithms, focused practice policies or instructions, and legal precedents derived from malpractice and other case law. We will briefly discuss some examples, with the understanding that, in practice, guidelines are often related to more than one of the following illustrations.

Models Drawn from Clinical Practice

The basis for most medical care in the past, and arguably the correct foundation for current care, was/is the totality of one's medical education and clinical experience, tempered by the individual patient situation at hand. Courts have long, and appropriately, held that physicians meet their standard of care when they exercise reasonable care, go through a good-faith process of clinical judgment, and make decisions that are consistent with legitimate teaching and experience in the field. Their decisions need not agree with the majority of accepted clinical knowledge, but they should agree with a respected minority.

Guidelines that rely on general clinical practice have the advantage of access to medical research and experience, as expressed in journal articles, textbooks, clinical meetings and symposia, and other professional communications. Such knowledge can be disseminated very rapidly, especially through today's electronic media and "new research" sections of professional conferences. On the other hand, the overwhelming mass of new information creates a responsibility in the reviewer to sift such information accurately and to be aware of the hallmarks of reliable and valid reports (as contrasted with unsophisticated studies, non-peer-reviewed communications, and "junk science"). Anyone charged with developing practice guidelines, or criticizing clinical practice itself, must be able to tell the "wheat" (e.g., what the legal profession describes as a "learned treatise" in a field of study) from the "chaff."

Medical staff protocols are a special example of this model, in which physicians themselves decide the theme and the substance of local care and generally provide mechanisms for review, exception, and consequences of practicing outside the protocol. At such a local level, monitoring is relatively easy and is directly related to individual practice. The protocols may be (and usually are) based on widely accepted clinical practice; however, the small group of authors and arbiters do not control clinical practice outside their local area. Thus, there are the advantages that most problems in protocol criteria can be recognized early, modification is easily accomplished, and any flaws will not affect regional or national care.

Practitioner influence on medical staff protocols is obvious; the impact of those outside the professional community (e.g., patients, payers) may (or may not) be small. When the local medical staff creates them, there is a danger of "inbreeding" in isolated professional communities and even a possibility that potential improvements in care will be avoided as threatening to the status quo. That danger is offset by such things as professional ethics, continuing education, licensing and accreditation requirements, awareness of malpractice trends, medical staff turnover, patient and community awareness of medical standards, and a need for quality improvement in competition with other facilities and organizations.

Models Drawn from Professional Organization Review and Consensus

Some of the best formats for practice guidelines have come from recent efforts by the American Psychiatric Association (APA). Spurred primarily by a wish to enhance the quality and the consistency of psychiatric care, but also by the realization that reasonable practice guidelines are key to the role and credibility of psychiatry in future health care scenarios, APA has preempted and/or eclipsed the scope and validity of most practice guidelines created by provider agencies (e.g., state mental health agencies or managed care organizations) and insurers. While occasionally criticized by some whose interests compete with the APA premise of "patient first" as being self-serving or "watered down," the APA guideline topics thus far examined have been treated fairly, with scrupulous attention to patient needs, exhaustive and very sophisticated literature review, broad professional input, and individual case flexibility.[3-5]

Smaller organizations attempting to develop national guidelines have sometimes produced less appropriate products. Both local/regional clinical associations and national ones with subspecialty focus and limited breadth of membership tend to produce guidelines or "standards" that reflect a provincial viewpoint, to the exclusion of important exceptions to their particular experiences. Whether caused by lack of resources, personalized or "guild" focus, or difficulty being aware of the "big picture" outside their organizations, this is the same problem that one encounters when any small group, such as a government or corporate committee, attempts to make rules for large, disparate populations of patients and clinicians.

Models Drawn from "Reasonable Physician" Expertise or Civil Case Law

The U.S. system of legal liability creates a powerful incentive for practice to an adequate standard of care and, indirectly, has created rough practice and documentation guidelines in several areas of psychiatry. Rightly or wrongly, "defensive" (and often costly) medical and psychological practice has sometimes evolved into a way of clinical life. For example, specific documentation of the absence of threat to others is common even in ordinary psychotherapy patients, for whom danger to others is so rare that its absence did not merit mention prior to the Tarasoff decision.[6] Risk of liability may also affect what kinds of patients a clinician decides—or is allowed—to treat. State law usually relegates scope of medical practice to the physician's judgment and conscience, the credentialing process, and the influence of the law's "malpractice remedy." Each of these exerts a powerful influence on both doctors and provider organizations as they decide when to treat and when to refer the patient elsewhere. Keeping a patient in a primary care environment when he or she needs specialty care, for example, is a prominent source of malpractice and contract liability.

Length of stay and choice of treatment are affected by case law that affirms the attending physician's responsibility for adequate care, regardless of administrative or financial constraint. A series of cases, beginning with *Wickline v. California*[7] and moving into psychiatry with *Hughes v. Blue Cross of Northern California*,[8] *Wilson v.Blue Cross of Southern California*,[9] and similar decisions in other states, has established a cause of action against payers for restricting physicians, but the cases have also reiterated the doctor's responsibility to protest countertherapeutic utilization review actions on the patient's behalf.[10]

Reimbursement parity between serious psychiatric disorders and general medical illness would imply that the psychiatrist must treat severe and chronic mental illness (SCMI) with definitive measures (including longer hospitalizations and more intensive follow-up) rather than with the episodic care encouraged by low annual and lifetime policy limits for mental illness. A few state civil cases suggest a right to reimbursement parity[11,12]; many others have been settled by payers in favor of plaintiffs/patients to avoid publicity or legal precedent. At least five states (California, Maine, Maryland, Texas, and Virginia) now have statutes that require parity for patients with SCMI.

Models Drawn from Government Agency or Statutory Entitlement
During the past two decades, unprecedented government influence on the practice of medicine, particularly in psychiatry, has been expressed through public sector practice, license restriction, and practice limitations, largely in the name of patient protection. These expressions of public policy are often without benefit of very much professional advice, but rather the result of political pressure from interest groups or of misunderstanding of clinical procedures or scientific reports. For example, some lay groups have caused several states to limit the availability of electroconvulsive therapy (ECT) to patients who need it, and fear of overutilization of inpatient care for adolescents has made it difficult in some locations to provide clinically recommended hospitalization.

Such clinical restrictions should not be considered legitimate by medical practitioners and should be resisted by the professional community. Nevertheless, they often find their way into clinical protocols via the health care organization's wish to create a "safe harbor" for risk management or reimbursement, bowing to social or political pressures, or to state or federal regulation.

State mental health agency clinical protocols are often influenced by similar nonclinical, nonscientific factors. In the author's experience, legislators and other elected officials often exert more influence than physicians. In some cases, this is for practical reasons, such as lawsuit settlement decrees or (often unfounded) liability concerns. In others, lay administrators' misunderstanding or responsiveness to special interest pressures can shape clinical practice by, for example, limiting legitimate polypharmacy and viewing psychotropic medications as unusually dangerous or "mind-altering." This creates bureaucratic (and often expensive) barriers to prompt and flexible care, such as additional paperwork, unnecessary consultations, or justification requirements that discourage even mildly controversial practices. Sometimes those obstacles are so onerous that legitimate procedures or treatments virtually disappear from practice, even when they are not technically "banned" (e.g., extending hospitalization in order to solidify therapeutic gains, observing patients without medication, or providing such treatments as specialized psychotherapy, ECT, antiandrogenic drugs, aversive conditioning, or innovative but unproved treatment options for refractory conditions).

Unfortunately, once set in government rule or policy, and unless patients are being harmed by institutional practices (not merely by omission of better or more flexible care), such restrictions are very difficult to remove. What may seem a harmless accommodation to consumer anxieties often later becomes the new "standard" by which other practices are measured and a new "floor" upon which further restrictions may be piled. For example, although written consent for psychotropic medication is rarely required by law and is not mandated for most other medications, many public and private sector mental health agencies, bowing to suggestions from lay consumers or risk managers, demand it. Once such a policy is established, many go on, unnecessarily, to require such things as complex documentation of all elements of informed consent (competency, knowledge, voluntariness) and even separate written consent for each medication (however similar) or dosage change.

Even when field psychiatrists and other caregivers are consulted (e.g., through opportunity to review drafts of rule or guideline proposals), they almost never actually make the decisions about guideline or policy content. Even so, the fact that decision makers are often laypersons is not as important as their general insulation from most practitioners and patients. Their ability to see the "big picture" and take a broader view of constituents, customers, and consequences is an advantage in most policy making; however, *patient care* policy should not be compromised in the same way one negotiates business, social, or political policy. To do so creates situations in which the product doesn't meet the real needs of any of the constituent groups, including those who directly provide or receive medical (psychiatric) care.

Developing High-Quality, Feasible Guidelines

Pilot Studies and Field Trials

One of the most important criticisms of practice guidelines is their frequent lack of extensive testing for clinical accuracy, quality, breadth, and feasibility. "Pilot studies" and "field trials" are both useful in this regard, but the latter are often left out of the practice guideline development process.

Pilot studies try to examine the new methodology quickly and inexpensively, using small populations and minimal investment to approximate its effects in broader use. They imitate the real world most closely if the process being developed is designed for small, independent, highly uniform sites. A McDonald's® hamburger recipe, for example, can be piloted in a few restaurants and be expected to produce the same product over and over (given the same ingredients and staff training) in other settings.

Useful *field trials,* in contrast, are slow and relatively uncontrolled but provide a much better predictor of real-world clinical experience. Medical care is not a "cookbook" process. Patients, their illnesses, their lives and families, and modern diagnostic and treatment modalities vary enormously. The most extensive and successful field trials are carried out by large professional or public health organizations, for example in the development of standard diagnostic nomenclature,[13] the American Psychiatric Association's several new practice guidelines,[3-5,14,15] and the clinical practice guidelines for depression in primary care settings developed by the

Agency for Health Care Policy and Research.[16,17] The results of field trials virtually always indicate that without broad testing, early versions of guidelines and standards—no matter how carefully crafted—have flaws that, if allowed to persist, would have produced significant unanticipated negative consequences.

Changes in Quality of Care

Specific influence of practice guidelines on quality of mental health care is difficult to measure, but outcome studies are starting to appear in the literature. Unfortunately most are small and tend to support the views of whatever group performed the study. Although some very broad field trials are in progress (by the Texas public mental health system, for example) the author is unaware of large-scale, scrupulously controlled outcome studies that either support or refute an association between clinical quality and practice guidelines *per se*.

Katon *et al.*[18] reported that a guideline recommending collaboration between psychiatric and primary care physicians increased intensity of treatment for major depression (but not "minor depression") in primary care settings and increased patient satisfaction. The differences in symptom improvement were statistically significant but not clinically striking and may have been due to better medication compliance in the collaboration group and/or to the group's receiving various kinds of special attention (e.g., frequent visits, educational videotapes).

Clinical Guidelines and Fiscal Issues

The medical and mental health professions were developing clinical guidelines and protocols long before external financial incentives became the primary visible forces in Western health care reform. There is a common, *but erroneous,* impression that fiscal concerns and clinical issues should be addressed together in practice guidelines. Various economic needs—sometimes patients' financial issues, but more frequently those of companies or governments—are unfortunately often expressed to the public in a way that suggests that increasing efficiency and saving money will improve both access to and quality of care.

It is important that both clinicians and laypersons understand that clinical and fiscal issues are quite separate. Despite some efforts by payers and managed care organizations to imply that cost-effectiveness is a clinical virtue, the driving force behind *their* practice guidelines is financial. There is nothing inherently wrong with limiting entitlements to private sector care or in pursuing health care business interests, provided those limits are appropriately disclosed in contracts signed by potential patients. However, once a clinical or doctor-patient relationship has been formed, physicians and physician executives must place their priorities in a different order: patient first, then finances.

Practice Guidelines and Statutory Practice Limitation

Government (particularly state government) sometimes strives not merely to protect patients but to broadly control the general practice of medicine. Psychiatry is often a target of such control, in part because it works with the mind, whose freedom of thought creates, perceives, and mediates many of the rights we all want to protect. Our work is more easily misunderstood than that of other specialties and professions. Laypersons do not appreciate our patients' illnesses as directly as they see a tumor, an infection, or a broken leg. They often do not perceive mental illness as serious or painful, and thus have trouble accurately assessing the treatment process and balancing the decision to treat with the consequences of not treating.

Further, detractors of modern psychiatry and mental health practices find an audience in government officials (both elected and agency administrators). It is easy to threaten legislators and civil servants with the prospect of controversy or negative publicity. The result can be laws that are unrelated to clinical wisdom or real patient need, that limit scope of practice, and that amount to ill-considered practice standards.

Although this chapter has referred primarily to practice guidelines within particular circumscribed settings, such as managed care organizations or public mental health systems, we have also seen that government sometimes becomes involved in practice procedures for all clinicians in its jurisdiction. License limitations are one example. Medicare practice guidelines might be another, since Health Care Financing Administration certification requirements affect mental health practice far beyond Medicare populations. A few papers suggest that OBRA-87 guidelines—clearly designed to limit federal reimbursement and not to improve care—may be a basis for so-called "best practices" in nursing home prescribing.[19] This author would vigorously disagree with the "best practices" inference and note a number of patient care problems that have been created by this most-bureaucratic, least-medical of guideline development processes.[20]

Physician Acceptance and Implementation

Administrators often believe that the best way to implement a practice guideline is simply to require its use. This approach may have limited success in settings in which physicians are employed and subject to administrative sanction; however, most doctors respond better to evidence that a guideline will be good for patients than they do to bureaucratic demands.

One reason many implementation strategies do not systematically change physician behavior is what Elson and Connelly[21] describe as lack of attention to "the involuntary time and mental processing constraints that have been clearly demonstrated to hamper physicians' ability to comply with guidelines." Good computerized records systems, with support for data collection and decision making, can ease some of the bureaucratic burdens and increase compliance; however, they have not been well studied in mental health settings. In another study of family practice guideline distribution, the authors found that no one dissemination format changed all relevant parameters of physician behavior. Communication using several media and frequent reminders was most effective, and social influence was an important factor.[22]

Nevertheless, in order to be effective and to be properly studied in the real world of patient care, practice guidelines must be widely used. In the final analysis, clinical relevance and national recommendations by peers are perhaps the best motivators. Once those are achieved, simple dissemination often creates good physician acceptance.

References

1. Maslow, A: *Motivation and Personality,* 2nd. Edition. New York, N.Y.: Harper & Row, 1970.

2. Woolf, S. "Practice Guidelines: A New Reality in Medicine. III: Impact on Patient Care. *Archives of Internal Medicine* 153(23):2646-55, Dec. 13, 1993.

3. American Psychiatric Association. *Practice Guideline for Psychiatric Evaluation in Adults.* Washington, D.C.: American Psychiatric Press, 1995.

4. American Psychiatric Association. *Practice Guideline for the Treatment of Patients with Substance Use Disorders: Alcohol, Cocaine, Opioids.* Washington, D.C.: American Psychiatric Press, 1995.

5. American Psychiatric Association. *Practice Guideline for Treatment of Patients With Bipolar Disorders.* Washington, D.C.: American Psychiatric Press, 1995.

6. *Tarasoff v. Regents,* 17 Cal. 3d 425, 551 P.2d 334, 131 Cal Rptr. 14 (1976).

7. *Wickline v. State of California,* 228 Cal Rptr 661 (Cal App 2 Dist 1986), 239 Cal Rptr 805 (Cal 1987).

8. *Hughes v. Blue Cross of Northern California,* 245 Cal Rptr 273 (Cal App 1 Dist 1988).

9. *Wilson v. Blue Cross of Southern California,* 271 Cal Rptr 876 (Cal App 2 Dist 1990).

10. Sederer, L. "Judicial and Legislative Responses to Cost Containment." *American Journal of Psychiatry* 149(9):1157-61, Sept. 1992.

11. *Arkansas Blue Cross/Blue Shield v. Doe,* 733 SW 2d 429, 22 Ark App 89 (1987).

12. *Kunin v. Benefit Trust Life Insurance Co.,* 696 F Supp 1342 (CD Cal 1988).

13. Sartorius, N., and others. "Progress toward Achieving a Common Language in Psychiatry. Results from the Field Trial of the Clinical Guidelines Accompanying the WHO Classification of Mental and Behavioral Disorders in ICD-10." *Archives of General Psychiatry* 50(2):115-24, Feb. 1993.

14. "Practice Guideline for Major Depressive Disorder in Adults." *American Journal of Psychiatry* 150(4, Suppl):1-26, April 1993.

15. "Practice Guideline for Eating Disorders." *American Journal of Psychiatry* 150(2):212-28, Feb. 1993.

16. Depression Guideline Panel. *Clinical Practice Guideline: Depression in Primary Care: Detection and Diagnosis.* Agency for Health Care Policy and Research publication 93-0550. Rockville, Md.: U.S. Department of Health and Human Services, 1993.

17. Depression Guideline Panel. *Clinical Practice Guideline: Depression in Primary Care: Treatment of Major Depression.* Agency for Health Care Policy and Research publication 93-0551). Rockville, Md.: U.S. Department of Health and Human Services, 1993.

18. Katon, W., and others. "Collaborative Management to Achieve Treatment Guidelines: Impact on Depression in Primary Care." *JAMA* 273(13):1026-31, April 5, 1995.

19. Slater, E., and Glazer, W. "Use of OBRA-87 Guidelines for Prescribing Neuroleptics in a VA Nursing Home." *Psychiatric Services* 46(2):119-21, Feb. 1995.

20. Lebowitz, B., and Gottlieb, G. "Clinical Research in the Managed Care Environment. *American Journal of Geriatric Psychiatry* 3(1):21-5, Winter 1995.

21. Elson, R., and Connelly, D.: "Computerized Patient Records in Primary Care: Their Role in Mediating Guideline-Driven Physician Behavior Change." *Archives of Family Medicine* 4(8):698-705, Aug. 1995.

22. Gorton, T., and others. "Primary Care Physicians' Response to Dissemination of Practice Guidelines." *Archives of Family Medicine* 4(2):135-42, Feb. 1995.

William H. Reid, MD, MPH, practices near Austin, Texas. He is Clinical Professor of Psychiatry at the University of Texas Health Science Center, San Antonio, and Adjunct Professor at Texas A&:M and Texas Tech medical schools. He is the former Medical Director of the Texas Department of Mental Health and Mental Retardation and often consults on clinical, forensic, and administrative psychiatry matters. His new book, Legal Issues for Psychotherapists, *will be published in 1999 by Zeig, Tucker, Inc.*

Epilogue

Theoretical and operational ambiguity has always been part of the nature of behavioral health care. However, change and the rate of change, and the fundamental essence of change in behavioral health care have promoted ambiguity to a position of near supremacy in behavioral health care's infrastructure. Our foundation is unstable; it's moving.

What was once professional financial security is now an arguable career proposition. Historical patients have become consumer stakeholders. Once clearly delineated behavioral health care discipline roles are now blurred and out of focus. Our workforce profile is altering its shape continually. Decisions about behavioral health care are made by entities in quarters that had no decision-making authority in the past. Data are collected almost faster than we can learn from or utilize them. "Scientific breakthroughs" have become so commonplace that we seldom see the phrase used anymore.

We find ourselves debating about basics such as the dichotomy of focusing behavioral health care services primarily on the individual or primarily on populations. We engage in arguments over esoterics such as to clone or not to clone human beings and human behavior. We are in a state of extreme flux.

For those who would be successful in behavioral health care, this situation is just a noted inconvenience in a time of exciting opportunity. Visionaries will see through the chaos and lead us toward new constructs of value in behavioral health care service delivery. But it won't be easy.

Even well-intentioned offerings such as this book involve jeopardy for those who will build the future of behavioral health care. That jeopardy is reinforcement of limited perspectives founded on limited knowledge bases.

To be successful, this book has to go further than its own textual substance. It must encourage readers to critically examine the current content of behavioral health care and even to challenge their concepts of behavioral health. To be successful, this book also has to encourage tomorrow's leaders to be today's innovators. The book has to applaud behavioral health care pioneers who generate what is positive and new—what others call change.

Today's behavioral health care leaders have a daunting task before them. They have to help others dismantle and improve on what they themselves have created so that motion in behavioral health care is forward. They must be flexible from core to periphery. They cannot strategize too long before action, or commit irrevocably to any single presumed future scenario. They must build on their knowledge base continually and master the skill of communicating their learning quickly and effectively. Today's leaders must also honor the changing profile of behavioral health care's most valuable assets, human beings who care for and about other human beings. And today's leaders must be willing to share all that may be beneficial with all who might benefit.

Sharing is intrinsic to humanity. The contributors to this book share themselves with you, the reader, as one more step in the promotion of behavioral health and well-being for all humankind.—F.B.

Index